Acts and Christian Beginnings

Acts and Christian Beginnings

The Acts Seminar Report

Edited by
Dennis E. Smith
and
Joseph B. Tyson

POLEBRIDGE PRESS
Salem, Oregon

Copyright © 2013 by Polebridge Press

All rights reserved. Printed in the United States of America. No part of this book may be used or reproduced in any manner whatsoever without written permission except in the case of brief quotations embodied in critical articles and reviews. For information address Polebridge Press, Willamette University, 900 State Street, Salem, OR 97301.

Cover and interior design by Robaire Ream

Library of Congress Cataloging-in-Publication Data
Acts and Christian beginnings : the Acts seminar report / edited by Dennis E. Smith and Joseph B. Tyson.
    pages cm
 Includes bibliographical references and index.
 ISBN 978-1-59815-135-0 (alk. paper)
 1. Bible. Acts--Criticism, interpretation, etc. I. Smith, Dennis Edwin, 1944- II. Tyson, Joseph B.
 BS2625.52.A25 2013
 226.6'06--dc23
                                                      2013028101

Table of Contents

Contributors vii

Preface ix

Abbreviations xi

   Introduction 1

   Chapter 1
      Beginning in Jerusalem (Acts 1:1–8:3) 21

   Chapter 2
      To Judea, Samaria, and Beyond (Acts 8:4–9:43) 93

   Map: The World of Acts: Chapters 1–12 122

   Chapter 3
      Antioch and Jerusalem (Acts 10:1–15:35) 123

   Map: The World of Acts: Chapters 13–20 178

   Chapter 4
      Paul in Asia and Greece (Acts 15:36–19:41) 179

   Map: The Journey of Paul to Rome According to Acts 244

   Chapter 5
      To the Ends of the Earth (Acts 20:1–28:31) 245

   Conclusion 329

Notes 343

Works Cited 347

Index of Ancient Sources 355

Index of Modern Authors 369

Cameo Essays

"Apostleship in Early Christianity," Joseph B. Tyson	34
"Artemis of Ephesus," Christine R. Shea	242
"The Association Model," Dennis E. Smith	49
"Comparing Paul and Luke on Paul's Conversion," Thomas E. Phillips	114
"Deconstructing the Resurrection Narrative in Luke-Acts," Dennis E. Smith	29
"The Gallio Episode," Dennis E. Smith	222
"The Gentile Mission Source," Richard I. Pervo	99
"Hellenists and Hebrews," Perry V. Kea	79
"The Itinerary of Paul," Dennis E. Smith and Joseph B. Tyson	206
"Jerusalem in Myth and History," Milton Moreland	44
"The Jews According to Acts," Shelly Matthews	268
"The Letters of Paul as Sources for Acts," William O. Walker, Jr.	116
"Names in Acts," Christine R. Shea	22
"Priscilla and Aquila," William O. Walker, Jr.	223
"Prison Breaks in Luke's Literary World," Dennis R. MacDonald	72
"Shipwrecks in Luke's Literary World," Dennis R. MacDonald	313
"The So-Called Noahide Laws," Nina E. Livesey	175
"Speeches in Acts," Richard I. Pervo	45
"Stephen," Shelly Matthews	90
"We-Passages in the Acts of the Apostles," Dennis R. MacDonald	191
"What Really Happened at the Jerusalem Council," William O. Walker, Jr.	173
"When Apostles Become Philosophers," Rubén Dupertuis	60
"Women in Acts," Shelly Matthews	193

Contributors

Rubén Dupertuis, Associate Professor of Religion, Trinity University, San Antonio, Texas

Perry V. Kea, Associate Professor of Biblical Studies, University of Indianapolis, Indiana

Nina E. Livesey, Assistant Professor of Religious Studies, University of Oklahoma at Norman

Dennis R. MacDonald, Professor of New Testament and Christian Origins, Claremont School of Theology, California

Shelly Matthews, Associate Professor of New Testament, Brite Divinity School, Texas Christian University, Fort Worth, Texas

Milton Moreland, Associate Professor of Religious Studies, Rhodes College, Memphis, Tennessee

Richard I. Pervo, retired, Minneapolis, Minnesota

Thomas E. Phillips, Dean of Library and Information Services, Claremont School of Theology, Claremont, California

Christine R. Shea, Professor of Classics, Ball State University, Muncie, Indiana

Dennis E. Smith, LaDonna Kramer Meinders Professor of New Testament, Phillips Theological Seminary, Tulsa, Oklahoma

Joseph B. Tyson, Professor Emeritus of Religious Studies, Southern Methodist University, Dallas, Texas

William O. Walker, Jr., Jennie Farris Railey King Professor Emeritus of Religion, Trinity University, San Antonio, Texas

Preface

The Acts Seminar

The Acts Seminar met from March 2000, to March 2011, under the leadership of Dennis E. Smith as chair, assisted by a subcommittee that included, at various times, Perry V. Kea, Richard I. Pervo, Robert M. Price, Christine R. Shea, Joseph B. Tyson, and William O. Walker, Jr. It presented its research twice yearly at the fall and spring meetings of the Westar Institute. Westar Fellows, which included members of the Acts Seminar, deliberated on the papers presented at each meeting and voted on the recommendations contained therein. A typical meeting would be made up of 25 to 35 scholars (Fellows) observed by a gallery of approximately 100 to 250 attendees from the general public (Associates). The meetings were public and available to any who wished to attend. Both Fellows and Associates voted at the meetings, but only the voting results of the Fellows are reported in this volume. Papers presented at the Acts Seminar have been published in the following special issues of the academic journal *Forum*: 3,1 (Spring 2000); 4,1 (Spring 2001); 5,1 (Spring 2002); Third Series 2,2 (Fall 2013); as well as in a number of other scholarly journals and monographs. Summary reports on Acts Seminar meetings since the fall meeting of 2006 have been published in the following issues of *Fourth R* magazine: 20,1 (January/February 2007); 20,5 (May/June 2007); 21,1 (January/February 2008); 21,3 (May/June 2008); 22,2 (March/April 2009); 22,4 (July/August 2009); 23,2 (March/April 2010).

This project could not have been completed without the research efforts of our colleagues in the Acts Seminar who contributed papers for the Seminar meetings. They are as follows: Rubén Dupertuis, Julian V. Hills, Perry V. Kea, Nina E. Livesey, Gerd Lüdemann, Dennis R. MacDonald, Shelly Matthews, Milton Moreland, Todd Penner, Richard I. Pervo, Thomas E. Phillips, Robert M. Price, Alan F. Segal, Christine R. Shea, F. Scott Spencer, Hal Taussig, William O. Walker, Jr., L. Michael White, Stephen R. Wiest, and Sara C. Winter.

In addition, a variety of Westar Fellows provided feedback at the various sessions of the Seminar.

We also wish to acknowledge the leadership and guidance of Robert W. Funk, whose shepherding of our project within the larger agenda of the Westar Institute was of significant importance to the success of our endeavor. Prior to his death in 2005, he was also a regular participant in our public deliberations. In addition, the organizational model he created for Westar Seminars, in which research is conducted by a team of scholars working under public scrutiny, provided the ideal setting and format for our agenda. The completion and publication of our project is therefore itself a memorial to the vision of Robert W. Funk, as is the case with all of the continuing work of the Westar Institute. We are also grateful to the Westar Board of Directors and to Larry Alexander and his team at Polebridge Press for their support as we completed this report.

The original goal for the project was to publish a red-letter edition of Acts on the model of the red-letter editions of the Gospels as published by the Jesus Seminar (see *The Five Gospels* and *The Acts of Jesus*). Well into the project, however, we began to realize that a red-letter edition of Acts was not feasible, since the Acts text cannot be broken down into its traditions. Instead, we adopted a format in which votes were taken not on traditions within the text of Acts but on components of its story. We trust the reader will find this to be a coherent format for presenting the results of the project.

Where available, we have used New Testament (NT) translations from the Scholars Version (SV). The translation of Acts is by Richard I. Pervo. It is reprinted from Richard I. Pervo, *Acts: A Commentary* (Hermeneia; Minneapolis: Fortress Press, 2009) and is used by permission. Unless otherwise noted, translations from the gospels are from Robert J. Miller, ed., *The Complete Gospels*, fourth edition (Salem, OR: Polebridge Press, 2010). Quotations from the Pauline letters are from Arthur J. Dewey, Roy W. Hoover, Lane C. McGaughy, and Daryl D. Schmidt, *The Authentic Letters of Paul* (Salem, OR: Polebridge Press, 2010).

Dennis E. Smith
Joseph B. Tyson

Abbreviations

1,2 Cor	1,2 Corinthians
1,2 Kgs	1,2 Kings
4 Macc	4 Maccabees
1 Pet	1 Peter
1,2 Thess	1,2 Thessalonians
1,2 Tim	1,2 Timothy
Col	Colossians
Deut	Deuteronomy
Eph	Ephesians
Exod	Exodus
Gal	Galatians
Heb	Hebrews
Isa	Isaiah
Jas	James
Jer	Jeremiah
Lev	Leviticus
LXX	Septuagint
Matt	Matthew
NRSV	New Revised Standard Version
NT	New Testament
Num	Numbers
OT	Old Testament
Phil	Philippians
Phlm	Philemon
Ps(s)	Psalm(s)
Rev	Revelation
Rom	Romans
SV	Scholars Version

Introduction

To the average layperson who is moderately acquainted with early Christian history, the Acts of the Apostles would be considered a reliable resource for Christian beginnings. After all, if we did not have Acts, how would we know our history? Acts just sounds right to us, because it is the only story of Christian beginnings we have. Scholars, who rightfully raise critical questions about the overall reliability of Acts, continue to use it as a default historical resource. The problem for scholars is that there have not been clear methods for determining when Acts is reliable and when it is not.

The Acts Seminar was formed as an attempt to bring order to the study of Acts as history. As a research seminar of the Westar Institute, the Acts Seminar was charged with the task to develop methods for determining the reliability of Acts and produce a comprehensive guide to Acts as history. The seminar held its first meeting in March 2000, and subsequently met twice a year until March 2011. During that period scholars representing a wide array of religious traditions and academic institutions participated in its deliberations. After a decade of research and deliberations by the Acts Seminar and other Westar Fellows, we are pleased to present the full report of the seminar in this volume.

The Top Ten Accomplishments of the Acts Seminar[1]

Members of the Acts Seminar began with a perspective firmly embedded in current scholarship as described above. That is to say, we knew that Acts needed to be critically assessed, but we did not anticipate how much we would have to rethink our understanding of Acts in order to do our job responsibly. We learned from each other, and thereby confirmed the genius of the seminar method for historical research. When we had arrived at our goal of assessing all of Acts and then looked back over our work, we were amazed at how far we had come. Here is a summary of those accomplishments.

1. The author of Acts was an accomplished storyteller/theologian who wrote a story with a decidedly apologetic purpose. He

did not write with an antiquarian interest or with a goal toward getting his history right. Nor did he simply stitch together sources he had collected. Rather we found that he was in complete control of his material and fully capable of making it say what he wanted it to say.

2. Acts was written in the early decades of the second century. This conclusion, which we only reached after we were well into the research agenda of the seminar, was seminal to our project. Up to this point, there has been a scholarly consensus that Luke-Acts as a two-volume work was written in the 80s CE. This dating has been fundamental for all proposals regarding the historical reliability of Acts, using arguments ranging from the view that the author was a companion of Paul to arguments that the reliability of Acts is proven by how well it tracks with the story of Paul's mission as found in his letters. Early on in its research the Acts Seminar, led by the foundational work of Richard Pervo and Joseph Tyson, overturned that consensus and found instead that Acts was written in the early second century. This conclusion has significantly undermined a vast segment of Acts scholarship that has relied on the 80s CE dating.

3. The author of Acts used the letters of Paul as one of his sources. This is a corollary of the revised dating of Acts. Another longstanding scholarly consensus has been that the writer of Acts did not have access to Paul's letters, primarily because Paul is not pictured as a letter writer in Acts and because Acts does not seem familiar with Paul's theology. Relying on groundbreaking studies by William O. Walker and others, the Acts Seminar concluded that Acts did indeed use the letters of Paul as a resource for its story of Paul, while relegating Paul's theology to the background. This conclusion is made even more likely whenever Acts is dated in the second century, since by then the letters of Paul were becoming widely known.

4. Except for the letters of Paul, no other reliable historical source can be definitively identified for Acts. Once Acts is dated in the second century, and is determined to have used the letters of Paul, then virtually all previous scholarship on the sources of Acts has to be rethought. Previous theories that reconstruct the historical sources used by Acts have been primarily based on the "remarkable" correlation of the story of Acts with the letters of Paul. This argument is buttressed by the perception that the author, by writing in the 80s CE, was either a participant in many of the events related

or knew people who were. Whenever Acts is defined as a second-century document which used Paul as a source, virtually all previous source theories have to be completely rethought. We found instead that Acts used a variety of "sources" like Josephus, Homer, Vergil, and the Septuagint (LXX). These materials, however, only provided background material or literary models for the Acts story. They were not sources for the story of Christian beginnings per se.

5. Jerusalem was not the birthplace of Christianity, contrary to the story Acts tells in chapters 1–7. The revised understanding of Acts we are proposing starts with the very beginning of the story. According to official Christian history as well as popular theology, the Pentecost story in Acts is firmly established as the official story of Christian origins. The Acts Seminar has shown through multiple studies that the entire Acts narrative of Christian beginnings in Jerusalem (Acts 1–7) has little historical value. This is a significant challenge to most theories of Christian origins.

6. Acts can no longer be considered an independent source for the life and mission of Paul. Rather we have found that the use of Paul's letters as a source is sufficient to account for all details of the life and itinerary of Paul in Acts. There is very little, if any, evidence for the use of independent sources, much less sources that can be proposed as historically reliable. As a result, we must rethink how we reconstruct the historical story of Paul without any reliance on or reference to the template created by the author of Acts.

7. Acts constructed its story on the model of the epic and related literature. This is a perspective on Acts that has been proposed in scholarly research for some time. What we accomplished in the Acts Seminar was to make this model much more functional in making hard decisions about the historical reliability of the story told in this way.

8. The author of Acts created names for characters as a storytelling device. Scholars have in the past commonly concluded that when names are preserved in the story, then they are probably based on historical personages. However, we have found that names in ancient narrative literature often had symbolic meaning appropriate to the stories in which they were found. This means that the name would therefore have been created by the author to lend verisimilitude to the story. The same phenomenon is found in Acts. The Acts Seminar has therefore concluded that names should not be used as an indicator of the historical reliability of the narrative.

9. Acts constructed its story to fit ideological goals. This is another perspective that the Acts Seminar inherited from previous generations of Acts scholarship. What is different is the rigor with which the Seminar applied this approach. We found that the ideological goals invariably emerged as the primary key to much of the content, form, and structure of the stories in Acts.

10. No longer can Acts be assumed to be historical unless proven otherwise. Rather, the burden of proof has shifted. Acts must be considered nonhistorical unless proven otherwise. This is the cumulative result of the accomplishments noted above.

There is another by-product of our research that we came to appreciate but were unable to address fully in this report. While Acts is highly questionable as a resource for first-century Christianity, it is a significant resource for understanding the issues and shape of the Christianity of its own day. As a product of the second century, Acts is a primary resource for understanding second-century Christianity. The Acts Seminar has addressed this issue with several papers, but research on this subject is still preliminary. It should be noted that interpreting Acts as *produced* in the second century is not the same as interpreting Acts as *read* in the second century and results in a different research methodology, a distinction not always made clear in current scholarship.

The Votes of the Fellows

This report is based on the conclusions reached by the Westar Seminar Fellows regarding the reliability of Acts as a historical resource. After the Fellows deliberated on the issues raised by the papers presented at the various meetings, they recorded their votes using the traditional Westar color-coded method (red, pink, gray, black). The colors represent differing levels of certainty regarding the probability or improbability of historical judgments reached by the Fellows. The definitions of the voting categories are as follows:

Red/Probable
- This information is virtually certain; it is supported by a preponderance of evidence and is accepted as probable.

Pink/Possible
- This information is not certain but is probably reliable as a whole or in part; it fits well with other evidence that is verifiable and so is accepted as possible.

Gray/Doubtful
- This information is unreliable as a whole or in part; it is not a clear fabrication but lacks sufficient supporting evidence and so is regarded as doubtful.

Black/Improbable
- This information does not fit verifiable evidence and/or seems likely to be a fabrication and so is regarded as improbable.

In this volume, the votes of the Fellows are labeled according to the color-coded system but are not printed in the colors indicated. Votes were tabulated according to weighted averages; thus in certain instances the votes might be scattered across the spectrum, but the weighted average allowed a conclusion to be reached that reflected the general consensus of the group.

The work of the Acts Seminar was collaborative throughout. In the spirit of that collaboration, while Smith and Tyson have written the bulk of this report, other members of the seminar have also provided supportive essays. The following introductory essays were written by a variety of individuals whose names are listed with their contributions.

The Date of Acts[2]

Richard I. Pervo

Early Christian texts are difficult to date, for both internal and external information is generally lacking. An example of internal information would be a reference to President Jimmy Carter as currently serving, which would locate a text in the years 1977–81. A 1940 newspaper column that mentioned Ernest Hemingway as the author of the recent book *For Whom the Bell Tolls* would constitute external evidence for dating that novel in 1940 or shortly before.

Acts was known and used ca. 180 CE by Irenaeus, Bishop of Lyons, and, in approximately the same period, by the *Acts of Paul*. It cannot be earlier than ca. 60, which is the date of its latest reported events (the imprisonment of Paul in Rome). As a means for narrowing this range one may identify datable sources used by the author. One of these sources was a collection, evidently, of the letters of Paul. This collection did not appear before ca. 100. Acts can also be shown to have used the later books of *Jewish Antiquities* by Flavius Josephus. Josephus finished this work in 93/4.[3] Thus Acts is later than 100. How much later? The latest probable date is ca. 130, based on the probability that the Pastoral Epistles (1–2 Timothy, Titus) and Polycarp of Smyrna may have known Acts.

Acts can also be shown to belong to the world of the Apostolic Fathers, namely the period in Christian history of ca. 100–150 CE. In addition to details of terminology and concepts, Acts is familiar with institutions that post-date 100. Notable among these is the existence of an order of widows (cf. Acts 6:1–7; 9:36–41). Organizations led by bishops, presbyters, and deacons are in place, if not unqualifiedly endorsed (cf. 6:1–7; 20:17–35). The misuse of funds (cf. 5:1–11; 8:14–25) and problems of deviant teaching echo concerns addressed by the Pastorals, Ignatius, and Polycarp, all representing issues of the first half of the second century CE. Although Paul is Luke's hero, he is not presented as someone who wrote or handled letters. This correlates with the fact that, in some circles after 100, Paul's letters had become controversial, even though a majority of believers utilized them.

Based on the above data as derived from the text of Acts, the most probable range of dates is ca. 110–120. Previous scholarship has tended to date Acts ca. 85, but a variety of recent studies have challenged this view and supported an early second-century dating.

The conclusions of the Fellows on the issue of the dating of Acts are as follows:

The Votes of the Fellows

Red/Probable
- Acts was written in the second century CE.

Black/Improbable
- Acts was written before the year 70 CE.
- Acts was written in the last quarter of the first century CE.
- Acts was written by a companion of Paul.

Marcion and the Date of Acts[4]

Joseph B. Tyson

If the book of Acts was composed in the period 110–20 CE, as argued in the previous essay, what social context might help to account for its appearance at this time? Studies of the history of Christianity in this period have shown that it was a time of great theological diversity and that no normative set of beliefs had yet emerged. One significant Christian movement was attached to the figure of

Marcion, who was probably the best known second-century "heretic." Irenaeus, Tertullian, and other later writers devoted more attention to Marcion than to any other single leader of the period.

The precise dates of Marcion's birth and death are unknown. He was probably born in the latter half of the first century CE in Sinope, on the Black Sea. Claims that his father was a Christian bishop have recently been challenged. Marcion had a successful ministry in Asia Minor and, before the middle of the second century, came to Rome, where he was initially accepted but finally condemned for views that Rome deemed heretical. He died a few years after 150 CE.

Marcion took his inspiration from the letters of Paul, most notably Galatians. He regarded Paul as the only authentic apostle of Jesus. He was deeply impressed with Paul's contrast of law and grace and concluded that these must be the domains of two Gods. One God was revealed in the Hebrew Bible as the creator, lawgiver, and judge of humankind. This God, thus, is identified with the created order, with Torah, and with the Jews, his chosen people. Marcion did not question the inspiration and authority of the Hebrew Bible; he interpreted it literally as the word of the creator-God but not as prophetic of the appearance of Jesus. The second God is the Father of Jesus Christ, completely unknown in this world before the appearance of Jesus in the fifteenth year of Tiberius Caesar (29–30 CE). This is the God of grace, love, and mercy. The work of Jesus was to release humankind from the creator-God into the domain of the God of grace.

Marcion and his followers actually developed the first Christian canon, without the Hebrew Bible but with ten letters of Paul and one gospel, which resembled the Gospel of Luke in today's NT. Although Marcion's opponents claimed that he "mutilated" the Gospel of Luke, some modern scholars question this assertion and maintain that the situation was reversed, that Marcion's Luke was taken over by "orthodox" Christians and enlarged. One of the more significant differences between the Marcionite and the "orthodox" versions of Luke is the inclusion of the birth narratives (Luke 1–2) in the latter.

Marcionite Christianity was so vigorous in the late second century that the number of adherents probably approximated or even outnumbered the "orthodox" in some places. There is evidence of its survival as late as the fifth century CE.

Although the author of Acts never mentions Marcion, some of the major themes in the book may be accounted for by supposing that its author intended to counteract some of the contentions of the Marcionite movement. For example, in the idyllic portrayal of the early believing community, the author of Acts stresses the community's fidelity to Jewish traditions and practices. The believers gather in the temple (Acts 2:46; 5:12), which is the setting for many of the episodes in the early chapters of Acts (see 2:46; 3:1, 2, 3, 8, 10; 4:1; 5:20, 21, 22, 24, 25, 26, 42). The believing community enjoys popular goodwill and esteem (see 2:47; 5:13), and apostolic healings are in great demand throughout the city (see 5:14–15). The participation of the apostles in the temple ritual is assumed. Peter and John go there "at the time of the 1500 [3:00 p.m.] service" (3:1), where they heal a man who had been lame from birth. Peter speaks in Solomon's portico (4:1), which subsequently becomes a regular meeting place for the Jesus community (5:12).

In addition, the characterization of Paul, who dominates the latter half of Acts, stresses his fidelity to Jewish beliefs and practices. In episode after episode, he begins his local mission with a visit to the synagogue, where he presents his message to Jews. The heart of his message in the synagogues is that Jesus is the fulfillment of Jewish expectations and prophetic promises. Readers who are steeped in the epistles of Paul may be surprised to learn that it was Peter, not Paul, who converted the first Gentile (Acts 10:1–11:18). The scenes in Acts where Paul is on trial portray him as a Torah-abiding Jew. In an appearance before the Jewish council, Paul submits to the high priest and quotes from the Hebrew Bible (23:5). Before the Roman governor Felix, Paul describes himself as a believing Jew: "I do revere our ancestral God and believe all that is commanded in the Law and written in the Prophets" (24:14). Paul reiterates his hope in the resurrection and calls attention to this hope as Jewish (24:15). He emphasizes his sacrifices in the temple and reminds us that he was captured while engaged in a ritual of purification (24:17–18). In a hearing before Festus, another Roman governor, Paul defends himself by saying that he has done nothing against the Jewish law or the Jewish people (25:8, 10). In the climactic hearing before Herod Agrippa, Paul firmly proclaims his Jewish allegiance (26:4–8).

Why does the author of Acts portray Paul in this way? If he wrote in the early second century, it is plausible to suggest that he would have been acquainted with some Marcionite contentions: that the creator God was not the father of Jesus Christ; that Jesus was not the Christ of Jewish expectation; that Paul was the only apostle of Jesus. The missionary method used by the Paul of Acts and his message to Jews stands in stark contrast to Marcionite theology. In Acts Paul repeatedly affirms the connection with the biblical prophets, a connection that Marcion vigorously denies. Marcion called Peter and the Jerusalem leaders "false apostles," but Acts elevates them and insists on their authentic appointment by the risen Jesus. Marcion thought of Paul as the only apostle, but Acts portrays him as being in total agreement with the others. Marcion drew a firm boundary between Judaism and Christianity, but Acts characterizes the apostles and Paul as faithful Jews, who fully observed Torah. Paul, before and after his conversion, is characterized as a loyal Pharisee. In these respects, the author of Acts appears to be reacting against certain fundamental features of Marcionite theology and constructing a vision of Christianity that includes a firm belief in the unity of God, a positive relationship to the Hebrew Bible, and a continuation of Jewish beliefs and practices.

These observations do not prove that Acts must be dated in the early decades of the second century. But if other evidence suggests that there are good reasons to date it at this time, as the previous essay contends, the Marcionite connection tends to confirm this date and provide a fitting context for its composition.

The Votes of the Fellows
Red/Probable
- A major factor behind the composition of Acts was the perceived threat posed by Marcion and Marcionite Christianity.
- One purpose of the composition of Acts was to provide assurance that Marcion's interpretation of Paul was wrong.

The Author of Acts
Dennis E. Smith

Irenaeus, a Christian bishop who wrote near the end of the second century, appears to be the first reader of Acts to identify the author as Luke, a companion of Paul.[5] The bishop was evidently thinking of the person mentioned in Col 4:14, Phlm 24, and 2 Tim 4:11. In all three of these letters, Luke is closely associated with Paul, and in Colossians he is described as "the beloved physician." Of the three letters, only Philemon is uncontested as an authentic letter of Paul, but Irenaeus would not have known this. Irenaeus also claimed that Luke wrote not only the Acts of the Apostles but also the Third Gospel (now known as "the Gospel according to Luke").[6] Following Irenaeus, it has become traditional to attribute both Acts and the Third Gospel to Luke, a companion of Paul and a physician. This attribution appears to find additional support in the so-called "we"-passages, which imply that the author was present at some of the events he described (see the cameo essay, "We-Passages in the Acts of the Apostles," p. 191).

Modern critical scholars have generally agreed that the same author is responsible for both Luke and Acts, but few have accepted the theory that a companion of Paul was the author. Members of the Acts Seminar agree with the majority of critical scholars. The possibility that the author was of Paul's generation is excluded if, as we contend, Acts was written as late as 115–20 CE.

The identification of the author of Acts as a companion of Paul encounters a number of problems. Why, for example, does the author make no explicit reference to Paul's literary activity? Why does he almost never make reference to his theological views as they are expressed in his letters? Why does he almost always deny the title *apostle* to one who vigorously claimed it? It seems that a companion of Paul would have known him better.

A disadvantage in denying the authorship of Acts to a companion of Paul is that we cannot provide a name for him. We think he is probably a Gentile, who was acquainted with the LXX and major Greek writings and adept in using accepted rhetorical techniques. But in the final analysis our author is anonymous. We will call him "Luke," not to imply that we know who he was, but only for the sake of convenience.

Sources in Acts

Perry V. Kea

In the opening preface to his Gospel, Luke acknowledges that he used written sources (see Luke 1:1–4). Most scholars hold that Luke used Mark's Gospel as his primary source and supplemented it with a hypothetical source called *Quelle*, the German word for "source" ("Q"), a collection of Jesus' sayings. Since Luke admits to using sources for his Gospel, it seems likely that he would have used sources for Acts. However, identifying sources for Acts has proven to be difficult.

Adolf von Harnack identified several hypothetical sources for Acts. For Acts 1–15, Harnack detected three sources. The first he called source A, and to it he assigned Acts 3:1–5:16; 8:5–40; 9:31–11:18; 12:1–24. Harnack expressed confidence in the historical reliability of this written source. To the second source B, Harnack assigned Acts 1–2; 5:17–42. He regarded the historical reliability of this material to be inferior to source A. Harnack identified a third source in the materials connected with the figures of Stephen, Barnabas, and Saul. Since the stories connect these three to both Jerusalem and Antioch, Harnack suggested a Jerusalem-Antioch source. For Harnack, Acts 6:1–8: 4; 11:19–30; 12:25–15:35 belong to this source. Beyond this, Harnack thought that Paul's personal recollection stood behind Acts 9:1–30, and that much of the rest of Acts came from Luke's personal records and recollections.[7] Harnack's views continue to be espoused by some scholars today. However, the participants in the Acts Seminar are more skeptical that such specific sources can be identified. The Fellows have identified other, less conventional sources.

Paul's Letters. Because Luke never refers to any of Paul's letters in Acts, it was once thought that Luke was not familiar with them. However, some scholars, such as William O. Walker, have argued that Luke knew Paul's letters and used them as sources for the Acts.[8] The early second-century date for Acts adopted in this commentary enhances the likelihood that Luke knew Paul's letters (see also the cameo essay, "The Letters of Paul as Sources for Acts," p. 116).

Acts 15, Luke's account of the Jerusalem Council, serves as an example. Paul provides an account of this meeting in Gal 2:1–10. Tensions between Paul and the Jerusalem leaders are evident in Galatians 2, but Luke completely masks them in Acts 15. In an ironic twist, Paul does not make a speech defending the Gentile mission in Acts 15. Luke gives that honor to Peter. Yet the speech he gives to Peter is based upon ideas and key terms in Galatians 2. In this way, Luke makes it appear that Paul's views were shared by Peter (and the rest of the Jerusalem leadership). Walker's study demonstrates that Luke does not follow Paul's account slavishly, but rewrites it to serve his own literary and theological purposes.

The Septuagint. Scholars have long recognized the importance, in some of the early speeches in Acts, of the Septuagint (the Greek translation of the Jewish Scriptures symbolized by the Roman numeral LXX). Like writers of that era, Luke was trained to compose speeches that were appropriate for the character and situation being described. Of the thirty-seven explicit OT (LXX) quotations in Acts, the vast majority of them occur in speeches addressed to Jewish audiences. It seems likely that Luke drew upon passages from the LXX.

We have a very clear example of this in Luke 4:16–30. Luke's version of this story is based on Mark 6:1–6. Mark describes how Jesus' hometown of Nazareth took offense at him when he visited and taught in the synagogue. Mark quotes only a single sentence from Jesus: "No prophet is disrespected, except on his home turf and among his relatives and at home" (Mark 6:4). That's not much for Luke to work with. So Luke significantly expands upon Mark 6:1–6 by adding material from the LXX. First, Luke has Jesus read several verses from the prophet Isaiah (61:1–2; 58:6):

> The spirit of the Lord is upon me, because he has anointed me to bring good news to the poor. He has sent me to announce pardon for prisoners and recovery of sight to the blind; to set free the oppressed, to proclaim the year of the Lord's amnesty. (Luke 4:18–19)

The audience's initial response is positive (Luke 4:22). At this point, Luke strings together three sayings of Jesus including the "disrespected prophet" statement he inherited from Mark 6:4. Luke returns to the LXX to complete his retelling of this story. Jesus tells two stories from 1 and 2 Kings about the prophets Elijah and Elisha (Luke 4:24–27). Both emphasize the care provided to non-Israelites, a Canaanite woman in the case of Elijah (1 Kgs 17:8–16) and a Syrian army commander in Elisha's case (2 Kgs 5:1–19). The hometown crowd explodes with rage and tries to kill Jesus, but he mysteriously escapes (Luke 4:28–30). When we compare Luke's account to Mark's, the differences are startling. Luke has significantly expanded Mark's scene by creating sayings material for Jesus. The majority of this new speech material comes from the LXX: in one case by direct quotation (the Isaiah passage) and in the other by summarizing stories about Elijah and Elisha.

Based on the above example, it seems likely that Luke would use the LXX for some of the speeches in Acts. Peter's Pentecost speech (Acts 2:14–36) is presented as his address to a large gathering of Jews who have observed Jesus' disciples speaking in tongues. Luke creates the speech around several quotations from the LXX. First, he cites Joel 2:28–32 (=Acts 2:17–21) to explain the phenomenon of speaking in tongues. Second, LXX Ps 15:8–11* (=Acts 2:25–28) serves Luke as a proof-text for the claim that Jesus was raised from the dead. Finally, Luke cites LXX Ps 109:1[9] (=Acts 2:34–35) as David's prediction about the coming of the Messiah, Jesus. The speech is 429 words in Greek. Of these, 189 (44 percent) come from the LXX.

---

*Because there are 151 Psalms in the LXX, the numbering of the Psalms differs slightly from the Hebrew Bible's numbering. Psalm 15 in the LXX is Psalm 16 in the Hebrew text.

The speech of Stephen in Acts 7 is particularly interesting. It is the longest in Acts. Here Luke uses the Septuagint in three ways. First, like Peter's Pentecost speech, Stephen's speech uses direct quotations from the LXX (for example, Amos 5:25–27 is cited in Acts 7:42–43). Fourteen of the thirty-seven OT quotations in Acts occur in this single speech (38 percent). Second, like the stories of Elijah and Elisha used in Luke 4:24–27, Stephen's speech summarizes various stories from the LXX. For example, in Acts 7:35–42, Luke recapitulates the story about ancient Israel's rejection of Moses' leadership and lapse into idolatry. And third, Luke sprinkles in biblical phrases to create an "Old Testament-like" tone to Stephen's speech. For example, at one point Stephen addresses his audience: "You obdurate creatures, cut off from the covenant in heart and hearing!" (Acts 7:51). This phrase imitates similar rebukes found in Exod 33:3, 5 and Jer 9:25.[10] Given the second-century date for Acts adopted in this commentary, Luke could not possibly have witnessed Stephen's speech. So he has created one. The LXX was a source for Stephen's speech in Acts.

Classical Literature. In today's world, few people have read the classical works of authors such as Homer and Euripides. But Dennis R. MacDonald reminds us that people in the Greco-Roman world were well versed in these works.[11] Students of that era were trained to *imitate* great literature. Luke would have been trained the same way. MacDonald points to a number of examples in Acts where Luke has used a story from a classic as the model for a story in Acts. One example will have to suffice.

Euripides' play *Bacchae* tells the story of the arrival of the cult of Dionysus in Thebes and the violent efforts of King Pentheus to stop it and its enthusiastic female devotees (maenads). Luke likewise describes the expansion of the new religion of Jesus in the face of violent opposition. MacDonald notes some of the parallels between the stories of Dionysus and Acts. The display of tongue speaking at Pentecost in Acts 2 recalls the divine madness of the women at the beginning of the *Bacchae*, including the charge of drunkenness. The prophet Tiresias interprets the women's mania as prophecy, just as Peter explains that God has poured out the holy spirit of prophecy on Jesus' followers (Acts 2:14–21). As Pentheus opposes Dionysius, so the Jewish authorities play the same role throughout Acts in their opposition to the Christian movement. When Pentheus imprisons the maenads and Dionysus, they miraculously escape. Similarly, when the high priest throws the apostles into jail, an angel breaks them out (5:17–26). MacDonald cites many other parallels and shared characteristics between Euripides' *Bacchae* and Luke's Acts. Perhaps it is not quite right to say that Euripides (and other classical authors) served as sources for Luke; but they certainly provided themes and story lines.

Luke's use of Paul's letters (a real source), the LXX, and Greek classics indicates that Luke was a skilled and creative writer. Creative writing does not exclude historical reliability, but clearly the two are not the same.

The Text of Acts
Richard I. Pervo

Since they were copied by hand, each copy of an ancient text differed from every other copy. Changes, varying in degree of importance, were introduced by accident and by design. The notion of intellectual property did not exist. Some changes came about because of editorial "improvements" and corrections. The text of the NT did not become standardized (and partially protected by the rubric of canonization) until the Middle Ages. Changes in texts occurred most rapidly in the first generation. The texts on which we base the NT today tend to be primarily from the fourth century, with substantial input from the third century and some from the second.

The text of Acts has come down in different editions. The version that is generally viewed as closest to the original is the "Alexandrian," a fourth-century edition with some corrections of grammar and syntax. The other early edition is known as the "Western" or, better, the "D-text."[12] Behind this edition—if it is a single edition—stands an earlier type of text that is sometimes superior to the Alexandrian. In many cases this edition is longer, as much as 9 percent longer in some sections, than the Alexandrian. At other points, such as Acts 27 (the voyage to Rome), it is shorter. Abridgment and expansion were characteristics of the transmission of ancient texts.

Many of the differences in the D-text are pedantic adjustments, as in Acts 5:17–26, where servants are reported as finding the prison empty at the beginning. Others add novelistic details, such as the provision of seven steps in 12:10, where Peter is escaping from prison. Still others enhance the status of Paul and the apostles and heighten animosity toward Jews. The D-text represents a stage of development between Luke's work and the style and mentality of the later second-century *Acts of Paul*. The D-text is generally considered secondary to the Alexandrian text because D-text readings tend best to be explained as alterations of the Alexandrian text rather than vice versa. The D-text demonstrates that second- (and third-) century readers of Acts did not regard it as a sacred and immutable book, but rather as a writing that could be revised as needed.

Acts, Myth, and History[13]

Joseph B. Tyson

Rudolf Bultmann taught us a great deal about the place and function of myth in the ancient world, and he suggested ways in which we can translate ancient myth for a post-Enlightenment era. Bultmann defined myth as

> the conception of the world as being structured in three stories, heaven, earth and hell; the conception of the intervention of supernatural powers in the course of events; and the conception of miracles, especially the conception of the intervention of supernatural powers in the inner life of the soul, the conception that men can be tempted and corrupted by the devil and possessed by evil spirits. This conception of the world we call mythological because it is different from the conception of the world which has been formed and developed by science since its inception in ancient Greece and which has been accepted by all modern men.[14]

The book of Acts certainly conforms to this definition. As a text from the ancient world, it speaks to us from the context that Bultmann described. Thus, we read of divine intervention in the choice of a successor apostle, of tongues of fire coming down and causing certain people to speak clearly in languages that are foreign to them, of healings by means of a passing shadow, of death seemingly caused by speech, of an angelic release from prison, of voices from the sky, of scale-like substances falling from formerly blind eyes, of multiple visions with divine messages, of inexplicable survivals of shipwreck and snake bite, and on and on. The author of Acts shares the worldview of his own time, which explains this-worldly events in terms of a world beyond.

More recent studies have focused attention on other meanings and functions of the concept of myth, and these studies further illuminate the role that Acts has played in the history of Christianity. Many students of myth stress the social function of traditional narratives in expressing, enhancing, and codifying belief, as well as in safeguarding and enforcing morality. Members of the Society of Biblical Literature's Seminar on Ancient Myth and Modern

Theories of Christian Origins have illuminated the role of myth-making in social construction, and they make use of this concept in their explorations of Acts.[15] They often speak of myths as charters for social organization and behavior.

The understanding of myth as charter illuminates the composition of Acts and the ways it has functioned in the history of Christianity. To be sure, the miraculous elements that Bultmann's definition stressed have impressed generations of Christians. But the role of Acts in constructing a myth of Christian origins may best be seen in its basic themes, which do not depend wholly on the miraculous. The author of Acts stresses the unitary character of the Jesus movement. He includes inspiring narratives that portray the unity and harmony of the earliest community and the authoritative role of twelve male apostles. Readers learn that, under the leadership of these apostles, disputes are easily settled and the community adheres to a practice of sharing wealth. In Acts the early Jesus community is faithful to the Hebrew Scriptures and to Jewish rites and traditions, despite the opposition of Jewish authorities. Readers of Acts learn that the Christian movement began in Jerusalem under the leadership of men appointed by Jesus, men who witnessed the resurrection and were commanded to remain in Jerusalem until they received the spirit. They also know that, although he was not an apostle, Paul allied himself solidly with the Jerusalem church and the apostles and that he engaged in missionary activity under their scrutiny. In all that the Christian leaders did they were guided by the divine, and everything they did was accomplished in an orderly fashion.

Acts is a charter myth, not only because its author adopts the mythological context that Bultmann described, but chiefly because the basic themes he employs dominate the story he tells. If we ask if the story could have been told differently, we have only to ask about a believer whose writings come from the very period that Acts describes—the letters of Paul. These letters give us an impression of a movement that was not so well organized, a movement with diverse factions and competing theologies. In the Pauline communities, problems do not appear to be easily resolved. In these communities there are apostles, and Paul insists that he is one. But there is no definite number of apostles, no requirement that they be associates of the historical Jesus, and no necessity that they all must be male. Although Paul acknowledges and respects the apostles who preceded him in the faith, he stresses his independence from them.

Acts is a charter myth, whose author composed an idyllic portrait of the early Jesus community. His narrative is governed by themes that support this portrait. He is writing at some distance in time from the events he describes, and he inevitably presents a perspective that is very different from that of an eyewitness such as Paul.

If the Acts of the Apostles is a charter myth, a myth of Christian origins, should it then be regarded as a source for historical study? Many studies of Acts have ignored its mythological character and answered the question of history in the affirmative. Some highly regarded studies of Christian origins are, for the most part, relatively uncritical replications of Acts. The study by Jean Daniélou and Henri Marrou is typical. The authors regret that Acts "covers only part of the history of primitive Christianity,"[16] but still regard it as of indisputable historical value. On Pentecost, they comment: "It is as impossible to write the history of the Church without starting from the descent of the Holy Spirit at Pentecost in the year 30, as to write the history of Christ without starting from the incarnation of the Word on the day of the Annunciation."[17] W. H. C. Frend accepts the structure of Acts as basic to his own historical construction.[18] Although he suspects that things might have been more complex than Luke allowed, he nevertheless accepts as historical the leadership of the Jerusalem church and the apostles, and he traces the development of the Christian movement through the Hellenists and Stephen.

More recent scholars have been more vigilant in distinguishing myth and history. Luther Martin makes the distinction clear: "If the texts produced by early Christians are to be understood as the products of their mythmaking, they cannot then count as historiographical documentation in support of events portrayed in their production."[19] Gerd Lüdemann says it even more provocatively:

> God or god should play no role in the historical investigation. The Acts of the Apostles must be investigated as all other religious or nonreligious texts are examined. And the rule that applies for historical science should also apply for theological science when it comes to the investigation of the historical records of Christianity.[20]

Martin and Lüdemann show that the reconstruction of the history of early Christianity cannot be accomplished without fully recognizing that the Acts of the Apostles, a source on which many historians have heavily depended, is a myth of Christian origins.

We cannot, however, rule out the possibility that a myth may include historical fragments. Narratives in the book of Acts, though dominated by nonhistorical themes, may very well contain historical materials drawn from earlier sources or traditions that rest on genuine historical reminiscences. This means that a study of Acts that is interested in history involves a most difficult task, namely the distilling of historical material from the myth. In the chapters that follow an effort has been made to do precisely this. Each chapter includes a section, entitled "In Search of History," which examines the possibly historical aspects of each narrative in Acts and discusses the ballots cast by members of the Acts Seminar on these potential historical aspects. While fully conscious of the power of Acts as a myth of Christian origins, we nevertheless intend to search for a history that might be contained within or behind its narratives. At the same time, given the probable date in which Acts was written, we may expect to find that it tells us as much or more about Christianity in the second century as in the first.

The Votes of the Fellows

Red/Probable

- The Acts of the Apostles is best understood as a myth of Christian origins.
- The use of Acts in historical investigation must include a consideration of the context within which it was probably composed.
- Historical data about first-century Christianity can be derived from Acts only where a credible case can be made for the existence of reliable underlying tradition that was used and perhaps modified in Acts.
- The Acts of the Apostles is more valuable for second-century Christianity than for first.

Pink/Possible

- The author of Acts used some ancient reliable traditions in the composition of the book.
- Critical historians can identify ancient reliable traditions that were used in the composition of Acts.

Black/Improbable

- The Acts of the Apostles should be employed as the basis for a historical study of Christian origins.
- The Acts of the Apostles is a primary source for Pauline biography or Pauline chronology.

The Design of This Book

The next five chapters of this book follow the order of chapters in Acts. Each of them contains translations of the sections under consideration, followed by two major segments. One segment consists of "Comments on the Story," which explores the probable meaning of the text as an early second-century reader might perceive it. Connections to other parts of Acts are indicated, and problems in understanding the narrative are explored. A second segment of each chapter is entitled, "In Search of History," which explores the likely historical reliability of the material under consideration. This segment generally includes a record of the votes of the Westar Fellows on issues connected with the particular section of Acts. Scattered through the chapters are a number of "Cameo Essays," which provide additional information or explore issues not covered elsewhere. A final chapter summarizes some of the conclusions to be drawn from this study. The book is not a commentary in the conventional sense, since many aspects of the composition of Acts will not be treated. It is our hope, nevertheless, that the book will serve to aid in the understanding of Acts and its bearing on early Christian history.

1
Beginning in Jerusalem
Acts 1:1–8:3

The Prologue

1 In the previous book, Theophilus, I dealt with all that Jesus did and taught from the beginning ²until that day when he was taken up after instructing the apostles whom he had been inspired to choose.

Comments on the Story

The beginning of Acts identifies this document as the second volume of a two-volume work, the first volume being the Gospel of Luke. Luke begins with a prologue addressed to Theophilus (Luke 1:1–4), and this dedication to Theophilus is repeated here, along with a reference to "the previous book." Such prologues are common in ancient literature and indicate that the author has literary pretensions and wishes the reader to know this.

In Search of History

The Prologue and History

The prologue to Acts is much abbreviated. It indicates a connection with the previous book, it renews the dedication to Theophilus, and it rehearses the main themes of volume one. The prologue of volume one, the Gospel of Luke, is much more extensive and contains typical features intended to assure the reader of the accuracy of the document it introduces. Some scholars have read the use of the prologues in Luke and Acts as an indication that the author is self-consciously identifying this work as a work of history. This argument is commonly used to make the case for the historical reliability of Acts. Paradoxically, the prologue is rarely cited as justification for arguing that Luke is the most reliable of the gospels. An analysis of the use of sources in the Gospel of Luke indicates a high level of creativity and reinterpretation as characteristic of this author. He is not one who tries to preserve a source just as he found it. Rather he feels free to change a source to fit his own theological needs. Since that is the case in the Gospel, it is difficult to maintain that sources for Acts would have been treated with a different level of respect and concern for accuracy. The Fellows therefore concluded that the prologue is unreliable as a marker of historical accuracy.

Theophilus

There is a tendency in Acts research to assume that proper names usually refer to historical figures, based on the idea that historical memory is the best explanation for the occurrence of proper names. However, examples from Greek and Roman literature illustrate how common it is in narrative texts that an author will provide, or better, create, a symbolic name for a character to fit the story within which the character is placed. The use of proper names also adds verisimilitude to a story. For these reasons, the Acts Seminar has adopted as a working hypothesis the position that names attested only in Acts should be assumed to be fictional unless there are good reasons for considering them to be historical. (see cameo essay, "Names in Acts," p. 22)

It is a standard feature of prologues to dedicate the work to a named individual who functioned as the patron for the writing of the document. In this case, however, the name Theophilus is suspiciously symbolic. Its meaning in Greek is "God-lover." The seminar therefore concluded that the character of Theophilus was most likely fictional.

The Votes of the Fellows

Red/Probable
- Luke used proper names to add verisimilitude to his story.

Gray/Doubtful
- Theophilus ("God lover"), to whom both Luke and Acts are dedicated, was a real person.

Black/Improbable
- The prologues of Luke and Acts indicate that Luke-Acts can be read as reliable history.

Names in Acts

A Cameo Essay by Christine R. Shea

The scholarly consensus once was that, although names in the Hebrew Scriptures had symbolic significance, NT names did not.

Recent work on the names *Stephen* ("Crowned [with the martyr's crown]") and *Damaris* ("Wife") reminds us that not all the names in Acts are personal—and, thus, historical. Yet, we should long ago have expected the names of Acts would contribute some special meaning to our understanding of the text, since:

1. Acts is the product of traditions that regard names as signifying. Thus, individuals likely know—and expect others to know—the meaning of their names. Julius Caesar, for example, being bald, was apparently embarrassed by one etymology of *Caesar*—"hairy"—and chose instead to derive it from the Carthaginian word for elephant, which suggests an ancestor who had killed an elephant in battle; thus, his coins have elephants.

2. In Greek and Roman traditional tales and the Hebrew Scriptures, characters often have names that give clues to their fates. This is a commonplace in epic: the chief suitor in the *Odyssey*, for example, is *Antinoos* ("Opposed Mind"). Greek and Roman historians, too, report that battles, for example, turned on the lucky or unlucky name of a general.

3. Speaking a well- or ill-omened name has divinatory meaning. The ancients regard the name as something conveying powerful magic: Odysseus is smart enough to conceal his true name from the Cyclops Polyphemus—for a time. When he reveals his name, Polyphemus uses it to call down evil on him. Acts has similar examples and apparently understands those examples in a similar way. In the account of Paul's arrest and trials in Acts 22–28, the two Roman governors are Felix and Porcius Festus. These two may be actual historical figures. Nevertheless, the use of their names here clearly conveys a sense of omen. *Felix* means "happy, lucky, blessedly happy"—it originally belonged to religious language. It will come to mean "happy like the blessed dead" in Christianity. *Porcius Festus* clearly suggests "a festal meal of pork" (*porcus* is a tame pig; *festus* pertains to religious feasts). Moreover, the names may give a hint to the outcome of the conflict between Paul and the Romans and may say clearly to the ancient reader what the true ending of the work is. *Felix* should be a word for the martyred dead who have found their way to heaven immediately. *Pig*, of course, is a Judeo-Christian ethnic joke, appropriate to people who kill Christians—Christians like Paul, perhaps.

4. Calling the name of supernatural figures, such as gods or the dead, has ritual significance in most of the cultures of the Mediterranean; and

5. Acts from its first words invites such analysis. The text is directed at one Theophilus, whose name has a significant meaning, "God-Lover," that might be thought to be too appropriate to be real (see Luke 1:3; Acts 1:1). If we persist in regarding this text as a historical document, we will forever be chasing Luke's friend Theophilus. But if we can concede that Luke intended us to use this text in a ritual context, to regard it as a living work reenacted with every reading, then the "God-Lover" is clearly you, dear reader. Luke has chosen to address the work to "God-Lover" because that is what he hopes will be the outcome of reading it. Naming the name would be understood as an omen. It would also serve as an instruction to watch for other significant names in the text.

There is another indication in Acts that names are carrying much more weight than we are accustomed to give them: name changes seem to mark a character's ascent to a higher level of spiritual—and social—significance. This should not seem unfamiliar to us; after all, Jesus himself acquires the name *Christ*.

In Acts 4:36 we have an example of a disciple, Joseph, whose name is changed when he is drafted into Christian society by the apostles. This example illustrates that a change in name signifies a change in status—a conversion from "out" to "in" group. This may reflect an actual ritual of the early Christian communities, a ritual that may linger on in the practice of taking a new name at Confirmation. This episode, then, may provide a founding myth for a Christian coming-of-age ritual. But whatever significance this story may have in ritual, it certainly functions to alert us to the symbolic significance of names and name *changes* in this narrative, the most notable example of which is Saul/Paul.

Resurrection Appearance, Instructions, and Ascension

1 ³For forty days after his passion he gave them numerous proofs that he was alive. He appeared to them and spoke about God's reign. ⁴During a meal, he directed them not to leave Jerusalem. "Wait here," he said, "to receive what the Father has promised, about which I have told you. ⁵John baptized with water. Before many days have passed you will be baptized with Holy Spirit."

⁶On one of these occasions the apostles asked Jesus: "Lord, are you going to reestablish the kingdom of Israel now?"

⁷"The choice of times and occasions is up to God, not you," he replied. ⁸"You will receive power after the Holy

Spirit has come upon you and you will be my witnesses in Jerusalem and in the rest of Judea, in Samaria, and to the ends of the earth."

⁹Then, as they watched, he was taken up, hidden from their sight by a cloud. ¹⁰As he went, they continued to stare into the sky, when two men in white suddenly appeared right next to them, and said: ¹¹"Why are you standing here looking into the sky, Galileans? Jesus has been taken up from your midst into the sky, from which he will return in the same way that you saw him leave."

Comments on the Story

The prologue alludes to the contents of "the previous book": all that Jesus had done and taught prior to his ascension, including some last minute instructions to his apostles. This is an adequate, if brief, summary of the Gospel of Luke, the only one of the canonical gospels to contain a narrative of the ascension of Jesus. In the last chapter of Luke we have a number of unique post-resurrection narratives: the walk to Emmaus (Luke 24:13–35); Jesus' appearance to the remaining eleven disciples in Jerusalem (24:36–49); and the ascension at Bethany (24:50–53).

A theme that ties Luke and Acts together is the centrality of Jerusalem. The Gospel of Luke differs from the other Synoptic Gospels in locating the post-resurrection appearances of Jesus in and around Jerusalem. By contrast, Matthew places the appearance to the disciples in Galilee (see Matt 28:16–20). Both in the last chapter of Luke and in the first chapter of Acts, Jesus' associates are told to remain in Jerusalem (Luke 24:49; Acts 1:4). In both it is envisioned that the preaching of the gospel will begin in Jerusalem and extend to the Gentiles (Luke 24:47; Acts 1:8).

Despite the common themes and linking narratives in Luke and Acts, there are striking differences. In Luke 24 the various narratives occur on the same day: the discovery of the empty tomb is set early on the day after the Sabbath (Luke 24:1); the walk to Emmaus is expressly said to be "on the same day" (Luke 24:13); the appearance to the eleven occurs just as the two companions return from Emmaus (Luke 24:33); and the ascension of Jesus occurs without further interruption. In Acts, however, the risen Jesus remains with his chosen ones for a period of forty days (Acts 1:3). The ascension in Luke is said to be at Bethany, and in Acts it is the "Olive Grove." Presumably, both are in the vicinity of Jerusalem, but they are not the same places.

Acts 1:4 repeats the words attributed to Jesus in Luke 24:49. The apostles are told to remain in Jerusalem until they receive a promise from the Father. In Luke the promise is described as "power from on high," while in Acts 1:5 it is the reception of the Holy Spirit. As we shall see, the promise is fulfilled in Acts 2. Yet another allusion to the Gospel shows up in Acts 1:5, which reports words of John the Baptist that are similar to those in Luke 3:16: "I baptize you with water; but someone more powerful than I is coming. I'm not fit to untie his sandal straps. He'll baptize you with holy spirit and fire." The allusion to fire is missing here in Acts 1:5, but in Acts 2:3 the coming of the spirit is said to be accompanied by "phenomena resembling jagged fiery tongues."

The consequence of the promise of the spirit is not crystal clear, either to the participants in the story or to the readers. The apostles wonder if it is to be the reestablishment of the kingdom of Israel (Acts 1:6); Jesus outlines a mission of the apostles in Jerusalem, Judea, Samaria, and the ends of the earth (1:8); at Jesus' ascension two men in white predict his return "in the same way that you saw him leave" (1:11). To the question about the kingdom of Israel, Luke has Jesus answer in words taken from Mark 13:32. Strictly speaking, Jesus' answer is not a denial of the re-establishment of the kingdom of Israel, but a command not to speculate about "times and occasions" (Acts 1:7). The fuller response in 1:8 focuses attention on the mission of the apostles, which includes a mission to Israel but extends to Gentiles. Acts 1:8 is frequently understood to be programmatic for Acts, a kind of outline for the book as a whole. Indeed, we will see that the apostles loosely follow a kind of itinerary, preaching first in Jerusalem, then in other parts of Judea, Samaria, and finally among Gentiles outside of the traditional land of Israel. The intent seems to be to stress that those who witness to Jesus are not to limit their mission to Jews but to include Gentiles. This is a major theme of the book of Acts.

The ascension of Jesus in Acts 1:9–11 constitutes a problem for the theory of the unity of Luke-Acts. If we read through the two books one after the other, we learn that Jesus ascended twice, from different locations and under different circumstances. As Ernst Haenchen astutely observed, "Two Ascensions—one on Easter Day (Luke 24.51), the other forty days after (Acts 1.9)—are one too many."[1] More recently, Mikeal C. Parsons has highlighted the literary significance of the story in its two contexts at the end of Luke and the beginning of Acts. He concludes: "Through the literary device of redundancy in the ascension narrative, [Luke] both ties his two volumes together with repetition, yet moves ahead to tell the tale of the early church by expanding the symbol."[2] According to Parsons, the ascension story is told differently in its two contexts in order to serve two different literary purposes. In Acts, it serves to separate the period of Jesus from the period of the church. The church, under the leadership of the apostles, remains in the world witnessing to the departed Jesus and waiting for his return. Notably, although the rest of the book of Acts devotes significant attention to the mission of the apostles (and later Paul), the pending return of Jesus is almost totally ignored.

In Search of History

The Acts story of the origins of the church in Jerusalem has dominated reconstructions of Christian origins from early times until the present. Because of the significance of Jerusalem origins to the overall narrative plot and theology of Acts, the Acts Seminar devoted multiple papers and discussions to this section of Acts. That theme begins with, and depends on, this story of resurrection and ascension.

The resurrection/ascension story with which Acts begins is a re-presentation of the resurrection/ascension story with which the Gospel of Luke ends. It is a sign that the two works were meant to be read as a whole. The story in the Gospel of Luke is constructed as an extension, and radical revision, of the story in Mark. The story in Acts is a variation of the story in Luke. Such variability in telling the same story is a literary motif in Luke, as seen in the three variable versions he provides of the story of Paul's conversion.

Luke's only historically reliable resource is Paul. In Galatians, Paul refers to the existence of a Christian group in Jerusalem three years after his "conversion" experience, thus up to four or five years after the death of Jesus (Gal 1:17–18). How long had that community been there? Since Luke's version of events is historically unreliable (see cameo essay, "Deconstructing the Resurrection Narrative in Luke-Acts," p. 29), it seems more likely that Mark's allusion to a flight to Galilee is closer to the truth. Jerusalem would have become a dangerous place for Jesus followers in the immediate aftermath of Jesus' execution. They most likely fled Jerusalem at that time and then returned at a later point after things died down. This is the version accepted by the Fellows as the most likely historical version.

Luke may have had another source of indistinct form and content, which Richard Pervo has labeled the "Gentile Mission Source" (see cameo essay, "The Gentile Mission Source," p. 99). This source could have provided some details about events in Jerusalem, but only for the purpose of justifying the Gentile mission. There is insufficient evidence to propose that any data that might have been derived from this source had any historical value.

The phrase "you will be my witnesses in Jerusalem and in the rest of Judea, in Samaria, and to the ends of the earth" (Acts 1:8) is a programmatic foreshadowing of the rest of the story in Acts. Since this is said by the risen Lord just prior to the ascension, it functions as a divinely uttered prophecy. Embedded in this narrative, therefore, is the idea that there was a singular beginning and orderly progression of the Christian movement that was divinely ordained. This becomes a standard theme throughout the story in Acts. Since this theme is so firmly embedded in the Lukan account, and since that account is so firmly founded on a Lukan fiction, the entire underlying framework of the story is judged to be unhistorical.

References
Pervo, "My Happy Home"
Smith, "Was There a Jerusalem Church?"
Moreland, "Reconstructing Jerusalem 'Christians'" and "An Early Christian Idea of the New Jerusalem"

The Votes of the Fellows

Red/Probable
- The death of Jesus initially resulted in a dispersion of the followers of Jesus from Jerusalem and any reaggregation occurred only later.
- The idea that there was a singular beginning of Christianity in Jerusalem is a Lukan literary fiction.
- Paul is the best witness for the presence and importance of a community of Jesus followers in Jerusalem.
- Neither the author of Acts nor his sources display an interest in the early Jerusalem church that extends beyond justification of the Gentile mission.
- Very little can be said about the nature, structure, organization, and beliefs of the Jerusalem church(es).
- "Jerusalem" functions in Luke and Acts as a symbol of continuity both with ancient Israel and with the Gentile mission.
- Luke has suppressed any data about a Galilean movement, including resurrection appearances, in favor of Jerusalem.

Pink/Possible
- When Paul makes his first trip to Jerusalem, three years after his conversion (ca. 35–38), there is an identifiable Jerusalem church.
- Paul explicitly confirms that there were other apostles in Jerusalem in the early years.

Gray/Doubtful
- Cephas and James lived in Jerusalem and thus were the leaders of the Jerusalem church.

Black/Improbable
- The disciples remained in Jerusalem after Jesus' death.
- The first church was formed in Jerusalem and all of Christianity spread from there.
- There was a singular beginning of Christianity.
- There was an orderly development of Christianity from its first beginning.
- The faith of the first disciples began with a resurrection event in Jerusalem.
- Acts is correct that the sole beginning of Christian faith was the resurrection.
- The Luke-Acts story of the ascension is historical.

Deconstructing the Resurrection Narrative in Luke-Acts

A Cameo Essay by Dennis E. Smith

The Gospel of Mark is our earliest known version of the death, burial, and empty tomb narrative. Mark does not have a resurrection-appearance narrative. However, there is a promise of a resurrection appearance from the divine messenger within the tomb. The key phrase is this (spoken to the women who have come to the tomb): "Go and tell his disciples, including 'Rock,' 'he is going ahead of you to Galilee! There you will see him, just as he told you'" (Mark 16:7). It should be noted that, according to Mark, the disciples are not to tarry one minute longer in Jerusalem. They are to go immediately to Galilee. The resurrection appearance would take place in Galilee, not Jerusalem. In fact, there is no indication that Jerusalem held any future promise for them at all.

Luke's empty tomb narrative is clearly built entirely out of Mark's story, but told in such a way as to support a different story of the post-resurrection actions of the apostles. The key phrase is this (spoken by the angelic messengers to the women): "Remember what he told you while he was still in Galilee: 'The Human One is destined to be turned over to sinners, to be crucified, and on the third day to rise'" (Luke 24:6–7). Notice how the reference to Galilee has been changed from a destination to a location where Jesus taught. Luke has radically altered Mark in order to tell a different story.

In Luke the disciples stay in Jerusalem for the resurrection appearances. Those appearances include the charge, "Stay here in the city until you are invested with power from on high" (Luke 24:49b; see also Acts 1:4). Following those instructions, Luke recounts an ascension story: "And while he was blessing them, it came to pass that he departed from them, and was carried up into the sky" (Luke 24:51; see also Acts 1:9).

This version of events is distinctive to Luke-Acts. Mark foresees a resurrection appearance in Galilee, but by no means in Jerusalem. Matthew, following Mark, provides a resurrection-appearance narrative on a mountain in Galilee (Matt 28:16–20). John contains resurrection-appearance narratives in both Jerusalem and Galilee (John 20:11–21:14). Paul refers to a varied succession of resurrection appearances without any geographic or temporal specificity, the last of which is an appearance to him (1 Cor 15:4–8), which would have taken place many months after the death of Jesus and in a location far from Jerusalem (Gal 1:15–17). Luke's story rules out the validity of any of these other stories. Only Luke recounts an ascension narrative, the function of which is to rule out any other resurrection appearances except those presented in Luke-Acts.

In conclusion, none of the other NT writers affirm in any way Luke's version of events; they appear to be oblivious to the existence of such a story of origins. The writer of Luke-Acts on the other hand, while familiar with other such stories, explicitly invalidates them all by ending his version with the ascension narrative. Luke's entire Jerusalem-origins narrative, from the resurrection appearances to the command to stay in Jerusalem to the distinctive events in Jerusalem, is built on a Lukan fiction, constructed to lay a foundation for the apologetic story he will tell in the rest of Acts.

The Constitution of the Twelve Apostles

1 [12]They then headed back to Jerusalem from Mount Olive Grove, which is about half a Sabbath's journey from the city. [13]They went up to the second-floor room in which they had been staying. These people were Peter and John, James and Andrew, Philip and Thomas, Bartholomew and Matthew, James the son of Alphaeus and Simon "the zealot," and Judas, son of James. ¹⁴All these men, as well as the women disciples and Mary the mother of Jesus and his siblings, devoted themselves to a common life of prayer.

¹⁵A few days later Peter arose to address the assembled believers, who then numbered about 120. ¹⁶"My fellow believers, the scripture about Judas, a prediction of the Holy Spirit through David, had to be fulfilled. Judas showed those who arrested Jesus where to find him. ¹⁷Judas belonged to our company and had a share in this ministry. ¹⁸While on the farm he had obtained with his ill-gotten gains, he fell flat on his face. His stomach burst open, and all of his insides poured out. ¹⁹Everybody in Jerusalem learned about this, and so they called the place 'Blood Farm'—'Akeldama' in their language. ²⁰Scripture says, in the Book of Psalms: 'His homestead is to become a deserted place where no one will live,' as well as 'Someone else is to assume his responsibilities.' ²¹For that we must have one of the men who have been with us from the Lord Jesus' arrival to his departure, ²²that is, from his baptism by John until he was taken up from us. This person must, like us, be a witness of his resurrection."

²³Two names were presented: that Joseph known as "Barsabbas," also known as "Justus," and Matthias. ²⁴After offering this prayer: "Lord, to whom all hearts are open, show which of these two you have chosen ²⁵to assume this place of apostolic ministry that Judas abandoned to go to his rightful place," ²⁶they cast lots. The lot indicated that Matthias was chosen to join the other eleven apostles.

Comments on the Story

These verses, which narrate the constitution of the twelve apostles, continue a theme that we found in the previous section—the centrality of Jerusalem. Lest the reader think that there has been a violation of Jesus' instructions to remain in the city, the author of Acts is careful to add that the distance from Mt. Olive Grove to Jerusalem was within the limits allowed by Jewish law, a Sabbath day's journey, traditionally one kilometer. Not only does the author insist on the centrality of Jerusalem but he also implies that the followers of Jesus continued to observe Jewish regulations.

The small group of Jesus' followers apparently occupied a single room in an upper story of a Jerusalem dwelling. The group consisted of the remaining apostles, some female followers, and Jesus' family. The piety and unity of this small community is stressed here. Unity is another of the major themes in Acts, whose author uses the Greek word *homothumadon* to express the idea of unanimity and agreement. The word is found more frequently in Acts than in any other NT writing (see Acts 2:46; 4:24; 5:12; 15:25).

The first specific act of this small community is to organize itself under the leadership of twelve apostles. Eleven who were chosen by Jesus himself remain and are named in Acts 1:13. The names on the list are identical with those in Luke 6:14–16, with the exception of the omission of Judas Iscariot in Acts. In his speech in Acts 1:15–22, Peter calls for the selection of a replacement for Judas. He states that Judas' action in turning Jesus over to the authorities, as well as his ultimate fate, were predicted in Scripture, and he quotes from Ps 69:26 and 109:8 to prove it. It is notable that Peter's description of the death of Judas differs from that in Matt 27:3–10, the only other such description in the NT. In Matthew, Judas repented and returned the money paid to him for the betrayal of Jesus; in Acts he bought a piece of property. In Matthew, Judas' death is a suicide; in Acts, it is apparently an accident. Despite these major differences, it is remarkable that both stories refer to a field known as the "Blood Farm."

The leadership of the community under a group of apostles is an integral concept governing the first major section of Acts. By means of Peter's speech in Acts 1:15–22, the author lays out his conception of apostleship. First, an apostle must be a man—the gender is specific—who had been with Jesus from the time of Jesus' baptism to his ascension. Second, there must be twelve and only twelve apostles.

The first requirement—that an apostle must be one who had been with the historical Jesus—takes us back to Luke 6:12–16, where Jesus chooses twelve of his disciples and gives them the title, apostles. The specific requirement, announced by Peter in Acts 1:21–22, is that an apostle must be one who had been with the eleven and with Jesus from the time when Jesus was baptized by John until the time of his ascension. It is clear from the narrative in Acts 1 that the eleven were with Jesus up to the ascension, as (presumably) were the nominees for Judas' position, Matthias and Joseph Barsabbas, and other unnamed persons. But, in the Gospel of Luke, none of them were present at the time of the baptism. Jesus' baptism was narrated in Luke 3, but the first disciples were not called until Luke 5. This discrepancy is probably not significant for our author, but an important effect of the requirement cannot be overlooked. The requirement that an apostle must have been a disciple of the historical Jesus has the effect of excluding Paul from the list, although he dominates much of the Acts narrative (but see comments on Acts 14:4, 14). Moreover, the exclusion of Paul from the apostolic group totally undermines Paul's own repeated and vigorous claims to the title (see, for example, Gal 1:1; 1 Cor 9:1–2) as well as his concept of apostleship (see the cameo essay, "Apostleship in Early Christianity," p. 34).

The second criterion—that the number of apostles must remain constant at twelve—is also announced in Peter's speech. Peter says that the death of Judas had left the apostolic group in a defective condition, and he quotes Ps 109:8 to affirm the need to select a replacement. The idea that there were twelve leaders, originally chosen by Jesus, is not unique to Acts, but the strict limitation on the number is stressed here. The selection of Judas' replacement by prayer and casting lots is understood as a way of determining the will of God. Matthias, the replacement apostle, serves to complete the group, but it is notable that he is never mentioned again in Acts.

In subsequent narratives in Acts we learn that the apostles are not only workers of miracles, exorcists, and healers but that they also have authority to determine authentic practice, appoint and dispatch missionaries, and delegate responsibility. By linking apostleship to the historical Jesus and restricting it to twelve named individuals, the author of Acts developed the concept of twelve apostles in order to provide for the church a clear line of authoritative successors to Jesus.

In Search of History

The Twelve

The idea that there was a group known as "the Twelve" is already found in Paul (1 Cor 15:5, 7). But the way in which Luke paints the Twelve as apostles is distinctive. Here in Acts a case is made that the Twelve needed to be maintained as such; thus, with the death of Judas, another must be chosen. The overall story serves to reinforce a theme in Acts, namely the idea that there was a clear line of authoritative successors to Jesus. When seen in this light, it is clear that the various elements of the story function to promote the larger Lukan theme. Several of those elements were isolated on the ballot and all received black votes from the Fellows. They include such features as the death of Judas, the limiting of the early leaders to twelve, and the necessity that an "apostle" was required to have known the historical Jesus.

The Characters

Luke provides a list of apostles, but its potential historical usefulness is limited. There are other such lists in the gospel tradition and the differences among them are so great that it is not possible to produce a single authoritative version (compare Mark 3:16–19; Matt 10:2–4; Luke 6:14–16; Acts 1:13). This fact in itself undermines the argument that the characters in Luke's list are all historical figures. Nevertheless, based on gospel data already analyzed in the Jesus Seminar, and on references in Paul's letters, one can argue that Peter and John were historical individuals. The pink vote on Peter and John affirms their historicity with some reservations about the stability of the category of "apostle."

The Votes of the Fellows

Pink/Possible
- The historical Peter was known as an apostle.
- The historical John was known as an apostle.

Black/Improbable
- After the death of Jesus, apostles in Jerusalem became the sole leaders of the church.
- After the death of Jesus, Peter and other leaders agreed that the number of apostles was to be limited to twelve.
- After the death of Jesus, Peter and other leaders agreed that apostles must have known the historical Jesus.
- After the defection and death of Judas, a replacement was chosen.
- The story of the death of Judas in Acts 1:18–19 is historical.
- All the names on the "official list" of Acts 1:13 are those of historical persons.

Apostleship in Early Christianity

A Cameo Essay by Joseph B. Tyson

The concept of apostleship changed radically in the decades between Paul and the author of Acts. For Paul, as we may understand from reading his uncontested letters, apostles were leaders of Christian communities who exercised extensive authority in ethical and theological matters. The reader of Paul's letters learns that, in the early communities, there was no universally accepted means of legitimation for apostleship, that there were disagreements among apostles and rival groups of them, that they were not exclusively male, and that the number of apostles was not limited.

For Paul, apostles were called by God, and there is no suggestion that a connection with the pre-resurrected Jesus was a requirement for him or for any other apostle. Indeed, Paul insisted that, as a witness to the risen Jesus, he had been chosen to be an apostle. He never claimed to have an acquaintance with the historical Jesus but, nevertheless, exercised apostolic authority in the churches he founded.

In the genuine Pauline letters at least seven apostles are mentioned by name: Paul (Gal 1:1; Rom 1:1; 11:13; 1 Cor 1:1; 9:1, 2; 12:12; 15:9), Barnabas (1 Cor 9:6), Cephas/Peter (Gal 1:18–19; 2:8), James (Gal 1:19), Andronicus (Rom 16:7), Junia (Rom 16:7), and Epaphroditus (Phil 2:25); in addition there is an indefinite number of unnamed apostles. The presence of a female apostle in this group should not be overlooked, especially when we consider the later development of the apostolic tradition. It is especially notable that Junia is mentioned without further qualification or characterization, suggesting that she enjoyed parity with the other apostles.[3] Further, although we can derive only a limited number of names from the genuine Pauline correspondence, there are no indications that the number of apostles was in any way restricted.

When we get to the Acts of the Apostles, almost everything is different. Apostles are still characterized as authoritative leaders of the believing community. They have authority to determine authentic practice, appoint and dispatch missionaries, and delegate responsibility. But now the criteria are different. Peter's speech in Acts 1:15–22 makes it clear that there are two criteria: first, an apostle must be a man who had been a disciple of Jesus; second, there must be twelve and only twelve apostles.

Given the time difference between Paul and Acts (about seven decades), it might be tempting to think of Acts as simply a modernization of an earlier tradition. In a certain sense this is the case, but it is important to ask why this author so pointedly differed from Paul, especially since he had great esteem for him and probably had access to some of his letters. It is likely that the context in which Acts was written required Luke to reject the rather fluid Pauline concept of apostleship and project his own. During this long interval the Christian movement experienced great growth and increasing diversity. As a result there would have been considerable uncertainty on the issue of apostleship, an issue that in the second century had more than an antiquarian component. Many would agree that apostles had considerable authority, but would disagree on the criteria or composition of the group exercising such authority and delegating it to later generations. The author of Acts may well have felt the need to offer some concreteness and structure in an effort to resolve the uncertainty. The concept of apostleship in the early first century emphasized a kind of experience that could not be empirically verified and lacked historical associations that might provide a basis for adjudicating competing interpretations. With the Pauline understanding of apostleship, it would be difficult to counter the influence of Christian groups that stressed spiritual elements rather than historical events. With the Pauline understanding of apostleship, it would be difficult to counter the influence of Marcionism, with its concept of Paul as the only true apostle. With discipleship to Jesus as a requirement for those to whom the church looks for authority, our author elevated history as a way to distinguish the "proto-orthodox" from the "heretical" Christian groups.

In the process the Pauline tradition suffered collateral damage. As one who was not one of the twelve disciples of Jesus, Paul could no longer be listed among the apostles, and thus a title that was dear to him was denied to the most engaging character in Acts.[4]

Pentecost and Peter's First Sermon

2 On the day of Pentecost the entire group was together. [2]A sudden noise from above, like the roar of a strong rushing wind, filled the house in which they were sitting. [3]Phenomena resembling jagged fiery tongues appeared. One of these settled upon each person. [4]All were filled with Holy Spirit and, all, directed by the Spirit to give utterance, began to speak in foreign tongues.

[5]Among the residents of Jerusalem were devout persons from every country under the sun. [6]In response to the noise a crowd flocked together, for each and every one of them heard these people speaking in their native languages. [7]In absolute bewilderment they exclaimed: "Aren't all these people who are speaking Galileans? [8]How can it be that each of us is hearing our original language? [9]There are

Parthians, Medes, Elamites, residents of Mesopotamia, [---], Cappadocia, Pontus, Asia, ¹⁰Phrygia and Pamphylia, Egypt, residents of Cyrenean Libya, visiting Roman citizens, ¹¹Jews by birth and Jews by choice, Cretans and Arabs. Yet we are hearing these Galileans glorifying God in *our own* languages! ¹²All were bewildered and perplexed, constantly asking one another "What is going on?" ¹³although there were some who made fun of the whole business by announcing, "They're full of cheap wine."

¹⁴At that Peter took his place with the other eleven apostles and addressed the crowd in a strong and solemn tone: "Judeans, and all residents of Jerusalem: there is something that you need to know, so please pay attention. ¹⁵Now these people are not, as you suppose, drunk. It's only 900 [9:00 a.m.]! ¹⁶No; this is what the prophet spoke of: ¹⁷'After this it shall come to pass'—God is speaking—'that I shall pour out some of my spirit upon the whole human race. Then your sons and daughters will prophesy. Your young people will become visionaries and your elderly will become dreamers. ¹⁸Yes; in those days I shall pour out some of my spirit upon the men and women who serve me. ¹⁹I shall provide portents in the sky above and signs on the earth below: blood, fire, and misty vapor. ²⁰The sun will be darkened and the moon take on a bloody hue before the arrival of the Day of the Lord, that great and glorious day. ²¹It shall come to pass that anyone who calls upon the name of the Lord will be saved.'

²²"My fellow Israelites, listen to what I have to say. There was Jesus the Nazorean, a man whom God brought to your attention by performing mighty deeds, wonders, and signs through him in your very midst. Of these things you are well aware. ²³You had Jesus killed, nailed up by wicked hands. He was betrayed—but this was in accordance with God's prior knowledge and fixed plan! ²⁴God cut loose Hades' dreadful cords and brought Jesus back to life, because death could not maintain its grip on him. ²⁵With reference to Jesus, David says: 'I foresaw that the Lord was always with me; because he is at my right side I shall not be perturbed. ²⁶Therefore my heart has been happy and my tongue full of joy. Indeed, my flesh will live in hope, ²⁷for you will not let my soul languish in Hades,

nor will you allow your sacred one to experience decay. ²⁸You have shown me the paths of life; your presence will fill me with gladness.'

²⁹"Brothers and sisters, if I may be candid with you about the patriarch David, he is dead and buried. His tomb remains in our midst today. ³⁰Since, then, he was a prophet and knew that God had solemnly 'vowed to him' that 'one of his descendants would sit upon his throne,' ³¹David spoke with foreknowledge about the resurrection of the Messiah when he said, 'He was neither left to languish in Hades, nor' did his flesh 'face destruction.' ³²Accordingly, God brought this Jesus back to life. To that fact we can testify. ³³Therefore, after he had been exalted to God's right hand and had received from the father the promised Holy Spirit, he poured it out in your sight and hearing. ³⁴David did not ascend into the heavens, but he does say, 'The Lord said to my Lord, "Take a seat at my right ³⁵until I make your enemies a resting place for your feet."' ³⁶The entire nation of Israel must recognize beyond any doubt that God has made him both sovereign and Messiah, this Jesus whom you people crucified."

³⁷These words stung the consciences of the audience, and so they said to Peter and the other apostles: "What shall we do, brothers?"

³⁸Peter replied, "Change your ways. All of you must be baptized in the name of Jesus [the Messiah] for the forgiveness of your sins. You will then receive the gift of the Holy Spirit. ³⁹The promise is for you, for you and your children and all those far away, whomever the Lord our God might invite." ⁴⁰Peter pressed his argument for some time, continually urging them: "Save yourselves from this unscrupulous generation." ⁴¹Those who accepted Peter's message were therefore baptized. On that day God brought three thousand persons into the community.

Comments on the Story

Acts 2 is the fulfillment of the promise in Acts 1 (1:4–5, 8; also Luke 24:49). The apostles were ordered to remain in Jerusalem until they had received the baptism of the spirit. Now they are still in Jerusalem and it is Pentecost, fifty days after the Passover season, when Jesus was executed. Pentecost is the Greek term ("meaning fiftieth") for the festival that is referred to in the Hebrew Bible as the "festival of harvest" (Exod 23:16) or the "festival of weeks" (Deut 16:10).

The scene is apparently the same upper room that was described in Acts 1:13. Again the unity of the group is noted: they are all together in this one room (2:1) when a sudden gust of wind fills the room and fiery tongues appear. The author of Acts may have intended to remind the reader of the narrative in Exod 19:16–19, when God appeared on Mt. Sinai. There the divine appearance was accompanied by wind and fire, as well as thunder, lightning, smoke, clouds, and a loud trumpet. A more likely allusion, however, is the story of Babel in Gen 11:1–9. The story in Acts appears to be the reversal of the Babel narrative. In Genesis it is said that all the people of the earth spoke the same language and that YHWH caused them to speak different languages to prevent them from achieving unlimited goals. In Acts 2, the people who speak different languages are able to hear about the mighty acts of God proclaimed in their native languages by Galileans, who know only their own language, presumably Aramaic. This phenomenon, called glossolalia, should not be understood as the speaking of an unknown language. The author of Acts appears to take special pains to make it clear to the reader that actual human languages are heard by a large variety of persons from different cultures.

We should probably assume that this first group of auditors is a Jewish audience. Although some texts omit the reference to Jews in Acts 2:5, others say that Jerusalem was occupied by devout Jews from every country. Acts 2:9–11 serves as an expansion of this phrase: among the devout Jews in Jerusalem were Parthians, Medes, Elamites, etc. Luke separates the earlier mission to Jews from the later one to Gentiles, which does not begin until the conversion of Cornelius in Acts 10. The phenomenon of glossolalia, therefore, serves to introduce the mission of the apostles to their fellow Jews.

There is a note of realism in Luke's reference to those who "made fun of the whole business by announcing, 'They're full of cheap [or new] wine'" (Acts 2:13). Apparent miracles do not convince everyone, and the author recognizes that there may be alternate explanations. Clearly, however, the mocking explanation is not satisfactory: it may explain the speaking of the Galileans, but are all the auditors also filled with cheap wine?

The speech of Peter in Acts 2:14–41 continues the theme of fulfillment. Not only did Jesus charge the apostles to remain in Jerusalem until they had received the spirit (Acts 1:4), but he also commanded them to be his witnesses first in Jerusalem (Acts 1:8). Peter's speech is the first explicit notice about the act of witnessing, an act that Peter stresses in Acts 2:32 in connection with the resurrection of Jesus: "to that fact we can testify" or, "of that all of us are witnesses."

In the early chapters of Acts Peter is the unquestioned leader of the community of Jesus' followers. One might find his lofty position surprising in view of the narrative of his denial of Jesus in Luke 22:54–62. Nevertheless, in the Gospel of Luke Simon Peter is clearly treated as among the closest confidants of Jesus and in some cases the spokesperson for the rest of the disciples. He is the first to be selected (Luke 5:1–11), and he is first in the lists of Luke 6:14–16 and Acts 1:13 (see also Luke 8:51; 9:20, 28–36; 22:8; 24:12). Despite Peter's weaknesses in the Gospel, his primacy among the apostles in Acts is beyond dispute. We have already noted his leadership in the constitution of the twelve apostles (Acts 1:15–22).

Peter's speech here is initially linked with the charge of drunkenness. He explains that 9:00 a.m. is too early for these people to be drunk and that the observed phenomenon is the fulfillment of prophecy, specifically Joel 2:28–32. One might wonder if Peter's speech is a continuation of the phenomenon of glossolalia, described above. Does Peter speak in Aramaic and the auditors hear him in their own languages? The author tells us nothing along these lines; he only has Peter address his audience as "Judeans, and all residents of Jerusalem," probably implying that the speaker and audience speak a common language.

Peter's speech here is the longest of those in the early chapters of Acts, but it shares basic themes with several of the later speeches, all of which are directed to Jewish people and their leaders. These themes are five in number:

1. Prophecy has been fulfilled. The quotation from Joel in Acts 2:17–21 is interpreted as fulfilled in the phenomenon of glossolalia. A quotation from Ps 16:8–11 in Acts 2:25–28 is understood as a prediction of the resurrection of Jesus. The key verse in this quotation is Ps 16:10. It is first quoted in Acts 2:27, but after observing that David, the presumed author of the Psalm, died and that his burial place is still known, Peter claims that the verse in question could not have applied to David. Then he quotes the verse again in Acts 2:31, but now with grammatical changes to show how it is to be interpreted: "He [the Messiah] was neither left to languish in Hades, nor did his flesh 'face destruction.'" The logic of the argument is that

David's words in the Psalm are true and authoritative but cannot apply to him; they must apply to Jesus, as a descendant of David. A similar argument is used to support Peter's claim about the ascension of Jesus. David, in Ps 110:1, seems to foresee himself as seated at God's right hand. But, according to Peter in this speech, it was Jesus, not David, who ascended to heaven, so the words must have been written prophetically to apply to him (Acts 2:34–35).

2. Jesus is the Messiah appointed for Israel. The course of Peter's argument here is significant. In Acts 2:22, he refers to Jesus as a man (*anēr* in Greek), a male human being. Then after reciting the events of his crucifixion, resurrection, and ascension, Peter concludes with the ringing announcement that "God has made him both sovereign [or Lord] and Messiah, this Jesus whom you people crucified" (Acts 2:36). This formulation is usually referred to as adoptionistic Christology. It seems to be the conviction of the Lukan Peter that God adopted the human Jesus after his crucifixion, thus Jesus *became* the Christ. This formulation is quite distant from later Trinitarian formulations, which claim that the Christ was an eternal divine being who became incarnated in the human Jesus. Indeed, it is a formulation that encourages the examination of Jesus' life as fully human and historical. It should also be noted that Peter's speech stresses the relationship of the Christ to Israel: Jesus is a Nazorean, who performed mighty works "in your very midst" (2:22) and became Messiah in fulfillment of Hebrew prophecy (2:36). These statements serve as strong affirmations of the permanence of the relationship between God and the Jewish people. There is no explicit indication that Jesus has a meaning for non-Jews, although Acts 2:39 may move in this direction. We shall see that in later chapters of Acts the mission to Gentiles becomes a dominant motif.

3. You Jews killed Jesus. The crucifixion of Jesus is, of course, fully narrated in the Gospel of Luke, where responsibility for the death of Jesus is a more complex matter (see Luke 22:66–23:25). The complexity is partly reflected in Acts 2:23: "You had Jesus killed, nailed up by wicked hands." The word translated here as "wicked" refers literally to lawless people or people without law. It is likely that the reference is to people without the Jewish law, that is, people without Torah. If so, Peter would be referring to the Roman authorities who actually administered Jesus' execution, but the meaning seems to be that these authorities were only carrying out the wishes of the Jews. The charge is repeated, but in more direct terms, in Acts 2:36, "this Jesus whom you people crucified." There is no difficulty in determining who the perpetrators are, since the audience is "Judeans and all residents of Jerusalem" (2:14), "fellow Israelites" (2:22), "brothers and sisters" (2:29). In these charges the author of Acts has contributed to a long history of Christian anti-Judaism, marked by claims about responsibility for the death of Jesus that are almost surely unhistorical.

4. God raised Jesus from the dead. Peter announces the resurrection of Jesus in every speech, where it serves as a counterpoint to the crucifixion. The structure of these announcements sets the negative action of the Jews against the positive action of God: Jews killed Jesus, but God raised him up (Acts 2:23–24). The announcement in 2:31–32 is not immediately accompanied by a statement about the crucifixion, but here it functions chiefly as a scriptural interpretation. Acts 2:36 forcefully highlights the opposition between the purposes of God and those of Peter's audience: "God has made him both sovereign and Messiah, this Jesus whom you people crucified."

5. Repent and be forgiven. Peter responds to a question from his audience by directing them to repent and be baptized for the forgiveness of their sins (Acts 2:38). In view of the earlier characterization of at least some residents of Jerusalem as devout (2:5), it is surprising that Peter says nothing about specific sins that require repentance. We can only surmise that the sin of killing Jesus is intended here, a sin so heinous that all the people of Israel must repent. Note also that the newly repentant and baptized will receive "the gift of the Holy Spirit" (2:38), presumably in the way that the original apostles had experienced.

Luke ends the speech with a note about its success: about three thousand persons were baptized and became members of the community. The community that, in Acts 1:13–14, could fit in one room had grown to 120 in 1:15 and now adds 3,000 more. In Acts 4:4 the community is said to include 5,000 men, in addition to unnumbered women and children.

In Search of History

This story is an inherent component of the Jerusalem origins theme in Acts, a theme that has already been discredited as historical in earlier discussions in this chapter. It is dominated by a lengthy speech by Peter. As argued in the cameo essay "Speeches in Acts" on p. 45, Luke created the speeches in Acts following the model utilized regularly by ancient writers to enhance their narratives.

The framing of Peter's speech includes the well-known reference to charismatic utterances. As a general phenomenon, such spiritual experiences were not uncommon in early Christianity, as evidenced by Paul (1 Corinthians 14). In this case, however, the phenomenon takes on a different characteristic. Instead of being an unknown language, as described in Paul, tongue-speaking in this case was characterized by speaking in a variety of languages, all at the same time. It is clearly being pictured as a miracle to characterize the beginning of a worldwide mission rather than as an individual spiritual experience. This theme is enhanced by the list of nations named in the listening audience, a list that was stitched together by the author of Acts on the model of the Roman quest for world domination. The framing of Peter's speech, therefore, is created by the author to provide an ideological context for the speech as a miraculous beginning for a mission "to the ends of the earth."

References
Pervo, "My Happy Home" and "What Athens has in Common with Jerusalem"
White, "The Pentecost Event"
Matthews, "Did Christianity Begin at Pentecost? Reflections on the Question"
Penner, "Did Christianity Begin at Pentecost? Beginnings and the Ends Thereof"

The Votes of the Fellows
Red/Probable
- Charismata such as tongues and prophecy were significant aspects of early Christian experience.
- A totalizing vision, modeled on the Roman quest for world domination, is one of the essential building blocks of Christianity that Luke attempts to construct.
- The author of Acts composed the speeches in his own words.

Pink/Possible
- The motif of speaking in tongues in Acts 2 functions rhetorically to display numinous power in this birthing moment without necessary connection to any actual early Christian charismatic experiences.

Black/Improbable
- The Pentecost miracle in Acts 2:1–13 happened.
- Christianity began with the events of Pentecost described in Acts 2.

- The formal speeches in Acts are historical records of what was said on the occasion.
- The formal speeches in Acts are summaries of what was said on the occasion.

Jerusalem in Myth and History

A Cameo Essay by Milton Moreland

Acts provides our most detailed account of early Christians in the city of Jerusalem. Yet this account is historically problematic on many counts. The early audiences and the author of Acts had no firsthand experience of the physical setting of Jerusalem. Once the city was completely destroyed in 70 CE, the city was in ruins and mostly uninhabited during the decades in which Acts was written and first read. Jerusalem had no significant population until Hadrian renamed the site as a new colonial town (*Aelia Capitolina*) in 135 CE. For the previous sixty-five years, Jerusalem was not a religious cult center. Thus this setting in the narrative has a complicated history at the time when Acts was first produced. It has to be considered as both a pre-70 cult center, and a post-70 setting that was memorialized negatively by the Romans in their imperial propaganda and positively by some early Christians who imagined the city as the place where their movement began.

Prior to its destruction in 70 CE, Jerusalem was a lively Jewish-Roman city that was still undergoing significant infrastructural improvements. The city, especially the temple compound, was completely rebuilt by Herod the Great in the closing decades of the first century BCE. Recent archaeological investigations have revealed that the building process continued right up until the outbreak of the war. Prior to the war, the city functioned like other Roman cities in the Eastern Roman Empire, with a theatre, hippodrome, schools, and, most importantly, a huge temple dedicated to the local deity. In the story of Acts, Jerusalem was presented as a Jewish city with exotic people, temple rituals and customs. The author appealed to stock images of temple and Roman administrative structures in his portrayal of the city. On the one hand, Jerusalem was represented as a cult city with strong priestly leaders. It was an international travel destination, patrolled by Jewish leaders and Roman soldiers. On the other hand, Jerusalem was presented as the site of preternatural Christian origins, directed by spirit-filled leaders who had easy access to the temple compound and directed many people to join the new movement.

For the author of Acts, and especially for his audiences, Jerusalem's complete destruction in 70 CE and its further decimation and rebuilding as a Roman city after the Bar Kokhba Revolt (132–35 CE) is an unspoken fact that lies behind the author's ability to claim the city as the place where Christianity began. Jerusalem's destruction is a factor in the story's basic theological and narrative logic: the author of Acts blamed the destruction of Jerusalem and the temple on the rejection of Jesus by the inhabitants of the city. In order to understand how the first audiences would have thought about Jerusalem when reading this narrative, we must consider the ways that the city was celebrated or memorialized in the Roman Empire—in multiple commemorative and creative venues (art, arches, coins, stories, etc.). In the decades following its demise, the Roman military victories in Judea were hailed as triumphs worthy of great fame and honor. Vespasian, Titus and Domitian, in the decade after the first revolt, and Hadrian, after 135, used their victories in multiple ways to bolster their imperial claims. The author and audiences of Acts did not know the city as an active place of veneration; rather, Jerusalem was a site of mythic imagination that was claimed and envisioned by authors who used this (ruined) site as a powerful narrative setting.

Speeches in Acts

A Cameo Essay by Richard I. Pervo

Ancient writers had a great deal of creative freedom when constructing a speech for a narrative, even if it was a historical narrative and even if a report of some sort was used as the source of a speech. One can note, for example, Josephus' use of biblical texts and Luke's use of Mark. In several respects, however, the speeches in Acts differ from the way speeches are employed by ancient historians. For example, speeches recorded by the historians tend to stand apart from the narrative, while those in Acts are normally parts of the narrative. The speeches in Acts comprise 30 percent of the book, while the amount of direct speech in the writings of Josephus, Polybius, and Dionysius of Halicarnassus is much less.

Among the reasons for attributing the speeches in Acts to Luke are the following: (1) Greco-Roman antiquity presumed that speeches included in works of literature, including history, were the work of the author rather than the putative speaker. (2) The speeches in Acts are Lukan in language, style and thought. (3) The speeches often play a role in the narrative. (4) The majority of the speeches are interdependent: they build upon and depend upon one another. (5) The speeches establish the unity of the narrative of Acts and the continuity of its plot and thought. (6) The speeches are directed to the readers of the book rather than to the dramatic audiences in the text. (7) In the ancient world means and motives for preserving speeches did not exist.

The First Christian Community Imagined

2 [42]The believers devoted themselves to the apostles' teaching, cultivation of unity, their meal, and their prayers. [43]Awe overtook everyone. The apostles became the agents of numerous portents and miracles. [44]All the believers remained together and shared everything. [45]They would sell their goods and property and distribute the proceeds to everyone on the basis of need. [46]Every day they met together in the temple and ate in homes, taking their food with happy and sincere hearts [47]that were filled with praise to God. Everyone approved of them, and the Lord increased daily the number of those who were being saved together.

Comments on the Story

The author of Acts skillfully alternates between narrations of specific incidents and general summaries of early Christian life. We observed a brief summary in Acts 1:14, and here we have a longer and more detailed one. Similar such summaries will be found a few chapters later (see Acts 4:32–35; 5:12–16). These verses present an idyllic portrait of the growing community. It is a community marked by adherence to apostolic teaching, cultivation of unity, common meals, and prayers. We learn nothing here about the prayers or the content of apostolic teaching (although the effect of the apostles' miraculous feats is noted). The features of unity and the meals receive just a bit more explanation.

The word translated here as "cultivation of unity" is the Greek *koinōnia*, usually understood as fellowship. It implies a close relationship among members, even a partnership. For Luke, *koinōnia* involves a sharing of possessions and support of the needy members by other believers who sell their property for this purpose. Luke will return to this topic in Acts 4:32–5:11.

In view of the powerful emphasis on the unity of the community, we should probably understand Luke's reference to meals to indicate the observance of common meals. To say simply that the members ate food, or even that they ate meals in their homes, adds nothing of any significance to this ideal portrait. But Luke probably intends to convey the impression of a Christian ritual, perhaps a primitive version of a eucharistic ritual that would have been familiar to second-century readers. Further, in Acts 2:46, he describes a community that is faithful to Jewish traditions but also practices unique Christian rituals: the believers meet daily in the Jewish temple but hold their own services, sharing meals together in homes of members. Here is a group trying to maintain its relations to two communities—Jewish and Christian—that second-century readers would recognize as distinct.

The idyllic nature of the community is beautifully described in Luke's words: they took "their food with happy and sincere hearts" (Acts 2:46).

In Search of History

The seminar concluded that the summary statement in Acts 2:42–47 was created by Luke as an idealization of the primitive Christian community, constructed out of literary utopian ideals and formulated to address issues of his own day.

The summary description also utilizes features of a Greco-Roman association. Luke probably described the early church in that way because his own community was a type of association. Scholarship has also shown that the communities described in the letters of Paul fit the model of an association. Therefore, the seminar concluded that the description contained in the summary statement of Acts, while not based on any identifiable historical sources specific to the Jerusalem church, nevertheless corresponds in some details to historical reconstructions of early Pauline communities (see the cameo essay, "The Association Model," p. 49).

However, the individual components of the description were judged to be a mixed bag. The Fellows agreed that the early communities met in homes and shared communal meals together (red) and that they emphasized caring for those in their number who were in need (pink). But they voted black on other features, including the use of prescribed prayers, the communal sharing of property, and the unified devotion to the teachings of the apostles.

While the Seminar was reluctant to confirm that baptism was practiced by *all* early Christian communities, as implied by the Acts story, it nevertheless gave a strong affirmation to the proposition that *some* early Christian communities practiced baptism. Sorting through the data about baptism is considered an as yet unresolved issue of Christian origins that goes beyond the study of Acts.

References

Smith, "Religious Practices of Early Christian Converts"

The Votes of the Fellows

Red/Probable

- The Greco-Roman association model is used by Acts as a literary model for the early Christian Jerusalem gatherings.
- The Greco-Roman association model is the model of the communities to which Paul related.
- The members of the early first-century Christian communities practiced communal meals.
- The members of the early first-century Christian communities met for communal meals in homes.
- Membership in some early first-century Christian communities was signified by baptism.

Pink/Possible

- The early first-century Christian communities emphasized caring for those in their midst who were in need.
- In the early first-century Christian communities, stories about miracles arose and were circulated.
- Some of the members of the early first-century Christian communities attended ritual activities at the temple in Jerusalem.

Gray/Doubtful

- The members of the early first-century Christian communities practiced a communal life style.
- The members of the early first-century Christian communities practiced prescribed communal prayers.
- In the early first-century Christian communities, miracles took place in their midst as signs of apostolic authority.

Black/Improbable

- The members of the early first-century Christian communities were unified in their devotion to the teachings of the apostles.
- The members of the early first-century Christian communities shared all of their properties.

The Association Model
A Cameo Essay by Dennis E. Smith

Luke's summary of the religious practices of the early Christian community is clearly an idealization, but it also reflects an organizational model that is comparable to the generic organizational form of Greek and Roman associations of Luke's day. Associations were ancient versions of "clubs" organized around a variety of common interests, such as a common occupation, common ethnic background, or common devotion to a particular deity. We know about associations especially because many of them posted their official bylaws, membership lists, and dedications on engraved monuments.

Associations held regular meetings at which they celebrated meals together. The meals were organized with an emphasis on decorum and orderliness. Disorderly conduct was considered to be disruptive to the unity of the community gathering and was punished by fines or even by expulsion. Members were especially expected to obey their elected leaders in all matters relating to the conduct of the meal. Members were required to pay dues that were used to provide for the regular community meals. Associations usually had patron deities whom they honored at their meals with libations and other acts of devotion—acts that we, today, might characterize as "worship."

Many of these features were also components of the organizational structure of Pauline communities, such as: (a) regular meetings for community meals (1 Cor 11:17–34) and (b) the importance of unity at their gatherings, as supported by the "bylaws" of the meeting (1 Corinthians 12, 14). It is likely that Paul's communities were easily recognized by his contemporaries as being variations of the associations of the day.

In comparison, Luke's idealized description emphasizes: (a) regular meetings for community meals, (b) obedience to their leaders, (c) the importance of unity in the community, and (d) a common treasury. He proposes this as the model for the Christian community for its very beginning. The tone of the passage, however, identifies it as an idealization created by the author; unlike the unruliness of the gatherings addressed by the association statutes and the letters of Paul, Luke's description pictures a group in complete and happy concord.

How is it that his description tracks so well with what we know of associations today? It is unlikely that he had actual historical resources for the earliest years of Christian groups that would have been this detailed about daily practices. Rather, since he proposes this as a model for the community of his own day, it is likely that many of these features were characteristic of his community as well.

Healings, Arrests, and Trials

3 While Peter and John were on their way to the temple precincts at the time of the 1500 [3:00 p.m.] service, ²a man who had been crippled from birth was being carried in— his people would place him at the gate called "Beautiful" every day to solicit alms from those entering the sanctuary. ³When he realized that Peter and John were on their way in, he began to beg alms from them. ⁴Peter, along with John, fixed his gaze upon the man and said: "Look at us." ⁵That he did, expecting to get something from them, ⁶but Peter said, "I have no money, but what I do have I shall give you. In the name of Jesus Christ the Nazorean get up and walk!" ⁷He then grabbed him by the right hand and raised him up. Strength immediately came to his feet and ankles. ⁸He sprang to his feet and began to walk about. Then he went into the sanctuary with them, leaping and walking and praising God. ⁹When everyone saw him doing these things, ¹⁰they recognized him as the fellow who had sat begging at the Beautiful Gate of the temple and were overcome with amazement at what had happened to him.

¹¹The man who had been healed would not let go of Peter and John. Meanwhile the people, filled with astonishment, flocked toward them in Solomon's colonnade. ¹²Peter addressed the gathered crowd: "My fellow Israelites, Why do you find this so remarkable? Why are you staring at us as if we, by our personal power or piety, have made him able to walk? ¹³The God of Abraham, the God of Isaac, the God of Jacob, the God of our forebears has honored his son Jesus. You people handed him over and disowned him to Pilate's face, after he had decided to let Jesus go. ¹⁴You, yes you, disowned the Holy and Just One, demanding the pardoning of a murderer ¹⁵and murdering him who opens the way to life. But God raised him from the dead. We are witnesses of him. ¹⁶God has made this person you see here, one well known to you, strong because of confidence in the

name of Jesus. The confidence that comes through Jesus has given him full health, and that right before your eyes.

[17]"I am certain, sisters and brothers, that you acted in ignorance, as did your rulers, [18]but God, who had predicted through all the prophets that the Messiah would suffer, fulfilled those predictions in the manner described. [19]Therefore, you must change your hearts and orient yourselves to God. Get the slates of your sins wiped clean, [20]so that God may provide relief from the pressures of this age and send Jesus, designated to be your Messiah. [21]He has to remain in heaven until the time for universal restoration arrives. Through the holy prophets God has spoken of that restoration from the beginning. [22]Moses said, 'Your sovereign God will raise up a prophet from your midst, just as he raised up me. Attend to whatever he tells you. [23]Anyone who does not attend to that prophet will be rooted out from the people.' [24]Every articulate prophet from Samuel on announced the coming of these days. [25]You are the heirs of the prophets and the covenant that God fashioned with your forebears when he told Abraham, 'Every family on earth will be blessed through your descendant.' [26]God raised up his son for you first of all and sent him to give each and all of you the opportunity to abandon your wicked ways."

4 While Peter and John were addressing the crowd, the priests, the chief of the temple police, and the Sadducees burst onto the scene. [2]These people were fed up with the apostles for teaching in public, specifically for arguing the case of Jesus as proof of the resurrection of the dead, [3]so they apprehended them and, as it was by now evening, had them put into custody until the next day. [4]Many who had heard the message became believers. The number of men alone had risen to about five thousand.

[5]The next day there was an assembly of their leaders, including the elders, the local legal experts, [6]and, notably, the high priest Annas, as well as Caiphas, Jonathan, Alexander, and the whole high-priestly clan. [7]They had Peter and John brought before them and asked, "By what power or with what name have you people done this?" [8]Directed by the Holy Spirit, Peter answered: "Leaders of the people, elders. [9]If we are being examined today regarding a good deed for a disabled person, that is, how he was

healed, ¹⁰all of you—and all the people of Israel—need to know that he stands before you in good health by virtue of the name of Jesus Christ the Nazorean, whom you people crucified but whom God raised from the dead. ¹¹This Jesus is the stone that, scorned by you, the builders, has become the keystone. ¹²There is no salvation by anyone else. There is no other name provided to mortals in the whole world through which salvation can be gained."

¹³The Council began to wonder when they saw the assurance with which Peter and John—mere amateurs in their view—spoke. They also realized that these men had been companions of Jesus. ¹⁴Since, however, the man who had been healed was standing with the apostles in plain sight, they could offer no refutation. ¹⁵After directing them to leave the chamber, the members of the council began to deliberate.

¹⁶"What shall we do about these people? The miracle they performed has become public knowledge in Jerusalem. It is as clear as day, and we cannot deny it. ¹⁷But, to quash further dissemination, let us enjoin them to make no mention of This Name to anyone." ¹⁸They recalled the two and charged them absolutely not to engage in proclamation or to give instruction in the name of Jesus.

¹⁹Peter and John replied, "It's up to you to determine whether it is right in God's sight to listen to you or to God. ²⁰For our part, we cannot desist from speaking about what we have seen and heard."

²¹They then let them go, after piling on additional admonitions, since public pressure prevented them from finding a pretext for punishment. Everyone was praising God because of what had taken place, ²²for the man who had been wondrously healed was over forty years old.

²³Once released the apostles went to their people and reported everything that the chief priests and the elders had said. ²⁴Whereupon they raised a unison prayer to God: "Master, maker of heaven, earth, sea, and all that is in them; ²⁵you said to our ancestors, through your servant David:

> Why did Gentiles rage,
> And peoples plot in vain?
> ²⁶The monarchs of the earth got ready for combat,

And the rulers came together,
Against the Lord and against the Lord's Messiah.

²⁷"In fact Herod and Pontius Pilate, with gentiles and Israelites, did come together in this city against your holy servant Jesus, whom you anointed. ²⁸They accomplished what your power and plan had previously determined would take place. ²⁹Take notice of their threats now, O Lord, and grant that your slaves may proclaim your message with complete boldness, ³⁰while you stretch forth your healing hand and bring about portents and wonders through the name of your holy servant Jesus."

³¹After their prayer was finished, the place in which they were gathered shook. All were filled with the Holy Spirit and continued to speak God's message boldly.

Comments on the Story

This material will be treated in six subsections: a lame man is healed (Acts 3:1–11); Peter's third speech (3:12–26); the apostles are arrested (4:1–7); Peter's fourth speech (4:8–12); the council deliberates (4:13–22); and the believers pray (4:23–31).

A lame man is healed (Acts 3:1–11). In the preceding summary section (Acts 2:42–47), we learned that the apostles had the goodwill of the people of Jerusalem, who stood in awe at the wonders and signs they performed. In 3:1–11 we have an example of the apostolic wonders, as Peter and John heal a forty-year-old man who had been lame from birth. We also learned in the summary that the early Jesus community adhered closely to the temple, and we read here that the healing took place as the apostles were headed to a 3 p.m. service in the temple. Authors of narratives frequently alternate between telling and showing, and here we have a good illustration of the strategy. In Acts 2:42–47 the author speaks in his own voice and tells the readers about the community. In 3:1–11 he recedes behind the story and shows the reader just what happened. Robert Funk used this story as a prime example of narrative showing. He wrote:

> The healing of the lame man in Acts 3:1–10 is shown or enacted: the reader is permitted to see and hear what transpires. The reader is made to observe the positioning of the lame man at the gate of the temple and the approach of Peter and John, and to listen in on the verbal exchange between the two. Peter then

takes the lame man by the right hand and lifts him up. The lame man, now cured, leaps up, walks around, enters the temple, and praises God, all visual confirmations of his cure: his healing is shown or enacted.[5]

Peter's third speech (Acts 3:12–26). As in chapter 2, where Peter interpreted the Pentecost phenomenon, here too he comments on the healing of the lame man (John is notably silent). In Acts 2 Peter corrected the explanation that the phenomenon of glossolalia was to be attributed to drunkenness. In Acts 3 he corrects the implied explanation that he and John had special powers, and he claims that it was God himself who healed the lame man. The two speeches also share a number of similar themes.

Prophecy has been fulfilled. Peter proclaims that Jesus is the prophet like Moses that Moses himself predicted, and he supports the claim by a quotation from Deut 18:15 (Acts 3:22). But not all such claims are backed up with quotations from the Hebrew Bible. In Acts 3:18 Peter says that all the prophets announced beforehand that the Christ would suffer, but no example of such a prophecy is included. In 3:24 he says that all the prophets from Samuel on predicted the appearance of Jesus, but again there is no quotation. In both of these cases it is difficult to know just what Scripture the author had in mind.

Jesus is the Messiah appointed for Israel (Acts 3:20). Jesus is given the status of God's servant (3:13), the ruler of life (3:15), the Messiah (3:18), and the prophet promised by Moses (3:22–23).

You Jews killed Jesus. In Acts 3:13–14 Peter charges his audience with delivering Jesus over to Pilate, demanding his crucifixion even after Pilate had pronounced him to be innocent, and calling for the release of a murderer. These verses remind the reader of the narratives in Luke, where Pilate repeatedly pronounces Jesus not guilty of the charges brought against him by the chief priests and their associates (Luke 23:4, 14, 22), and where the crowd calls for the release of Barabbas (Luke 23:18–19). In Acts 3:15 Peter heightens the accusation by claiming that the Jews are guilty of "murdering him who opens the way to life." The accusation is mitigated only by the recognition of ignorance (3:17), but it is difficult to know if ignorance is excusable. Since the concession is followed immediately by the proclamation that the suffering of the Messiah was foretold in Scripture, one might conclude that if those in Peter's audience had understood the Scriptures, they would not have been ignorant of what they were doing in denying and killing Jesus. In any event, their ignorance seems to serve as a ground for repentance and forgiveness, as Acts 3:19 suggests.

God raised Jesus from the dead. The contrast we saw in the first speech between the actions of the Jews and the actions of God is manifest again here in Acts 3:15: Peter charges that Jews murdered the one who opens the way to life, but God raised him up. The raising of Jesus is probably intended also in 3:13, where God's glorification of Jesus is set over against Jewish betrayal and denial. Peter concludes the speech with another proclamation of the resurrection, coupled now with the announcement that God sent the resurrected Jesus first to the Jews to give them the opportunity to repent (3:26). This is a remarkable combination of themes: Jewish rejection of the author of life has brought about for them the first prospect of beginning a new life.

Repent and be forgiven. As in Peter's second speech, the goal here is to bring about repentance on the part of the audience. In Acts 3:19–20 Peter promises that Jewish repentance will bring about "relief from the pressures of this age" and will hasten the time of Jesus' return.

In addition to these now familiar themes, the speech of Peter in Acts 3 has some other features that deserve our attention. In Acts 3:13, there is a specific linking of Jesus with the God of Abraham, Isaac, Jacob, and contemporary Jews: God is the God of *our* forebears. We have already called attention to a reference to Moses in 3:22 and another to Abraham in 3:25, where Peter identifies his fellow Israelites as heirs of the prophets and the Abrahamic covenant. These verses may not be surprising to a modern audience, but in the second century, when Marcion and other Christians rejected the God of Israel and denied that the Hebrew prophets had predicted the coming of Jesus as Messiah, the Lukan emphasis is of great importance. Luke must surely have known of these variant Christian theologies. He rejected such views and insisted on a vital and lasting connection between Jesus and the God of Israel.

In Acts 2:46 we learned that the apostles and their followers spent a lot of time together in the Jerusalem temple. It seems fitting that the healing of the lame man should take place in the temple area, at the "Beautiful" gate, and that Peter and John were there for a regular service of prayer. Solomon's colonnade at the temple is the setting of Peter's third speech. The precise locations are less important than the fact that Luke places the action within the temple complex. Ernst Haenchen is probably correct in observing that "Luke evidently enjoyed no direct personal knowledge of the Temple."[6] Indeed, the temple had been long destroyed at the time Luke was writing. Still the setting should impress the reader with the sense of piety that the author attributes to Peter and John. The attempt of the early believers to continue a relation to Jewish traditions is an impressive emphasis in Acts. We shall see, however, that the center of Jewish worship will soon become a site of conflict.

The apostles are arrested (Acts 4:1–7). The conflict begins when powerful Jewish leaders—priests, the temple police, Sadducees—descend on the apostles and arrest them. The authorities do not charge the apostles with illicit action in regard to the lame man but rather with teaching and proclaiming the resurrection of Jesus. Does Luke mean to say that holding such views was regarded as illegal? Or is it because Peter and John taught in public, or in the temple? Since the setting for this teaching was Solomon's colonnade, ostensibly a part of the temple complex, it is likely that behind the priestly disapproval of apostolic teaching there lies an equally important objection about their teaching in the temple area. The opponents of the apostles are convinced that their teaching is a misuse of the temple itself, and their objections will become more explicit in later chapters of Acts. Readers of Luke may recall a major section of that gospel that dealt with Jesus' teaching in the temple (Luke 19:47–21:38). Luke notes that Jesus taught daily in the temple and was supported by the people but opposed by those leaders who controlled the temple. Just as Jesus made the temple the scene of his teaching, just so must the apostles attempt to occupy the temple and use it as a place of teaching. Just as Jesus was accepted by the people, so are the apostles, who persuade some five thousand more men to believe (Acts 4:4). But just as Jesus was opposed by the priests, so are the apostles. Luke describes a formidable array of opponents, including priests, police, Sadducees (4:1), the high priest and members of his family (4:6). Notably absent from this group are Pharisees, who in Luke were often shown in debate with Jesus. But if the charge against the apostles is that they were teaching about resurrection, the absence of Pharisees may not be so surprising. In the Gospel Luke had noted that it was Sadducees who rejected belief in resurrection (Luke 20:27), and in a later narrative he will exploit the difference between the two groups and turn it to Paul's advantage (see Acts 23:1–10).

Peter's fourth speech (Acts 4:8–12). We should expect Peter in this speech to defend himself and John against the charges of the Jewish leaders, and this is what we get. But Peter deftly uses his defensive speech as a further evangelistic opportunity. He asks about the specific charge: are we under investigation because of the healing (Acts 4:9)? If so, says Peter, it is by the name of Jesus that this happened, and only in Jesus is salvation possible (4:10–12). This charge is not, however, the one that initially motivated the priests. Acts 4:2 says that they were "fed up" with the apostles because they were teaching.

Most of the customary themes do not appear in this speech, but we do have reference to the death and resurrection of Jesus, cast in the usual form: you people crucified Jesus, but God raised him up (Acts 4:10). There is, however, a quotation of Ps 118:22 in Acts 4:11: the rejected stone (Jesus) has become the keystone. The same verse was quoted in Luke 20:17, where, in the parable of the vineyard, it was applied to the son of the vineyard owner, who was killed by the tenants.

Near the end of this short speech Peter introduces a somewhat surprising theme of the exclusivity of salvation through Jesus. Although Luke does not pursue the issue here, it becomes clear as the narrative proceeds that Jewish reliance on God without Jesus is not sufficient.

The council deliberates (Acts 4:13–22). The council is unable to retain or punish the apostles and can only release them with the order to cease their teaching. The apostles reply that they must obey divine rather than human orders. The members of the council faced a complex dilemma. For one thing they knew that the apostles had popular support that was likely to grow. In addition the council members were unable to deny that the lame man had been healed, since he was present at the hearing, and so they must acknowledge the power of Peter and John. For these reasons they released them with a stern warning. Peter and John (now speaking together), however, gave notice that they had no intention of obeying the orders of the council. The contrast between popular support and the opposition of leaders is especially marked here, and readers might be encouraged to reflect on the similar situation of Jesus, as described in the Gospel of Luke. Luke writes that the authorities, who intended to have Jesus executed, were unable to arrest him because of his popular support (see, for example, Luke 19:47–48).

The believers pray (Acts 4:23–31). When Peter and John returned from their examination by the council and reported on its results, the community of believers "raised a unison [*humathamadon*] prayer to God" (Acts 4:24). We have been told about the community in prayer before, but we don't always hear the words. In

Acts 1:24–25 there is a brief prayer prior to the casting of lots to determine the right successor to Judas. Here in Acts 4 there is a longer prayer asking God to grant boldness (*parrēsias*, 4:29) to the preachers.

The prayer is directed to the creator of "heaven, earth, sea, and all that is in them" (Acts 4:24). The address to God as creator is common in Jewish prayers, but some Gnostic and Marcionite Christians of the second century would have objected to it, feeling that the materials of creation were unworthy of the high God. Luke rejects these views and so portrays the early Christian community as squarely affirming the one God as creator of all. In addition he associates the community with Jewish Scripture by referring to David and "*our* ancestors" (4:25).

The prayer affords us an opportunity to see how, through his characters, the author of Acts interpreted Scripture. The prayer quotes from Ps 2:1–2 in Acts 4:25–26 and then interprets the Psalm in the following verse (4:27). The Psalm lists those who oppose the Lord and the Lord's anointed one. The list includes Gentiles, peoples, monarchs, and rulers, and the interpretive verse says that those arrayed against Jesus were Gentiles, Israelites, Herod, and Pontius Pilate. The identification of peoples with Israelites is common. Evidently Herod is taken as a monarch, and Pilate as a ruler. It is often thought that these verses from Psalm 2 guided Luke in his portrayal of the trial and execution of Jesus, and there is much to commend this view. Notably, it is only in Luke among the canonical gospels that Herod appears in the trial narratives. But there is no exact fit between the trial scenes in Luke and the interpretation of the Psalm as we have it in Acts, for in Luke neither Herod nor Pilate found Jesus guilty. Indeed, it is only the Israelites, more specifically the Jewish leaders, who insisted on his execution.

Acts 4:31 confirms that the believers' prayer was answered positively. The verse seems to indicate that a kind of mini-Pentecost occurred on this occasion. Everybody was filled with the Holy Spirit, and they kept speaking boldly, although there is no hint that the phenomenon of glossolalia was repeated.

In Search of History

This text contains four clusters of data that, together, hold its narrative together and determine its lack of historical credibility.

1. The first such cluster is the healing story at 3:1–10. The Fellows reviewed the evidence that this story is based largely on the healing

of the paralytic in Luke 5:17–26 and other similar accounts. Miracle stories as a literary genre were common in the ancient world and functioned as the means to promote emperors, philosophers, and other religious leaders as individuals marked with the power of the divine. They occur in early Christian literature, both canonical and noncanonical, as a means to counter the propaganda of their competitors in the culture. Though some individuals, including Jesus, may have accomplished healings that could be considered miraculous by standards of the day, the stories themselves must be judged as a group. The Jesus Seminar determined that the miracle stories of Jesus are nonhistorical as a group, but that Jesus was likely to have been an exorcist.[7] This same principle has been applied to the data in Acts. Perhaps healings took place in the early Christian communities, but the stories in Acts, since they rely on common literary motifs, do not provide evidence of that. This is further buttressed by the fact that this story betrays features common to other such stories in the gospel tradition, most notably Luke 5:17–26.

2. The second cluster of data is made up of speeches and other quoted dialogue (Acts 3:11–26, 4:8–12, 16–20, 24–30). This type of material in Acts has been determined to be the creation of the author and to lack historical value (see cameo essay, "Speeches in Acts," p. 45). This rules out a major portion of the material in this text.

3. The third cluster of data is the description of opposition of Jewish leaders, leading eventually to an arrest and trial (Acts 4:1–22). This fits a pattern that is a major apologetic motif in Acts; it will become a standard feature of the narrative of Paul's missionary travels. This narrative also functions as an elaboration of the healing story (see 4:14, 22) and so cannot stand independently of it. Therefore, this cluster of data is also judged to be nonhistorical.

4. Another theme occurs at various points throughout this narrative, the theme of "bold speaking" (Acts 4:13, 29, 31). The Greek term used here is *parrēsia*. It is a term used to characterize the speech of philosophers, particularly in contexts of opposition. It is used with this function throughout Acts (2:29; 9:27, 28; 13:46; 14:3; 18:26; 19:8; 26:26; 28:31). The term is part of a larger apologetic theme in Acts to portray early Christian leaders as philosophers, modeled after the literary portrayal of Socrates and other philosophers in the Greco-Roman world. More specifically, Acts utilized the term *parrēsia* in stories of opposition and stories which evoke the claim of a divine commission, all of which served the larger apologetic purposes of Acts. The Fellows were convinced by these arguments and

determined that the use of this theme in Acts is an apologetic device that lacks historical validity (see also the cameo essay, "When Apostles Become Philosophers," p. 60).

References

Dupertuis, "*Parrēsia*, Opposition, and Philosophical Imagery in Acts"
Pervo, "My Happy Home"
Smith, "Rethinking the Acts Story"

The Votes of the Fellows

Red/Probable

- Luke composed the miraculous healing in Acts 3:1–10 on the basis of Luke 5 and similar accounts.
- *Parrēsia* ("free speech") is used in Acts in an intentional attempt to echo philosophical literary imagery.
- *Parrēsia* is consistently associated with stories of opposition in Acts.
- *Parrēsia* is used in Acts in contexts which evoke the claim of a divine commission authorizing the right to speak "with boldness."
- *Parrēsia* is used in Acts to portray Christian leaders as Socratic figures.
- The use of philosophical imagery in Acts is an apologetic device to legitimate Christianity as a movement led by true philosophers.

Black/Improbable

- Acts provides historical evidence that Peter was a miracle worker.
- The characterization of the early Christian leaders as "bold speakers" is an historical datum.
- Acts 3:1–26 is historical.
- There was widespread support in Jerusalem for the early followers of Jesus.

When Apostles Become Philosophers
A Cameo Essay by Rubén Dupertuis

No other death in the ancient world was as well known as that of Socrates. By the early Roman imperial period, Socrates had become the pre-eminent martyr, the prototype of the philosopher unjustly accused, tried, and executed. His prominence is due, in part, to being the subject in some of the writings of his students, Plato and

Xenophon, which became standards of the Greek educational curriculum. In the literature of the late Hellenistic and early Roman periods, Socrates' death became a widely imitated model of how to die nobly. Given the importance of Socrates as a cultural model at the time, it is unsurprising that the author of Acts effectively "Socratizes" the apostles.

A good place to see this is in the description of Paul's visit to Athens in Acts 17:16–34. Acts describes Paul addressing (*dialegomai*) people in the market place every day (Acts 17:17), using the precise terms Plato used to describe the activities of Socrates that eventually got him in trouble.[8] Paul soon encounters some philosophers, some of whom refer to him as "a dilettante" (*spermologos*) and others who take him to be a promoter of "alien gods" (*xenon daimonion*, Acts 17:18). Paul is then taken to the Areopagus, where the philosophers say to him, "May we learn what this novel doctrine you are talking about is? Since you are propounding alien ideas, we certainly wish to know just what point you are trying to make" (17:19–20). The accusations against Paul echo the charges against Socrates, which Plato records as follows: "Socrates is guilty of corrupting the youth and of not honoring the gods the city honors, but other *new deities*."[9] Xenophon records a similar version of the charge: "Socrates is guilty of not honoring the gods honored by the state and of *introducing* other *new deities*. He is also guilty of corrupting the youth."[10]

While Paul may not be formally on trial in Athens, the change in venue to the Areopagus does create a trial-like situation. For although the Areopagus is not the site of Socrates' trial in the literary tradition, by the early Roman Empire the association of that site with being questioned or judged was relatively common in literature. In addition, while Paul's subsequent speech is not a formal "apology" or defense, it certainly has the feel of one, given that he is responding to questions and concerns that evoke the accusations for which Socrates was brought to trial in Athens.

The speech Paul delivers to the inquisitive philosophers on the Areopagus continues the echoes of Socratic traditions. His first words, "Gentlemen of Athens," recall Socrates' manner of addressing the Athenian jury in the first lines and throughout Plato's *Apology*.[11] Paul then notes the Athenians' religiosity, which is manifest in the inscription "to an unknown god" (Acts 17:23). Paul volunteers to fill in the details of this god, whom they already have on their radar. Central to Xenophon's defense of Socrates in his *Memorabilia* is the argument that Socrates' religious practices were not foreign, outlandish, or weird, but were at their root really not different from the practices of any other devout Athenian. Similarly, although Paul may be using terms the Athenians don't recognize, he is really only speaking in greater detail about something they already accept. By placing Paul's subject under the heading of something they already acknowledge, however obliquely and not without some ignorance (17:30), Paul avoids "introducing" new deities, the charge leveled at Socrates and the concern voiced by the philosophers whom he is addressing.

Paul concludes his speech by introducing the notion of God's judgment:

> God will overlook past failures that were due to ignorance. For the present, God invites all people everywhere to change their lives, for God has set a time at which he intends to judge the world justly by a man he has selected, in proof whereof God has raised this man from the dead. (Acts 17:30–31)

At first glance this may not sound particularly Socratic, but Socrates also spoke of a judgment after death. At the end of Plato's *Apology*, Socrates sees his impending death as a good thing, for it might allow him to be judged by truly righteous judges.[12] And while Socrates' understanding of life after death is surely different from Paul's (or Luke's), both conclude their speeches with this subject.

Acts' description of Paul's activity in Athens, the famous home of Socrates, is rich with echoes of the Athenian philosopher. Paul is, put simply, dressed in Socratic garb.

Sharing Possessions in the Community

4 ³²The body of believers was one in heart and soul. Not even one of them would say, "That's mine," about any of their possessions, but they held all in common. ³³The apostles continued to give very powerful testimony to the resurrection of the Lord Jesus, and all enjoyed an abundance of divine favor. ³⁴None of them was in need, for all who owned land or houses sold those objects and placed the ³⁵proceeds at the disposal of the apostles; they were distributed in accordance with need. ³⁶Joseph, a Levite from Cyprus, whom the apostles nicknamed "Barnabas" ("preacher"), ³⁷had a piece of property. He sold it and gave the money to the apostles.

5 Now a man named Ananias (whose wife was Sapphira) sold a piece of property. ²With the connivance of his wife, he withheld some of the proceeds and placed the balance at the disposal of the apostles. ³Peter said, "Ananias, why did you let Satan move you to lie to the Holy Spirit and withhold some of the proceeds from your land? ⁴Wasn't that property yours to keep? Once you sold it, wasn't the money at your disposal? What gave you the idea to do this? You have not lied to mortals but to God." ⁵When Ananias heard this, he dropped dead. Terror struck all who witnessed this exchange. ⁶The young people then covered him and took the body out for burial.

⁷Three hours later his wife, who was unaware of what had happened, showed up. ⁸Peter asked her, "Tell me, did you sell the field for X amount?"

"Yes, for X."

⁹"Why did you two agree to challenge the Spirit of the Lord? Look, those who buried your husband are at the door. They will be carrying you out, too." ¹⁰She dropped dead at his feet. The young people came back and, finding her dead as well, removed her for burial next to her husband. ¹¹Dread terror struck the entire community and everyone who learned what had happened.

Comments on the Story

This section begins with another summary (Acts 4:32–37), similar to those in the first two chapters of Acts. Again we are told that the community enjoyed remarkable unity and that the apostles continued to preach the resurrection of Jesus.

The focus in Acts 4:32–37 is on the financial aspects of community life. The topic had been introduced in 2:44–45 but is dealt with more fully here. The general impression we gain from the two summaries is that the community eliminated poverty among the members by supporting the needy. What is not clear is just how Luke imagines that this was done. We first read that the members of the community held all things in common (2:44; 4:32). Then it is said that whoever had possessions would sell them and distribute the proceeds to those in need (2:45; 4:34–35). In 4:35 the apostles appear to be the brokers in this arrangement. As a result it would be possible to say that the members of the community held all things in common and that poverty would be reduced if not eliminated. To say that no one claimed private ownership of property suggests that the practice was compulsory, but the stories of Barnabas and of Ananias and Sapphira imply that it was voluntary.

Luke follows the summary section with two exemplary narratives, one positive the other negative. Joseph Barnabas is cited as an example of those who sold property and gave the proceeds to the apostles (Acts 4:36–37). Whether Barnabas, who will reappear later in Acts alongside Paul, is to be regarded as a typical or an outstanding example is not clear, but he would hardly be an example at all if he did what he did only under compulsion.

The story of Ananias and Sapphira serves as a negative example for the reader (Acts 5:1–11). This married couple, members of the community, sold property as did Barnabas, but they held back some of the proceeds from the sale for themselves, claiming that the contribution to the apostles was the entire amount they earned. Peter first called in Ananias, whom he condemned for lying to God, and Ananias suddenly died. Then Peter dealt with the wife, who admitted her complicity in the deceitful arrangement, and she too fell over dead. Both were buried immediately, and great fear came over the whole community.

Here is a place in Acts where showing and telling are not compatible. The author has told us that no one regarded property as his/her own and that any owners of property sold it and laid the proceeds at the feet of the apostles (Acts 4:32–37). But now the author shows us a narrative about members of the group who departed from this ideal (5:1–11). The author's stress on unity and community in the group of believers would appear to be subverted by this narrative.

To be sure, the culprits are punished for their sin. But it is fair to ask why they were not given an opportunity to repent. In the speeches of Peter that we have examined from earlier chapters, his message to potential converts is to repent and be forgiven (Acts 2:38; 3:19–20). But no such message is given to Ananias and Sapphira, who are summarily judged and punished. Are we to conclude that, according to Luke, it is only nonbelievers who may repent and be forgiven and that a different standard applies to the baptized? The question of post-baptismal repentance is one with which Christians have struggled for centuries. It is said that the emperor Constantine postponed his own baptism until just before death in order to avoid the possibility of committing a sin that might not be forgiven.

We return to the question of whether the kind of community life that Luke shows and tells here is thought of as voluntary or compulsory. Acts 4:32 tells us that no one regarded property as his or her own, thus suggesting that participation was compulsory. But the statement of Peter to Ananias in 5:4 stresses the voluntary aspect: "Wasn't that property yours to keep? Once you sold it, wasn't the money at your disposal?" The tension here may be another example of conflict between telling and showing. It is, however, likely that Luke wanted the reader to understand the practice as a spontaneous expression of mutual love among members of the community. In this sense, the donation of proceeds from the sale of property is voluntary but (almost) everybody participates.

In Search of History

This story functions as an elaboration of the theme Acts introduced in 2:43–47, where the author presented a utopian view of the ideal community. A central component of that idealization was the idea that the members "would sell their goods and property and distribute the proceeds to everyone on the basis of need" (Acts 2:45). That summary idealization is repeated here and then elaborated with a hard-hitting sermonic story that was intended to send a message to Luke's own community.

The first component of Luke's elaboration is to add a small positive anecdote as a balance to the negative example that will follow. We have earlier argued that names in Acts are freely created by the author using the ancient technique in which the name is considered descriptive of the individual's character (see the cameo essay, "Names in Acts," p. 22). Here we see the author self-consciously following that principle. His source is Paul, who identifies Barnabas as one of his early co-workers (1 Cor 9:6; Gal 2:1, 9, 13). Luke will expand on the role of Barnabas later in his narrative. Here he provides a back-story for Barnabas, one that he has created out of a rather vague etymology that he creates for his name: "preacher" or more literally "son of consolation" (Greek: *huios* ["son"] *paraklēseōs* ["exhort" or "comfort"]).[13] While later in the story Barnabas will be spotlighted as a co-preacher with Paul, here it is the "comfort" theme that is spotlighted. In short, the Barnabas anecdote is created out of an etymology of his name. Adding the detail that his first name was Joseph, a detail not found anywhere else in the NT, further enhances Luke's point that "Barnabas" is a nickname meant to describe his character.

The negative example is provided by the story of Ananias and Sapphira, two characters whose names are distinctive primarily in the fact that they are clearly Jewish in origin. This is a miracle story, which downgrades its credibility from the outset; miracle stories follow a literary genre and are notoriously unreliable as historical records. It also lacks plausibility in some of its minor details, such as the immediate burial of Ananias without an appropriate ceremony or any consultation with his wife. Furthermore, according to Jewish law property ownership belongs wholly to the husband, so that the wife's guilt in these matters would normally be lessened. Finally, it is striking that she is a widow at the point when she stands before Peter, thus giving her a special status in the community, a status that Peter does not acknowledge.

Julian Hills concluded that the story is a "theological fiction." The ultimate battle is between the power of Satan and the power of the Holy Spirit ("why did you let Satan move you to lie to the Holy Spirit," Acts 5:3). Within that divine drama there is also an emphasis on the apostolic authority of Peter and the importance of sharing possessions within the community, both of which are major themes in Luke-Acts.

References
Hills, "Equal Justice"

The Votes of the Fellows
Red/Probable
- The story of Ananias and Sapphira is a theological fiction, designed to contrast the power of Satan with that of the Holy Spirit.
- Luke transformed a tradition about a dispute over community funds (Acts 5:1–11) into a utopian ideal that met Deuteronomistic standards.

Black/Improbable
- Ananias and Sapphira were members of the early Jerusalem community.
- Ananias and Sapphira perished at Peter's word and/or presence.

An Arrest and a Prison Break
5 ¹²The apostles worked numerous miracles and portents among the people. They now frequented the Portico of

Solomon in a body, ¹³and no outsiders ventured to get too close to them, while the general public sang their praises. ¹⁴Indeed, men and women alike joined the community in droves. ¹⁵The crowds were so large that people would actually put their sick out on the street in beds and stretchers, so that Peter's shadow might fall upon one or another of them as he was passing by. ¹⁶The populace of those towns near Jerusalem flocked in, bringing the ill and those tormented by impure spirits, all of whom were made well.

¹⁷As a result, the high priest and his colleagues, that is, the Sadducees, turned green with envy. ¹⁸They seized the apostles and had them held in official custody. ¹⁹An angel of the Lord opened the prison doors at night and escorted them out, saying, ²⁰"Go take your place in the sanctuary and proclaim to the public everything about this way of life." ²¹In response they went to the sanctuary at dawn and began to teach.

When the high priest and his colleagues arrived, they convoked the council, that is, the entire Israelite Senate, and then sent instructions to the jail for the prisoners to be conveyed to court. ²²The agents dispatched for this task did not find them in the prison and returned with this report: ²³"We found the prison-house locked and well secured, with guards at the doors, but, when we opened the doors, we didn't find any one inside!"

²⁴When they heard this information, the chief of the temple police and the leading priests couldn't figure out what was going on. ²⁵At that moment someone came in and announced, "Listen! Those people whom you had put in prison are standing in the temple teaching the populace!" ²⁶Thereupon the police chief and his men set out to bring them back, with a minimum of force, since they were afraid that the populace would stone them.

²⁷The authorities arraigned the apostles before the council for examination by the high priest: ²⁸"We strictly enjoined you not to teach in 'this name,' but look at what you've gone and done: *filled* Jerusalem with this teaching! In addition, you are trying to make us responsible for this fellow's death!"

²⁹"We must obey God rather than mortals," replied Peter and the other apostles. ³⁰"Our ancestral God raised Jesus, whom you took and hung upon a cross. ³¹Divine

power exalted him to become Leader and Savior, in order to give Israel opportunity to change its heart and find forgiveness for sins. ³²As for us, we are witnesses of these matters, as is the Holy Spirit that God gives to those who are obedient."

³³Cut to the quick, the audience was eager to kill them. ³⁴At that point a learned and universally revered Pharisee named Gamaliel took the floor. After directing that the defendants be removed for a while, ³⁵he spoke:

"My fellow Israelites, think carefully about what you propose to do to these people. ³⁶Some time ago Theudas rose up in rebellion, claiming that he was someone special. He gained about four hundred adherents, but, after he had been eliminated, all of his followers were dispersed, and the movement evaporated. ³⁷Subsequently, at the time of the census, Judas of Galilee also rose up and gathered a pack of rebels. He also perished, and all of his followers were put to flight. ³⁸My advice in this matter is that you keep your distance from these people. Let them go, for, if this scheme or enterprise happens to be of human origin, it will be thwarted, ³⁹but, if it is of divine origin, you will not be able to thwart them. Be careful to avoid conflict with God!" They found his argument persuasive. ⁴⁰The officials then recalled the apostles and, after beating them, released them with the command to cease speaking in the name of Jesus.

⁴¹The apostles left the Sanhedrin rejoicing that they had been deemed worthy to suffer abuse for the sake of the Name. ⁴²They continued to teach and to proclaim that Jesus is the Messiah, day after day, both in the temple and in houses.

Comments on the Story

In this section the author of Acts gives us narratives that might be called "the apostles versus the Jewish council." The section is bracketed by two summaries. It may be outlined as follows:

Summary (Acts 5:12–16)

The apostles are arrested, escape, then are rearrested (Acts 5:17–26)

The hearing before the council (Acts 5:27–40)

Summary (Acts 5:41–42)

Summary (Acts 5:12–16). By now the reader is accustomed to the author's alternation of telling by way of summary sections and showing by way of vivid narratives. So here again we have a summary, with emphasis on the customary aspects of early Christian life. The community is all together (*homothumadon*), meeting at Solomon's portico (or colonnade). The miracles of healing performed by the apostles attract major attention among the populace of Jerusalem and its environs. Just by lying under Peter's shadow, some people are healed. And the community grows by leaps and bounds, as both men *and women* join the others. Recall that in 4:4 the author had mentioned only men.

Even in this brief summary the author has left us with a tantalizing problem. In Acts 5:13 he has, "none of the rest dared to join them" (NRSV). But in the following verse we read that great numbers of believers were added to the community. Who are "the rest" who dared not join the community? And how are they to be distinguished from the many who did join up? The author doesn't give us much help in understanding this apparent contradiction. Pervo has smoothed things out a bit by his translation: "No outsiders ventured to get too close to them, while the general public sang their praises. Indeed, men and women alike joined the community in droves." Even here it is not clear who the outsiders are, although there appears to be a connection with the fear that followed the deaths of Ananias and Sapphira (5:11). The author clearly wants to stress the popularity of the apostles and the growth of the community, but he cannot hide his awareness that there were holdouts, some people whose fear prevented them from even approaching the believing community.

The apostles are arrested, escape, then are rearrested (Acts 5:17–26). Here it is all the apostles who are arrested, as were Peter and John in Acts 4. The opponents are more briefly described as the high priest and Sadducees, but they are essentially the same as in the previous chapter. As before, the apostles are imprisoned for the night to await trial the following morning. Readers of Luke will recall the trial of Jesus, which also began with an arrest at night, an overnight incarceration, and a hearing the following morning (see Luke 22:47–71). In the narrative here the council encounters an unusual situation. As they convene for the morning hearing, the apostles have gone missing. They have escaped during the night, but it is no ordinary prison break. Rather an angel arranges it and commands the apostles to go to the temple and preach. As members of the council wonder what is going on, someone reports that the apostles are in the temple, and so they are arrested again and brought before the council. Even at this point the Jewish leaders are compelled to tread carefully because of the popular support enjoyed by the apostles, and so they have them arrested with a minimum of force.

The apostles would seem to be in a difficult situation. The angel of the Lord commands them to preach in the temple, in direct violation of the gag order previously issued by the council. But there is no doubt which order they will obey. In 4:19–20 Peter and John announced that they had no intention of obeying the council's orders, and so it is no surprise that they all now are found preaching in the temple. The temple has become a battleground. The believing community convenes in the portico of Solomon, and the apostles intend to use the temple as a place to proclaim their message about Jesus. But the authorities—priests and Sadducees—prevent them and bring them up on serious charges. Control of the temple is here being contested. The earliest readers of Acts surely knew that it had been destroyed long ago, and they must have interpreted the preaching of the apostles as an attempt to take it over for Christian purposes. The destruction of the temple would, thus, be seen as justified in the light of the rejection of the apostolic proclamation by the priestly leaders.

The hearing before the council (Acts 5:27–40). The long-anticipated hearing finally begins with an examination before the high priest, who charges the apostles with disobeying the previous order to cease preaching about Jesus. He also says that the apostles tried to blame them—apparently the members of the council—for the death of Jesus. Both charges are justified: the apostles preached in violation of the council's order, and Peter repeatedly charged Jews with the death of Jesus. Then it is the turn of the apostles to answer the charges, which they do in verses 29–32. Notably, this speech is delivered by "Peter and the other apostles" (5:29). Does this mean that the Twelve spoke in unison or that Peter spoke, with the consent and support of the others? The essence of the speech is the affirmation of 4:19, which is repeated in 5:29: "We must obey God rather than mortals." But themes that we heard in previous Petrine speeches recur here: You killed Jesus, but God raised him. You must repent and be forgiven. The members of the council are ready to execute the apostles, but one of their number, Gamaliel, cautions them. He advises the council to leave the apostles alone. If, he says, their work is from God, nothing will stop it, but if it is merely human, it will not succeed. His cautionary words prevail, and the council releases the apostles, after beating them and reissuing the order against speaking in Jesus' name.

Gamaliel saves the apostles from being executed, but Luke does not describe him as a quasi-believer. His speech displays a kind of pragmatism and caution but not conviction. He includes no examples of movements that were God-inspired, but he cites a pair of examples to illustrate the point that humanly-derived movements are bound to fail. Theudas and Judas led two failed movements. In Gamaliel's speech the order is explicitly chronological: "Some time ago Theudas rose up in rebellion. . . . Subsequently, at the time of the census, Judas of Galilee also rose up and gathered a pack of rebels" (Acts 5:36–37). These citations are historically backward—Judas is to be dated in 6 CE, while Theudas led a rebellion in ca. 44 CE. Richard Pervo is probably correct in claiming that the error is to be attributed to Luke's reading of Josephus, who dealt with Theudas before Judas, though not indicating that this was the chronological order.[14] Of even greater interest is the fact that the rebellion under Theudas had not yet occurred at the time when Gamaliel supposedly gave this speech. In the chronology of Acts we are still within the first year after the crucifixion of Jesus, some fourteen years before the Theudas rebellion. Luke and his readers in the early second century might well have known of Theudas, but Gamaliel would not. From the perspective of the narrative itself, it is manifest that we have here a speech written by Luke, not one delivered by Gamaliel.

Summary (Acts 5:41–42). Luke concludes this section with a brief summary, telling the readers that the apostles were joyful to suffer abuse for the sake of the name of Jesus and reminding them that the apostles continued their activity of preaching in the temple and in houses. They confirmed their commitment to obey God rather than mortals and continued the contest for control of the temple.

In Search of History

This section begins with a summary statement that is characteristic of Luke's style and fits well in its context as a follow-up to the manifestation of Peter's awesome power in the previous pericope. It is therefore a Lukan creation that is not based on any identifiable historical data. The reference to the "Portico of Solomon" (Acts 5:12) is intriguing since, as mentioned in the comments above, this was written at a time when the temple was long gone. It is a reference whose purpose is to lend further credibility to Luke's overall apologetic theme, in which the community originates in Judaism even while it is in constant conflict with its leaders.

The prison break story is one of three such stories in Acts. Each of them can be paralleled to similar stories in Greek literature (see the cameo essay, "Prison Breaks in Luke's Literary World," p. 72). Ancient writers made a practice of copying such motifs for use in their own compositions, and Luke is no exception. In this case, the prison break story emulates a similar story in Euripides' *Bacchae*. It is therefore judged to be a literary creation and has no claim on history.

The prison break story is couched in a narrative of Jewish opposition, arrest, imprisonment, and trial, all of which is common plot material in Acts and thus has the markings of Lukan creation. Within that narrative is found a long speech and other quoted dialogue which ultimately derive from the author (see the cameo essay, "Speeches in Acts," p. 45). The upshot is that nothing in this narrative qualifies as historical data.

References
MacDonald, "A Mimetic Interpretation of Prison Breaks in Acts"

The Votes of the Fellows
Red/Probable
- Acts 5:17–33 is written to emulate the prison break of the maenads in Euripides' *Bacchae*.
- Acts 5:17–33 is a Lukan fiction.

Prison Breaks in Luke's Literary World
A Cameo Essay by Dennis R. MacDonald

The Acts of the Apostles narrates three prison breaks. In 5:17–32 one reads that an angel emptied a Jerusalem prison of its apostolic residents; in 12:1–17 another angel repeated this feat by freeing Peter; and in 16:24–34 an earthquake did the trick for Paul and Silas in Philippi. Most critics attribute these accounts to Luke's fondness for the genre of the "door opening," which could include the opening of the door to Jesus' tomb in the Gospels (Mark 16:2–4, Matt 28:1–4, Luke 24:1–3, and John 20:1).

Prison escapes characterize the mythology of Dionysus, and the most popular versions appear in the *Bacchae* by Euripides, a tale of hostility to the expansion of a new, enthusiastic religion from Asia Minor. A soldier notifies Pentheus, the king of Thebes, of the escape of the Maenads, the god's female followers:

> The Bacchant women you shut up—those you arrested
> and bound in chains at the public prison—
> they have fled, freed!
> They are leaping around the meadows calling on their god,
> Clamor.
> The chains loosened themselves from their feet,
> without a mortal hand, the bars of the door were undone.[15]

Pentheus still will not repent, so Dionysus reveals his power to him directly. Although shut up in a stable for a prison, the god produces fire and earthquake and tells his Maenads that he himself "shook the house." When the doors fly open, the king fears that his prisoner might escape, so he draws his sword to slay him; but he vainly stabs a look-alike phantom. He drops his sword in exhaustion; "though he was a man, / he dared to wage war on a god."[16]

Pentheus then emerges from the ruins astonished to discover that his prisoner has not escaped. Dionysus tells him, "We will wait for you. We will not flee."[17] The messenger reports what he had seen in the hills. After listening to a litany of outrageous activities performed by the women, the king decides to rid Greece of this religious scourge from the East once and for all. But the god warns him not to do so: "I would rather sacrifice to him than kick against the goads, / a mortal raging against a god."[18] This last quotation appears in Acts 26:14 on the lips of Jesus to Saul the persecutor! In the end, Pentheus' own mother, a Maenad, mangles him.

Many scholars have recognized the parallels between prison escapes in the *Bacchae* and in Acts 5 and 16, whether by direct imitation or by the ubiquity of Dionysian traditions in Luke's world.[19] Peter's prison break in Acts 12 often is grouped with Dionysian tradition as well, but Luke probably used a different literary model for this account.[20]

According to the final book of Homer's *Iliad*, Priam, the king of Troy, sets out with his guards on a dangerous journey to ransom the body of his son Hector from Achilles. The god Hermes, Zeus' *angelos*, meets them and leads them to the camp. With his wand, the god then puts the guards to sleep and magically opens the barred gates and door to Achilles' quarters. After Priam negotiates the release of the body of Hector, he dines with his son's murderer and sleeps under his roof. In the middle of the night Hermes again comes to him and warns him to leave.

> Hermes stood over Priam's head and spoke to him, saying:
> "Old man, you have no concern for harm—the way you are still sleeping
> among your enemies—since Achilles has spared you."
>
> So he spoke, and the old man was terrified and woke his herald.
> Hermes yoked the horses and mules for them,
> and he himself swiftly drove them through the camp. No one knew about them.[21]

The parallels with the prison break in Acts 12 are uncanny. An "angel of the Lord" comes to the prison at night and, while the guards are sleeping, wakes Peter and unshackles him. The angel and the apostle pass undetected past the guards, whom the angel apparently had put to sleep. They come "to the iron gate that leads to the city. This opened to them on its own accord" (Acts 12:10). The angel then departs, as Hermes did after leading Priam safely from the enemy camp.

The Seven Are Chosen

6 Around that time, as the number of followers continued to grow, those who spoke Greek charged those who spoke Aramaic with unfair treatment of Greek-speaking widows in the daily ministry. ²The Twelve convened a community meeting, at which they announced: "It is undesirable for us to neglect proclamation of God's message in order to administer charity. ³Please choose for yourselves, sisters and brothers, seven men of your number who are well recommended and notable for their spiritual and intellectual capacity. We shall place them in charge of this function, ⁴while we shall continue to devote ourselves to prayer and to the ministry of proclamation." ⁵The entire community approved of this solution. They chose Stephen, who was notable for his strong spiritual convictions and gifts, Philip, Prochorus, Nicanor, Timon, Parmenas, and Nicholas from Antioch, a convert to Judaism. ⁶They presented these seven to the apostles for prayer and the laying-on of hands. ⁷Proclamation of God's message expanded; the number of followers in Jerusalem increased substantially, including priests, a large number of whom began to embrace the faith.

Comments on the Story

Just two chapters after Luke reports the deceit of Ananias and Sapphira, he turns to yet another problem internal to the fledgling community. Now we learn that, although the number of members is increasing, there are complaints about the treatment of some of the widows. The Twelve, presumably the apostles, convene the entire group and propose a solution. They propose a division of labor, in which they, the apostles, will continue to engage in prayer and preaching, while a group of seven men is to be put in charge of administering charity (literally, "serving tables"). All agree, and the Seven are selected and ordained. Luke concludes the story with a brief summary calling attention to the continued growth of the community and especially to the large number of priests who become believers.

Luke seems to be more interested in stressing the solution to the problem than in describing the problem itself. As a result, he has left us with only a vague impression of the issue. Questions abound. Among them: Who constituted the groups involved? What was the complaint? What were the Seven commissioned to do?

In the translation above, the contending groups are called, "those who spoke Greek" and "those who spoke Aramaic." Earlier versions have "Hellenists" and "Hebrews," respectively (Acts 6:1). Either way, the context of Acts 6 demands that we understand both groups as Jews believing in Jesus. The setting is still Jerusalem, and no Gentiles have yet been converted to the believing community. Thus, the distinction is most likely a linguistic one. Hellenists would be Jewish Christians who speak Greek, and Hebrews would be Jewish Christians who speak Aramaic, a language related to Hebrew and used by Jews in the first century. If this is Luke's meaning, it behooves us to ask why differences in language would precipitate a practice in which some of the most vulnerable members of the community were being neglected.

Evidently the Greek speakers complained that their widows were being overlooked in "the daily ministry" (Acts 6:1). The NRSV makes the neglect specific by translating the phrase as "the daily distribution of food." We should probably be reminded of Luke's earlier statements about the believers taking food in their homes (2:46) and about the common ownership of property and the absence of needy persons (2:44–45; 4:32, 34–35). These summaries portray a community engaged in common meals supplied by the apostles from a common purse. Thus, it would be reasonable to think of them actually distributing food to those in attendance. Such a practice is confirmed in Acts 6:2, where the Twelve contrast preaching with serving tables (here translated as "to administer charity"). In this process some widows who spoke Greek were overlooked. Although Luke does not dwell on the point, we should note the fact that it is the Aramaic-speaking apostles (or their delegates) who are neglecting the Greek-speaking widows. He tells us so little about this problem that we gain no idea of why such a neglect might have occurred. Further, the incident would subvert Luke's insistence that there were no needy people in the community. His vagueness about the whole matter may indicate a kind of discomfort, as it is not likely that Luke would want to impugn the apostles or call attention to needy believers.

At one level the solution to the issue seems reasonable. There should be a division of labor, and the apostles should not be expected both to preach and to serve tables. But at another level, the solution does not seem to be quite appropriate. Although the serving of tables is regarded as secondary to preaching, the qualifications required of the table-servers are rigorous. They must be highly regarded by members of the community and filled with spirit and wisdom (Acts 6:3). Further, two members of the group — Stephen and Philip — are later portrayed as vigorous preachers, and there is no hint that they had anything to do with the distribution of food. Finally, all the members of the group of seven have Greek names. Six of them would be Greek-speaking Jews, while one — Nicholas — is an Antiochene convert. If the issue is the neglect of Greek-speaking widows, how does the appointment of a group of Greek-speaking men solve it? Is it to be presumed that the Greek speakers are more fair-minded than the Aramaic speakers? Or should we now expect the Aramaic-speaking widows to be the ones overlooked in the daily distribution?

These observations and questions have led many commentators on Acts to conclude that something more is at stake than Luke allows the reader to see. Just what that might be, however, cannot be known with certainty. Narratives of Stephen and Philip show these two as performing pretty much the same functions as the apostles — working miracles and preaching. Whatever the issues may have been, Luke's narrative about a group of twelve and a group of seven probably indicates that he knew of some controversy between them but intended to do everything possible to minimize it.

He made the appointment of the seven to cohere with the authority of the Twelve, but the stories of Stephen and Philip that follow suggest that a body of believers functioned independently of the apostles.

In Search of History

According to the chronology of Acts, when this story takes place the community is still confined to Jerusalem, the conversion of Paul has not yet taken place, and the Gentile mission is far into the future. The story is therefore placed within the first two to three years of the birth of the Christian movement. Yet it is already a community that has developed a stable sense of leadership (the Twelve), rituals of appointment (laying-on of hands), and an organized system of community care. In a remarkably short period of time, it has developed a social structure in which widows can be singled out from among its number as a classification of members to be given special attention. These components of the story are anachronistic and unsuited to the time period in which they are placed. Such a remarkable pace of development is unknown among the communities of Paul, as evidenced by Paul's letters, and is contrary to the probabilities of group social development. For these reasons alone, the story is found to be lacking in historical credibility.

Nevertheless, as noted in the comments above, there are intriguing inconsistencies in the story that raise questions about whether there is a source behind it. Why does Luke not describe the problem in more detail? Why does he not provide a conclusion in which the problem is shown to be resolved? Why does he reveal only to moderate the existence of a dispute within the community between groups of members identified solely by their language traditions? These issues cannot be resolved by assuming that the story is based on historical events in the early years of Christian beginnings, contrary to a long tradition in scholarship; there are simply too many historical anachronisms in the story. At best, one might propose that the story masks a controversy in Luke's own day, a period in which there existed such features as a stable sense of leadership, rituals of appointment, a class of widows, and a nascent organized system of community care. The characters of "the Twelve" and "the Seven" would then provide a model for apostolic leadership transition that the author is proposing to his community.

Since the story has no historical basis or source tradition lying behind it, the list of seven names is undermined as a useful record of historical characters from the early Jerusalem community. Five of the characters appear only here. The two others, Stephen and Philip, become important literary characters in subsequent stories in Acts. All of the names function as devices for verisimilitude in a story that is otherwise Luke's creation. There is no historical core with which to connect them as actual figures from the early period.

The history of the interpretation of this text in the Seminar offers an interesting case study in the development of its research methodology. At the first meeting of the Seminar in March 2000, a paper was presented by Stephen Wiest in which he summarized current scholarship and argued for the basic historicity of the text. At that time, the Seminar still assumed a date of ca. 80 CE for the composition of Acts. While all of Wiest's proposals were not accepted, the basic idea that there was a probable historical core to the story remained, and the text was tabled for future discussion.

In a 2007 paper, Perry Kea proposed that there was a Lukan structure underlying the story but that the "Hellenists" and the "Seven" were historical. His argument was based on a longstanding consensus in scholarship on this text. During the discussion of this paper, the Seminar made a significant methodological breakthrough. The realization grew that dating Acts in the early second century changed how we assess the potential historicity of the Acts story. Previous scholarship, based on a date of ca. 80 CE, had assumed historicity for the stories in Acts based on a perception of the historical reliability of its source materials. We now realized that a later dating, and the likelihood that Acts used Paul's letters as a source, changed the burden of proof and undermined the bases on which most previous arguments had been built. Thus a majority of the Fellows rejected claims to historicity and concluded that both "the Hellenists" and "the Seven" are more likely to be narrative devices than historical references. In the cameo essay, "Hellenists and Hebrews" (p. 79), Kea provides a summary of the Seminar discussion and the resulting state of the discussion regarding historical probabilities in this text.

References
    Wiest, "The Story of Stephen"
    Kea, "The Hellenists and the Hebrews"

The Votes of the Fellows
Gray/Doubtful
- The Hellenists of Acts 6:1 were Greek-speaking Jews.
- The Hellenists of Acts 6:1 were diaspora Jews.

- The list of the Seven in Acts 6:5 is a pre-Lukan tradition.
- The Seven belonged to the Hellenists.

Black/Improbable
- The Hellenists of Acts 6:1 were Gentiles.
- The Seven were selected by the Twelve.
- The Seven served as overseers/administrators for the Hellenist community in Jerusalem.
- At least two of the Seven, Stephen and Philip, were evangelists.
- The Hellenist community of Jesus' followers in Jerusalem was persecuted.

Hellenists and Hebrews
A Cameo Essay by Perry V. Kea

Acts 6 abruptly introduces two groups, the Hellenists (*Hellēnistai*) and the Hebrews (*Hebraioi*). We are told that in Jerusalem the Hellenists complain that their widows are not receiving an equitable share of food with the Hebrews (Acts 6:1). The apostles are called in to settle the dispute. They appoint seven men to serve as table waiters, thereby providing for an equitable sharing of the food resources. However, these men do not behave as table waiters. One of them, Stephen, is described this way: "Endowed with power and favor, Stephen began to perform remarkable miracles among the people" (6:8). Shortly after this report, Stephen is charged with blasphemy and placed on trial before the Jewish council (6:9–12). A second "Hellenist," Philip, appears as an evangelist in Acts 8.

The meaning of the term "Hellenists" is unsure. It does not occur in literature before its mention in Acts 6. Many think it refers to Greek-speaking Jews. Many Jews lived outside of Palestine and spoke Greek as their primary language. It was common for these Jews to visit Jerusalem. Some even relocated to Jerusalem. In support of this was the discovery of a first-century Greek inscription for a synagogue located in Jerusalem[22]. This indicates the existence of a Greek-speaking Jewish community in Jerusalem. According to this view, Luke intended the term "Hellenists" to refer to Greek-speaking Jews who had become members of the Jesus movement. The Hebrews then would be Hebrew- (or Aramaic-) speaking Jews, perhaps native to Palestine, who were followers of Jesus.

The second occurrence of the term "Hellenists" is in Acts 9:29. In 9:26–30, the recently converted Saul visits Jerusalem and argues with the Hellenists about Jesus. They look for a way to kill Saul, so he is hustled away by the believers. Obviously, if "Hellenists" means Greek-speaking Jews, those mentioned here are not Jesus' followers.

The third instance of "Hellenists" occurs in Acts 11:20. Luke picks up the story from 8:1. Luke reported that Stephen's death prompted a persecution of Jesus' followers, forcing them to leave Jerusalem. In 11:19 Luke tells us that these followers traveled to Phoenicia, Cyprus, and Syrian Antioch preaching the word "to Jews only." Luke then adds that some of these followers also spoke to the "Hellenists". But identifying Hellenists with Greek-speaking Jews does not work here. One would think that the Jews to whom the word was spoken in 11:19 were Greek-speaking too. What is the difference between the Jews mentioned in 11:19 and the (presumably) Greek-speaking Jews (Hellenists) in 11:20?

However, the manuscript evidence is uncertain at this point. Some of our ancient manuscripts of Acts read "Greeks/Hellenes"(*Hellēnas*) instead of "Hellenists." If the original word was "Greeks," Luke would be saying that these early followers preached only to fellow Jews at first, but that in Antioch they began to include non-Jews, that is, Greeks, in their missionary efforts. This clearly makes better sense of 11:19–20. Some scholars have suggested that Luke used "Greeks" and "Hellenists" interchangeably. That might explain the appearance of both terms in the different manuscripts of 11:20, but it does not make good sense of 6:1 and 9:29.

If Luke intended "Hellenists" to refer to Greeks, that is, non-Jews, it is hard to explain the presence of non-Jews in the company of Jesus' followers so early in the story (Acts 6 and 9). In Acts 10 and 11, Luke goes to great lengths to rationalize the mission to non-Jews. If "Hellenists" means non-Jews in 6:1 and 9:29, Luke's failure to explain their presence in the Christian community before Acts 10–11 is a mystery.

When the Fellows of the Acts Seminar voted on whether the Hellenists were Greek-speaking Jews, they were almost evenly split (0.49 weighted average=a vote indicating doubtful historicity). Given the above difficulties, the Fellows did not have confidence that they could reach historically reliable conclusions.

The Martyrdom of Stephen

6 ⁸Endowed with power and favor, Stephen began to perform remarkable miracles among the people. ⁹Opposition arose from some who belonged to the Synagogue of Former Slaves, whose members came from Cyrene and Alexandria. People from Cilicia and Asia also engaged in debate with Stephen, ¹⁰but were helpless against the wisdom and vigor of his message. ¹¹These people thereupon prompted some to allege: "We have heard this fellow uttering blasphemies against Moses and God!" ¹²Their allegations agitated not only the general public but also the elders and the legal experts, who ambushed and kidnapped Stephen, then took him to the council. ¹³There they produced lying witnesses, who said, "This character incessantly denounces the holy place and the Torah. ¹⁴We have heard him claim that this fellow Jesus the Nazorean will destroy this place and alter the practices that Moses gave us." ¹⁵When all those who were seated in the council chamber glared at Stephen they saw that his face was as radiant as an angel's.

7 The high priest asked, "Are these charges true?"

²"Fathers and brothers, please listen," he replied. "Our glorious God appeared to our ancestor Abraham while he was in Mesopotamia, before he settled in Haran: ³'Leave your land and your relatives and go to the land that I shall show you,' God said.

⁴"So Abraham left the land of the Chaldeans and settled in Haran, from which, following the death of his father, God had him relocate in this land that you now inhabit. ⁵God did not, however, provide him with even so much as a square meter of it, but did promise to award it to him and to his descendants thereafter, although Abraham was then childless. ⁶God said, in effect, that 'his descendants would be aliens in a foreign land, whose inhabitants would enslave and abuse them for four hundred years. ⁷I shall condemn the nation that enslaves them, and they shall thereafter leave it and serve me in this place.' ⁸God then made a covenant ratified by circumcision with Abraham. Therefore, when Isaac was born he circumcised him on the eighth day, as did Isaac for his son Jacob, who did likewise for the twelve patriarchs whom he sired.

⁹"The patriarchs, however, became jealous of Joseph and sold him into slavery in Egypt, but God was on his side, ¹⁰rescuing him from all his afflictions and bestowing upon him wisdom and charm that won the favor of

Pharaoh, the king of Egypt. God made him the governor of Egypt and put him in charge of Pharaoh's household. [11]Then all of Egypt and Canaan experienced a famine, which brought terrible affliction. Our ancestors could find no provisions. [12]When Jacob heard that there was grain in Egypt he sent our ancestors to Egypt for the first time. [13]On their second visit Joseph revealed himself to his brothers, and thus Pharaoh learned about Joseph's family. [14]Joseph then sent for his father Jacob and his entire family, seventy-five persons altogether. [15]So Jacob went to Egypt, where he himself died, as did the patriarchs. [16]Their bodies were transported to Shechem and placed there in the tomb that Abraham had acquired for a sum from the offspring of Hamor.

[17]"When the time for fulfillment of the promise God made to Abraham was drawing near, the Israelites in Egypt spread and increased, [18]until there came a king who did not recall Joseph. [19]He exploited our race and oppressed our ancestors, compelling them to expose their infants so that they would not survive. [20]At that time Moses was born. This divinely beautiful child was nurtured in his father's home for three months, [21]but after he had been exposed, Pharaoh's daughter claimed him and reared him as her own son. [22]Moses learned all that Egyptian wisdom had to offer and became persuasive in speech and effective in action.

[23]"When he had attained the age of forty, Moses decided to pay a visit to his kindred, the Israelites. [24]While so doing he found one of them being abused. Moses came to his aid and gave his Egyptian oppressor what he deserved: death. [25]He presumed that his kindred understood that God was using him to rescue them, but they did not. [26]On the very next day, he came upon some Israelites fighting and sought to settle the dispute without violence. 'You belong to the same people,' he said. 'Why are you harming each other?' [27]The aggressor rebuffed him. 'Who appointed you as our ruler and judge? [28]Are you going to kill me, just as you killed that Egyptian yesterday?' [29]At that Moses fled and took up residence as an alien in Midian, where he fathered two sons.

[30]"Forty years after he had left Egypt, while he was in the desolate region around Mount Sinai, an angel appeared

to Moses in the flame of a fiery bush. ³¹Taken aback by the sight, he drew close to investigate, when the voice of the Lord erupted: ³²'I am the God of your ancestors, the God of Abraham, Isaac, and Jacob.' Moses became too frightened to investigate further. ³³The Lord said: 'Remove your sandals, for the place where you are standing is holy ground. ³⁴I have fully observed the misery of my people in Egypt, and have heard their groans; I have come down to deliver them. So now I am sending you to Egypt.'

³⁵"Moses was the one whom they repudiated by saying, 'Who appointed you as ruler and judge?' Moses was the one whom God sent with the assistance of the angel who appeared to him in the bush to be both ruler and redeemer. ³⁶Moses led them out after he had worked portents and miracles in Egypt and at the Red Sea and, for forty years, in the wild. ³⁷Moses it was who told the Israelites 'God will raise up a prophet like me for you from among your number.' ³⁸Moses was the one who was with an angel that spoke to him on Mount Sinai during the wilderness assembly and there received vital precepts. ³⁹Our ancestors, who also were with him, did not choose to be obedient to Moses, but rebuffed him and turned their hearts toward Egypt. They said to Aaron: ⁴⁰'Manufacture some gods to carry in front of us, for we do not know what has happened to this Moses who led us out of the land of Egypt.' ⁴¹They then concocted a calf, made offerings to this idol and took pleasure in their handiwork. ⁴²So God turned away and abandoned them to their worship of heavenly bodies. As the book of the Prophets says: 'Did you bring me animal and other sacrifices during those forty years in the wilderness, house of Israel? ⁴³No, but you did take the tent of Moloch and the star of the god Rompha, those images that you fabricated in order to worship them. I am going to remove you to some place east of Babylon.'

⁴⁴"While they were out in the wild, our forebears had the tent of testimony, fashioned by Moses in compliance with the instructions given by the one who had spoken with him and in accordance with the design that he had been shown. ⁴⁵Our forebears carried this tent with them while later, under Joshua, they dispossessed the gentiles whom God expelled, and they retained it until the time of David. ⁴⁶God approved of David, who asked to provide an

abode for the house of Jacob, ⁴⁷yet it was Solomon who actually built a temple for God. ⁴⁸Nonetheless, the Most High does not inhabit abodes of human manufacture. This is how the prophet puts it: ⁴⁹'The sky is my throne and earth my footstool. What kind of a dwelling could you fashion for me,' says the Lord, 'or where shall I take my rest? ⁵⁰Did not I create all these things?'

⁵¹"You obdurate creatures, cut off from the covenant in heart and hearing! You, like those who went before you, always line up against the Holy Spirit. ⁵²Which of the prophets did your forebears neglect to persecute? They murdered those who foretold the coming of the righteous one! Now that he has come, you betrayed and murdered him. ⁵³You received the Torah through angelic agency, but you have not observed it."

⁵⁴The audience gnashed their teeth in rage at his slashing words. ⁵⁵Stephen, on the other hand, was brimming with inspiration. He gazed upward and saw the nimbus of divinity and Jesus standing to God's right.

⁵⁶"I see heaven revealed," he proclaimed. "The Son of Man is standing at the right side of God."

⁵⁷At this his hearers shrieked, stopped their ears, and rushed at him en masse. ⁵⁸They thrust Stephen outside of the city limits and proceeded to stone him. The witnesses left their coats in the care of a young man named Saul. ⁵⁹As he was being pelted with stones, Stephen invoked the Lord, saying, "Lord Jesus, accept my spirit." ⁶⁰He then knelt and, after crying out with a loud voice, "Lord, do not hold this sin against them," Stephen died.

8 Saul was in favor of this murder. That same day saw the beginning of a virulent persecution of the church in Jerusalem. All but the apostles fled into the countryside of Judea and Samaria. ²Some devout men buried Stephen and raised a loud lament over his body. ³Saul began to wreak havoc against the church. He entered one house after another to drag out both men and women and toss them into jail.

Comments on the Story

Luke uses the story of Hebrews and Hellenists (Acts 6:1–7) to introduce narratives about two of the Seven, Stephen (6:8–8:3) and Philip (8:4–40). The extensive concentration on Stephen, and especially his speech, shows that this section of Acts was very important to the author. There are three phases of this section: Stephen's arrest; Stephen's speech; Stephen's death and the subsequent persecution.

Stephen's arrest (Acts 6:8–15). Stephen is said to be a worker of miracles, who became so prominent that he drew opposition from members of certain Jerusalem synagogues and from the public at large. Apparently Luke is thinking of synagogues that were organized by Jews who had been slaves in the Diaspora but who had gained their freedom and then relocated to Jerusalem. After debating unsuccessfully with Stephen, members of these synagogues induced some people to allege that he had blasphemed against Moses and God. These allegations so stirred up the people and some of their leaders that Stephen was taken before the Jewish council, charged—falsely according to Luke—with speaking against the temple and the Torah and claiming that Jesus had threatened to destroy the temple and change Mosaic Law.

Several things are notable in this brief paragraph. For the first time in Acts we learn of opposition from synagogue members and leaders as well as the general public. Indeed, the earlier chapters of Acts made it clear that the apostles had strong popular support, so strong that the temple authorities were unable to move against them (see Acts 4:21; 5:26). The author of Acts consistently associated priests and Sadducees with the temple (see 4:1; 5:17), and now he identifies elders and scribes ("legal experts" in our translation) with synagogues. So, in his scheme of things, opposition from synagogue leaders and the general public has been added to that from temple authorities.

The charge of blasphemy against Stephen might remind readers of similar charges against Jesus in the Gospel of Luke (see Luke 5:21; 22:71). Blasphemy is usually understood as the breaking of the third commandment against wrongful use of the name YHWH (see Exod 20:7; Deut 5:11), but here in Acts it seems to reflect a broader interpretation. Stephen is charged with demeaning God, Moses, the temple, and the Torah. It is also said that he claimed that Jesus threatened to destroy the temple and change the law. In the Gospel of Luke, Jesus did predict the destruction of the temple (see Luke 21:5–6), but Luke, unlike Matthew and Mark, did not have Jesus' accusers say that he would be the one to destroy it (see Matt 26:61; Mark 14:58; in John 2:19 Jesus himself issues the threat against the temple). As for changing Mosaic law, the Gospel of Luke could serve as a basis for this accusation, especially in regard to Sabbath observance (see e.g. Luke 6:1–11; 13:10–17; 14:1–6).

Stephen's speech (Acts 7:1–56). The entirety of Acts 7 is devoted to the trial of Stephen, most of it to his speech, the longest one in the book. In response to the high priest's question, Stephen immediately launches into a summary of Israel's history, from Abraham to Solomon. Most of the attention is devoted to Abraham, Joseph, and Moses. Stephen calls attention to Abraham's relocating from Chaldea to Haran and finally, to "this land that you now inhabit" (Acts 7:4). Presumably, Abraham's final destination is the land of Israel, home to the members of the Jewish council as well as Stephen. God promises that Abraham's descendants will possess this land, although at the time Abraham had no descendants. The promise is ratified by the covenant of circumcision.

The story of Joseph is summarized, and Stephen tells of his being sold into Egyptian slavery and his divinely aided rise to power. When a famine arose in Canaan, his father and brothers found help from Joseph in Egypt, where they remained. But after some years, a Pharaoh who did not recall Joseph oppressed the descendants of Jacob and required them to expose their infants to death.

Stephen then turns to the story of Moses. He tells of his birth, his exposure as an infant, and his rescue by Pharaoh's daughter. Although rebuffed by some of his own people, Moses was called by God to be the ruler and redeemer of Israel. The speech of Stephen stresses the difficulties of Moses, both before and after the Exodus. The people of Israel questioned his right to be a judge over them, and even after the departure from Egypt they did not accept his leadership. Instead, they manufactured a calf, which they worshiped. During the forty years in the wild, Moses designed a "tent of testimony," the specifications of which were divinely communicated to him. Stephen claims that this tent remained among the people through the time of David. But then Solomon built the temple, although, in Stephen's s view, God does not live in anything built by humans.

Stephen concludes his speech by accusing his compatriots of perennially opposing the Holy Spirit and killing all the prophets and, finally, Jesus. He accuses the people of Israel of disobedience to God's Torah. The speech produces the expected reaction of rage from the audience, but Stephen reveals his vision of heaven opened and Jesus standing at God's right.

As important as Stephen's speech is to Luke, we must ask about its relevance. How can this speech be an answer to the charges brought against Stephen? According to the narrative he is accused of blasphemy against God, Moses, Torah, and temple—major aspects of Jewish religious life in the first century. But Stephen neither affirms nor denies any of the charges; indeed, there is no explicit reference to them in the speech. It is true that, in many similar treatments, martyrs do not directly address the charges against them, but the question of the appropriateness of Stephen's speech is especially perplexing. How is a history of ancient Israel fitting in its present context? Further, what is the point of the speech? We could easily imagine some members of the council, after listening respectfully for several minutes, rising up to demand that Stephen get to the point.

And yet, a close reading of the speech will show that it is relevant. It is true that Stephen neither affirms nor denies that he attacked the temple. But his analysis of worship-centers in Israel's history contrasts the "tent of testimony" with the temple that Solomon built in Jerusalem, and it is clear that Stephen prefers the former. He affirms that God does not dwell in any one place and certainly not in humanly constructed buildings. Stephen does not deny that Jesus threatened to destroy the temple; rather he implies that it was a mistake to build it in the first place. If we place the speech in the context of Luke's literary work, we may see it as the culmination of attempts by Jesus and the apostles to make it a place for Christian proclamation and teaching. Jesus made such an attempt, but he was executed. The apostles made several attempts but they were arrested. Stephen now delegitimizes the Jerusalem temple as a divinely authenticated place of worship. Readers of Acts in the second century, who knew that the temple had been destroyed many decades before, might not applaud the Romans for burning it down, but Stephen's speech would not lead them to regard its destruction as an act against God.

The speech also demonstrates the falsity of the charge that Stephen demeaned Moses and the law. There is nothing but praise for Moses but blame for the people of Israel for their disobedience to him. At the end of the speech Stephen accuses the members of the council of disobeying Torah. He even endorses a fundamental aspect of Jewish observance, namely circumcision. In view of the role that this practice is to play later on in Acts, it is remarkable that nothing negative is said about it here. It is referred to as a covenant that God made with Abraham, which was faithfully observed by the patriarchs (Acts 7:8). It is true that Stephen does not deny that he attacked Torah or that Jesus intended to alter the Mosaic laws, but the speech makes it clear that this charge was false. Indeed, it may be said that Stephen turned the tables on his inquisitors: it is you, not I, who have demeaned Torah.

It is also useful to ask why Luke had Stephen cite OT passages so extensively. The answer should be sought not in terms of the appropriateness of such citations for Stephen and his audience, but rather for Luke and his. To be sure, citations of the Scriptures might tend to create a bond between Stephen and members of the Jewish council. But, if, as we believe, Acts was written in the early second century, we may ask the question differently. What would it mean for Luke's readers that these Scriptures are so extensively quoted? In the early second century, some Christians were raising fundamental questions about the Hebrew Scriptures. Marcionite Christians attributed the inspiration of these writings to the creator God, who was not the God of Jesus, and denied that the prophets foresaw his advent. Other Christians made use of the Hebrew Scriptures but linked their interpretations to polytheistic ideologies. In Stephen's speech the author of Acts affirms the validity of the Hebrew Scriptures as the word of the one God, and he ties them tightly to belief in Jesus. For Luke the God of the OT is the God of Jesus, and the Hebrew prophets predicted his coming. In Acts, Luke weaves a complex ideology that distances Christians from Jews but retains a basic conviction of the inspiration and authority of the Hebrew Scriptures.

In this light it is important to observe that the version of Scripture on which Luke relied was the Greek translation of the OT, the Septuagint (LXX). Perhaps it was appropriate for Stephen, who had previously been identified as speaking Greek, to use the LXX, although his audience would presumably have been familiar with the Scriptures in Hebrew. The reality is, however, that the author of Acts used the Greek because this is the version he and presumably his readers knew and revered.

Stephen's death and the subsequent persecution (Acts 7:57–8:3). After the speech Stephen is hauled outside the city and stoned to death. As he dies he calls on God to forgive his oppressors as Jesus had done in Luke 23:34 (although the authenticity of the text is questionable). In Acts 8:1, Luke introduces Saul, whose name will later be changed to Paul and who will play a dominant role in the latter half of the book. Here it is said that he held the coats of those engaged in the stoning of Stephen, which he approved. In 8:3 Saul is shown to be a vehement persecutor of the Jesus movement, and the implication of Luke's words is that Saul instigated a persecution that led to the flight of believers from Jerusalem. Only the apostles remained in the city.

Luke seems to envision the killing of Stephen as the action of several stone-throwers. The Mishnah, a text reflecting Jewish practices that was compiled in the late second century, describes stoning differently. The victim is thrown off a cliff and, if he survives, a large boulder is rolled down to crush him. It is not certain, however, that the rules of the Mishnah were known as early as the writing of Acts or the time of Stephen. It is possible that Luke's source described a lynching that Luke transformed into a judicial execution or that Luke intentionally described the actions of the Jewish council as illegal.

We will read much more about Saul/Paul as we work through Acts.

In Search of History

In a 2001 paper, Perry Kea proposed that the Stephen story, and Stephen's speech, were fashioned by Luke on the basis of models he found in the Septuagint. He also recommended that the core data that an early Christian named Stephen met a violent death may have been historical. The Fellows agreed with the former proposal but were unsure about the argument that Stephen and his martyrdom may have been historical.

In a 2007 paper, Shelly Matthews proposed that the story of Stephen's martyrdom fails on several criteria to qualify as historical. In addition, she gave special attention to the themes of the story in which Jews as a group are stereotyped as killers of Christians. She thus argued not only that the story is unhistorical but also that the traditional reading of it as historical has been closely associated with an anti-Jewish agenda in the writing of Christian history (see the cameo essay, "Stephen," pp. 90). Both the Fellows and the Associates affirmed her arguments with strong votes in favor.

In addition, the Fellows were persuaded that the material about Saul and the persecution of the Jerusalem church is unhistorical. It was noted that, while Acts 8:3, about Saul's persecuting activity, is generally confirmed in the Pauline letters, his specific acquaintance with the churches of Judea is contradicted in Gal 1:22.

References

    Wiest, "The Story of Stephen"
    Kea, "The Septuagint as a Source" and "The Speech of Stephen"
    Matthews, "The Stoning of Stephen" and *Perfect Martyr*

The Votes of the Fellows

Red/Probable
- The speech of Stephen is a creation of the author of Acts.
- Luke composed the speech of Stephen using a variety of OT (LXX) texts organized on the model of a "history of Israel."
- Luke modeled the account of Stephen's accusation and stoning on the Naboth incident (1 Kgs 21:8–13).
- There is no necessary and singular relationship between the events of history and the language used to translate those events into historical narrative.
- Decisions about how to translate the "raw events" of history into the language of a historical narrative have ethical consequences.
- The story of the stoning of Stephen fails both the criteria of multiple attestation and dissimilarity.
- It is anachronistic to speak of "Jews" killing "Christians" in the first century of the Common Era.
- There is no ethical good to come from speaking of Jews killing Christians in the first century of the Common Era.
- The story of the stoning of Stephen in Acts constructs "the Jews" as a negative category.

Gray/Doubtful
- Behind the speech attributed to Stephen lies a Hellenistic Jewish or Jewish Christian source.

Black/Improbable
- The speech of Stephen in Acts 7 is an historically accurate summary of what Stephen said during his trial before the Sanhedrin.
- Stephen and his martyrdom are historical events.
- Saul/Paul was present at the stoning of Stephen.
- Saul/Paul persecuted Christians in Jerusalem/Judea.
- The dispersal of Jesus' followers from Jerusalem because of a persecution precipitated the spread of the Jesus movement.
- Soon after his conversion in Damascus, Paul attempted to join the Christian community in Jerusalem.

Stephen

A Cameo Essay by Shelly Matthews

Stephen is the sole follower of Jesus whose death is detailed in vivid coloring in Acts: a charismatic Jew associated with the "Hellenists," singled out for leadership and then subject to false charges, which are refuted in a long and eloquent speech culminating in counter charges of prophet-persecution and Christ-killing. After Stephen announces his vision of the Son of Man, he is dragged out of the city and stoned by a Jewish mob. The death, at the close of the Jerusalem section of Acts, ignites a severe persecution causing all except the apostles to scatter, with some traveling as far as Antioch, the place where the followers of Jesus were first called Christians (cf. Acts 11:19–26).

A translator wishing to highlight Luke's penchant for symbolic names might choose the English word "Crown" to designate this first martyr, for Crown is the English equivalent of the Greek *Stephanos*. Through employing the name, Luke taps into developing associations among early Christians between bearing witness (*martyreō*) to Jesus as Messiah, and the crown received in the afterlife as a reward for suffering death on behalf of that witness (1 Cor 9:25; Rev 2:10; 3:11; Jas 1:12; 2 Tim 4:8; cf. 4 Macc 17:15).

Yet, to recognize the significance of the name is to scratch only the surface of the rich symbolism with which this pericope is freighted. Stephen serves as a link between Jesus in the Third Gospel and Paul in Acts. Like both Paul and Jesus, Stephen is sent by God to deliver prophetic oracles, rejected by Israel, subjected to false charges, and persecuted in Jerusalem.

The significance of the Stephen story lies foremost, however, in the differences between his fate and the fates of Jesus and Paul. In a narrative in which the author is trying to carve out a space for Christians in the empire by depicting Roman officials as positively as possible, and non-believing Jews as negatively as possible, Luke faces the conundrum that tradition laid the deaths of both Jesus and Paul at the hands of Roman officials. His solution is (a) to diminish Roman responsibility for Jesus' death, while highlighting Jewish culpability; (b) to avoid the narration of Paul's death at Roman hands altogether, while inserting numerous plots by Jews to kill Paul; and (c) to craft the murder of Stephen, the first and prototypical Christian martyr, as a purely Jewish affair, outside of Roman purview. The fact that Stephen dies through stoning by a riotous Jewish mob underscores the non-Roman/barbaric nature of the deed, since Romans regarded stoning (unlike crucifixion!) as an improper resort to violence, employed only by barbarians and rebels.

No ancient source outside of Acts attests to Stephen, until the time of Irenaeus, who clearly depends on Acts for what he knows of this martyr. It is thus impossible to ascertain whether a historical figure named Stephen did in fact exist, whose death inspired the story, or whether Luke invented the story out of whole cloth. Violence is a commonplace of imperial occupation, and it is plausible to imagine that sometimes that violence turned inward, such that in the case of Roman-occupied Judea, a Jesus-believing Jew named Stephen "got in a fight" with non-believing Jews and was subsequently killed.

The tragedy of this story, in terms of the long history of Western depictions of Jews as killers of Christians, is not that Luke conjures here a historically impossible situation—a Jesus follower being killed by non-believing Jews. It is, rather, that this author's telescopic narrative of one, and only one, significant death beyond the crucifixion of Jesus—that of a merciful Jesus follower by merciless Jews—has become canonized as a foundational event in Western consciousness. Such telescoping veils both the magnitude and imperial circumstance of first-century bloodshed in this region of the ancient Mediterranean. If it is accepted as *the* historically significant encounter between believing and non-believing Jews, it forecloses the possibility of imagining ancient Jewish-Christian relations in more complex and multiform ways.

As a counter tradition to Acts' simplifying, binary depictions of virtually all non-believing Jews as violent, and all Jesus believers as suffering at their hands, crystalized here in the Stephen pericope, one might consider Josephus' version of the death of James, the brother of Jesus.[23] Among the remarkable details of this account is Josephus' claim that at the death of James, Pharisees were "burdened by grief." Thus Josephus, in distinction from Acts, provides a glimpse of possible alliance and even sympathy among Jews who otherwise disagreed over the significance of Jesus.

2

To Judea, Samaria, and Beyond
Acts 8:4–9:43

Philip, Peter, and John in Samaria

8 ⁴Meanwhile, those who had fled proclaimed the message in the course of their travels. ⁵Philip, for example, went to the city of Samaria and began to tell the people about the messiah. ⁶Large crowds hung on his every word, for they not only heard his message but could also see the miracles that he performed. ⁷Impure spirits departed with loud shrieks from many who were possessed, while many of the infirm and disabled were healed. ⁸There was loud rejoicing in that city.

⁹Prior to all this an individual named Simon had practiced magic in the city. The populace of Samaria held him in awe. He claimed to be a great person. ¹⁰All classes of people, from top to bottom, now became devoted to him and exclaimed, "He is the Power of God called 'Great.'" ¹¹The cause of this devotion was the awe evoked by Simon's long-standing feats of wizardry. ¹²Yet, when they came to believe Philip's message about God's reign and the name of Jesus Christ, they, men and women alike, began to have themselves baptized. ¹³Even Simon came to believe and, after his baptism, became a firm adherent of Philip; when he saw miracles and other powerful deeds occurring, he was astonished.

¹⁴When the apostles at Jerusalem learned that Samaria had accepted God's message, they sent Peter and John to visit them. ¹⁵After the two had arrived, they prayed that the converts might receive the Holy Spirit, ¹⁶for the Spirit had not yet fallen upon any of them. They had merely been baptized in the name of the Lord Jesus. ¹⁷After praying, the apostles laid their hands upon them, and the converts started receiving the Holy Spirit. ¹⁸When Simon observed that the Spirit was conveyed through the imposition of

apostolic hands, he offered them money, [19]saying, "Bestow upon me this power, so that anyone upon whom I lay my hands may receive Holy Spirit."

[20]Peter replied, "The hell with you and your money, for you have decided that you can acquire with cash that which God supplies gratis. [21]There is no place or role for you in this enterprise, for your heart is not right with God. [22]Abandon this wickedness and beg the Lord in the hope that he will perhaps forgive your wicked intention, [23]for I am aware that you have been snared and poisoned by evil." [24]"Will all of you please intercede with the Lord for me," Simon answered, "entreating that none of these things you have mentioned will happen to me."

[25]After speaking about what they had seen and heard and proclaiming the message, Peter and John set out for Jerusalem. On their return journey, they preached the gospel in a number of Samaritan villages.

Comments on the Story

Readers will recall the instructions of Jesus given in Acts 1:8, which directed the apostles to remain in Jerusalem until they receive the Holy Spirit and then go out to proclaim the gospel in Judea, Samaria, and the ends of the earth. Up to this point, the city of Jerusalem has been the setting for all the episodes in Acts. Now it is time to widen the scope, and the author focuses next on Samaria. It is notable that, although Acts 1:8 is a broad outline for the action in the book, Luke does not follow it rigidly. Acts 1:8 has Judea then Samaria; but the actual episodes in Acts occur in the reverse order.

Philip (presumably one of the Seven appointed in Acts 6:5, not one of the apostles listed in 1:13) goes to Samaria and preaches with great success. A special convert, Simon, had been practicing magic there but was so impressed with Philip's preaching that he became devoted to him. The apostles, who were still in Jerusalem at this time, sent two of their number, Peter and John, to Samaria to follow up on Philip's work. People in Samaria had been baptized, but Peter and John laid hands on them, and they received the Holy Spirit. Simon was so amazed at this turn of events that he offered to buy the rights to do as Peter and John had done. But Peter rebuked him for this attitude and encouraged him to repent. The episode ends with Simon imploring Peter and John to pray for him, and then the apostles return to Jerusalem.

Samaria was at the time a mixed community, with Gentiles in the majority. But traditionally the region was associated with descendants of the Northern Kingdom of Israel, people who could claim a special relationship with Jews to the South. Although it is not impossible that the author of Acts intends the readers to understand that Philip preached to Gentiles in Samaria, it is far more likely that he thinks of the converts as Samaritans. The movement of the narrative in Acts is gradual—from preaching aimed at Jews of Jerusalem in Acts 1–7 to a mission to Gentiles beginning in Acts 10. In between we should think of persons who are peripherally related to the Jews in Judea—first Samaritans and then diaspora Jews. The course of the narrative is not strictly orderly, but its general course is clear.

The vocabulary used by the author in Acts 8:4–13 calls attention to a certain parallelism between Philip and Simon. The use of parallelism is clearer in Greek than in English translation. The author uses the same word—expressing the idea of *eager listening*—to describe the responses to both Philip and Simon: the crowd *eagerly listened* to Philip (8:6); everybody *eagerly listened* to Simon (8:10, 11). Similarly we have the same word to describe the two proponents: Simon is called *great* (8:9, 10), and Philip performs signs and *great* deeds (8:13). A word for "amazement" is used for both: Simon *amazed* people (8:9, 11) but later was *amazed* at the deeds of Philip (8:13). The parallelism between the two is also suggested by the description of Philip as performing miracles (8:6, 13) and Simon as practicing magic (8:9). Perhaps the author would place these performances on different levels, but it is hard to see this in the narrative at hand. Nevertheless, it is clear that the narrative moves toward a lowering status for Simon. He thinks that he is *someone great* (8:9) but later stands amazed at the *greatness* of Philip (8:13).

Philip retreats from the scene when the apostles Peter and John arrive in Samaria. What is the function of the apostles? Are they sent to inspect the work of a non-apostolic preacher, or is their presence necessary in order to validate Philip's activity? It does not seem that Peter and John were sent simply to see what was going on, since when they arrive they engage in an activity that extends Philip's work. Philip had baptized people in the name of Jesus, but no one had yet received the Holy Spirit. The apostles correct this situation by laying hands on the baptized, and with this ritual the believers receive the spirit. This must imply that we have here another Pentecost, although there is no description of people speaking in tongues. The major point is that the apostles must put a stamp of approval on the activity of other Christians and supply what might be missing. We shall see, however, that Luke is not consistent in requiring apostolic hands after baptism (see Acts 8:38). Even so, the author strongly stresses apostolic authority in the early church.

The story of Simon recalls some aspects of the story of Ananias and Sapphira (Acts 4:32–5:11). In both narratives we meet apparent believers who commit offenses, and in both cases money is the root of the problem. Ananias and Sapphira do not fully disclose their profits, and Simon offers to purchase a power from the apostles. It may be tempting to think that Simon's commitment to the Jesus movement is not genuine, since his offer to purchase the power to deliver the Holy Spirit may betray a continued belief in magic. But a major difference between the two stories is that, while Ananias and Sapphira are not given an opportunity to repent but are summarily punished for their misdeed, Simon is invited to repent (8:22). Does he? He certainly shows fear of punishment and asks Peter and John to pray for him, but, as for the quality of Simon's later life Luke says nothing. The story ends inconclusively, and we do not know if Simon received forgiveness and continued in the Christian movement. Early readers of Acts apparently did not think so. Irenaeus, writing at the end of the second century, regarded him as the father of all heresy.[1]

In Search of History

The introductory phrase at Acts 8:4 identifies the persecution of Stephen in Jerusalem as the reason for the gospel being spread from Judea to Samaria. Since the Stephen story has already been judged to be a creation of the author (see discussion of chapters 6–7), the entire story of the Samaritan mission becomes suspect by association. The story is also driven by the themes and purposes of the writer of Acts such as the fulfillment of the command/prophecy of the risen Lord (1:8), the affirmation of the Holy Spirit (8:7, 13–17), and certification by Jerusalem apostles (8:14–17; see also 6:5–6). Because the story so closely tracks with the overall purpose of Acts, the Fellows concluded that the story is a Lukan creation.

The Votes of the Fellows

Red/Probable
- Luke was responsible for bringing Philip, Simon, Peter, and the Ethiopian eunuch together and shaping their narrative profiles.

However, even though Luke shaped the story here, he may also have derived some of his data from a source identified as the "Gentile Mission Source."

The Gentile Mission Source is a hypothetical source that presents its own distinctive version of the origins of the Gentile mission. The main proponent of the theory is Richard Pervo (see the cameo essay "The Gentile Mission Source," pp. 99). The significance of Pervo's Gentile Mission Source is that, unlike previous source theories, it is based on the view that Acts was written in the early second century and used Paul's letters as a source. The Seminar gave a pink vote ("Borderline Historical") to the overall proposal that the Gentile Mission Source was a major source behind Acts 1–15. The pink vote in this case is significant, since it indicates an acceptance by the Seminar of the general proposal but not necessarily all of its particulars (see, for example, the discussion of the Stephen story in Chapter One). The characteristics of the source as proposed by Pervo received more definitive votes. The proposed point of view and purpose of the Source was enthusiastically endorsed.

As detailed in the cameo essay, the existence of such a source does not make it historical. The question of history has to be addressed separately and, in this case, there is very little in the source that can be affirmed as history. In essence, it is a "story," and its primary value is that it witnesses to the existence of more than one story about the origins of the Gentile mission.

The Votes of the Fellows

Red/Probable
- The Gentile Mission Source reflects the viewpoint of believers at Antioch and addressed various controversies among followers of Jesus.

Pink/Possible
- The major source behind Acts 1–15 was an account of the origins of the Gentile mission (the Gentile Mission Source).
- The Gentile Mission Source was a model for the structure of Acts.

Gray/Doubtful
- The Gentile Mission Source told the story of the conversion of Cornelius.

Black/Improbable
- Acts allows a confident reconstruction of the contents, order, form, and theological viewpoint of the Gentile Mission Source.

- The Gentile Mission Source removes all doubt that the origins of the Gentile "law-free" mission were in Jerusalem.
- The Gentile Mission Source is an excellent guide to the pre-Pauline theology of the church in Antioch.

The Seminar concurred with Pervo that the source can be identified only in a fragmentary form, especially since Luke has so thoroughly incorporated whatever it contained into his own literary program. Consequently it cannot be mined for much of historical value. The primary value of the source is not that it provided historical data for the writer of Acts, but that it provided a model for how to tell the story that Acts wanted to tell. In essence, it functioned as a "source" much as did the LXX, epic literature, and novelistic literature.

The Characters

Philip. The Philip of these stories is identified later in Acts as "Philip the Evangelist, one of the Seven" who had "four unmarried daughters endowed with the gift of prophecy" (Acts 21:8–9). It is Acts 8 that establishes Philip's career as an evangelist. Luke may have based his account on a character by that name in the Gentile Mission Source. But the form and chronology of the story are Luke's own, developed to serve his literary and theological purposes. Since the Gentile Mission Source, like Acts, is a story with an agenda, there is not sufficient data to affirm the historicity of "Philip the Evangelist" in either version of the story (see also the votes on Acts 6:1–7, pp. 78–79).

Simon the Magician. This character, also known as Simon Magus, has played a significant role in early Christian literature. According to Justin Martyr, there was a magician named Simon who came from Samaria and migrated to Rome where, during the reign of Claudius, he achieved a degree of fame for his wondrous deeds.[2] The Seminar voted that this character may have been historical and thus gave Simon a vote of "Pink/Possible." What this vote does not affirm is the story Acts tells. It is likely that the author of Acts used data about this character in his story to lend it verisimilitude, much as he used references to other historical characters in his otherwise fictional stories elsewhere in Acts.

Peter (and John). Peter is clearly the lead character; John plays no active role in the story except as a concurring witness. We know Peter was a historical personage based, at the least, on Paul's references to him in his letters. What is at question here is whether what is said about Peter in this story should legitimately be included in a historical biography of the real person. The speech of Peter in Acts 8:20–23, like the rest of the speeches, is judged to be the creation of the author (see the cameo essay, "Speeches in Acts," p. 45). The identity of Peter as a leader of the Jesus community at Jerusalem in the early years of the movement was addressed in Chapter One. It was judged to be an historical datum based on the letters of Paul; it is therefore an instance where Acts used Paul's letters as a source. However, Luke has taken Paul's brief reference to Peter's leadership in Jerusalem (Gal 2:9) and extended it into a larger narrative of his own. In this story, Peter and John provide the important connection with Luke's theme in which the Gentile mission must be authorized, at least initially, by the leadership from Jerusalem. Their presence in this story is due entirely to Luke and does not qualify as historical data.

References

Pervo, "Is There a There There?"
Spencer, "A Waiter, A Magician, A Fisherman, and a Eunuch"

The Votes of the Fellows

Pink/Possible

- A popular charismatic figure named Simon worked wonders among the Samaritans.

The Gentile Mission Source

A Cameo Essay by Richard I. Pervo

The Gentile Mission Source is a revised version of the "Antioch Source" previously proposed by Adolf Harnack and others. It is close to that source in content but different in function. It is a hypothetical document and can be isolated only through the identification of material that contrasts with what is typically Lukan in vocabulary and style and/or in ideas. However, since the author of Luke and Acts tends to recast sources in his own style, ideological tensions will more clearly attest to the presence of this source.

Luke prefers that all missions be initiated and carried out under the aegis of Peter and the other early leaders. Jarring exceptions to this principle occur in Acts 6–8, which describes the ministries of Stephen and Philip, as well as in 11:19–26, which narrates the beginning of the Gentile mission in the Syrian metropolis of Antioch. In addition, Paul's initial missionary work lacked direct sanction from Jerusalem (9:20–25). Finally, the so-called "First Missionary Journey of Paul" (Acts 13–14) was launched from Antioch without a consultation with the apostles in Jerusalem (13:1–3). On the principle that Luke would not concoct such unseemly irregularities, the existence of a source is highly probable.

The data base includes, with varying degrees of probability, the following texts (or portions thereof): Acts 2:1–13; 4:36–37; 6:1–6; 6:8–7:60 (minus 7:1–54); 8:1–13, portions of 10:1–48 and 11:19–26; 12:12–17, portions of 13–14, 15:19–21. These texts support the following summary of the nature of the source:

1. Antioch is the place of origin and viewpoint. Its likely date of composition was in the last quarter of the first century.
2. The objects of the source were (a) to locate the origins of the Gentile mission in Jerusalem and (b) to exhibit Antioch as its showcase. What it knows of Jerusalem is viewed through the lens of Antioch.
3. The chief criterion for legitimacy was charismatic: verification through wonders, in particular, prophetic and ecstatic activity.
4. Although not anti-Pauline, the source held that Paul was originally subordinate to Barnabas.
5. The existence of mixed communities required Gentiles to make certain compromises on matters of purity and to be tolerant of Jewish observances.
6. The source's apostolic patron was Peter, who welcomed Gentile believers but promoted compromise for the sake of unity. Matthew, located in the vicinity of Antioch by most scholars, has a similar view.
7. At an earlier stage this source viewed the Seven (Acts 6:1–5) as its authorities rather than the Twelve.

The perspective of the Gentile Mission Source influenced nascent Christianity through two literary channels, in particular, the Gospel of Matthew and Luke/Acts. The "primacy of Peter" is part of this heritage, as is an approach to community life that prefers moderation to perfection and looks to compromise. That viewpoint emerges in the Pauline tradition with Ephesians.

From the historical perspective the source is useful for its hints about how one non-Pauline mixed community of believers understood itself. Of actual history it contributes very little, beyond confirming that Barnabas was senior to Paul in Antioch, that Paul functioned during that period (which lasted more than a decade,

Gal 2:1) as an agent of the Antiochene church, and that Peter, who prevailed in his argument with Paul (Gal 2:11–14), enjoyed high status in Antioch thereafter.

The most vexing question is the nature of the Gentile missionary movement's Jerusalem background. The source identified the Seven as Greek-speaking Diaspora Jewish members of the Jesus movement who came into conflict with other (non-Jesus movement) Diaspora Jews over Torah, but associates of the Seven do not proselytize among Gentiles until they reach Antioch. This picture is credible, but "credible" does not mean "factual." Much about the background of Barnabas (and even Paul) remains unclear. Barnabas probably had Jerusalem associations. Nothing is known about an early mission to Damascus or why Paul was in that region.

The cracks in Acts that Luke could not successfully paper over indicate that other stories existed. On the missionary center of Antioch there are marks of three such stories: Paul's, the source's, and Luke's. The chief historical value of the Gentile Mission Source is its warning that other stories existed, some of which have disappeared and others of which have been altered beyond recognition.

Philip and the Ethiopian Eunuch

8 ^{26}A messenger of the Lord said to Philip: "Travel at noon along the desert road that leads from Jerusalem to Gaza." ^{27}So Philip set out. Just then a eunuch from Ethiopia, an official in charge of the treasury of Candace, their queen, was on his way home from a pilgrimage to Jerusalem. ^{28}He was reading the prophet Isaiah while seated in his chariot. ^{29}The Spirit said to Philip: "Go up and get close to his chariot."

^{30}When Philip caught up with him, he heard him reading Isaiah. "Do you really perceive what you are perusing?" he asked.

^{31}"How could I possibly understand without someone to guide me?" he replied, and then invited Philip to come up and sit with him. (^{32}This was the passage he was reading: "As is a sheep, he was led to slaughter, and, as a lamb taken to the shearer is mute, so he did not open his mouth. ^{33}In his humiliation the judgment against him was lifted. Who will tell the story of his times, because his life has been removed from the earth?")

^{34}The eunuch said, "Please tell me, about whom does the prophet make this statement, himself or someone else?"

³⁵Using this passage as a starting point, Philip opened his mouth and told him the message about Jesus. ³⁶In the course of their journey they came upon some water. The eunuch exclaimed: "Look, water! Is there any reason why I cannot be baptized?" ³⁸He ordered that the chariot be halted. Philip and he both descended into the water, where Philip baptized him. ³⁹When they arose from the water, a spirit of the Lord removed Philip from the scene. The eunuch did not see him again, but he resumed his journey filled with joy. ⁴⁰As for Philip, he appeared at Azotus, from which point he began to travel along the coast, preaching the gospel in all the cities as far north as Caesarea.

Comments on the Story

If Acts 1:8 is to be a guide to the course of the gospel message, we should expect the geographical settings in this section of Acts to be important. Recalling that 1:8 had outlined the route of apostolic witness as beginning in Jerusalem and moving to Judea, Samaria, and the end of the earth, we noted that the actual order in Acts placed Samaria before Judea (see comments on Acts 8:4–25). We would expect the next episode to take place in Judea, and, at least by implication, it does. Luke calls no explicit attention to this, but the incident involving Philip and the eunuch takes place on the road that runs from Jerusalem to Gaza. This would probably locate the incident somewhere in Judea, although Luke gives no specific indications, except to describe the road in question as "desert" or "deserted." But at the end of the story, Philip resumes his travels, going now from Azotus (Ashdod) to Caesarea, and preaching in all the cities along the way. These cities would be in Judea, even if Luke does not specifically say so.

Some scholars have noted that Ethiopia, the eunuch's home, was often thought of as the end of the earth. So, perhaps, Luke is here signaling that the gospel has achieved the goal of Acts 1:8, since a representative from the end of the earth has received the gospel. If this is so, then we must ask why the book does not simply end at this point. Since we have more than half of Acts yet to come, we should probably understand this narrative as a foreshadowing of the later outcome.

A major question has to do with the ethnicity of the eunuch. Is he a Jew or a Gentile? It is surprising that Luke does not say which he is, but perhaps he has given some indications. At first glance, it would seem that the designation of the eunuch as Ethiopian would settle the issue: an Ethiopian is a Gentile. As a eunuch he would seemingly be barred from attendance at temple observances in Jerusalem (see Deut 23:1; but see Isa 56:3–5), and his high rank as guardian of the Queen's treasury would suggest that he is not Jewish. But, according to Acts 8:27–28, he is associated with Jewish matters: he has been in Jerusalem for the purpose of worshiping, and now he is reading from the Jewish Scriptures. These individual indications do not settle the issue. In favor of the identification of the eunuch as Jewish: one can be both Ethiopian and Jewish, and there are several Jewish texts that focus attention on Jews who have achieved high positions in Gentile countries. In favor of his identification as a Gentile: nothing prevents Gentiles from going to Jerusalem and entering the Court of the Gentiles; and Gentiles may certainly read the Bible in its Greek translation.

If the individual indications do not conclusively tell us who the eunuch is, perhaps the placement of the story helps. In Acts 10:1–11:18, we will meet a Gentile named Cornelius, who will be converted by the apostle Peter. Luke places a great deal of emphasis on this relatively long narrative and later has two major characters refer to it as the first conversion of a Gentile (see Peter's words in Acts 15:7 and James's in 15:14). If Cornelius is the first Gentile convert, the Ethiopian eunuch cannot be. Luke's vagueness about his identity is intriguing, but narrative consistency requires that the eunuch be a Jew, albeit a peripheral one, a eunuch from the Diaspora. The narratives about Philip's work among the Samaritans and his conversion of the eunuch from Ethiopia represent an in-between situation: they come after the mission to Jerusalem Jews but before that to Gentiles.

Luke's esteem for the Jewish Scriptures is evident here, as it is throughout Luke and Acts. The concluding chapter of the Gospel of Luke has similarities to the passage here. In both there is a focus of attention on the Hebrew prophets and the theme of the suffering Messiah. In Luke 24:27, 44–46, Jesus opened the minds of his followers to "every passage of scripture that referred to himself." Here "Philip opened his mouth and told him [the eunuch] the message about Jesus" (Acts 8:35). The claim that the Hebrew prophets predicted the coming of a suffering Messiah is important to Luke (see, e.g., Luke 18:31–33; 24:25–27, 44–46; Acts 3:18; 26:22–23), but it is only here that a specific text is cited to support the contention. The passage is Isa 56:7–8, quoted in the LXX version. The eunuch's question about the text is entirely appropriate: about whom does the prophet speak (Acts 8:34)? A reader might be reminded of

Peter's Pentecost speech, where he quoted from a supposed writing of David and claimed that, as prophecy, David did not speak of his own resurrection but that of Jesus (see 2:25–35). Philip does not directly answer the eunuch's question but proclaims the gospel of Jesus. The implication is clear, however: Isaiah was not speaking of himself but of Jesus.

After the eunuch asks about baptism, both he and Philip get into the water, and Philip baptizes him. We noted that in the previous episode, those converts who were baptized by Philip did not receive the spirit. Neither does the eunuch, but in this story no apostles come down to complete Philip's task. Instead the spirit sweeps Philip off to Azotus, and he preaches in the cities between there and Caesarea. Clearly Luke has a sense of the significance of baptism (see also the discussion above, pp. 94–96) but no rigid conception of its connection with the reception of the spirit.

In Search of History

With this story, Philip's mission is complete (for now; but see Acts 21:8). In this cycle of stories, beginning at 6:1–5 and continuing through the Samaria (8:4–25) and Eunuch (8:26–40) stories, Philip has emerged as a precursor for Luke's developing profile of the Gentile mission witness. He was the first to take the message beyond Judea to Samaria, and now he is the first to go to "the ends of the earth," as represented symbolically by Ethiopia and as empowered dramatically by the direct action of the Holy Spirit.

The story of the Eunuch is beautifully crafted. It follows the same pattern as the Emmaus story, written by the same author (Luke 24:13–32). In both stories: (a) a traveler, or travelers, are joined by the miraculous appearance of God's messenger, (b) the messenger of God asks a probing question, (c) the question leads to a discussion on the nature of the Christ event, (d) the traveler(s) respond sacramentally (breaking bread; baptism), and (e) the messenger is abruptly and miraculously transported to another location.[3] The story is so tightly crafted that it leaves little room for proposing a source, not to mention a historical core, behind it.

Along with the story of Philip in Samaria above, this story functions in the larger narrative of Acts as a *foreshadowing story*. Even though the official extension of the mission to Gentiles lies ahead in the narrative (Acts 10–11), this story anticipates the move to the larger Gentile world ("the ends of earth") with a compact narrative that references the themes of the Gentile mission: the itinerant missionary being compelled by the Holy Spirit, the encounter with and teaching of an archetypical outcast (on this theme see also Luke 5:29–32; 6:20–23; 7:22–23, 36–50; 19:1–10), a successful conversion signified by baptism and a sign of discipleship ("resumed his journey filled with joy," Acts 8:39), and the departure of the missionary to other mission fields. The Seminar concluded that the story contained little if any historical data. Above all, the circumstances whereby Philip met up with the eunuch were judged to be nonhistorical.

The Characters

Was the eunuch an historical character? The omniscient narrator tells us several things about the character in the chariot that are not specifically made known to Philip in the narration: he is (a) an Ethiopian, (b) a eunuch, (c) an official in the court of Queen Candace, and (d) either a Jew or a Gentile Godfearer, having just returned from a trip to the temple in Jerusalem. There are no clues in the story itself about how the narrator might have known such things about a historical character. Nevertheless, as seen in the votes below, the Fellows left open the possibility that some historical traditions may lie behind this story. Overall, however, the eunuch serves a symbolic function to fit the literary purposes of the author of Acts. In ancient lore, Ethiopia symbolized a faraway, exotic place ("the furthest of humans").[4] Its dark-skinned inhabitants were characterized in literature as wealthy, wise, and militarily powerful. This eunuch is no exception. He travels with a servant, indicating wealth, and is a literate student of the Jewish Scriptures, indicating he was well-educated. He was a high official in the court of the queen, whose dynastic title in Ethiopia was "Candace." His identification as a "eunuch" is consistent with that role, since eunuchs often served as officials at royal courts. The force of the story has been characterized in this way: "Within a context of travel among foreigners, the episode dramatizes the movement of Christianity to figures whose power is expressed in their own wealth and wisdom and in the military might of the groups they represent, and yet these figures choose to submit themselves to the authority of Luke's ultimate patron deity."[5]

References

    Pervo, *Acts*, "Is There a There There?"
    A. Smith, "Do You Understand?"
    Spencer, "A Waiter, A Magician, A Fisherman, and a Eunuch"

The Votes of the Fellows

Pink/Possible
- In writing Acts 8, Luke had access to historical traditions.
- Philip the evangelist played a role in the Ethiopian eunuch's conversion.
- There was a eunuch who was a royal officer from Ethiopia who made a pilgrimage to Jerusalem.
- The conversion of the Ethiopian eunuch to Christianity is historical.

Black/Improbable
- The dramatic circumstances surrounding Philip's evangelization of the Ethiopian eunuch are historically reliable.

The Conversion of Saul

9 Now Saul, who still fulminated murderous threats against the disciples of the Lord, approached the high priest ²to request that he issue letters to the synagogues in Damascus authorizing him to take back to Jerusalem in chains any adherents of the Movement he might find there, women no less than men.

³As he was nearing Damascus in the course of his journey, a light from above suddenly engulfed him. ⁴He fell on the ground and heard a voice saying to him,

"Saul, Saul, why are you persecuting me?"

⁵"Who are you, Lord?"

"I am Jesus, whom you are persecuting. ⁶Now get up and enter the city. You will be told what you must do." ⁷Those traveling with Saul were standing there speechless, for they heard the voice but saw no one. ⁸After Saul had been picked up from the ground and opened his eyes, he could not see, so they took him by the hand and led him into Damascus. ⁹For three days he remained blind and neither ate nor drank.

¹⁰In Damascus there was a disciple named Ananias, whom the Lord addressed in a vision:

"Ananias!"

"Yes Lord."

¹¹"Go to Straight Street and inquire at the house of Judas for a man from Tarsus named Saul. He is at prayer

[12] and has seen [in a vision] a man named Ananias enter and place a hand upon him to restore his sight."

[13] "Lord, many people have told me about this character and all of the horrible things that he has done to your people in Jerusalem. [14] Now he is here with authority from the high priests to arrest everyone who calls upon your name."

[15] "Get going, because this man is the medium I have selected to carry my name to gentiles, monarchs, and Israelites. [16] I shall show him how much he will have to suffer for the sake of my name." [17] Ananias went to the house and laid his hands upon him, with these words: "Brother Saul, the Lord has dispatched me—Jesus, who appeared to you on the way here—so that you might see again and be filled with the Holy Spirit." [18] At that moment a flaky substance fell from his eyes, and his sight returned. Saul got up and was baptized. [19] After he had taken some nourishment his strength revived.

Saul spent some time with the disciples in Damascus, [20] where he set right out to preach about Jesus in the synagogues, proclaiming, "He is the son of God." [21] This bewildered his hearers, who wondered, "Isn't this the fellow who wreaked havoc on those who call upon the name of Jesus in Jerusalem? Hadn't he come here so that he might take those of this ilk back to the high priests in chains?" [22] Yet Saul worked even harder. He dismayed the Jews of Damascus by proving that Jesus is the Messiah. [23] After this had gone on for some time, the Jews concocted a plot to kill him. [24] Saul caught wind of it: They were keeping a twenty-four-hour watch at the city gates so that they might apprehend and slay him, [25] but his disciples took him by night and let him down by lowering him in a hamper from an aperture in the wall.

[26] Upon his arrival in Jerusalem, Saul attempted to associate with the disciples, but they were all afraid of him because they were unwilling to believe that he was one of them. [27] Then Barnabas took charge of Saul and conducted him to the apostles. He related how Saul had seen the Lord on his expedition and what Jesus had said to him. He further reported how vigorously Saul had preached in the name of Jesus at Damascus. [28] Saul thereupon became part

of their company in and around Jerusalem. He preached vigorously in the name of Jesus and ²⁹engaged in contentious debate with the Hellenists, who launched an effort to kill him. ³⁰The believers discovered this, so they escorted him to Caesarea and sent him to Tarsus.

³¹The church throughout all Judea, Galilee, and Samaria then began to enjoy a time of peace. It grew in quantity and quality, living in reverence for the Lord and with the support of the Holy Spirit.

Comments on the Story

This account is one of the best known narratives in the book of Acts. Saul, previously said to be a participant in the execution of Stephen and a leading opponent of the church, asks the high priest for letters allowing him to go to Damascus to arrest believers and bring them back to Jerusalem, presumably for trial and punishment. But, as he approaches Damascus, he sees a bright light and hears a voice asking, "Why are you persecuting me?" The speaker identifies himself as Jesus and instructs Saul to proceed to Damascus and learn there what to do next. Saul is blinded by the vision and remains so for three days afterward, but is taken on to Damascus to meet with a believer there named Ananias. Meanwhile Ananias receives a vision of the Lord, who instructs him to meet with Saul. Ananias initially expresses doubt about Saul, since he knows his reputation as an enemy of the believers, but he nevertheless obeys the Lord's instructions. He seeks out Saul, cures his blindness, lays hands on him, and baptizes him. Saul then begins to preach in the synagogues of Damascus, meets opposition from Jews in that city, but escapes to go to Jerusalem. In Jerusalem he is first met with suspicion from the believers there, but Barnabas introduces him to the apostles, who accept him as a fellow-believer. After meeting lethal opposition from a group called "Hellenists," he is sent on to Caesarea and Tarsus. The author of Acts concludes the narrative with a summary statement to the effect that the whole church then enjoyed peace and grew numerically. It seems that the conversion of Saul made all the difference.

At first Acts 9 appears to be yet another in a series of remarkable conversions, following that of Simon and the Ethiopian eunuch, and preceding the conversion of Cornelius. In Acts 1–7 the stress was on groups of people who accepted the apostolic message and on the numerical growth of the church, but now as the author moves us out into Samaria, Judea, and Syria, the focus is on individuals. But when we look closely at these narratives, we learn that there is more to them than the conversion of isolated individuals. The conversion of Simon is tantamount to that of Samaria; the eunuch stands for Ethiopia; the conversion of Cornelius in Acts 10–11 will signify the opening to Gentiles. What about Saul in 9:1–31? Here a major persecutor of Jesus suddenly becomes a believer, who will in turn be persecuted. Indeed, Saul/Paul is to become the leading character in the second half of Acts. From a literary perspective it is appropriate that he be introduced through a narrative such as we have here. We should also note that the story of Saul's conversion is told three times in Acts (9:1–31; 22:1–16; 26:9–18), a fact that demonstrates its importance to Luke. There are similarities and differences among these three accounts, and we shall examine them in comments on chapters 22 and 26.

Here, however, we note the relationships of the story of Saul with those in the surrounding chapters. In all the stories there is a demonstration of the power of God. Simon of Samaria is converted when he sees the miracles at work through Philip. The meeting of Philip with the Ethiopian is divinely ordered and arranged, as is the encounter between Peter and Cornelius. With Saul, we have a remarkable vision, divine instructions, and a healing of blindness. A major difference is that there is no further mention in Acts of Simon, the Ethiopian, or Cornelius, but Saul, whose name will be changed to Paul, becomes the leading character in the later chapters. Clearly the most significant aspect of this narrative is Saul's conversion from being a vehement persecutor of the Jesus movement to becoming its chief spokesperson.

Despite the familiarity of this narrative, there are some puzzling details. In his letter to the Galatians, Paul tells about his early experience, and there are interesting similarities and differences. In the cameo essay, "Comparing Paul and Luke on Paul's Conversion" (p. 114), these details are further examined and subjected to historical criticism. Here we are more interested in certain aspects of the story that need some clarification.

For example, although Saul's vision in Acts 9:3–6 is central to the whole narrative, it is remarkably elusive. Saul, it says, saw an intense light and heard the voice of Jesus. Those with him also heard the voice but saw no one. But did Saul see anyone? The text only says that he saw a light from the sky, which blinded him. Acts 9:8 emphasizes Saul's blindness: despite the fact that his eyes were open, he could see nothing. A few verses later (9:12), we learn—from the Lord's words to Ananias—that Saul had another vision, this time seeing Ananias and being healed of his blindness. This vision was not narrated and would not be continuous with what was reported in verses 3–6; we can only assume that it occurred during the three days of Saul's blindness.

In Damascus, Ananias expresses reluctance to accept Saul's experience as genuine, and, in Jerusalem, the believers are similarly suspicious. Their distrust is understandable within the context of the narrative. But what is the motivation for the fierce opposition to Saul on the part of the Jews in Damascus and the Hellenists in Jerusalem? Apparently the opposition of Jews in Damascus is continuous with that of the authorities in Jerusalem, who arrested and tried the apostles. As the book proceeds we shall see Jews more and more in the role of opponents of the Christian leaders and their message. The role of Hellenists is, if anything, more perplexing. In Acts 6:1 we read about a division between Hebrews and Hellenists. There we concluded that Hellenists were Greek-speaking Jews who accepted the gospel. Here, however, Hellenists can hardly be believers: Saul contends with them as he had with Jews in Damascus, and they plot to kill him. Luke never casts believers in such malicious roles. Apparently Luke wants us to understand these Hellenists as Greek-speaking Jews, but not believers like those in Acts 6:1.

Although the central experience in Acts 9 is that of Saul, he does not appear to be alone. How does Luke intend for readers to understand the several references to undefined groups?

- In 9:7 the narrator calls attention to those travelling with Saul and what they experienced. Surprisingly, they heard the voice that spoke to Saul but saw no one. If so, they must also have heard the words uttered, and so they would have understood that Saul was directed to proceed to Damascus.
- In 9:8 "they" led the blinded Saul into Damascus. Who constituted this group is left indefinite.
- In 9:19 we read that Saul was with "the disciples" in Damascus, but this group is not further defined.
- The oldest manuscripts of 9:25 say that "his disciples" assisted Saul to escape from Jewish opponents. Again we have an undefined group.

Do we have multiple undefined groups here: fellow travelers (9:7), escorts (9:8), pre-Saul believers (9:19), Saul's converts (9:25)? The complexity is somewhat reduced if we understand that, in all these cases, Luke refers, however obliquely, to the same group. If so, we learn that Saul was accompanied by a group of assistants, who then escort him to Damascus, continue to support him throughout his mission in that city, and provide for his security. Saul's assistants in persecuting the church continue as his disciples.

Not all references to "disciples" are to supporters of Saul. When he arrives in Jerusalem he meets with a group of disciples who doubt the genuineness of his conversion (Acts 9:26). It is only due to the intervention of Barnabas that the believing community accepts him. We met Barnabas earlier, in Acts 4:36–37, as an example of honesty and generosity, whose action was contrasted with that of another Ananias and his wife Sapphira. It is not surprising to find him here as a close associate of the apostles. Luke says that Barnabas introduced Saul to them, told them of the events in Damascus, and convinced them that he was to be trusted. How did Barnabas obtain this information? Luke gives us no clue, but by portraying Barnabas as the one who introduces Saul to the apostles, Luke attributes to him a certain priority, which will be confirmed in Acts 13:1, where Barnabas is named ahead of Saul.

Despite the prominence of Saul (and Barnabas), Acts maintains a careful distinction between them and the apostles. Saul may preach and debate in Damascus without apostolic authentication, but in Jerusalem his alliance with them seems to be essential. In our translation of Acts 9:28, Saul "became part of their company" (literally "he went in and out among them"). The literal translation is reminiscent of the description in Acts 1:21 of the requirements for apostolic designation: "For that we must have one of the men who have been with us from the Lord Jesus' arrival to his departure" (literally, "during all the time that the Lord Jesus went in and out among us"). The public association of Saul with the apostles may signify their approval of him, but even so he is not one of them. The relation of Saul/Paul to the apostles will continue to intrigue us as we read on.

In Search of History

Since he used the biographical data from Galatians 1–2 quite liberally, Luke was clearly familiar with Paul's own version of this story (Gal 1:15–16; see the cameo essay, "The Letters of Paul as Sources for Acts," p. 116). However, Luke preferred another version, in which Paul's conversion was narrated in a more elaborated style.

A comparison between the two stories is provided in the cameo essay "Comparing Paul and Luke on Paul's Conversion" (p. 114). Because Paul's story is a first person autobiographical account, it is to be preferred over Luke's version for historical data, as affirmed by the vote of the Seminar.

Luke's version is a radically reworked account that refutes aspects of Paul's account. It appears to have been based on what Richard Pervo characterizes as a novella about the punishment and subsequent healing of a notorious enemy of God, a narrative that was then reshaped into a conversion story about Saul.[6] However, when Saul responds to the divine epiphany with "who are you?" (Acts 9:5), he is responding as would a polytheist ("which deity are you"). This represents an appropriation of the story to make Paul into a model of a Gentile convert, a perspective that can also be traced in the Deutero-Pauline letters (Eph 2:3, 3:8; 1 Tim 1:12–17). Since Luke wants to emphasize the Jewishness of Paul, it is not likely that he would have composed the story. Pervo therefore proposes that Luke adapted a pre-existing story of Paul's conversion. The Seminar concurred with his recommendation.

Luke's editing of the story emphasized Paul's participation in violent persecution of the followers of Jesus. This is not consistent with Paul's own account or with Roman law (see the cameo essay, "Comparing Paul and Luke on Paul's Conversion," p. 114). Consequently, the Seminar voted that this portrayal of Paul was not historical.

In Gal 1:15–24, after recounting briefly his christophany experience and his call to preach to Gentiles, Paul then outlined where he went next. His agenda was to establish that he was not beholden to Jerusalem for his authority. He made the following points: (a) immediately after his "conversion" he did not confer with anyone else; (b) he went to Arabia, (c) then to Damascus; and then (d) three years later he went to Jerusalem, where he saw Cephas and James but none of the other leaders there. This conflicts with the Acts account in which Paul (a) went to Damascus to receive instruction from Ananias (with no specific mention yet of a call), (b) preached to Jews in Damascus, where they plotted to kill him and he had to escape in a basket, and (c) went to Jerusalem, where he was introduced by Barnabas to the apostles as a whole, where he preached, and where once again his life was threatened so that he had to be rescued by "the believers." There are radical differences in these two stories. Luke's version can be accounted for as part of his program to emphasize Jewish opposition and persecution, as well as to promote the idea that all mission work was undertaken under the leadership of the Jerusalem apostles. Taking these themes of Luke into account, the Seminar voted to accept Paul's account as historical and Luke's account as fictional.

There was some suspicion that Paul might be overemphasizing the trivial nature of his visit to Jerusalem, so the Seminar voted pink ("Borderline Historical") on Paul's claim that he was not recognized in Jerusalem.

The story in Acts 9:23–25 of Paul's escape from danger in Damascus is derived from Paul's own account in 2 Cor 11:33–34. There is a significant difference in these two accounts, however (see the cameo essay, "The Letters of Paul as Sources for Acts," p. 116). In Paul's account, he escapes from a danger posed by King Aretas; in Acts he escapes from the threat of Jewish persecution. It is quite clear that Luke has taken Paul's story and adapted it to fit the themes of his story. The Seminar therefore voted for the historicity of Paul's account and the fictional nature of the story in Acts.

References

Kea, "Second Corinthians" and "Miscellaneous Saul Stories"
Pervo, "Converting Paul" and *Dating Acts*
Walker, "Acts and the Pauline Corpus Revisited"

The Votes of the Fellows

Red/Probable

- Galatians 1 is the single primary source of information about Paul's change of orientation toward the Jesus Movement.
- The source behind Acts 9:1–19a was a revised edition of a fictional story told about Paul.
- Sometime after his conversion, Paul visited Jerusalem (Acts 9:26, 28; Gal 1:18).
- Directly after his conversion, Paul went to Arabia (Gal 1:17).
- Three years later Paul visited Jerusalem (Gal 1:18).
- Paul went to Jerusalem to visit Peter and James (Gal 1:18–19).
- After visiting Jerusalem, Paul traveled to the area of Tarsus, Cilicia (Acts 9:30; Gal 1:21).
- An attempt was made to seize Paul in Damascus.
- The Ethnarch of King Aretas attempted to seize Paul.

Pink/Possible

- Paul remained unrecognized in Jerusalem (Gal 1:22).

Black/Improbable
- Paul was responsible for the incarceration and death of Jesus-people.
- Paul went to Jerusalem for public preaching and debate (Acts 9:28).
- While Paul was in Jerusalem, Hellenists sought to kill him (Acts 9:29).
- The Jews of Damascus attempted to seize Paul.

Comparing Paul and Luke on Paul's Conversion
A Cameo Essay by Thomas E. Phillips

Acts narrates Paul's transformation in chapter nine and then has Paul speak about this transformation twice in his defense speeches before various Roman courts (Acts 22 and 26). Paul's letters explicitly refer to this event only once (Gal 1:13–17), but repeatedly allude to his former persecution of the church (Phil 3:4–6; 1 Cor 15:8–9; cf. 1 Tim 1:12–17).

The only primary source for this story, Gal 1:13–23, contains five central claims: that Paul (1) practiced zealous obedience to the Law, (2) persecuted the church, (3) experienced a christophany, (4) was called to proclaim Christ among the Gentiles, and (5) had no significant contact with the Christian leaders in Jerusalem in temporal proximity to this event.

First, as he discussed his "former life in Judaism," Paul left little doubt about his own early commitment to the Law ("way beyond most of my contemporaries," Gal 1:14). Second, Paul acknowledged that he had persecuted the church and tried to destroy it (Gal 1:13). Third and fourth, Paul claimed that God revealed his Son to him so that he would proclaim him among the Gentiles (Gal 1:16). Finally, Paul insisted that his message resulted from this revelation and not from any human source (Gal 1:16b–17). Paul explained that he didn't visit Jerusalem until three years later—and that he saw only Peter and James during that brief fifteen-day stay (Gal 1:18–19). In utmost seriousness, Paul promised, "I do not lie!" (Gal 1:20) and even added a further claim that the churches in Judea did not even know him by sight at that time (Gal 1:22).

The first four elements (obedience to the Jewish Law, persecution of the church, a christophany, and a call to the Gentiles) are echoed elsewhere in Paul's letters (1 Cor 15:8–9; 1 Cor 9:1; Phil 3:4–6; Rom 1:13; 11:13). However, Paul's claim in Galatians not to have had early interaction with the Jerusalem leaders appears to be contradicted by what he says in 1 Corinthians 15. Here he speaks of having been taught ("received," 1 Cor 15:3) the basic gospel message separate from his christophany (1 Cor 15:8).

Acts tells a more dramatic story, but does so in three different versions. The Acts accounts are sometimes internally inconsistent (who heard the heavenly voice? [Acts 9:7; cf. 22:9]), but they tend to work with the five elements from Paul's letters. First, two of the three reports in Acts specifically state Paul's zealous obedience to the law (22:3; 26:5) and the third account seems to presume such obedience (Paul operates under the authority of the high priest, 9:1).

Second, all three accounts report Paul's persecution of the church (9:1–2; 22:4, 8; 26:10, 15), but Acts intensifies the violence. Paul persecutes "women no less than men" (22:4; cf. 9:2), utters "murderous threats" (9:1), and even seeks the death penalty against believers (22:4; 26:10). These reports of Paul's violent persecution of the church are not historically plausible. Roman law would not have allowed the high priest in Jerusalem to remove people forcibly from Damascus and bring them back to Jerusalem for execution. Only the Romans could extradite and pronounce death sentences. The more historically plausible Pauline letters make no explicit claims of violence as a part of Paul's "persecutions" (the SV's "how aggressively I harassed" is far superior to the NRSV's "violently persecuted" in Gal 1:13, where the NRSV unfortunately reads Acts back into Paul's letters).

Third, Paul's cryptic account of his christophany (Gal 1:15–16) is significantly rewritten in Acts and made into a dramatic encounter on the road to Damascus, with the inclusion of such stock religious symbols as a heavenly light, a divine voice, and metaphorical blindness.

Fourth, Paul's call to preach to the Gentiles is included in all three Acts accounts (9:15; 22:17–21; 26:15–17), but each version is different, and all three differ from Paul. In Paul, the call is made part and parcel of the christophany. In Acts 9:1–16, only Ananias (and the reader) is informed about Paul's call to the Gentiles; Paul is oddly excluded. In Acts 22:17–21, Paul learns about his call while praying in the Jerusalem temple. In Acts 26:15–17, Paul's call is part of the christophany itself, bringing this account more in line with Paul's version but with a great deal of dramatic license.

After the christophany, according to Acts, Paul immediately went to Damascus where Ananias baptized him (9:10–19; 22:11–13; 26:20) and to Jerusalem where he preached publicly (9:26–27; 22:17; 26:20). In Paul's own account, however, he went to Damascus and

Arabia and was unknown in Judea at the time (Gal 1:11–23). This fabricated Pauline visit to Jerusalem in Acts 9 is likely part of Acts' larger agenda to make Paul subservient to the apostles in Jerusalem.

The Letters of Paul as Sources for Acts
A Cameo Essay by William O. Walker, Jr.

Although Paul is the main character in the second half of the book of Acts, the author never so much as hints that Paul ever wrote any letters. Moreover, his portrayal of Paul differs at significant points from that to be found in Paul's letters. For these reasons, there was widespread scholarly agreement during much of the twentieth century that Luke simply was not aware of the letters. In recent years, however, many scholars have concluded that Luke knew at least some of the letters of Paul and used them as sources. The primary evidence consists of numerous rather striking verbal parallels between specific passages in Acts and specific passages in the letters and, to a lesser extent, some significant substantive and ideational parallels.

A particularly noteworthy example of such parallels appears in Acts 9:23–25 and 2 Cor 11:32–33—two accounts of what almost certainly was the same incident. According to Acts, the Jews in Damascus plotted to kill Saul (later known as Paul), but he became aware of their plot. The Jews *"were watching* the gates both day and night in order that they might kill him [presumably as he attempted to escape from the city], but his disciples took him by night and *let him down through the wall, lowering him in a basket"* (Walker's translation). In 2 Corinthians, Paul reports that "the governor under King Aretas *was guarding* the city of Damascus in order to arrest [him] and he *was lowered in a basket* through a window *through the wall* and escaped from his hands." The primary difference between the two versions concerns the identity of Paul's opponent. Was it a governor or was it the Jews? Since Acts has a tendency to blame the Jews for all of Paul's difficulties and to exonerate the civil authorities, Acts appears clearly to be secondary. Therefore Paul's report in 2 Corinthians likely served as the source for Luke's account of the same incident in Acts.

Even more striking is Peter's speech at the Jerusalem Conference (Acts 15:7–11), in which a significant portion of the account is paralleled in Paul. Like Paul, Peter attributes his appointment as missionary to Gentiles to divine decree (Acts 15:7; cf. Gal 2:7–8) and cites reception of the Holy Spirit as validation for the Gentile mission (Acts 15:8; cf. Gal 3:2–5). Consistent with the signature themes of Paul's preaching, Peter in Acts 15 proclaims that salvation comes through "faith" (Acts 15:9; cf. Gal 2:16), attributes salvation to "grace" (Acts 15:11; cf. Gal 1:6, 15; 2:9), refers to the Law as a "yoke" (Acts 15:10; cf. Gal 5:1), and emphasizes divine impartiality (Acts 15:9; cf. Gal 2:6).[7]

To be sure, it is Peter who speaks in Acts and Paul in Galatians, but the transfer of ideas and even words is explainable in terms of what appears to be Luke's desire to "Paulinize" Peter—that is, to portray him as in essential agreement with Paul's understanding of the gospel. The goal of such a "Paulinization" was apparently not the exaltation of Peter but rather the "rehabilitation" of Paul in the minds of Christians who may have viewed his popularity among the Marcionites and other "heretics" as an indication that he was a "maverick" who stood outside the mainstream of a developing "orthodoxy." In any case, the parallels between Acts 15:7–11 and Galatians almost certainly indicate that Luke was here dependent on Galatians.

Numerous other parallels between Acts and the Pauline letters have been detected by a variety of scholars (see especially Pervo, *Dating Acts*, 111–33). Particularly significant is the fact that such evidence points not to just one or two of the letters but rather to a number of them, including the pseudonymous Colossians and Ephesians. This suggests that Luke was familiar with a collection of letters. Such a collection most likely would not have existed until near the end of the first century or early second century, but since Acts is now dated to the early second century the use of the letters is not improbable.

Why does Luke fail to mention the letters or even the fact that Paul wrote letters? Apparently Luke wished to downplay any differences between Paul and the Jerusalem apostles, especially Peter. He wanted to claim (or perhaps co-opt) Paul for the emerging "orthodox" consensus, and he likely regarded the letters as roadblocks in the path toward such a goal.

Peter in Lydda and Joppa

9 [32]While visiting all of the communities Peter came in due course to the people of God dwelling at Lydda. [33]There he discovered a man named Aeneas, who had been confined to his cot by disability for about eight years. [34]"Aeneas," he said, "Jesus Christ has made you well. Rise and tend to your bed." Aeneas got right up. ³⁵When all the dwellers in Lydda and the coastal plain saw him, they converted.

³⁶In Joppa lived a disciple named Tabitha (which means "gazelle"). She abounded in good works and charitable acts. ³⁷While Peter was in the vicinity, she fell ill and died. They washed her corpse and laid her out in an upper room. ³⁸When the disciples learned that Peter was in Lydda, which is not far from Joppa, they sent two men who importuned him, "Please come to us as soon as possible." ³⁹Peter went with them. When he got there all the widows presented themselves, weeping as they showed him the clothes and coats that Dorcas had made while she was with them. ⁴⁰Peter had all of them leave the room, then knelt down in prayer. Addressing his attention to the corpse, he said, "Tabitha, get up." She opened her eyes, saw Peter, and sat up. ⁴¹After helping her up with a hand, he summoned all of God's people, including the widows, and presented her alive and well. ⁴²The news spread all over town, and many came to believe in the Lord. ⁴³Peter stayed in Joppa for some time, lodging with a tanner named Simon.

Comments on the Story

Luke is not yet ready to tell the story of Paul's mission. Rather he turns immediately to Peter and focuses attention on him for the next several chapters. Peter appears to be making a tour of the new communities of believers, and he arrives in the Judean towns, Lydda and Joppa. In Lydda he meets up with a certain Aeneas, who has been bedridden for eight years, and he heals him. In Joppa, he is called upon to rescue a believer named Tabitha, and he brings her back to life. The healing in Lydda results in the conversion of that town and the surrounding territory, and the resurrection in Joppa issues in conversions there.

That Peter is the focal character here, after the dramatic narrative of the conversion of Saul, may come as a surprise. But we should know by now that Luke is intent to stress the primacy of the apostles, and so even the story of Paul must wait. We are apparently to understand that Peter is on some kind of tour of the new communities, but Luke does not tell us what the purpose is. Recall that Peter and John came to Samaria following the mission of Philip and that they approved and completed his work. But in these Judean towns Peter does not preach in order to induce repentance, nor does he baptize or lay hands on anyone. The apparent purpose of Peter's visits at this point would be to provide encouragement and support for the fledgling communities of believers. Furthermore, it is important to observe that the members of these communities are Jewish converts. The first Gentile convert—Cornelius—will appear in the next chapter of Acts.

The recipient of Peter's aid in Lydda—Aeneas—bears a famous name. It is not unknown as a Jewish name at the time, but Luke's first readers would certainly think of that Aeneas of whom Vergil sang (see the cameo essay, "Names in Acts," p. 22).

Tabitha (Dorcas in Greek) is introduced as an example of the ideal believer. She was a disciple who "abounded in good works and charitable acts" (Acts 9:36). After her death, the widows show Peter the clothing she had made, apparently to bring her good works to his attention. The implication is that Tabitha made the clothing and donated it to the widows, who lovingly display her handiwork.

The raising of Tabitha here is reminiscent of the resurrection of the widow's son in Luke 7:11–17 and of Jairus' daughter in Luke 8:41–42, 49–56. Although all of these narratives describe a recovery of life after death, they should not be confused with those dealing with the resurrection of Jesus. Tabitha, the widow's son, and Jairus' daughter are raised to resume life on earth, and it is presumed that they will die later. Jesus, however, is raised to eternal life. It is especially clear in Luke-Acts that Jesus' post-resurrection life is qualitatively different from all others. Not only does he overcome death, but he is transported to a different plane, as the story of the ascension in Acts 1:9–11 makes clear.

At the end of Acts 9 Peter is in Joppa, staying in the home of a tanner by the name of Simon. This will be Peter's location in the narrative of Acts 10–11.

In Search of History

The two miracle stories recounted here follow patterns found in the miracle stories of Jesus in the Gospels. The Jesus Seminar judged most such stories to be literary constructs and thus nonhistorical.[8] Stories about the apostles as miracle workers abound in Acts as they do in the apocryphal Acts. The Acts Seminar voted that these stories, like most of those in the Gospels, are, as a group, not to be considered historical evidence that the apostles were miracle workers.

The Characters

If the stories are not historical, then what about the named characters? There is a pattern in Acts to provide names of individuals whose stories are significant in some way. This functions to give these stories verisimilitude. The Acts Seminar looked at the use of names as a whole and judged that it is quite probable that the author created names for his stories, much as symbolic names were frequently created in Greek and Roman narrative literature, particularly epic and novelistic literature (see the cameo essay, "Names in Acts," p. 22). Consequently the Seminar voted red ("Probable") on the proposition, "Names of characters found only in Acts are often assigned for theological or symbolic reasons." This proposition, by using the terminology "often," is intended to shift the burden of proof to any argument for the historicity of named characters found only in Acts.

Both names in these two stories qualify as symbolic. In the first story, the name Aeneas, while not unknown in Jewish circles, was a literary name of epic significance to Romans. He was the mythological hero of Vergil's *Aeneid*, whose saga eventually led to the founding of Rome. It is a name synonymous with Rome itself. The story of Peter healing a crippled Aeneas served as a subtle symbol for the power of the gospel to heal a "crippled" Rome.

Tabitha is emphasized as a symbolic name in the story itself when it is translated into Greek, "Dorcas," which means "gazelle." Here the fact of the symbolism is emphasized while its symbolic meaning in the story remains obscure. In a literary culture in which symbolic names were routinely utilized, this name, in a story that is already determined to be fictional, appears to be fictional as well.

Luke is known for his emphasis on stories about women (but see the cameo essay, "Women in Acts," p. 193). Like Lydia (Acts 16:11–15, 40) and Priscilla (18:1–3, 26), Tabitha is a textile worker, a trade that Luke associates with women who emerge as community leaders.[9] Tabitha also shares characteristics with the women of Luke 8:1–3, who had been healed and consequently served as benefactors for the community. Tabitha's benefaction consisted in the making of garments for the community, which the text celebrates as "good works and charitable acts" (Acts 9:36), a phrase reminiscent of Peter's description of Jesus as one who "went about doing good" (10:38). As is the case in Acts 6:1–6, the reference to an order of widows in the community makes the story late first or early second century, at which time such orders existed.[10] Peter's healing miracle functions to restore Tabitha to her role in the community. In the Lukan community, the story would function to give an apostolic imprimatur to the work of such women as community benefactors.

References
>Pervo, *Acts*
>Seim, *Double Message*
>Shea, "What Isn't in a Name?"
>D. Smith, "Rethinking"
>Spencer, "Women of 'the Cloth'"

The Votes of the Fellows
Red/Probable
- Names of characters found only in Acts are often assigned for theological or symbolic reasons.
- The name Aeneas occurs in Acts 9:33 because of its symbolic value rather than because it was historically factual.
- The name Tabitha, or Dorcas ("gazelle"), in Acts 9:36 occurs because of its symbolic value rather than because it was historically factual.

Black/Improbable
- Acts provides historical evidence that Peter was a miracle worker.

The World of Acts: Chapters 1–12

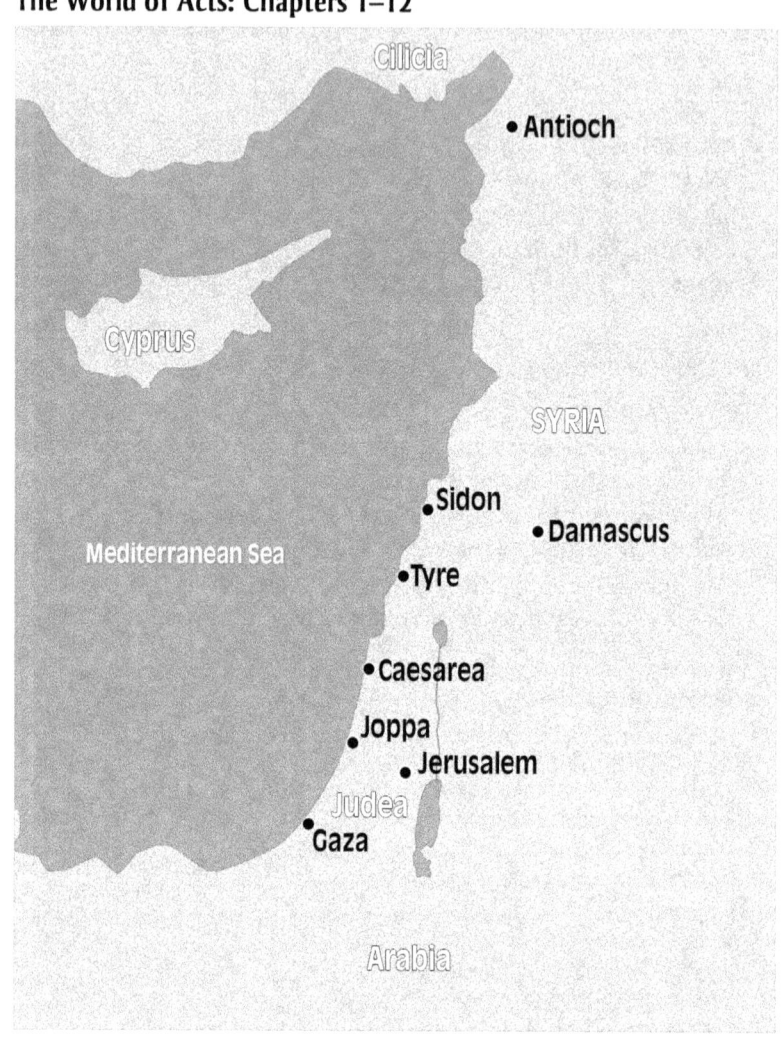

3

Antioch and Jerusalem
Acts 10:1–15:35

Peter and Cornelius: The Gentile Mission Begins

10 There lived in Caesarea a centurion of the Italian Cohort named Cornelius. ²He was a pious and God-fearing individual, as was his entire household. Cornelius gave generously to the people of Israel and was constant in prayer to God. ³One day at about 1500 hours [3:00 p.m.] he had a vision in which he distinctly saw an angel of God, who came in and said, "Cornelius!"

⁴Gazing at him in awe, the centurion said, "What may I do for you, lord?"

"God is mindful of your devotions and charitable acts. ⁵Therefore, please send some men to Joppa to invite one Simon, surnamed Peter, ⁶who is staying with Simon, a tanner, whose house is on the seashore."

⁷When the angel who addressed him had left, Cornelius summoned two of his household slaves and a pious soldier from his staff. ⁸After explaining the entire matter to them, he sent them off to Joppa.

⁹The next day, around 1200 hours [noon], as their journey was bringing them close to the city, Peter went up to the roof to pray. ¹⁰He began to feel hungry and decided to have a meal. While this was being prepared, he fell into a trance. ¹¹He had a vision of an object like a large cloth suspended by its four corners that descended from the opened sky to the ground. ¹²In it were all the four-legged animals and reptiles of earth and all the birds of the sky. ¹³A voice said: "Go kill and eat these creatures."

¹⁴"Certainly not, sir," he answered. "I have never tasted anything that was unclean and impure." ¹⁵The voice from above spoke again: "Stop designating 'unclean' what God has made pure." ¹⁶This was repeated twice more, after which the whole apparatus was hauled back up into the sky.

[17]While Peter was struggling to make sense of the vision that he had seen, the men who had been sent by Cornelius had obtained directions to Simon's house and arrived at the door. [18]They called out, "Is Simon surnamed Peter a guest here?"

[19]As Peter continued to try to figure out the vision, the Spirit said: "Listen! Two men are here, looking for you. [20]So go downstairs and accompany them, no questions asked, for I have sent them." [21]So Peter went down and said to the men, "I'm the person you're looking for. What has brought you here?"

[22]"Centurion Cornelius has sent us. He is an upright and reverent person, well recommended by all Jewry. He has been directed by a holy angel of God to invite you to his home so that he may hear what you have to say." [23]Peter then invited them to come in and receive some hospitality.

The next day Peter set out with them, accompanied by some of the believers from Joppa, [24]and on the following day he reached Caesarea. In expectation of their arrival Cornelius had invited his relatives and close friends. [25]As Peter was about to enter, Cornelius came to meet him, falling to his knees in homage. [26]At this Peter pulled him up, saying, "Please stay on your feet; I too am a mortal." [27]Peter continued to converse with him as he entered the house, where he found a sizable gathering.

[28]"All of you are aware," he said, "that it is taboo for Jews to associate intimately with or to visit those of another race, but God has shown me that no person is unclean or impure. [29]I therefore came when summoned. Please explain why you have asked me to be here."

[30]"Three days ago," replied Cornelius, "I was at home praying at 1500 hours [3:00 p.m.], when an elegantly dressed man appeared before me and said: [31]'Cornelius, God has heard your prayers and is mindful of your charitable acts. [32]Therefore send to Joppa and invite Simon surnamed Peter who is staying with Simon a tanner by the seashore.' [33]That I promptly did, and you have been so kind as to come. We are now gathered, in the sight of God, to hear what the Lord has directed you to say."

[34]"I am beginning to grasp," replied Peter, "that God really is nondiscriminatory [35]and accepts all who revere him and conduct themselves properly, regardless of national or

ethnic background. ³⁶God issued the message of peace to the Israelites through Jesus Christ (he is the sovereign of all people). ³⁷You are familiar with what happened throughout Judea. It began in Galilee, following the baptism that John proclaimed. ³⁸You know about Jesus of Nazareth, who, when God had invested him with the power of the Holy Spirit, went about doing good and healing all who were oppressed by the devil, because God was with him. ³⁹We can attest to all that Jesus did in Jewish territory and at Jerusalem. There they actually put him to death by hanging him on a tree, ⁴⁰but God raised him two days later and arranged for him to be seen—⁴¹not by everyone but by us, witnesses selected by God in advance. We regularly ate and drank with him after God raised him from the dead. ⁴²He charged us to proclaim to the people and to testify that he is God's appointed judge of the living and of the dead. ⁴³The prophets are in full agreement that all who believe in him will obtain release from sins through his name."

⁴⁴While Peter was still speaking, the Holy Spirit fell upon all who were listening to his sermon. ⁴⁵All the Jewish believers who had accompanied Peter were amazed that the gift of the Holy Spirit had been bestowed even upon the gentiles, ⁴⁶for they heard the audience speaking in tongues and praising God. Peter said, ⁴⁷"There is no reason why these people, who have received the Holy Spirit just as we did, cannot be baptized with water, is there?" ⁴⁸He thereupon directed that they be baptized in the name of Jesus. After this they invited Peter to stay for several days.

11 News that gentiles had also welcomed God's message came to the apostles and other believers in Judea. ²When Peter got back to Jerusalem, the circumcised took issue with him: ³"Why did you enter the home of uncircumcised men and eat with them?" ⁴Peter undertook a point by point explanation. ⁵"I was in Joppa, saying my prayers, when a trance came upon me. I had a vision of an object like a large cloth that descended from the sky, suspended by all four corners. It came right down in front of me. ⁶As I carefully scrutinized it, attempting to figure out what it meant, I saw tame and wild animals, reptiles, and birds. ⁷A voice told me: 'Peter, go kill and eat *these creatures*.' ⁸'Certainly not, sir,' I answered. 'I have never tasted anything that was unclean or impure.' ⁹The voice from the sky spoke again: 'Stop designating "unclean" what God has made pure.' ¹⁰This was repeated two more times, and then the whole apparatus was hauled back up into the sky. ¹¹At that very moment three men appeared at the house where I was staying. Cornelius had sent them to find me. ¹²The spirit told me to go with them, avoiding distinctions. Together with these six believers we went there and entered the man's house. ¹³He then told us how the angel had appeared in his home and said, 'Send to Joppa and summon Simon Peter. ¹⁴He will tell you how you can be saved—you and your household.' ¹⁵Shortly after I began to speak, the Holy Spirit fell upon them—just as upon us in the beginning. ¹⁶I remembered the Lord's words: 'Now John baptized by means of water, but you will be baptized with Holy Spirit.' ¹⁷Since, therefore God had bestowed upon them a gift identical to that which we received when we came to faith in the Lord Jesus Christ, could I try to block God's path?"

¹⁸These words stilled their objections and brought forth praise: "Look at that! God has also offered the gentiles conversion to new life!"

Comments on the Story

The narrative of Peter and Cornelius is of great importance to the author of Acts. The reader has been prepared for the story of the conversion of the first Gentiles by the previous chapters of Acts, especially the stories of Philip's activites among the Samaritans and with the Ethiopian. Belief is no longer confined to Judea. Now we have some sixty-six verses telling of the complex circumstances that led to the baptism of the first Gentiles. The theme of divine leadership pervades the entire narrative, as God makes his will known through visions, trances, and spiritual visitations. Certainly it is Luke's conviction that this important event in the history of the Christian movement was not the product of human activity or conviction but only came about because of divine intervention.

The complexity of the narrative requires that we first recognize the units that make it up. The story unfolds in seven scenes.

Scene 1: Cornelius' vision (Acts 10:1–8). The story begins in Caesarea, and the reader will recall that Philip ended up there after his meeting with the Ethiopian eunuch (Acts 8:40). Cornelius is introduced as a Roman centurion and a man of great devotion to God. Clearly his piety is characterized in Jewish terms: he fears

God, gives generously to the Jewish people, and prays constantly. It is notable that the first non-Jew to embrace the Christian movement was, according to Acts, very close to Judaism. Luke would place him among the Godfearers, those Gentiles who were deeply attracted to Jewish beliefs and practices and associated with synagogues but had not become proselytes. Such persons are often mentioned in Acts, but the most prominent is Cornelius. Luke also stresses the point that Cornelius' piety extends to his family and household. Even one of his soldiers is said to be devout (10:7). We cannot lose sight of the fact that, for Luke, the Christian breakthrough to Gentiles was a gradual process.

In his vision Cornelius sees a divine messenger, who tells him to send and summon Peter from Joppa (see Acts 9:43). Luke notes that Peter is staying at the home of another Simon, a leatherworker or tanner, whose work would have put him in touch with animal skins and subjected him to suspicion and contempt from fellow Jews.

Scene 2: Peter's Vision (Acts 10:9–16). The setting of time is important throughout this narrative. Cornelius' vision occurs at 1500 hours (3:00 p.m.), and Peter's at about noon the following day. Peter has gone to the rooftop of Simon's house to pray, and he becomes hungry. As the meal is being prepared, he goes into a trance and sees the skies opened and a large sheet descending to earth. On the sheet are all mammals, reptiles, and birds—apparently a phrase that is meant to include all known animals, without distinction of whether Jewish law permitted their consumption or not. Although the heavenly voice commands Peter to kill and eat these animals, Peter firmly rejects the command: he has never eaten forbidden food. Then Peter is told not to regard those things that God has cleansed as unclean. The voice speaks three times and Peter three times refuses, and then the sheet ascends back into the sky.

Scene 3: Peter and Cornelius' servants (Acts 10:17–23a). Peter is quite perplexed about the meaning of the vision when the visitors from Cornelius arrive in Joppa. The visitors, who extol Cornelius' piety, explain that a divine messenger had ordered him to have Peter summoned to Caesarea, so that he and his household may hear Peter speak. The visitors then are invited by Peter to stay with him in Simon's house overnight.

Scene 4: Peter and Cornelius (Acts 10:23b–33). Again we should note the settings in time. The embassy from Cornelius arrives in Joppa just after Peter has his vision. This sets their arrival as less than twenty-four hours after Cornelius had his vision. The visitors stay overnight in Joppa, and the following morning they, with Peter and some of his associates, set out for Caesarea.

When the group arrives, Cornelius approaches and kneels before Peter, who reproaches him. Peter then tells the group assembled by Cornelius that God had shown him that "no person is unclean or impure" (10:28). Apparently, this is Peter's and Luke's interpretation of the vision in 10:9–16, and we shall return to examine this more extensively below. In any event, Peter now is ready to enter the home of a Gentile, and Cornelius and his company are ready "to hear what the Lord has directed you [Peter] to say" (10:33).

Scene 5: Peter's speech (Acts 10:34–43). Peter's speech is a development of his interpretation of the vision in 10:28. "God really is nondiscriminatory and accepts all who revere him and conduct themselves properly, regardless of national or ethnic background" (10:34–35). This would seem to be Luke's primary justification of the Gentile mission. Israel is a favored people only in the sense that the message of Jesus was first announced among them, but Peter emphatically asserts that Jesus is "the sovereign of all people" (10:36). He then succinctly summarizes the life of Jesus, highlighting his death and resurrection. He notes that not all in Israel were witnesses to Jesus' resurrection and claims that those who did witness it were chosen ahead of time and were selected to eat and drink with Jesus after his being raised from the dead. Although he is not accompanied by the other apostles on this occasion, he feels free to include them in his speech (note the "we" in 10:39). The reader of the Gospel of Luke will recall the episode in 24:36–49, in which Jesus ate with his disciples and commissioned them as witnesses. Peter concludes his speech by claiming that all the prophets had announced forgiveness of sins through Jesus, but there is, notably, no specific reference to a Hebrew prophet.

Scene 6: The Conversion of Cornelius (Acts 10:44–48). The spirit falls on the assembled congregation while Peter is still speaking, and the Gentiles begin to speak in tongues. Peter has them baptized and then remains with Cornelius for several days. In an allusion to Acts 2, this incident is often thought of as the Gentile Pentecost, and this seems to be Luke's understanding, since he has Peter comment that the spirit fell on them just as it did on the first believers (Acts 10:47; 11:17).

Scene 7: Peter at Jerusalem (Acts 11:1–18). A reader may be inclined to think that the story about the conversion of Cornelius and his household is over at the end of Acts 10. In response to remarkable divine activity, the major apostle has announced that God is not partial and that Gentiles are not inherently unclean. The spirit came upon those assembled by Cornelius, and they began to speak in tongues just as occurred at Pentecost in Acts 2. It would seem that their baptism would end the story.

But there is yet another scene, precipitated by criticism of Peter by other Jewish Christians in Jerusalem. It may surprise the reader to learn that their criticism is not that he allowed Gentiles to be baptized but that he ate with them (Acts 11:3). In any event, after Peter retells the story of his vision and his meeting with Cornelius, the other apostles agree that "God has also offered the gentiles conversion to new life!" (11:18).

The story of Peter and Cornelius is very important to the author of Acts. Its length alone is evidence of its significance. In addition there are a number of repetitions. The narrator tells the story of Cornelius' vision (Acts 10:3–6); then Cornelius tells it to Peter (10:30–32), and Peter refers to it before the other apostles in Jerusalem (11:13–14); the narrator tells the story of Peter's vision (10:9–16); Peter repeats it before the Jerusalem apostles in 11:5–10 and alludes to it again in 15:7. Repetitions in Acts appear to be signals of significance, as in the case of the three stories of the conversion of Paul (9:1–18; 22:6–16; 26:12–18). Clearly, the story of Peter and Cornelius is crucial to the narrative of Luke-Acts as a whole.

This long and complex narrative has its share of problems. Among the problems is an apparent conflict between Peter's vision and his interpretation of it. On its surface the vision itself (Acts 10:9–16) seems to constitute the annulment of Jewish dietary regulations. The sheet that Peter saw coming down from the sky contains, "all the four-legged animals and reptiles of earth and all the birds of the sky" (10:12), and Peter is ordered to kill and eat. The inclusive character of the vision and the command is forceful. (As Peter describes the vision in Acts 11, it is less clearly inclusive.) Among the quadrupeds would be camels, rock badgers, hares, and pigs, all specifically prohibited in Leviticus 11. The specific mention of reptiles serves as a convincing clue that the command of Acts 10:13 is inclusive (see Lev 11:42). To be sure, some permitted animals would be included, but nothing is said about separating them from those that are prohibited. If we should wonder why Peter could not have eaten only the permitted foods, we should note that any mixture of permitted and prohibited animals would have rendered all of them unclean by contact. Peter's response to the divine command is exactly what we should expect from an observant Jew: "I have never tasted anything that was unclean and impure" (Acts 10:14).

But what then does it mean for the heavenly voice to say to Peter, "Stop designating 'unclean' what God has made pure" (Acts 10:15)? Within the context of the vision, it is apparent that the dietary regulations of Leviticus 11 are being overhauled. The former prohibitions are no longer operative, and believers are now permitted to eat whatever is set before them, even if it includes pig, lizard, eagle, or buzzard.

Dietary regulations are of great significance for the Gentile mission that the author of Acts will now begin to describe. Gentile hostility toward Jews frequently involved suspicions that rooted in what appeared to them to be social isolation, and the isolation was almost altogether a result of Jewish adherence to dietary regulations and laws of purity. Such regulations quite simply impeded social relations between Jews and Gentiles. But after experiencing the vision, Peter provides lodging for Cornelius' ambassadors (Acts 10:23) and later enjoys his hospitality for several days (10:48). Although Luke does not specifically say that Peter ate with Gentiles, the reference to an extended stay would clearly include partaking of meals.

Indeed, it is the eating with Gentiles that seems to have disturbed the other apostles in Judea, who ask Peter, "Why did you enter the home of uncircumcised men and eat with them" (Acts 11:3)? They do not ask how it was that Peter had Gentiles baptized, although Peter addresses this issue; instead, they are critical of his eating with Gentiles in a Gentile home and so (presumably) not adhering to the food laws. The entire narrative seems to revolve around issues of food and commensality.

But when Peter finally arrives at an interpretation of his vision, nothing is said about food. The vision perplexed him, and he struggled for some time to understand it (Acts 10:17, 19) but finally came to interpret it as signifying God's acceptance of Gentiles: "God has shown me that no person is unclean or impure" (10:28). A figurative meaning is here substituted for the literal meaning of the vision itself. But even here, Luke shows the reader what the connection is between the literal and the figurative. Peter prefaces his interpretation of the vision by observing that "it is taboo for Jews to associate intimately with or to visit those of another race" (10:28). As Peter interprets the vision, it permits social intercourse between

Jews and Gentiles, but we must not forget that a primary aspect of such intercourse frequently involves food.

As we read on through Acts, we learn that it is Paul, not Peter, who is primarily responsible for the Gentile mission. Clearly, Paul is the hero of Acts, and it is surprising that he is not the one to initiate the mission to Gentiles. In his letter to the Galatians, Paul himself pointed to an agreement that he had made with the Jerusalem leaders to the effect that he, Paul, was to be regarded as apostle to the Gentiles while Peter was apostle to Jews (Gal 2:7–9). We have seen that Luke prepared for the arrival of Paul on the scene by narrating his calling and early activities in chapter 9.

In view of these considerations it is important for the reader to understand why it is Peter rather than Paul who has the distinction of opening the Christian movement up to Gentiles. The reason must lie with the author of Acts, who stresses apostolic authority throughout this section of the book. The stress begins in Acts 1 with the appointment of the Twelve as witnesses to the life, death, and resurrection of Jesus and continues in Acts 10:39–41, where Peter calls himself a witness to these things. Paul, who is not an apostle in the eyes of the author of Acts, could not have made this claim. For our author, such a momentous act as the conversion of the first Gentile must involve an apostle. The point will be confirmed in Acts 15:7, when Peter reminds the assembled council that *he* was the one through whom God acted to bring the gospel to Gentiles.

But even the agency of the leading apostle is not enough. Peter must finally justify his actions before the other apostles and believers in Jerusalem (Acts 11:1–18). We have here a situation that is reminiscent of the story of Philip and the Samaritans. Philip's act in baptizing Samaritans was authenticated when the apostles sent Peter and John to investigate (8:14–18). For Luke, the story of the first Gentile conversion is not over until the apostles as a body give their stamp of approval and agree that "God has also offered the gentiles conversion to new life!" (11:18).

In Search of History

As noted in the discussion above, this story from beginning to end is marked by characteristic themes and motifs of Lukan authorship. It tells a Lukan version of the origin of the Gentile mission and tells it in a Lukan way, with motifs such as miraculous divine guidance and an emphasis on the centrality of apostolic leadership. It is Luke's story throughout and contains very little that might be considered a tradition used by Luke.

Especially notable is the importance given to Peter in this story, a theme that is central to Luke's interests and contrary to Paul's version of events (Gal 2:1–10). Indeed, Luke clearly knew Paul's version, but chose for his own reasons to reverse the roles of Peter and Paul and put in Peter's mouth the defense of the Gentile mission that was characteristic of Paul (see the cameo essay, "What Really Happened at the Jerusalem Council?" p. 173).

Dietary Laws and the Gentile Mission

In this story, Jewish dietary laws emerge as key issues in the Gentile mission. This is consistent with references in Paul, in which dietary laws must be addressed whenever there is a mixed group of Jews and Gentiles (Gal 2:11–14; Rom 14:1–15:13; and perhaps 1 Cor 8:1–13). How the idea developed that Gentile converts need not follow dietary laws is not accounted for in a consistent way in early Christian writings. For Paul, the death of Jesus meant that Gentiles were now acceptable to God as Gentiles and therefore need not submit to circumcision or follow dietary laws. For Mark, it was Jesus who preached that dietary laws were now annulled (Mark 7:18–19).

Acts is not only distinctive in its version but also inconsistent with the versions of Mark and Paul. After all, if Jesus had taught this, would not Peter have known? And if Peter had received the vision indicated in the Acts story, why would he be represented in Paul as the missionary to the circumcised (see Gal 2:7–8)? The Acts story has the clear markings of a Lukan composition; consequently, the Acts Seminar voted black ("improbable") on the basic facts of the story. On the other hand, it is quite possible that Peter's reputation after his death might have included some of the features utilized in Luke's story, so the Seminar gave a gray vote ("doubtful") to that concept.

Dietary laws remained an issue in early Christianity up to and including the early second century when Acts was written. In Paul's account of the Christian meal at Antioch, which took place in the 40s, Peter ate with the Gentiles at first but then withdrew to eat at a separate table under pressure from "those who were advocating circumcision" (Gal 2:12). It appears that by this time, and in this location, the status of dietary laws in the Christian movement was beginning to be in a state of flux. How early that happened is hard to say, but the Seminar affirmed as "possible" the proposition that the change began to take place within a decade or two after the death of Jesus. By this time also, based on Paul's story in Galatians 2, eating with Gentiles appeared to have been an occasional, if not normative, practice for Peter.

Cornelius and Godfearers

The story is very specific in giving a name to a centurion convert from Caesarea. This is often taken to be a sign that a historical character, or at least a tradition about such a character, lay behind this story. Luke, however, is quite fond of using names as a means to lend verisimilitude to his stories. Since this is clearly a pattern in Luke-Acts, names should not in themselves be considered to be references to real people (see the cameo essay, "Names in Acts," p. 22).

Acts is the earliest document to mention the category of "Godfearers" as a designation for Gentiles who were sympathetic to Judaism (Acts 10:2), many of whom became generous benefactors of the synagogue. Indeed, Luke's stress on Godfearers may rightly be considered a Lukan motif. Whether they existed as early as the date for the event portrayed in Acts is difficult to affirm, but clearly Luke in his own day knew of such individuals.

References

Pervo, *Acts*
Tyson, "Guess Who's Coming to Dinner"

The Votes of the Fellows

Red/Probable
- Peter himself ate with Gentiles.

Pink/Possible
- Within a decade or two after the death of Jesus, some Jewish Christians abandoned the Jewish dietary regulations and thus opened the way for Gentile and Jewish Christians to eat together.

Gray/Doubtful
- Peter was described by others as having divine authority to pronounce judgments about acceptable and unacceptable food.
- Petrine claims of authority to pronounce judgments about acceptable and unacceptable food were challenged by others in the early church.

Black/Improbable
- Peter had a vision in which his traditional views on acceptable and unacceptable food were modified.
- Peter claimed to have divine authority to pronounce judgments about acceptable and unacceptable food.

The Story of the Antioch Church

11 [19]Now those who had fled as a result of the oppression that broke out because of Stephen traveled through Phoenicia, then Cyprus, until they came to Antioch. They proclaimed the message to Jews only. [20]Among them were some Cypriotes and Cyreneans who, when they reached Antioch, began to proclaim the message about the Lord Jesus to all who spoke Greek. [21]The Lord was on their side, so that a large number turned to him in faith. [22]When this news came to the attention of the church in Jerusalem, they sent Barnabas to Antioch. [23]After he had arrived and seen the very grace of God at work, he was overjoyed and set out to urge that all remain true to the Lord with heartfelt resolve. [24]Now Barnabas was a fine man, notable for his spiritual gifts and conviction. His work resulted in a huge increase of believers. [25]Barnabas then went to Tarsus to seek out Saul, [26]whom he located and brought back to Antioch, where they worked together in the community for an entire year and instructed a huge number. Indeed, it was in Antioch that the followers of Jesus were first labeled "Christians."

[27]Around that time some prophets came to Antioch from Jerusalem. [28]One of them, Agabus, made an inspired indication that a dreadful famine would fall upon the entire civilized world. (This famine occurred during the reign of Claudius.) [29]The followers of Jesus arranged to send support to the believers in Judea, all contributing in accordance with their resources. [30]They sent Barnabas and Saul to deliver this offering to the elders.

Comments on the Story

At first glance, this section of Acts may appear to be a follow-up to the story of the conversion of Cornelius. That narrative in Acts 10:1–11:18 justifies the mission to Gentiles, and so 11:19–30 may show how the mission was implemented. But there is no reference to the Cornelius story in the later verses, and the section reads as a narrative that is quite independent of it. Indeed, the author reaches back to notes that he had included much earlier. Those notes appeared in 8:1, 4, where our author had stated that a persecution arose after the death of Stephen that issued in the scattering of members of the Jerusalem church. All were scattered except the apostles. Now we learn that those who were so scattered travelled north to Phoenicia and Cyprus, finally settling in Antioch. Thus we have a focus on a non-apostolic group of believers from Jerusalem, who conduct evangelistic missions to the North.

This group preached only to Jews, but some of their converts, when they got to Antioch, began to approach Hellenists (here translated as those "who spoke Greek," Acts 11:20). The term Hellenist has been used in other contexts in Acts (6:1; 9:29), where the meaning is less clear than here. Here it is used in contrast to Jews, and so it is almost certainly equivalent to Gentiles. Thus we have another narrative about an initiative to non-Jews, this one focusing on Antioch. Some scholars think that the disjuncture between the story of Cornelius and the mission in Antioch is a sign that Luke is incorporating various sources that originated from different locations. This may be, but it is difficult to resist the judgment of Henry J. Cadbury, who said that the expectation of an orderly account that narrates an evolutionary development is a modern expectation. Rather, Cadbury wrote, "Luke's real interest is not the evolution of an institution, but the gradual attainment of God's predestined purpose."[1] Acts therefore tells of "repeated beginnings of Gentile Christianity."[2]

Even if this narrative is derived from an earlier source, we can see signs of Luke's hand in it. Not only is there an allusion to an earlier section of Acts, but there is also the use of an important Lukan motif that we have observed in several other narratives. Just as the mission of Philip to Samaria required authentication from the apostles (Acts 8:14–17) and just as Peter's acceptance of the household of Cornelius required approval from the apostolic group (11:1–18), so here the mission in Antioch is followed by a visit from a Jerusalem emissary (11:22). But there is a surprise: the emissary is not an apostle. It is Barnabas who is sent from Jerusalem. We previously learned that Barnabas was an exemplary member of the Jerusalem church, who had sold his property and donated the proceeds to the community (4:36–37). Later Luke notes that he was close to the apostles and introduced them to Saul (9:27). In the present paragraph he is described as "a fine man, notable for his spiritual gifts and conviction" (11:24).

Barnabas preaches successfully at Antioch, but his major literary function is to bring Saul back into the narrative. After threats from Hellenists in Jerusalem, Saul is sent back to Tarsus for his protection (Acts 9:30). Barnabas, who is in Jerusalem at the time, knows of this, and so in 11:25 he goes to Tarsus to bring Saul to Antioch. So begins a partnership that will continue for some time.

An episode within this section tells of a universal famine predicted by one Agabus, said to be a prophet from Jerusalem (Acts 11:27–30). Believers in Antioch readily agreed to send funds to relieve their brothers in Judea. One may wonder how, if the famine is to be universal, the Antioch church had discretionary funds to donate, but this problem seems to be of no concern to Luke.

Finally, we should not bypass Luke's comment that "it was in Antioch that the followers of Jesus were first labeled 'Christians'" (Acts 11:26). Although the term is not Luke's favorite for designating the believers, his awareness of it is significant. It suggests a distancing of the followers of Jesus from other groups, notably Jews, a distancing that is historically more appropriate in the second century than in the first. The term "Christian" is rare to nonexistent in first-century writings, and its use here and in 26:28 supports the theory that Acts was written in the second century, by which time the nomenclature was becoming standard (see also 1 Pet 4:16).

In Search of History

This section was probably created out of a tradition from Antioch (see the cameo essay, "The Gentile Mission Source," p. 99), but it has been so thoroughly adapted to the Lukan literary context that the content of the source can no longer be definitively isolated. What the story does witness to is an Antioch version of Christian origins that included such details as the prominence of Barnabas and the connection of the term "Christians" with Antioch. For Luke, Barnabas plays the role of mediator between Paul and Jerusalem, and sets up the eventual dominance of Paul in the Gentile mission. This section sets up the partnership of Barnabas and Paul in Antioch and the interconnection between Antioch and Jerusalem that anticipates the Pauline story of the Jerusalem conference that Acts will adapt in chapter 15.

The term "Christian" was most likely applied to the Jesus followers by outsiders, and perhaps arose in Antioch, as claimed here, or in Rome.[3] It was not used as a self-designation of the movement in Paul or any early Christian writings of the first century until perhaps the 90s. The claim here by Acts that it arose as early as the 30s or 40s is therefore unhistorical.

The claim that Paul is from Tarsus is specific to Acts (9:11, 30), and is not found anywhere in Paul. Since it plays a prominent role in the plot of Acts (see 21:39), its credibility as an historical datum is suspect.

References

Pervo, *Acts*
White, "The First Christians"
Winter, "Antioch in Acts"

Encounters with Herod

12 At that time King Herod began to attack some members of the church. ²He had John's brother James put to the sword. ³When he observed that the Jews approved of this, he proceeded to arrest Peter also, whom he seized during the Days of Unleavened Bread ⁴and placed in custody, setting a guard of four squads of four soldiers each. Herod intended to bring Peter to public justice once the feast was over. ⁵Peter therefore remained in custody while the church prayed fervently to God in his behalf.

⁶On the night before Herod was going to bring him to justice, Peter was sleeping, cuffed with two chains between two guards while two others kept watch outside the door. ⁷Suddenly an angel of the Lord appeared and a light shone in the facility. The angel aroused Peter with a blow in the side and said, "Get up quickly!" The shackles fell from his hands. ⁸The angel then said: "Belt up your robe and put on your sandals." Peter complied. "Put on your coat and follow me," the angel continued. ⁹Peter followed him out, not knowing that the angel had actually done all this, for he imagined that it was a vision. ¹⁰They passed by the first guard station, then the second, coming finally to the iron gate that leads to the city. This opened to them on its own accord. They went out and traveled a block, at which point the angel suddenly left him.

¹¹At that Peter came to his senses and exclaimed: "Now I know that the Lord really did send an angel and that he has delivered me from Herod and all the expectations of

the Jewish people!" ¹²Once he had realized this, he proceeded to the house of Mary, who was the mother of John surnamed Mark, where a large group had gathered for prayer. ¹³A maid named Rose came in response to his knock on the courtyard gate. ¹⁴When she recognized Peter's voice, she became so excited from joy that she did not open the gate, but dashed back in to announce that Peter was standing outside. ¹⁵"You're crazy!" was their answer, but she was so persistent in her claim that they began to say, "It's his guardian angel." ¹⁶Meanwhile, Peter continued knocking, so they opened the gate and, upon seeing him, were astonished. ¹⁷Peter gestured that they should be quiet and then related how the Lord had led him out of prison. "Tell James and the believers about this," he said, before leaving them and going elsewhere.

¹⁸The following day the soldiers were confused about what had become of Peter. ¹⁹After Herod had looked for him without success, he interrogated the guards, disposed of them, then left Judea to pass some time in Caesarea.

²⁰Herod was furious with the people of Tyre and Sidon. They approached him jointly, because their region depended upon Herod's realm for its food supply. After securing the support of Herod's chamberlain, Blastus, they petitioned for an amicable resolution of the conflict. ²¹On the day fixed for the formalities, Herod took his place on the throne, vested in his royal garb, to deliver a public address. ²²The populace kept chanting: "This is a god's voice, no mere mortal's!" ²³An angel of the Lord immediately struck Herod with a blow, because he had not given proper honor to God. He died from an infestation of worms.

²⁴Proclamation of God's message expanded and abounded. ²⁵Barnabas and Saul returned to Antioch from Jerusalem after completing their mission of relief. They took with them John surnamed Mark.

Comments on the Story

The theme of opposition to the followers of Jesus plays a major role throughout Acts. We observed this theme in the early chapters, where apostles were arrested and interrogated by Jewish priests and the council (Acts 4:1–22; 5:17–42). Luke later stressed the role of Saul as an agent of the high priest and, until his conversion, a major persecutor of the new movement (8:1, 3; 9:1–2). The execution of Stephen was followed by a persecution that dispersed all Jerusalem believers except the apostles (8:1). But then Luke noted in 9:31 that the entire believing community enjoyed peace after the conversion of Saul.

The peace of Acts 9:31 is suddenly shattered when Herod takes action against the leaders of the Jesus movement. No longer are the apostles safe, as Herod executes one of them and arrests another. The reader quickly recognizes that a new phase of opposition has begun in Acts 12, with the full power of government focused against the believers. Luke refers to the persecutor as "King Herod," usually identified with Agrippa I, a grandson of Herod the Great and ruler of various Jewish territories from 37–44 CE. But Luke is less interested in the actual history than in the character of the opposition. Just as a Herod was implicated in the trial of Jesus in Luke (23:6–12), so is a Herod the initiator of violence against the apostles in Acts.

Luke also remarks that "the Jews" approved of Herod's action (Acts 12:3), and from here on in the narrative of Acts the term "Jews" is used to designate major opposition to the Christian movement. One wonders what happened to the abundant support and admiration the Jesus believers enjoyed from Jews in the early chapters of Acts.

Luke is careful to identify the first apostolic martyr as James the brother of John. This would be one of the two sons of Zebedee who became disciples of Jesus (see Luke 5:10; 6:14; Acts 1:13). Luke apparently wanted to distinguish this James from the one named later in this narrative at Acts 12:17.

But the focus of Acts 12:1–17 is not on James but on Peter, heretofore portrayed as the leader of the apostles. There are nuances here that remind the reader of the trial and death of Jesus as narrated in Luke 22:66–23:25. In the case of both Jesus and Peter the time is Passover; in both cases a Herod is involved.

Peter's arrest creates a perilous situation, and so the church engages in fervent prayer (Acts 12:5). For what did the church pray? Did the believers pray that God would sustain Peter as he approached martyrdom, or did they pray for his release? Although the author of Acts does not specifically answer these questions, he shows that the believers were unprepared for what happened. They could not believe that Peter had been released and stood before them. The reader may be struck with the fact that, although the believers had been praying for Peter, they could not believe that their prayers were answered. And yet, Luke has portrayed something profoundly human: people can indeed pray for something that seems so improbable that, if it should happen, they would find it almost impossible to believe it.

The narrative has not only human interest but also humor. Think of Peter, aroused from sleep and directed to get dressed. He is sure that he is still dreaming, and it is necessary for the angel to give him specific directions on what to wear. He is slow to realize what has happened (Acts 12:7–10; see also 10:17, 19, 28, where Peter ponders for a long time before understanding his vision). When he finally arrives at his destination and knocks at the gate, the maid recognizes his voice but leaves him standing there, while she tries to convince her masters that it is he (12:14–17).

When finally the group recognizes Peter, he is able to direct them to communicate with James and the brothers (Acts 12:17). Obviously this is not the James who was named in 12:2 as the brother of John. There is another James listed in Luke 6:15 and Acts 1:13, who is designated as James the son of Alphaeus. But since, in both references to this James, the name of the father is included, it is unlikely that this is the person Luke has in mind here. Instead, Luke introduces a character who will play an increasingly significant role in the story of the believers in Jerusalem. Indeed, in 15:13; 21:18, this James appears to carry immense authority in Jerusalem. He is probably to be identified with the James who is frequently mentioned by Paul and characterized as the brother of the Lord (see Gal 1:19; 2:9, 12; 1 Cor 15:7). His authority in Jerusalem would explain Peter's directive in Acts 12:17: an event such as the release of Peter should be reported to the leader of the community. But readers should not overlook the fact that, according to the list in 1:13 and the specifications in 1:21–22, this James is not an apostle. Further, 12:17 notes that after meeting with believers in Jerusalem, Peter went to an unspecified location. He will turn up again at the Jerusalem conference in 15:7, but never thereafter. Effectively, Luke is here alluding to the end of apostolic leadership in Jerusalem and the transfer of authority to a non-apostle. Clearly this is a significant event, and possibly not a harmonious one, but Luke has chosen to omit the details and provide only a tantalizing allusion to it.

In Acts 12:18–23, Luke returns to a focus on Herod and narrates his death in Caesarea. The position of this narrative suggests that the death of Herod is a payback for his treatment of the apostles. After all, the agent of his death is an angel of the Lord, just as an angel is the agent of Peter's release from prison. But Luke does not stress this relationship and rather attributes Herod's death to his arrogance in accepting the plaudits of those who shouted out, "This is a god's voice, no mere mortal's!" (12:22). The villainy of Herod is more than matched by his self-importance, and he must die an agonizing and humiliating death. Readers are reminded of the death of Judas in 1:16–20.

Luke concludes this chapter with a summary note about the increasing success of the believing community and then mentions the travels of Barnabas and Saul (Acts 12:24–25). We last read of them in Acts 11:30, where it was said that they were sent from Antioch to Jerusalem with relief money. According to the best attested texts, Acts 12:25 should read: "Barnabas and Saul returned to Jerusalem." The problem is that, according to 11:30, they are already in Jerusalem, and the following narrative locates them in Antioch (see 13:1). For these reasons, Pervo has chosen to translate the verse as "Barnabas and Saul returned to Antioch from Jerusalem after completing their mission of relief" (12:25). Either Luke inadvertently wrote "to Jerusalem" when he intended "from Jerusalem," or a very early copyist introduced this mistake. In any event, it is worth noting that, according to Acts, Barnabas and Saul were in Jerusalem during the Herodian persecution but were not affected. Luke seems to have lost sight of them until the last verse of Acts 12.

Finally, Luke introduces John surnamed Mark (Acts 12:25), who will appear briefly in later narratives. His mother apparently owned the house where the believers were praying for Peter and finally received him (12:12).

In Search of History

This prison-break story, like the two others in Acts (5:17–32, 16:24–34), is based on a literary model that is widely found in ancient narrative. This one shows special connections to a story about Priam's escape from Achilles in Homer's *Iliad*, as argued by Dennis MacDonald (see the cameo essay, "Prison Breaks in Luke's Literary World," p. 72). It is an elegantly constructed story showing Luke at his best as a storyteller. It functions as a component of Luke's overall theological aims, as nicely summarized in 12:11: "Now I know that the Lord really did send an angel and that he has delivered me from Herod and all the expectations of the Jewish people." Not only does the story reestablish Peter as God's divine agent, it does so by reasserting the theme that God is in charge of this story and is the one who initiates the action. This affirmation of Peter takes place as a judgment against both Herod and "the Jewish people" and thus also feeds into Luke's theme of anti-Judaism and supersessionism. Because the prison break story is constructed out of identifiable literary models and fits so well into Luke's theological program, it has nothing to commend it as historical.

Herod is clearly a villain here, but later in Acts, Roman officials will be presented more sympathetically. Herod as a villain is a traditional literary motif; the family of Herod was widely thought of as cruel and violent. As indicated in the voting record, the Fellows concluded that there may be a historical core to the report that Herod had James killed.[4]

The Herod trajectory then concludes with his gruesome death. Josephus has a similar story.[5] Such stories are common in popular lore as "good riddance" stories about hated figures. Luke's source is most likely Josephus, whose story refers to Agrippa I, a name for the ruler Luke does not use. Both stories take place in Caesarea and connect the death of the monarch with a public event in which he is praised too highly, thus providing a literary justification for his impending death, which follows quickly and unexpectedly. Luke changes the context of the story, however, and connects it by association with a series of Herod stories, including his execution of James and imprisonment of Peter. Luke's purpose is literary, not historical.

Luke juxtaposes the execution of James with his story of Peter's jailbreak. This creates something of a dissonance since God seems to favor Peter over James. The dissonance, however, serves to emphasize that God's actions are not for the purpose of protecting everyone but instead are a part of a larger plan. Thus, while the killing of James may have historical credibility, the imprisonment of Peter does not, especially since it cannot be affirmed without also affirming the prison break itself. The episode with "Rose" (Rhoda in Greek, Acts 12:13–17), the servant who answers the door, is such an inherent part of the miraculous escape from prison that it cannot be affirmed as having any historical core to it. Even the name Rhoda must be excluded, since this story is the only thing Luke tells us about her. Furthermore, to provide a name for his characters is a storytelling device he frequently uses (see the cameo essay, "Names in Acts," p. 22).

References

>MacDonald, "Luke's Emulation of Homer" and "Mimetic Interpretation of Prison Breaks"

The Votes of the Fellows

Red/Probable
- Acts 12:1–17 is written to emulate Priam's escape from Achilles in the last book of the *Iliad*.
- Acts 12:1–17 is a Lukan fiction.

Pink/Possible
- Agrippa 1 executed James, "the brother of John."

Gray/Doubtful
- Agrippa imprisoned Peter.

Black/Improbable
- Peter experienced a prison break.
- Rhoda was a historical figure.

Antioch Commissions Barnabas and Saul

13 The community at Antioch included prophetic teachers: Barnabas, Simeon, known as "Blacky (Niger)," Lucius from Cyrene, Manachen, a childhood companion of Herod the Tetrarch, and Saul. ²Once, while they were engaged in worshiping the Lord and fasting, the [Holy] Spirit said: "Be so good as to reserve Barnabas and Saul for the task to which I have called them." ³Therefore, after fasting and prayer, they laid hands upon the two and sent them on their way.

Comments on the Story

With the return of Barnabas, Saul, (and John Mark), Luke is ready to focus attention once again on the church at Antioch. The reader will remember that converts from Cyprus and Cyrene began to preach to Gentiles at Antioch (see Acts 11:20) and that the church there sent Barnabas and Saul to Jerusalem in the effort to provide help during a famine (see 11:30). There may be a suggestion that some time has passed between Acts 12:25 and 13:1. The former verse (as emended) noted that Barnabas and Saul travelled from Jerusalem to Antioch after the death of Herod. In 13:1 the two have become leaders of the church there, along with three others: Simeon, Lucius, and Manachen. It would be difficult to imagine that they achieved this high position immediately upon their return from Jerusalem.

This is a diverse group of leaders. Barnabas is a Levite from Cyprus; Lucius is from Cyrene; Manachen is an old friend of Herod

Antipas and presumably from Galilee; Saul is a diaspora Jew from Tarsus. The origin of Simeon is not identified, but the nickname "Blacky (Niger)" may suggest that he is from Africa.

It is notable that the leaders in Antioch are called prophets and teachers, or as here translated, "prophetic teachers." None of them is said to be an apostle, and clearly none of them would qualify according to Luke's standards (see Acts 1:21–22). We have already seen that Luke is now describing a post-apostolic age (see comments on 12:1–25). Even so, we shall see that, in a certain sense, practices of the church in Antioch need to be approved by the leaders in Jerusalem (see 15:1–35).

Despite the absence of apostles, the community is devout and is led by the Spirit, which directs the leaders to separate Barnabas and Saul for a special task that will be narrated in what follows. It is tempting to think of the episode described in Acts 13:3 as an ordination ceremony. If so, it included three stages: fasting, prayer, and the laying on of hands. The practice of laying on of hands has been described previously in Acts, where it seems to be used for different purposes. In 6:6 the Twelve laid hands on the Seven as a seal of approval; in 8:17, Peter and John laid hands on Philip's converts in Samaria to authenticate his activity; in 9:12 it is said that Saul will recover his sight through the laying on of hands; and in 9:17, Ananias fulfills this prediction. Here in 13:3 it is part of a solemn ceremony in which the church dedicates two missionaries to an awesome task.

Interestingly, John Mark is not mentioned in this scene. He must be in Antioch, since he travelled there with Barnabas and Saul from Jerusalem (see Acts 12:25). But apparently our author does not think of him as a leader in the church at Antioch, although later on he notes that John accompanied Barnabas and Saul as they fulfilled their commission (see 13:5).

In Search of History

There are three components to this brief story that deserve attention. The first is its overall plot, in which the story takes shape by means of divine agency. The choice of Barnabas and Saul foreshadows the eventual importance of these two for the Gentile mission, which itself began by divine agency (see Acts 10:1–11:18). This is one of Luke's apologetic emphases; it is not an historical item. The list of "teachers and prophets" in Antioch is impressive and may derive from an Antioch source. But it lacks any clear mooring in history since it is connected specifically with this miraculous story created by Luke. The appointing of Barnabas and Saul by means of laying on of hands is most likely anachronistic for the time of Paul; it is a practice more commonly associated with the late first- to early second-century Christian community (see 1 Tim 1:18, 4:14; 2 Tim 1:6). That Barnabas and Paul were in some way designated as official representatives of the Antioch community can be learned from Paul's letters (see Gal 2:1–14). This, however, is not the historical story of that appointment.

References
Kea, "Miscellaneous Saul Stories"

The Votes of the Fellows
Gray/Doubtful
- At Antioch, Barnabas, Simeon, Lucius, Manaen [Manachen], and Saul were recognized as teachers and prophets.
- Barnabas and Saul were appointed to do missionary work on behalf of the church at Antioch.

Black/Improbable
- Barnabas and Saul were appointed to do missionary work on behalf of the church at Antioch in a ritual that included the laying on of hands.

Barnabas and Saul in Cyprus
13 ⁴Thus dispatched by the Holy Spirit, the two proceeded to Seleucia, where they caught a ship to Cyprus. ⁵When they arrived in Salamis they began to proclaim the message of God in the Jewish synagogues. John was with them as an assistant. ⁶After crossing the entire island they reached Paphos, where they came upon one Bar-Jesus, a Jewish practitioner of sorcery and prophetic quackery. ⁷He was in the retinue of the proconsul, Sergius Paulus, a cultured man. Sergius sent for Barnabas and Saul, whom he asked to expound to him the message of God. ⁸Elymas the magician (for that is what his name means) argued with them in an effort to deflect the proconsul from the faith. ⁹In response Saul, also known as Paul, was motivated by the Holy Spirit to fix his eye upon Elymas and ¹⁰say: "You satanic creature, master of every foul trick and unscrupulous technique, you enemy of anything that is upright, must you always

attempt to turn the straight ways of the Lord into crooked paths? ¹¹Look, you have got the Lord's attention. For some time you will be blind, deprived of the light of day." At that moment mist and gloom overtook him. Elymas began to grope about in search of a guide. ¹²When the proconsul saw what had happened, he was utterly astonished at the teaching about the Lord and became a believer.

Comments on the Story

The first mission of Barnabas and Saul, assisted by John Mark, takes them to Cyprus, the homeland of Barnabas. They preach in synagogues in Salamis and then travel across the island to Paphos, which served as the capital. There they meet with the proconsul, Sergius Paulus, and with a magician in his entourage.

This brief narrative contains a number of perplexing notes but also makes use of a major theme. It is a theme that is introduced here and will reappear in many of the following narratives of the mission of Paul, who, on his arrival in a new locality, will preach first in the synagogue. The theme may be Luke's way of honoring Paul's theological protocol as announced in Rom 1:16: "first Jews and then Greeks." We shall see that Luke develops this theme into a full agenda for Paul: the Jews hear the gospel but, for the most part, reject it, and this opens the way for the missionaries to approach Gentiles (see Acts 13:13–52; 14:1–7; 17:1–15; 18:1–17; 19:1–10). The present narrative does not fully develop the theme, since we learn nothing about the reaction of those in the synagogues. Barnabas and Saul do, however, travel from Salamis to Paphos, where they meet and convert a leading Gentile government figure.

Among the perplexities in the narrative is the use of more than one name for a character. The better-known name for Acts' hero is introduced in Acts 13:9, where the author refers to "Saul, also known as Paul." Here is a turning point in Acts: before 13:9, the character is always called Saul; afterward he is Paul (except in references to his conversion). This sounds like a change of names, but Luke states in 13:9 that the one person bore both names all along. It is notable that, in his genuine letters, Paul never refers to himself as Saul; it is only in Acts that this name appears. Its use implies that the author of Acts wanted to stress the Jewish character of Paul, and this is a theme that we shall observe later in the book. Luke gives Paul the name of the first king of Israel and thereby intimates that his main character has deep Jewish roots.

The other character with a double name is the magician, known both as Bar-Jesus and Elymas (Acts 13:8). Actually, the author claims that the latter name is a translation of the former. The former is clearly Semitic, but Elymas is not, so far as can be determined, a Greek word. The problem here is reflected in the textual tradition, which provided other names for the magician. It is not likely that the author of Acts created these names, since he probably would not have called this character Bar-Jesus, meaning "son of Jesus," and he must not have understood the meaning of the name "Elymas." The names must, therefore, have been part of an earlier tradition that Luke received.

Despite the perplexities, we should not miss the main point of the story: the conversion of a high-ranking Roman official despite formidable opposition. Opposition comes from the magician, who is described in three terms: he is a sorcerer, a false prophet, and a Jew (Acts 13:6). By this point in Acts, readers will not be surprised to find these terms used to describe an opponent of the Jesus believers. Remember Simon, the magician in Samaria, who at first opposed Philip (8:4–25). A similar character will turn up in 19:11–20. As for Jews, the author of Acts, from 12:3 on, counts them among the opponents of the believers. The opposition of Bar-Jesus/Elymas is, however, not a serious challenge for Paul, who vehemently curses him and announces his punishment (13:11). He becomes temporarily blind, as had Saul himself on the road to Damascus (9:8–9).

The proconsul, by contrast, is described as a cultured man, although one may ask why he has such a reprobate as Bar-Jesus on his staff (Acts 13:7). He summons Barnabas and Paul and wishes to hear their message (13:8). After the encounter with Bar-Jesus/Elymas, Sergius Paulus becomes a believer (13:12). It is notable that Luke does not share with his readers the content of the preaching of Barnabas and Paul, but he nevertheless attributes the conversion of Sergius Paulus not only to his reaction to what had happened to Bar-Jesus but also to his hearing of the teaching about the Lord.

In Search of History

This story presents in a nutshell the essence of Luke's interpretation of Paul's mission and sets up much of the action that is to follow. As discussed above, the Lukan components include: the divine guidance of the Holy Spirit, the beginning at the synagogue, the encounter with a Jewish detractor, and the subsequent conversion of a representative Gentile. The miracle story that lies at the heart of this narrative is also a Lukan characteristic. The entire narrative, therefore, is manifestly a product of Luke's own creativity.

Does it contain any information that might be historical? Two bits of data stand out: the change of Saul's name to Paul and the conversion of a specifically named individual, Sergius Paulus. Names in themselves are not markers of historical veracity, as already pointed out in the cameo essay on "Names in Acts" (see p. 22). The idea that Paul was once called Saul is unique to Acts; it is nowhere to be found in Paul's letters. It was not uncommon to have both a Jewish name and a Greek name, as is seen, for example, with Cephas/Peter. But it is striking that Paul himself, who referred to Peter as "Cephas" (see 1 Cor 1:12; 3:22; 9:5; 15:5; Gal 1:18; 2:9, 11, 12) never mentioned that he had ever had the name Saul. Such a detail would have been useful for his defense of the legitimacy of his Jewish heritage in such texts as Gal 1:14, Phil 3:4–6, and Rom 11:1. On the other hand, Acts makes it a point to identify Paul, along with the rest of the apostles, as embedded in Judaism. To call him Saul is a brilliant means for making that point. In this narrative, he takes on his Greek name at the point when he secures his first Gentile convert, symbolic of the fact that from this point on his mission will be primarily directed to Gentiles. Thus the use of the name Saul to this point in the narrative has a literary rather than historical purpose. Sergius Paulus is so convenient a character for this story that he must be a creation as well. By giving Paul's first Gentile convert the same name as Paul, Luke makes a narrative move in which he seals the solidarity of Saul with the Greco-Roman mission field.

After one removes the features of Lukan composition, there is nothing left to the story except the itinerary itself. The existence of an itinerary source, a source that contained very little, if anything, except a list of places Paul visited in their correct order, is no longer tenable as a working hypothesis (see the cameo essay, "The Itinerary of Paul," p. 206). Therefore, we conclude that the itinerary in this text is not based on independent, reliable data but rather is most likely the creation of Luke himself.

References

Shea, "Names in Acts 2"

The Votes of the Fellows

Gray/Doubtful

- The Sergius Paulus story in Acts is derived from a story found in Galen.

Black/Improbable
- Paul the letter writer was once called Saul.
- Paul converted a Roman official named Sergius Paulus.

Paul and Barnabas in Antioch of Pisidia

13 ¹³Paul and his companions sailed from Paphos to Perga in Pamphylia. John, however, left them and went back to Jerusalem. ¹⁴Meanwhile, the others left Perga and traveled on to Antioch of Pisidia, where they went to the synagogue on the Sabbath and took a seat. ¹⁵Following the readings from the Torah and the Prophets, the synagogue officials extended this invitation, "Brothers, if you have a sermon, please deliver it."

¹⁶In response Paul stood up and indicated that he would speak. "My fellow Israelites and you that revere God, please listen. ¹⁷The God of this people Israel chose our ancestors. During their stay in Egypt he fashioned them into a great nation and subsequently brought them out of that country with a substantial display of force. ¹⁸Over some forty years he cared for them in the wilderness. ¹⁹After eradicating seven nations in the land of Canaan, he conferred it upon the Israelites. ²⁰Roughly 450 years later God appointed judges, who served until the time of the prophet Samuel. ²¹At that point the people demanded a king, so God appointed Saul, son of Kish, from the tribe of Benjamin, who ruled for forty years ²²until God removed him and elevated David to the throne, with this recommendation: 'I have found David, the son of Jesse, a man after my own heart. He will do everything that I want.' ²³As promised, God has produced a savior for Israel from David's descendants: Jesus. ²⁴John spoke of Jesus before his appearance, while he was proclaiming baptism and a change of heart to all the people of Israel. ²⁵As his mission was drawing to a close he used to say, 'What do you imagine that I am? I am *not* "the one," but after me will come one whose sandal straps I am not fit to untie.'

²⁶"My fellow believers and heirs of Abraham's line, as well as those of you that revere God, this message of salvation was directed to *us*. ²⁷For the residents of Jerusalem, together with their leaders, failed to recognize

Jesus. In condemning him they brought to fulfillment the declarations of the prophets, which they also failed to perceive, although these are heard every single Sabbath. ²⁸These people demanded to Pilate that he be executed, failure to find him guilty of any capital crime notwithstanding. ²⁹When they had brought to pass all that had been written about him, they removed him from the cross and placed him in a tomb. ³⁰Yet God raised him from the dead. ³¹Over the course of many days he appeared to those who had traveled with him from Galilee to Jerusalem. They are his witnesses to the public, ³²while we are here to announce the achievement of the promise made to the ancestors. ³³God has fulfilled it for us their heirs by raising Jesus, as the first Psalm says, 'You are my son; today I have become your father.' ³⁴To indicate that the one raised will never return to the decay of death, God says, 'To you I shall offer the Davidic promises, which are sacred and inviolable.' ³⁵In support of this God says in another place, 'You will not allow your sacred one to experience decay.' ³⁶Now David served God's purpose in his own generation, after which he died, was buried with his ancestors, and *did* experience decay, ³⁷but the one whom God raised did *not* experience decay.

³⁸"There is something you need to know, my fellow believers: through this person comes to you a message of forgiveness of sins. ³⁹Through Jesus all who have trust are acquitted of everything for which the law of Moses has no remedy. ⁴⁰Be careful, therefore, that you do not experience the judgment announced by the prophets: ⁴¹'Take a look, you scoffers, be astonished, and then drop dead! I am going to do something in your lifetime, an act that you will not believe even if you are told about it.'"

⁴²As they were leaving, Paul and Barnabas were urged to say more about their message on the following Sabbath. ⁴³After the service many Jews and observant converts congregated about the two, who exhorted them to hold fast to God's grace.

⁴⁴When that Sabbath arrived, almost the entire city had gathered to hear the Lord's message. ⁴⁵When the Jews saw the size of the crowd, they were filled with jealousy and attempted to refute Paul's arguments with slanderous claims. ⁴⁶Undaunted, Paul and Barnabas said, "We were obliged to

preach God's message to you first. Since you reject it and show that you are unworthy of eternal life, we are therefore going to turn to the gentiles. ⁴⁷That is what the Lord has directed us to do: 'I have made you a light for the gentiles and a means of salvation to the ends of the earth.'"

⁴⁸When the gentiles heard this, they were overjoyed and praised the Lord for the message they had received. All who were destined for everlasting life became believers. ⁴⁹The message about the Lord was disseminated throughout the entire region. ⁵⁰In response, the Jews aroused their influential women sympathizers and the leaders of the city and inaugurated a persecution of Paul and Barnabas, whom they drove out of their jurisdiction. ⁵¹So the two shook of the dust from their feet in judgment against them and moved on to Iconium. ⁵²Their followers, however, continued to abound in joy with the presence of the Holy Spirit.

Comments on the Story

Paul, Barnabas, and John Mark arrive now in Asia Minor, and the mission begins in earnest. In the narrative about Cyprus (Acts 13:4–12), we noted a theme that now appears in all its fullness. This is the theme that governs Luke's descriptions of most of the activities of Paul: he preaches to Jews, meets with limited success but overwhelming rejection and then goes to Gentiles, who respond positively. Acts 13:13–52 is a narrative presentation that is governed by this pattern, and it is a model for much of the rest of Acts.

At the heart of this section is a speech of Paul at the synagogue in Pisidian Antioch (Acts 13:16–41). The speech may remind readers of the sermon of Jesus in Luke 4:16–30, which also was delivered in a synagogue. That sermon was initially received well, but at the end Jesus was almost stoned to death. In a similar way, after Paul speaks in Pisidian Antioch, many Jews and proselytes join up with the missionaries, and Paul is invited to speak again. But a week later there is nothing but opposition, and eventually the Pauline party is forced out of town.

Paul's speech also has a number of resemblances to the speech of Stephen in Acts 7. Both begin with references to early Hebrew history, although different phases are stressed. Stephen's recital goes from Abraham to Solomon, while Paul's covers the time between the Exodus and the reign of David.

The most impressive resemblances are between the sermon of Paul and those of Peter in the early chapters of Acts. Peter's sermons generally covered five topics: prophecy has been fulfilled; Jesus is the Christ appointed for Israel; you Jews killed Jesus; God raised Jesus from the dead; repent and be forgiven. All these points are included in Paul's speech in Acts 13, but with some variations.

Prophecy has been fulfilled. The recital of Hebrew history moves very quickly from the Exodus to David and focuses on this king's notable descendant Jesus. Paul quotes several OT passages to support his claims about the fulfillment of prophecy in Jesus. He quotes from Ps 2:7 in Acts 13:33, to support his contention that Jesus fulfilled the promise to David. Then he quotes from Isa 55:3 and Ps 16:10 in a complex argument to show that a promise that ostensibly was made to David actually was meant for Jesus. The verse from Psalm 16 seems to say that the speaker, traditionally thought to be David, would not experience decay. But Paul argues that, since David died and his body decayed, the promise could not have applied to him. It applied, rather, to Jesus, whose body was revivified and so did not suffer destruction. The reference to Isaiah 55 is to a verse the meaning of which is obscure but which the Lukan Paul quotes to support his point that promises made to David were meant for Jesus. However torturous the exegesis may be, the point is clear: prophets foretold the things about Jesus.

Jesus is the Messiah appointed for Israel. Paul affirms that God has brought a savior *for Israel* (Acts 13:23). He makes the Jewish context clear in 13:26: "My fellow believers and heirs of Abraham's line, as well as those of you that revere God, this message of salvation was directed to *us*."

You Jews killed Jesus. This charge has been adapted for an audience of diaspora Jews. Paul does not hold his audience guilty but states that it was the Jews in Jerusalem and their leaders who put Jesus to death (Acts 13:27). He goes on to say that those Jews asked Pilate to execute Jesus (13:28), here reflecting the narrative in Luke 23:13–25. An interesting disagreement with the narrative in Luke occurs, however, in Acts 13:29, where Paul says that these same Jewish people and leaders laid Jesus in a tomb. Readers of the Gospel of Luke will remember that it was not the opponents but a sympathizer, Joseph of Arimathea, who had Jesus buried (see Luke 23:50–54).

God raised Jesus from the dead. The resurrection of Jesus constitutes God's answer to the act of the Jewish people and their leaders in putting Jesus to death (Acts 13:30).

Repent and be forgiven. Paul's sermon does not include an explicit call for repentance, although the members of the audience in the synagogue are warned to beware "the judgment announced by the prophets" (Acts 13:40). The promise of forgiveness is clearly announced, but with a difference. Luke here makes a rare nod to a characteristic Pauline concept by using a term that is thoroughly discussed in his letters to the Romans and Galatians. It is the Greek term *dikaioō*, usually translated with the appropriate form of the verb "to be justified," or, as here, "to be acquitted." Moreover, a contrast is made between the power of the Mosaic Torah and the justification through Jesus. These notes seem to have the flavor of some of the letters of Paul. But, in a way that does not wholly reflect the Pauline concept, Luke associates justification with the forgiveness of sins. Paul generally characterizes justification as an act of God in regarding a person as in the right, rather than as forgiving past misdeeds. C. K. Barrett rightly observes that "on a central question of faith Luke shows his devotion to Paul but less than full understanding of his theology."[6]

The story at Pisidian Antioch is governed by the narrative pattern that we have already observed. But there are points of detail that do not fully conform to the pattern. Paul's synagogue audience does not appear to be offended by the reference to the ineffectiveness of Mosaic Torah but instead exhibits only a positive response to the message about Jesus. Many Jews and proselytes join with Paul and Barnabas, who are invited to speak again on the following Sabbath (Acts 13:42–43). But after the second appearance of the missionaries, we read that "the Jews" become jealous of the large crowd, presumably of Gentiles, that Paul and Barnabas attracted (13:45). They contradict the speakers, stir up some women and principal citizens, and cause the missionaries to be run out of town (13:50). The reaction of Paul and Barnabas is to shake the dust from their feet and announce that, henceforth, they will go to Gentiles (13:46–47, 51). To some extent this reaction is inappropriate, since not all of the Jewish people who heard the message of the missionaries rejected it. But it seems that the author of Acts spins the account so that readers inevitably come away with negative impressions of Jews. The movement of the narrative has been from an initial acceptance of Paul's message by some Jews to a final rejection by "the Jews." The positive response of many Jews from Pisidian Antioch is valued by the implied author as less significant than the opposition of that body he increasingly refers to as "the Jews" (13:45, 50). Although he tells of some missionary success, the impression the author conveys to the reader is that Jews as a whole rejected the Christian message.

The incident at Pisidian Antioch concludes with a solemn announcement by Paul and Barnabas. "We were obliged to preach God's message to you [Jews] first. Since you reject it and show that you are unworthy of eternal life, we are therefore going to turn to the gentiles" (Acts 13:46). Support is provided by a quotation of Isa 49:6 in Acts 13:47. The announcement is a summary statement of the pattern that we have already observed and, as such, is not surprising. It is troubling, however, that the announcement will be repeated twice more in Acts (see 18:6 and 28:28) and that, after the first two announcements, Paul and company return to evangelize Jews. A reader who is not confused at this point has probably not been paying attention.

The confusion results from the author's stress on the protocol that dominates the Pauline missions: to Jews first and then to Gentiles. Luke uses the accustomed literary pattern in individual narratives and then summarizes the pattern in the three solemn announcements in Acts 13:46; 18:6 and 28:28. The juxtaposition of individual narrative and summary may cause confusion, but at the same time the reader learns that no effort has been spared to present the Christian message to Jews. In view of their efforts and Jewish rejection, the missionaries are free, indeed obligated, to go to the Gentiles.

At the beginning of this section the author subtly notes that changes have taken place in the leadership of the mission in central Asia Minor. In Acts 13:13, for the first time Paul is named ahead of Barnabas, probably indicating that he now has become the chief missionary. Then in what follows Paul is the speaker and Barnabas the mute companion. In addition, John Mark has gone back to Jerusalem for unspecified reasons. The incident may appear to be inconsequential until we read in Acts 15:37–38 that Barnabas and Paul had a parting of the ways because of John Mark's departure. Whatever John's reason for leaving the group, the Paul of Acts interpreted it as a kind of desertion that cast doubt on his reliability. In Gal 2:13 Paul indicates that his split with Barnabas was the result of a serious theological conflict. We probably should see here that Luke is aware of certain issues that brought about the break-up of Barnabas, John Mark, and Paul, but that he minimizes the difficulty as much as possible. In any event, the author's attention will increasingly focus on Paul as the chief missionary.

It is also notable that, with the ascendancy of Paul, Luke has just about forgotten about the apostles. But this is not quite the case, because there is one interesting note in the speech of Paul at Pisidian Antioch: in Acts 13:31–32 he makes a reference to the post-resurrection appearances of Jesus to the witnesses who travelled with him from Galilee to Jerusalem. The reader will recall the forty days of such appearances to the apostles noted in Acts 1:3. In 1 Cor 15:8, where Paul gives a catalogue of post-resurrection appearances, he pointedly includes himself; but not in Acts. On the contrary, here he makes a distinction between the original witnesses and himself: "They [the apostles] are his witnesses to the public, while we [Barnabas and I] are here to announce the achievement of the promise made to the ancestors" (Acts 13:31–32). Luke has not forgotten that, despite their spirit-led work as missionaries to Gentiles, Paul and Barnabas are neither apostles nor witnesses to the resurrection. In the following chapter we shall see, however, that this view appears to be compromised.

In Search of History

The second stop on Paul's journey follows what is taking shape as a standard pattern: they first preach in the synagogue, they are eventually rejected by the Jews, and they then turn to the Gentiles, where they win converts. This time some new wrinkles are added, most notably a lengthy speech, a characteristic of Luke's storytelling technique (see the cameo essay, "Speeches in Acts," p. 45). This story also introduces the recurring theme of organized Jewish persecution. These characteristics mark the story as Luke's creation.

In Acts 13:46, the term "undaunted" translates the Greek word *parrēsiazomai*, which literally means "to speak boldly or freely." It is a term widely used in ancient literature to characterize the bold speech of the philosophers. It is used here and elsewhere in Acts as a means to present the apostles as philosophers in their own right (see the cameo essay, "When Apostles Become Philosophers," p. 60). This insight provides us with another tool for evaluating Luke's creative methodology and was strongly affirmed as such by the votes of the Fellows.

The Votes of the Fellows
Red/Probable
- *Parrēsia* ("free speech") is used in Acts in an intentional attempt to echo philosophical literary imagery.
- *Parrēsia* is consistently associated with stories of opposition in Acts.

- *Parrēsia* is used in Acts in contexts that evoke the claim of a divine commission authorizing the right to speak "with boldness."
- *Parrēsia* is used in Acts to portray Christian leaders as Socratic figures.
- The use of philosophical imagery in Acts is an apologetic device to legitimate Christianity as a movement led by true philosophers.

Black/Improbable
- The characterization of the early Christian leaders as "bold speakers" is an historical datum.

Another theme of Luke's apologetic is presented here. A corollary of the theme of Jewish opposition to Paul and the apostles is the theme that this opposition becomes a primary reason for the Gentile mission. Here that idea is stated in an explicit, programmatic fashion, "We were obliged to preach God's message to you first. Since you reject it and show that you are unworthy of eternal life, we are therefore going to turn to the gentiles" (13:46). According to the Acts story, but not the letters of Paul, Paul always preached first to the Jews in the synagogue, then, when he was rejected, he took his mission to the Gentiles. This is a key point for the plot of Acts and is repeated as Paul's last words in Acts, "God's salvation has been offered to the gentiles. They shall listen" (28:28). This theme functions as part of an underlying supersessionist theme in Acts, in which Judaism is indicted as having been rejected by God in favor of Christianity. Luke may have derived this concept from Rom 1:16, "first Jews and then Greeks," but he took it in a direction that Paul never intended. Paul's theology on this subject was that "God has not given up on the people of Israel whom God already embraced in faithful love" (Rom 11:2; see the complete argument in Romans 9–11). The supersessionist theology that Acts attributes to Paul can in no wise be considered historical (see also the cameo essay, "The Jews according to Acts," p. 268).

References

Dupertuis, "Opposition and Philosophical Imagery"
Pervo, "The Gates Have Been Closed"

Paul and Barnabas in Iconium

14 Paul and Barnabas followed the same procedure in Iconium as at Antioch. They went to the Jewish synagogue and spoke as before, with the result that a very large number of both Jews and Greeks came to believe. ²However, the Jews who were not convinced poisoned the minds of the gentiles against the believers.

³The missionaries nonetheless remained for a substantial time, vigorously proclaiming their message about the Lord's grace. God verified their claims by the miracles and portents he enabled them to perform. ⁴The citizenry split into two factions, one supporting the Jews, the other the missionaries.

⁵When gentiles and Jews, including their leaders, resolved to attack and stone them, ⁶they caught wind of it and escaped to the cities of Lycaonia, that is, Lystra, Derbe, and the adjacent territory. ⁷There they continued to proclaim the message.

Comments on the Story

This section is more of a summary than a report of a specific incident. Luke signals in Acts 14:1 that the literary pattern that was used in the story of Pisidian Antioch will also govern this section. The missionaries speak in the local synagogue (although no sermon is recorded) and meet with some success. But unbelieving Jews create overwhelming opposition, and Paul and Barnabas flee to another place.

Even in this short passage there are some difficulties for the reader. After the unbelieving Jews turned the Gentiles against them (Acts 14:2), the missionaries nevertheless remained in Iconium for "a substantial time" (14:3). Then we read that the town was divided among supporters of the Jews and supporters of the missionaries (14:4). Finally, it seems that the whole town was arrayed against Paul and Barnabas, as both Jews and Gentiles intended to stone them (14:5). Apparently the supporters have ceded control to the more numerous opponents.

A special problem appears in Acts 14:4, where a division among the people is reported. Our translation has "The citizenry split into two factions, one supporting the Jews, the other the missionaries." The word translated here as 'missionaries' represents the Greek *apostoloi*, i.e., apostles. The problem is that, according to the definition that Luke himself provided in Acts 1:22, Paul and Barnabas cannot be apostles. Neither had been a follower of Jesus during his lifetime, and neither is included in the official list of Acts 1:13 (with Matthias added, 1:26).[7] Many scholars attribute the use of the term to Luke's reliance on a source, which probably used it in a sense different from that of Luke. Others might suggest that Luke was influenced by those letters where Paul insists on his own status as apostle. Still others would suggest that Luke himself introduced the term, either inadvertently or intentionally. If Luke used a source or was influenced by the Pauline letters, or if he inadvertently introduced the term, we could conclude that he was only human and excusable for a minor inconsistency. If, however, we think that Luke intentionally referred to Paul and Barnabas as apostles, we might then say that, by this point in the narrative, the missionaries have achieved a status that was hitherto denied them. Against this judgment, however, we should note that, although Paul is clearly the hero of the latter half of Acts, he is never again referred to as an apostle (except perhaps for a textually dubious reference in 14:4). It seems most reasonable to suppose that the Pauline claim of apostleship has rubbed off on Luke. But whatever alternative we select to account for the appearance of the term here, we must not assume that the criteria for apostleship that were so carefully worked out in Acts 1 have been compromised.

In Search of History

This text is a classic compendium of the literary themes of Luke's story, and it is presented in a self-conscious way: "followed the same procedure . . . as before" (Acts 14:1). Even though it is presented as a report on the next stop of the journey, it functions as a summary statement of Paul's mission method throughout Acts. They begin at the synagogue; they win many converts there; they are opposed by Jewish leadership, resulting in a split between Jews and Gentiles; they perform miracles that function to substantiate their claims to divine guidance; the entire citizenry is caught up in the conflict; the missionaries then escape before violence overtakes them. It has all the marks of Lukan authorship and thus no claims to historical validity.

Paul and Barnabas in Lystra and Derbe

14 ⁸[At Lystra] there sat a lame man whose feet had been crippled from birth and who had never walked. ⁹Once, as he was listening to Paul, Paul turned a searching gaze upon him and realized that he believed that he could be cured.

¹⁰"Stand up straight on your feet," he shouted. The man jumped up and began to walk.

¹¹When the crowd saw what Paul had accomplished, they cried out: "The gods have come down to visit us in human form!" ¹²They acclaimed Barnabas as Zeus and, since he was the principal speaker, Paul as Hermes. ¹³The priest of the Temple of Zeus Before the City brought bulls and garlands to the gates so that he and the crowd might offer sacrifice.

¹⁴When the missionaries Barnabas and Paul perceived what was happening, they tore their coats and dashed out into the crowd, shouting, ¹⁵"Good people, why are you doing this? We are mortals, just like you. We would tell you to abandon these idle rites and embrace the living God, who made the heavens, the earth, the sea, and all that they contain. ¹⁶In the past God permitted all peoples to go their own way, ¹⁷yet even then God could be recognized in the good things given you, including rain from above that brings bountiful harvests and the food that you happily receive." ¹⁸Through this argument they were able—barely—to dissuade the crowd from sacrificing to them.

¹⁹Then Jews from Antioch and Iconium arrived on the scene and were able to win over the crowd. After deluging Paul with stones they hauled him outside of the city, presuming that he was dead, ²⁰but, when his followers had gathered about him, he got up and went into the city. On the next day he set out with Barnabas for Derbe.

Comments on the Story

Three incidents make up the story of Paul and Barnabas in Lystra: the cure of a lame man (Acts 14:8–10); the attempt to make sacrifices to the missionaries (14:11–18); and the stoning and recovery of Paul (14:19–20).

The cure of the lame man by Paul (Acts 14:8–10) may remind readers of a similar story told of Peter in 3:1–10. In both cases a man who had been lame from birth is healed by a command to stand up and walk. The healing by Peter was connected with the temple of the Jews in Jerusalem; the healing by Paul with a temple to Zeus in Lystra. Parallels between Peter and Paul are notable in Acts, and they indicate the author's stress on the compatibility between the two leaders.

While the miraculous cure by Peter led to his arrest (Acts 4:1), the one by Paul led to an incredible acclamation (14:11–18). He and Barnabas were hailed as gods: Barnabas as Zeus, the chief god, and Paul as Hermes, the messenger of the gods. (Something similar happened to Peter in Acts 10:25–26, when Cornelius fell before him and worshipped him). At Lystra, the people are apparently so awestruck by the healing of the lame man that they prepare to make sacrifices to the missionaries, who, of course, raise strenuous objections and barely succeed in restraining the crowd.

But Jews from Antioch and Iconium arrive and succeed in turning the crowd against the missionaries, and they stone Paul, leaving him apparently dead (Acts 14:19–20). Paul, however, is still very much alive, and he finds support from some converts. He goes back into Lystra and then journeys on to Derbe.

It is fascinating to observe the interplay among these three incidents. Crowd responses to miracles are frequently stressed in Acts, but here there seems to be an overreaction if there ever was one. It is notable that Paul did not explicitly name Jesus when he cured the lame man, but the reader knows, if the crowd at Lystra does not, that he came to evangelize the residents. The irony is evident here: proclaimers of the one God are thought to be two of the old ones. Barnabas and Paul are so revered that the crowd and the local priest of Zeus prepare to offer sacrifices to them (Acts 14:13). The missionaries are scarcely able to convince the people that they are merely humans, but then visiting Jews seem easily to persuade them that Paul (why not Barnabas?) should be executed (14:19). The crowd that hailed the missionaries as gods has become a lynch mob.

Despite the ruckus, Paul and Barnabas are able to preach a short sermon (Acts 14:15–17). This one is notable not only because it is apparently spoken by two missionaries in unison, but because it is the first in Acts that is directed to Gentiles, i.e., Gentiles who were not associated with synagogues. Notice again the absence of a mention of Jesus. The whole point of the sermon is monotheism: the creator God, who provides for human sustenance through the bounties of nature, is the only God. Paul could have preached this sermon before his conversion. It focuses attention on a basic theological point on which many Christians (excluding Marcionites) could make common cause with Jews. Perhaps Luke means to suggest that this is only the first part of Paul's sermon and that he would have gone on to proclaim salvation through Jesus. But it is more likely that Luke is saving up for a fuller presentation of the Pauline message to Gentiles and will record that sermon in connection with Paul's visit to Athens (Acts 17:16–34).

The author of Acts makes no allusion to the presence of a synagogue in Lystra. For this reason, the narrative here does not follow the usual pattern that governs the stories of Paul's missionary efforts. He does not initially preach in a synagogue and then, after rejection, go on to Gentiles. But one element in the pattern does survive even here. Although Luke has to import them from other locations, it is nevertheless unbelieving Jews who oppose Paul and turn the crowd against the missionaries. A reader who follows these narratives can hardly fail to be impressed with the cumulative impact of Luke's presentation of Jews. They are unflagging in their efforts to oppose Paul and bring about his defeat wherever he goes, and in Lystra they succeed in stoning him and leaving him for dead. Paul, however, will not be deterred by a mere attempt to execute him: he continues bravely to obey his divine orders to carry the gospel to Gentiles.

Despite the problems in this section, the probable intent of Luke comes through: to show that, although the word of God may meet with opposition and misunderstanding, its power cannot finally be extinguished.

In Search of History

The themes that are summarized in the previous narrative are here played out in more detail. The story of Paul healing a lame man follows classic miracle story format. Such stories occur throughout the ancient world and attribute healing powers to a variety of famous figures. Because such stories are so common, it is clear that they are literary in nature, not historical reports. Consequently, the Fellows concluded that such stories in Acts cannot be claimed as historical. The rest of the story functions as an elaboration of the miracle story, told with great panache by Luke but without any claims to historical validity.

An interesting feature to the story is its allusion to the story of Baucis and Philemon as found in Ovid.[8] It is a story of an elderly couple of simple means who are visited by two strangers who ask for hospitality. The pious couple invites them in and feeds them the best they have. To their amazement, however, the meager portions they place on the table are miraculously increased in size. It is then that they realize that the two strangers are gods in disguise, namely Zeus and Hermes. The gods have tested them, and, having passed the test, they are rewarded lavishly. The surrounding village, however, is destroyed, because no one in the village would offer hospitality to the strangers. This story follows a popular story motif widely found in the ancient Mediterranean world; the Jewish version, about Abraham and Sarah, is found in Genesis 18–19. There were doubtless other versions (as suggested by Heb 13:2), but the reference here to Barnabas as Zeus and Paul as Hermes suggests an allusion to the Ovid story. Luke was widely read in ancient literature and made use of references from a variety of sources (see, for example, the cameo essays, "Prison Breaks in Luke's Literary World," p. 72; "When Apostles Become Philosophers," p. 60; and "Shipwrecks in Luke's Literary World, p. 313). This story is another such instance in which Luke has borrowed liberally from story models in the literature of the day. Even though he has replaced the hospitality theme with a miracle story, the theme of gods in disguise betrays this as a story that is indebted to literary models.

References
Smith, "Rethinking the Acts Story"

The Votes of the Fellows
Black/Improbable
- Acts provides historical evidence that Paul was a miracle worker.

Paul and Barnabas Return to Antioch

14 [21]Proclamation of the message in Derbe produced numerous followers. The two then made their way back through Lystra and Iconium to Antioch. [22]In each city they fortified the followers spiritually and encouraged them to remain firm in the faith. Their theme was: "There are many obstacles on the path to the dominion of God." [23]They also ordained presbyters in each community, who, after prayer and fasting, were commended to the Lord in whom they had placed their trust.

[24]The two passed through Pisidia and came to Pamphylia. [25]After proclaiming the message at Perga, they went down to Attalia [26]and sailed from there to Antioch, where they had been entrusted to God's grace for the activity that they had now completed. [27]On their arrival they assembled the community and reported all that God

had accomplished with them, in particular that God had opened a door of faith for the gentiles. [28]There they remained with the followers for a considerable time.

Comments on the Story

This section bears traces of being a summary, similar to those we met in the early chapters of Acts (see 2:42–47; 4:32–35; 5:12–16). But it adds some information we had not had before. Paul and Barnabas return to those cities they had just visited—Derbe, Lystra, Iconium, Pisidian Antioch—preaching the gospel and fortifying the believers. It is surprising that Luke has his heroes return to these locations so soon after the horrifying events that caused their departures, but there is no recurrence of such tribulations. The preceding narratives had left the impression that the number of converts in the individual locations was slim to none, but now we learn that communities were established in each place. The appointment of presbyters is intended to provide at least minimal organization for the fledgling communities, since the founding missionaries cannot remain in the area. The members of these churches are told that they must face persecution for the sake of the dominion of God. One wonders if they needed to be told this, since they had witnessed the persecution of Paul and Barnabas, but perhaps Luke fears that readers will think that only the leaders face such tribulation.

The return to Antioch in Syria completes the journey, and Paul and Barnabas announce that they have accomplished the task given them at the start of it (Acts 13:2–3). Although there was no explicit mention of a mission to Gentiles when Paul and Barnabas were commissioned, at the end of it the missionaries announced that "God had opened a door of faith for the gentiles" (14:27). The reader will recall that, for the most part, the door for the Gentiles was opened when most of the Jews rejected the message of Paul, but Luke clearly does not think of this as an accidental set of events. Paul had been designated as missionary to Gentiles (as well as to kings and Jews) as early as Acts 9:15. After Peter's report of the conversion of Cornelius, the apostles agreed that God had granted repentance to Gentiles (11:18), and here Paul and Barnabas make a similar claim after the mission in Asia Minor. The announcement in 14:27 is a celebratory acknowledgement that the purpose for which Paul had been converted has now been fulfilled. It also serves to set up the issue that Luke will have his characters face in the next chapter: the conditions under which Gentiles may be admitted to the community of Jesus believers.

In Search of History

This summary section provides a quick linkage in Luke's itinerary so as to bring Paul and Barnabas back to Antioch. The itinerary and its stories are all Luke's creation. They provide a setup for the event that will be recounted in Acts 15 in which Paul and Barnabas will report their success with the Gentiles to the leaders in Jerusalem. Luke derived the Jerusalem conference story from Paul and has created the narrative in chapters 13 and 14 to provide an appropriate prelude to the conference.

This text contains one other bit of data that should be noted. In the context of a summary statement that characterizes the regular missionary practice of Paul and Barnabas, Acts 14:23 says, "They also ordained presbyters in each community." As a title for a Christian leader, "presbyters" is a term that is first used in the late first and early second centuries (see 1 Tim 5:17, 19; Titus 1:5; 1 Pet 5:1, 5). It represents Christian leadership in the period when Luke writes, but is an anachronistic term for the Christian community in the late 40s, the time of Luke's story.

The Jerusalem Council

15 Some people from Judea arrived and began to teach the believers, "Unless you are circumcised in accordance with Mosaic practice, you cannot be saved." ²That claim set off a divisive partisan controversy in which Paul and Barnabas took a strong stand against the visitors' position. It was decided that those two, as well as some others, would go to Jerusalem to lay this conflict before the apostles and elders. ³After being sent off by the community, they journeyed through both Phoenicia and Samaria. Their detailed reports about the conversion of the gentiles became an occasion of great joy to all the believers who heard them. ⁴Once they arrived in Jerusalem they were welcomed by the community, the apostles, and the presbyters, to whom they reported all that God had accomplished with them. ⁵In response, some converts who belonged to the Pharisaic party stood up and insisted, "It is necessary to circumcise them and direct them to observe the Law of Moses."

⁶The apostles and the presbyters assembled to consider this matter. ⁷After a lengthy debate, Peter arose and said:

"My fellow believers, you are well aware that God long ago selected me from your number as the one from whose lips the gentiles would hear the gospel message and come to believe. ⁸God, who knows what humans really think and feel, approved of these gentiles by giving them the Holy Spirit that was also given to us. ⁹God, who purified their souls also by giving them the faith, made no distinctions between them and us. ¹⁰Why, therefore, are you now challenging God by imposing a burden upon his followers that neither we nor our forebears have been able to tolerate? ¹¹On the contrary, we believe that both we and they are saved by the grace of the Lord Jesus."

¹²The entire assembly listened in silence while Barnabas and Paul set out all the miracles and portents that God had performed for the gentiles through their agency. ¹³When they had finished, James said: "My fellow believers, please listen. ¹⁴Simeon has explained how God first acted to raise from the gentiles a people of God. ¹⁵With this understanding the utterances of the prophets are in agreement. Scripture says: ¹⁶'Thereafter I shall return and rebuild David's demolished dwelling; that which has been torn down I shall erect again. I shall restore that dwelling, ¹⁷so that the rest of humanity may seek out the Lord, even all the gentiles who belong to my people. Thus says the Lord who does these things, ¹⁸known since long, long ago.'

¹⁹"It is therefore my verdict that harassment of gentile converts cease, ²⁰but to direct them to abstain from idolatrous food, prohibited sexual relationships, and meat from animals that were strangled or not drained of blood. ²¹For Moses has always had his exponents and is read everywhere every week in every synagogue."

²²The apostles and presbyters then resolved, the entire community concurring, to send selected representatives to Antioch with Paul and Barnabas. Those chosen were Judas Barsabbas and Silas, two leading believers. ²³They were to deliver the following letter:

"Dear gentile brothers and sisters in Antioch, Syria, and Cilicia: ²⁴Inasmuch as it has come to our attention that some of our number have been causing trouble for you by making, without our authorization, subversive assertions, ²⁵we have unanimously resolved to select delegates and send them to you along with our well-beloved Barnabas and Paul, ²⁶who have devoted their lives to the name of our Lord Jesus Christ. ²⁷The delegates we have sent are Judas and Silas. They will personally provide oral confirmation of our decision. ²⁸For we, with the Holy Spirit, have resolved to impose upon you no obligation beyond the following essentials: ²⁹to abstain from foods that have been offered to idols or contain blood or have been killed by strangling, as well as from prohibited sexual relationships. You will be in good standing if you avoid these things.

Best Wishes, Your brothers and sisters, The Apostles and the Elders."

³⁰The delegates were sent on their way and traveled to Antioch, where they called a meeting of the full community, at which they delivered the letter. ³¹After it had been read aloud, the believers were delighted with the reassurance it conveyed. ³²Both Judas and Silas were prophets. They edified the believers with a great deal of spiritual comfort and sustenance. ³³The two spent some time there and were then sent back, with the community's blessing, to those who had dispatched them. ³⁵Paul and Barnabas, however, remained in Antioch and continued to teach and preach, along with many others, the message about the Lord.

Comments on the Story

Acts 15 tells of a very important meeting of apostles and elders in Jerusalem at which an agreement is reached about the requirements for Gentile salvation. It is interesting to note that requirements for Jewish admission to the Christian movement did not become an issue. The meeting was precipitated by vigorous controversy as to the necessity of male circumcision. Paul and Barnabas are leading contenders on the side against imposing the requirement, and they are sent from Antioch to Jerusalem to meet with the apostles and elders and to reach an authoritative solution to the problem. At the meeting Peter speaks against the requirement, supported by Paul and Barnabas, and then James announces that only four requirements are to be imposed on Gentile believers. This decision meets with the unanimous approval of the apostles, presbyters, and members of the community, and it is communicated by letter to believers in the North.

An attentive reader may be confused when encountering Acts 15. One may well wonder if the issue of circumcision had not already been settled. After all, in Acts 11:18 the apostles had affirmed the acceptance of Gentiles, and there was no mention of circumcision. The missionary efforts of Paul and Barnabas in Asia Minor (Acts 13–14) brought in more Gentiles, and nothing was said about specific requirements. Now we hear of certain believers in Antioch and of Pharisaic believers in Jerusalem demanding that male Gentile believers be circumcised. Moreover, although the meeting in Jerusalem is said to be about the necessity of circumcision, the judgment that is reached at the end of the meeting seems to ignore this issue.

Some scholars think that things are a bit out of order here or that Luke has misunderstood the nature of the controversy. Paul, in Galatians 2, told of a similar controversy, but it was about Gentile and Jewish believers eating together, not about requirements for salvation (see the cameo essay, "What Really Happened at the Jerusalem Council?" p. 173). It is likely that Luke used the Pauline material in Galatians but intentionally shaped the narrative to support his own literary and theological purposes.

Luke's purposes may be discerned by observing some of the dominant themes in the book as a whole. Two of those themes are at work in the narrative before us: (1) the divine authorization of the Gentile mission; and (2) the fidelity of the Jesus movement to Jewish traditions and practices. In Acts 15 these themes nearly collide with one another.

1. The divine authorization of the Gentile mission has been a prominent theme in several sections of Acts that we have already observed. One need only be reminded of the story of Peter and Cornelius (Acts 10:1–11:18) and of the mission of Paul and Barnabas in chapters 13–14. Divine guidance dominates these narratives as God communicates his purposes through visions and miracles. As early as the narrative about the conversion of Saul we learn that he was chosen by God to bring the gospel to Gentiles (as well as to Jews and rulers, see Acts 9:15).

It is incontestable that the inclusion of Gentiles is a dominant theme in Acts 15. Their inclusion is shown to be a cause of rejoicing in Phoenicia and Samaria (Acts 15:3) and, by implication, among the apostles and presbyters in Jerusalem (15:4). Peter reminds the group of his role in converting the first Gentiles, and he argues that this should be a model for subsequent Gentile conversions, since God granted them the Holy Spirit in the same way as with the original apostles and since God made no distinctions (15:7–11). No additional burdens should be imposed, Peter maintains. Paul and Barnabas follow Peter and tell of the signs and wonders done among Gentiles (15:12). Clearly the inclusion of Gentiles in the believing community is intended by Luke to be seen as a positive factor and is in accord with divine authorization. God set aside Peter to present the gospel to Gentiles, gave the spirit to Cornelius, and underscored the work of Paul and Barnabas with signs and wonders. Divine leadership of the community is shown also by James's reference to Scripture and his interpretation that the quotation from Amos 9:11 accords with the inclusion of Gentiles in the believing community.

2. Fidelity to Jewish traditions and practices has also been stressed in preceding narratives, especially in the early chapters of Acts. The believers gathered in the temple (see Acts 2:46; 5:12), the central setting for many of Luke's episodes (see also Acts 3:1–3, 8, 10; 4:1; 5:20–22, 24–26, 42). The participation of the apostles in the temple ritual is assumed. Peter and John go there "at the time of the 1500 [3:00 p.m.] service" (3:1), where they heal a man who had been lame from birth. Peter speaks in Solomon's portico (3:11), which subsequently becomes a regular meeting place (5:12). We have also noted that, in the narratives in Acts 13–14, Paul and Barnabas almost invariably begin their missions with visits to the synagogue, telling us that the gospel is intended for Jews first of all. The theme of fidelity to Jewish traditions and practices appears also in the narratives that follow Acts 15, and we shall note them when we come to these passages.

Despite his positive treatment of the inclusion of Gentiles, Luke seems intent in Acts 15 on stressing the Jewish character of the believing community. This is the case despite the fact that there is controversy about the requirement of circumcision for Gentiles and despite Peter's puzzling characterization of Torah observance as an unbearable yoke (Acts 15:10). To be sure, the resolution announced by James (15:20, 29) is depicted as not troubling to Gentiles, but it nevertheless constitutes the minimal retention of significant requirements from Torah. It is misleading to think of Acts 15 as maintaining Gentile freedom from the law. We should rather think of it as an illustration of the Lukan stress on the believing community's fidelity to Jewish traditions and practices and should underscore the point that the four requirements—"to abstain from idolatrous food, prohibited sexual relationships, and meat from animals that were strangled or not drained of blood" (15:20)—are set forth by Luke as minimal Jewish practices for Gentile believers. Luke seems intent that the requirements in the decree be understood as Torah for Gentiles. The decree does not abolish the distinction between Jew and Gentile, since circumcision is not required for the latter, but it binds believing Gentiles to adhere to that part of Torah that is meant for them (see the cameo essay, "The So-Called Noahide Laws," p. 175).

We are to conclude that the Jerusalem conference determined that, although it is not mentioned in the decree, circumcision and adherence to the entire Torah are not to be required of Gentile believers. But adherence to certain observances is requisite.

Precisely what the decree requires is not, however, clear. Our translation suggests that three items in it relate to Jewish dietary regulations: one may not eat food offered to idols, meat from an animal that had been strangled, or meat that contained blood. The other item "prohibited sexual relations" translates the Greek word, *porneia*, the root of the English term, pornography. The word clearly denotes sexual relations and may designate appropriate degrees of marriage, but it probably is best to understand it as prohibiting those sexual relationships that were understood to violate the commandment against adultery (see Exod 20:14). Further, the prohibition of blood may, rather than alluding to a dietary regulation, be a way of citing the commandment against murder (see Exod 20:13). Some early versions of the decree add the obligation to observe the golden rule (see Luke 6:31). The precise meaning of the decree may never become clear, but we may at least say that Luke intends for readers to understand that Gentile Christians are under obligation to remain faithful to some minimal Jewish observances.

Acts 15 also contains a puzzling feature about the leadership of the Jerusalem community. We know that the author of Acts stressed the unity and harmony of the believing community as exemplified by the leadership of the apostles. Apostolic leadership was important in a number of passages in Acts, as we have observed. In Acts 15, although the apostles are included among the leadership group, they are accompanied by the presbyters, heretofore unmentioned. More surprising, however, is the role of James in Acts 15. In the way Luke organizes the Jerusalem conference, it appears that James is the unchallenged leader: Peter, a real apostle, is allowed to speak first, but it is James who announces the decision; Paul and Barnabas present their case, but we do not learn what they actually say. The focus is on James, who settles the issue by quoting from Scripture, adding an obscure interpretation, and announcing the requirements expected of Gentile believers. Luke tells us nothing about this James, but it is important to note that he is not, in Luke's terms, an apostle. Recall that an apostle of the same name had been executed in Acts 12:2. Most scholars identify the James of Acts 15 with the brother of the Lord, who is known from the letters of Paul (see Gal 1:19; 2:9, 12; 1 Cor 15:7).

Pervo's translation of Acts 15:19 suggests that James is the authoritative spokesperson not only for the Jerusalem church but for the church as a whole: "It is therefore my verdict ..." Some scholars prefer a translation that suggests that James is announcing a consensus of the apostles, presbyters, and members. In either case, the emergence of a non-apostolic leader in Jerusalem is surprising. The only note that might prepare the reader for this surprise is the statement of Peter in Acts 12:17, where he directed that James be informed of his miraculous release from prison. It is reasonable to conclude that Luke knows about a changing of the guard in Jerusalem but does not wish to focus attention on the circumstances that led to the change. That the change is not a temporary one is shown by the fact that neither Peter nor any other apostle appears again in Acts and that, when next we have a narrative located in Jerusalem, the leaders are James and the presbyters (see Acts 21:18–25).

At the end of this narrative we meet two new characters—Silas and Judas Barsabbas—who accompany Paul and Barnabas back to Antioch with the letter from the Jerusalem church. Their task is to explain the Jerusalem decision and encourage the believers. Later in Acts, Silas will take the place of Barnabas as Paul's leading associate, but we will not hear again of Judas Barsabbas. Interestingly, the same nickname, Barsabbas, is given to one Joseph, who lost out to Matthias in the election to replace Judas Iscariot as the twelfth apostle (see Acts 1:23).

The significance of this incident for the author of Acts is demonstrated by the way he prepares for it and especially by the repetition of the decree. It appears first in the announcement of James (Acts 15:20) and again, in nearly identical wording, in the letter that was sent to Antioch, Syria, and Cilicia (15:29). It will be quoted once more in Acts 21:25. It appears that Luke does not want his readers to miss the point: Gentile believers need not be circumcised and committed to total Torah observance, but their fidelity to minimal practices must not be compromised.

In Search of History

There *was* an actual conference in Jerusalem. We know this because Paul tells us about it in Gal 2:1–10. Scholars once thought that Acts was an independent account of the same conference from another perspective. Now we know better. The arguments are summarized in the cameo essay "What Really Happened at the Jerusalem Council?" by William O. Walker, Jr. (pp. 173).

As pointed out in the cameo essay, our knowledge about the Jerusalem conference must be based entirely on Paul. Once one concludes that Acts used Paul for this account, it becomes difficult to identify any other sources used by Acts. Based on the information in Paul, there was widespread agreement among the Fellows about the fact of the conference and the probable leading figures who took part. The nature of the meeting and its conclusions also derive from Paul, yet, as noted in the cameo essay, even Paul must sometimes be taken with a grain of salt. Because of this unpredictable aspect to Paul's story, the Fellows struggled to define the historical probability of some components of the event.

The nature of this event has implications for how we view the nature of early Christian communities and their leaders. Many components of the Acts story seem clearly to have been composed by Luke to fit his apologetic goals. For example, like other Christian community meetings in Acts, the Acts version of the meeting is marked by agreement and concord, in contrast to the tensions and conflicts that are prominent in Paul's story. In addition, what Paul reveals, and Luke tries to gloss over, was an inherent tension early on among prominent leaders in the nascent Christian community about the place of Gentiles in the movement.

The Votes of the Fellows
Red/Probable
- A meeting was held in Jerusalem in the mid-to-late 40s to address the issue of Gentile Christians and circumcision/other issues of Torah.
- Paul, Barnabas, James, Peter, and at least one other group ("false brothers/Pharisees") were at the center of a multi-sided conversation in Jerusalem that took place at that meeting.
- The meeting was memorable for its coming to terms with major differences concerning the participation of Gentiles in activities related to those invoking the name(s) of Jesus/Christ.
- At points in the meeting Paul, Peter, James, the "false brothers" and/or "Pharisees," and Barnabas all had different notions of how Jews and Gentiles should be together within the movement(s).

- The account of a church meeting at Jerusalem in Acts 15 needs to be read within the context of other community meetings described by Luke.
- The community meetings described in Acts serve the narrative structure and theological agenda of the book.
- Luke promotes a picture of Christian meetings as cohesive assemblies willing to endorse the decisions of their leaders.
- The early Jesus community was less harmonious than the author of Acts pictures it to be.
- There was competition among the leaders of the early Jesus community.
- The history of the early Jesus movement was marked by internal conflicts, struggles for leadership positions, and policy disagreements.

Pink/Possible
- There was an effective conclusion or agreement which came out of the meeting.
- Peter and James were accommodating enough to the perspectives of Paul and Barnabas at least to continue conversation and hospitality, a convention whose favor was returned by Paul and Barnabas at Antioch (but which in that very process broke down).
- Peter and James disagreed on some matters concerning Gentile participation.
- Paul and Barnabas disagreed on some matters concerning Gentile participation.
- Paul broke off conversation with the group he called the "false brothers."

Gray/Doubtful
- Acts 15:1–35 was based on an unwritten tradition.
- The purpose of the meeting was more dialogue and less agreement.

Black/Improbable
- Acts 15:1–21 was based on a written source.
- Acts 15:22–29 was based on a written source.

The unusual nature of the "decree" regarding dietary laws, which is found only in Acts, deserves special comment and is analyzed in the cameo essay, "The So-Called Noahide Laws," by Nina Livesey.

As pointed out in the cameo essay, Paul showed no familiarity with the dietary restrictions on Gentiles as contained in the Acts account. At numerous points in his letters, he addressed meals of Christian communities without reference to dietary restrictions. For example, in Rom 14:1–15:13, he referred to a community meal that included both Jewish Christians and Gentile Christians. He acknowledged the dietary restrictions of the Jewish Christians and urged that the Gentile Christians practice hospitality by allowing for variations in the menu, not by adopting a common menu. Consequently, the Acts account of a Jerusalem council "decree" regarding Gentile diet cannot be considered historical. The origin of the decree, whether it derived from a post-Pauline context in early Christianity or whether it derived from Luke, is yet to be determined.

References

    Winter, "Antioch in Acts"
    Kea, "Source Theories"
    Pervo, "Community Meetings"
    Segal, "Acts 15 as Jewish and Christian History"
    Taussig, "Jerusalem as Occasion"
    Tyson, "Themes at the Crossroads"
    Smith, "Two Speeches and a Letter"

The Votes of the Fellows

Black/Improbable
- The issuing of a "decree" at the Jerusalem meeting specifying the four laws for the Gentiles is historical.

What Really Happened at the Jerusalem Council?
A Cameo Essay by William O. Walker, Jr.

Both Acts 15:1–21 and Gal 2:1–10 report a gathering in Jerusalem involving Paul, Barnabas, and leaders of the Jesus movement in Jerusalem, at which a controversy regarding circumcision of Gentile converts was decided in favor of Paul's argument that such circumcision not be required. There are major differences between the accounts, but most scholars agree that both refer to the same event, which is often labeled the "Jerusalem Council." Because Paul was present at the gathering but the author of Acts presumably was not, Gal 2:1–10 is the primary source for what happened, and Acts 15:1–21 is, at best, a secondary source. Recently, however, the Acts Seminar has concluded that the major—and perhaps the only—source for Acts 15:1–21 is in fact Gal 2:1–10 and that differences between the two accounts stem solely from the theological/apologetic agenda of Acts and imaginative literary artistry of its author. Thus, Gal 2:1–10 is the *only* historical source for "what really happened" at the Jerusalem Council.

According to Gal 2:1–10, Paul went to Jerusalem with Barnabas "in response to divine direction," and they were accompanied by Titus. Paul privately discussed with "those who were reputed to be leaders" the gospel he was preaching among the Gentiles, and, despite opposition from some "pretending friendship," his gospel was approved by "those who were reputed to be leaders," Titus, a Greek, was not compelled to be circumcised, and "the reputed pillars" (James, Cephas, and John) gave Paul and Barnabas "the right hand of fellowship" that the latter should go to the Gentiles and the former to the circumcised. The only stipulation was that Paul and Barnabas "remember the poor," which, Paul says, he was eager to do.

We cannot assume, however, that Gal 2:1–10 reports the facts exactly as they occurred. There was a lapse of time between the Jerusalem Council and the writing of Galatians, and, given the frailties and propensities of human memory, Paul may well have forgotten some of what happened (see 1 Cor 1:14–16, where he acknowledges a failure of memory), he may have "remembered" things that did not happen, and he certainly would have interpreted what happened (or what he remembered as having happened) in light of his subsequent experience. Human memory—including Paul's—is never a completely reliable guide to what happened in the past. Moreover, we must keep in mind Paul's own theological/apologetic agenda in Galatians and his rhetorical strategies for promoting this agenda. He wishes to persuade his readers that obedience to the Law, and particularly circumcision, is not necessary for salvation. Everything in the letter, including the autobiographical materials, is subordinated to this goal. Anything that might be extraneous or stand in the way of achieving this goal is, no doubt, simply omitted or perhaps altered. In short, we really do not know exactly what happened at the Jerusalem Council. We have only Paul's report, and it is surely both incomplete and anything but unbiased.

Two or more generations later, the author of Acts alters what Paul wrote in order to promote a quite different theological/apologetic agenda—namely, that of downplaying any conflict between Paul and other leaders of the Jesus movement and drawing Paul into the mainstream of an emerging "Proto-Catholic" consensus.

Whereas Paul reported that he went up to Jerusalem "in response to divine direction," Acts says that Paul, Barnabas, and others were appointed (presumably by leaders of the Jesus movement in Antioch) to go to Jerusalem and consult with the apostles and elders. Whereas Paul reported that Titus accompanied him along with Barnabas and, apparently, that Titus figured prominently in the circumcision debate, Acts says simply that "some others" went with Paul and Barnabas, making no mention of Titus. Whereas Paul reported that he met "in private" with "those who were reputed to be leaders" (apparently James, Cephas, and John), Acts says that Paul, Barnabas, and the others met with "the apostles and elders." Whereas Paul reported no speeches at the meeting, Acts includes speeches by Peter and James, with James delivering the decisive pronouncement. Whereas Paul reported that he and Barnabas were admonished to "remember the poor," Acts makes no mention of this admonition. Most significantly, whereas Paul claimed a clear victory for himself and Barnabas so far as circumcision was concerned, Acts reports something of a compromise: circumcision will not be required, but Gentile converts must "abstain from idolatrous food, prohibited sexual relations, and meat from animals that were strangled or not drained of blood" (Acts 15:20). In short, Acts 15:1–21 is an altered and embellished rewriting of Gal 2:1–10.

The So-Called Noahide Laws

A Cameo Essay by Nina E. Livesey

Three times Acts (15:20, 29; 21:25) informs its hearers and readers of laws the Jerusalem apostles and elders require of Gentiles. These laws are commonly called the "Apostolic Decree" and include the abstention from idolatrous food, from prohibited sexual relationships, from animal meat that was strangled, and from blood. The prohibition against blood is ambiguous: it could either refer to meat that contains blood or to bloodshed. The former meaning is more likely correct because in each of the three narrations of the Apostolic Decree, the Greek words for strangled and blood occur side-by-side, suggestive of their association. Furthermore, the sense of eating blood of animals relates well to the other prohibitions in that they all directly or indirectly refer to idolatry. The laws of the Decree emerge from the context of a discussion that was underway about how Gentiles may be saved (Act 15:1). The pronouncement of these laws is anomalous because in another and earlier account of Paul's meeting with Jerusalem apostles, the source for the Acts report, there is no mention of any laws required of Gentiles; there is only the suggestion that they remember the poor (see Gal 2:1–10).

If the earlier account of Paul's meeting in Jerusalem does not discuss these laws, from where do they derive? Did the author of Acts draw on an authoritative predefined list of Jewish laws set aside for Gentiles? Such an assumption is highly unlikely, since, so far as we know, no such list was in existence at that time. The earliest known codification of Jewish laws pertaining to Gentiles, the Noahide laws, is found in the third-century *Tosefta*,[9] a text that post-dates Acts by a full century or more. The text reads as follows:

> Seven commandments were the sons of Noah commanded: (1) concerning adjudication (*dinim*), (2) and concerning idolatry (*avodah zarah*), (3) and concerning blasphemy (*qilelat ha-shem*), (4) and concerning sexual immorality (*giluy arayot*), (5) and concerning bloodshed (*shefikhut damim*), (6) and concerning robbery (*ha-gezel*), (7) and concerning a limb torn from a living animal (*eber min ha-hayy*).[10]

Unlike the laws of the Apostolic Decree, the Noahide laws were intended more generically for all humanity, and not strictly for Gentile salvation or conversion. They were to serve as "natural laws," which any just person could be expected to follow. As is evident, there is only a loose connection between the laws in the *Tosefta* and the laws in Acts. The laws in Acts are not only fewer in number, but also—with their emphasis on those things not to be consumed—pertain primarily to issues of ritual purity. The prohibition against blood probably concerns its consumption rather than the act of taking the life of another human being.

While it is improbable that Luke drew on the Noahide laws as found in the *Tosefta*, a likely source for the Apostolic Decree is the Levitical laws, intended to apply to non-Jews who reside among Jews. These laws have many points in common with those mentioned in Acts. According to Leviticus, Jews as well as non-Jews were to abstain from offering sacrifices to other gods (Lev 17:7), from eating blood, especially that of animals (Lev 17:10–15), from incest, and from adultery (Lev 18:6–20). Leviticus also refers to the avoidance of things torn by wild animals (Lev 17:15) which connects with the notion of strangulation mentioned in Acts 15:20. The Hebrew word for strangulation is *terefah* and refers to meat that wild beasts have hunted (*preyed-upon meat*). The laws in Acts, like the Levitical laws, discuss a combination of ritual and moral obligations. In addition, the laws in Leviticus resonate with the laws in

Acts in that they allude to salvation: they come with the warning that those who do not heed them will be utterly destroyed (Lev 17:9, 14; 18:29).

The laws in Acts, with which Paul shows no familiarity, conform to Luke's overall purpose. Like the author's other and numerous references to things Jewish, the synagogue, and Jerusalem, they serve rhetorically to create a sense of continuity with Judaism, a bridge between the ancient and respected religion and the emerging Christ-believing sect.

The World of Acts: Chapters 13–20

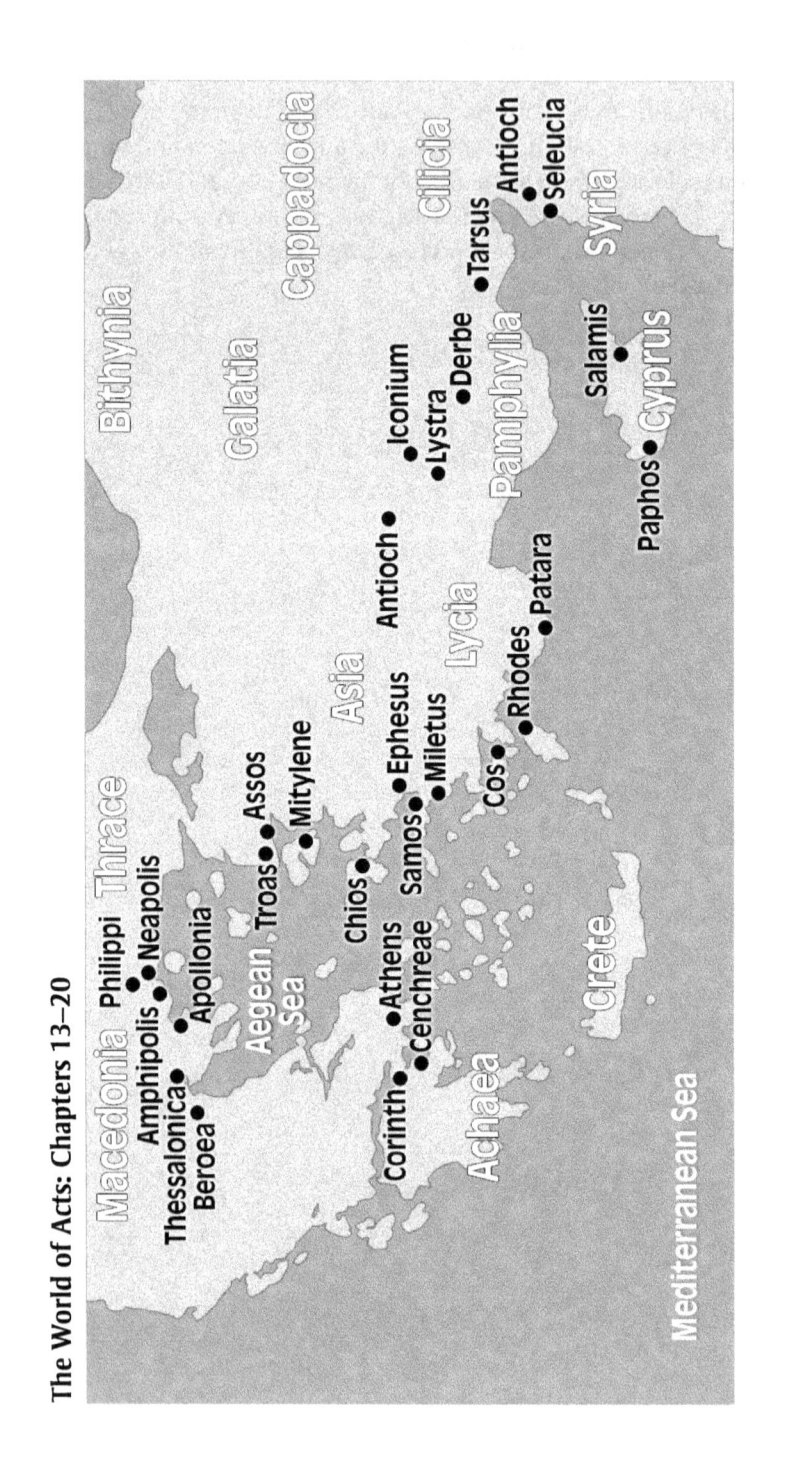

4
Paul in Asia and Greece
Acts 15:36–19:41

Paul and Barnabas Separate

15 ³⁶Some days later Paul said to Barnabas: "Let us go back and visit the believers in every single city where we proclaimed the message about the Lord so that we may see how they are faring." ³⁷Barnabas wanted to take John Mark along with them, too, ³⁸but Paul was of the view that they should not take him along, since he had abandoned them in Pamphylia rather than remain with them on their task. ³⁹There ensued a quarrel that ended with their separation. Barnabas set sail with Mark for Cyprus, ⁴⁰while Paul chose Silas and, after the believers had commended him to the Lord's gracious care, set out. ⁴¹He proceeded through Syria and Cilicia, fortifying the communities.

Comments on the Story

This is clearly a transitional section in Acts. It moves the action from the decisions of the Jerusalem Council to the resumption of Paul's missionary travels. It is, however, an important transition, marking a significant change of personnel. In the mission narrated in Acts 14, the main actors were Paul and Barnabas; in what follows the focus will be on Paul, supported by Silas.

Luke seems to be aware that the breakup of Paul and Barnabas was the result of a sharp disagreement between them. In Galatians, Paul characterized the disagreement as theological, involving questions about Jewish and Gentile believers eating together. Peter, he says, ate with Gentiles, but withdrew from this practice when representatives from James arrived in Antioch. Paul writes that "even Barnabas was carried away by their duplicity" (Gal 2:13). Although Paul does not explicitly state that this precipitated a breakup of the two, he characterizes Barnabas as siding with the opposition. Luke chose to suppress this information, which he obtained from

Galatians, and elected to portray the cause of the breakup as Paul's suspicion of John Mark's reliability.

Despite the disagreement with Galatians, the story in Acts hangs together quite remarkably. Readers may have wondered about the previous references to John Mark. He first appeared in the story of Peter's remarkable release from prison. The believers were meeting in John Mark's mother's house in Jerusalem, where Peter surprisingly turned up (see Acts 12:12). Then when Paul and Barnabas left Jerusalem for Antioch, they took John Mark with them (12:25). He accompanied the two missionaries on their journey through Cyprus (13:5) but, when they arrived in Perga, in Pamphylia, he returned to Jerusalem (13:13). No explanation was given there of Mark's return, and the reader is left to wonder about it. Even here in Acts 15:38, the Lukan Paul does not cite the cause, but he has no hesitation in pronouncing it to be an act of desertion. Indeed, Luke, departing from his usual habit of downplaying inner-Christian controversy, states that the disagreement between Paul and Barnabas was sharp and led to the separation of the two missionaries. Further, Luke uses a word for desertion that was also used in early Christian writings to designate apostasy, i.e., the denial of one's faith.

The breakup, however, does not diminish the mission in any way. Barnabas and Mark go to Cyprus, and Paul and Silas to Syria and Cilicia. Silas, the reader will recall, was one of the delegates chosen by the Jerusalem church to accompany Paul and Barnabas to Antioch, Syria, and Cilicia, and to deliver the decree of the Council (Acts 15:22). Luke had told how he and Judas Barsabbas had done much to encourage and strengthen the believers (15:32). In the narratives that follow, Silas will accompany Paul in successful evangelism and painful persecution.

This is the last we will hear of Barnabas and Mark (and Judas Barsabbas) in the book of Acts, and this transition section prepares for this change as well. Luke simply notes that one pair sails off to Cyprus, but all his attention is focused on the other pair. Paul and Silas receive the support of the congregation at Antioch, and the author follows their movements thereafter. In fact, however, the author almost loses sight of Silas at this point. It is Paul and Silas who set out in Acts 15:40, but in the following verse it is *he*, i.e., Paul, who goes through Syria and Cilicia.

In Search of History

This text presents Luke's version of Paul's split with Barnabas. That there was a split he could have surmised from Gal 2:13, where

Paul refers to a serious theological difference between Paul and Barnabas. Luke creates another reason for their split. He introduces two minor characters into the story, Mark and Silas. Mark's connection with Barnabas is likely derived from Col 4:10, where Mark is identified as the cousin of Barnabas, an identification that Luke does not use. Silas is perhaps Luke's version of Silvanus, who appears frequently in the epistles as a co-worker with Paul and, along with Timothy, is part of Paul's mission activities in Greece (see 2 Cor 1:19; 1 Thess 1:1–2; 2 Thess 1:1). The overall story functions to establish a turning point in Paul's status as a missionary. Whereas up to this point he was identified by his association with Barnabas, now he is on his own. These components of the narrative, from Paul's explanation for distrusting Mark to the change in Paul's status in relation to Barnabas, all relate to the underlying structure that is unique to Acts. Since these details are so closely connected with Luke's narrative, there is no reason to think that any of this is historical.

Paul, Silas, and Timothy to Lystra and Derbe

16 In due course Paul also reached Derbe and Lystra. At Lystra there was a follower of Jesus named Timothy, the son of a believing Jewish woman and a gentile. ²The believers in Lystra and Iconium gave Timothy good recommendations. Paul resolved to have this man accompany him. ³He accepted Timothy as a colleague and circumcised him because of the Jews in those parts, all of whom were quite aware that Timothy's father had been a gentile. ⁴As they went about the various cities, they delivered the decrees promulgated by the apostles and elders in Jerusalem and instructed people to abide by them. ⁵The communities were strengthened in the faith and grew daily in number.

Comments on the Story

As this narrative begins, we are led to expect a resumption of Paul's missionary travels. He seems intent on revisiting the scenes of his previous missions, Derbe and Lystra. But the focus suddenly shifts to highlight a surprising incident. A believer named Timothy is introduced, and there is a detailed notice about his parents: his mother is a Jewish believer, and his father a Greek, presumably an adherent of traditional Greco-Roman religion. In terms of the narrative flow, it would appear that both mother and son had been converted by Paul on his previous visit to Lystra (Acts 14:8–20). In the meantime, Timothy had become well known in his hometown and the surrounding area. Paul's interest in Timothy as a potential co-missionary is not surprising, but his willingness to have him circumcised is very perplexing.

To readers of the Pauline letters, the circumcision of Timothy would appear to be a violation of Paul's deepest principles. But Luke has already subverted some aspects of the Pauline letters, and he may be doing so here as well (see comments on Acts 15:1–35). In Gal 2:3, the Greek Titus was not compelled to be circumcised, but in Acts 16:3 Paul seems to require it of the mixed-breed Timothy. Alternatively, Luke may have been influenced by an allusion to a rumor that he found in Gal 5:11. This verse reflects a charge that Paul continued to practice circumcision, whether in respect to Jewish or Gentile believers is not stated. Perhaps Luke believed the charge was true.

Even in Acts, Luke had shown that Paul was opposed to the imposition of circumcision on male Gentile believers. He and Barnabas had engaged in debate on this topic in Antioch (see Acts 15:1–2). But was Timothy—whose mother was Jewish and whose father was Gentile—regarded as a Gentile or a Jew? It is frequently asserted that Jewish practice was matrilineal, that is, a child's religion would be that of the mother, so that sons of Jewish mothers would normally be circumcised. In this case, Timothy would have been regarded as Jewish. But recent studies have suggested that, although this is the current practice among Jews, it does not go back to the early centuries.[1]

In any case, Luke does not cite such alleged Jewish practices. Rather he maintains that Paul circumcised Timothy because of the Jews in Lystra. Although this does little to clarify the episode, it reveals to the reader something about Luke's literary intentions. These intentions will become clearer when we examine the narratives that tell of Paul's trials (Acts 21–28). A major issue in the trials is Paul's attitude toward Jewish beliefs and practices, and Luke will there have him defend himself as a faithful Jew and devout Pharisee. Although the circumcision of Timothy is not cited in the trial narratives, it nevertheless prepares the way for the Lukan defense of Paul. Indeed, in Acts 21:21, James calls attention to a widespread belief that Paul teaches "all Diaspora Jews to renounce the Law of Moses, telling them that they should stop circumcising their sons or observe our practices." Luke certainly thinks this charge is false, and later in Acts 21 he shows how Paul countered it. But Luke also subverts it here. Whether or not matrilineal descent was observed as early as the time of Acts, the author regarded Timothy as Jewish, and he wanted to avoid any suspicion that Paul was against the circumcision of male Jews. Luke seems willing to go to any extreme to dispute a portrayal of Paul such as that of Marcion, in which Paul is believed to be opposed to all things Jewish. Thus, he includes Acts 16:3 so that the reader will be prepared to recognize the anti-Pauline charge of 21:21 to be patently false.

Acts 16:4–5 confirms the image of Paul in the previous verses. He continues to support the decision of the Jerusalem conference, which, as the reader will recall, required Gentile believers to adhere to certain Jewish regulations (Acts 15:20, 29). To be sure, the Lukan Paul is brave, adventurous, and religiously zealous. But the adjective, "conservative," would be an appropriate addition to the list.

In Search of History

This story presents data about Timothy that is not found anywhere in Paul's letters but nevertheless appears to be a variation of a text from Paul. As argued by William O. Walker, Jr., and Richard Pervo,[2] this narrative is parallel in many respects to a similar story in Paul's version of the Jerusalem conference, only with the opposite purpose. Paul's story is about Titus, who is identified as a Greek ("Hellene") and whose identity in the narration is closely tied to that of Paul. He was not compelled to be circumcised even though some, "pretending friendship," wanted that to happen (Gal 2:3–5). Luke omits that story from his version of the Jerusalem conference but uses its bits and pieces to create this story. Here it is Timothy whom Paul chose to accompany him (Greek: "with him") and whose father is a Greek ("Hellene"). Paul chooses to have him circumcised "because of the Jews in those parts." It is striking that the story is all about Paul's decision, not Timothy's. Timothy would clearly have had this identity all his life, so why be circumcised only now? The answer, of course, is that Luke's Timothy is created to appear in this scene and serve a narrative role in Acts. The Timothy whom Luke creates is a hybrid, part Greek and part Jewish, making him in a sense a narrative stand-in for the hybridity of the church in Luke's story. At this point in the narrative, Paul's task is to present to all of his Gentile churches the decree about following the Jewish food laws, and for this task Luke's Timothy is an ideal companion.

The same *modus operandi* can be seen in Luke's Gospel, when he takes Mark's story of the anointing of Jesus at a meal by an unnamed woman, relocates it, and reconstructs it to tell a different story (compare Luke 7:36–50 and Mark 14:3–9), or when he does the same with Mark's version of Jesus' rejection at Nazareth (compare Luke 4:16–30 and Mark 6:1–6).

Because the story is crafted out of data found in Paul but reconstructed to fit Luke's purposes in Acts and at the same time to contradict Paul, it was judged by the Fellows to be nonhistorical.

References
Livesey, "Circumcision"
Walker, "The Timothy-Titus Problem"
Pervo, *Dating Acts*, 86–88.

The Votes of the Fellows
Red/Probable
- Luke's Paul bends to the wishes of the Jews.
- Luke creates a Paul who continues to engage in Jewish practices.

Gray/Doubtful
- The theme of matrilineal descent in Acts 16:1–5 identifies the text as a product of the second century.

Black/Improbable
- Paul had Timothy circumcised.

A Vision Sends Paul to Macedonia
16 ⁶They then traversed Phrygia and Galatian territory because the Holy Spirit had vetoed proclamation of the message in the province of Asia. ⁷When they were near the eastern border of Mysia, they attempted to travel north toward Bithynia, but the Spirit of Jesus would not allow them to do so. ⁸So they skirted Mysia and came to Troas. ⁹There came to Paul at night a vision of a Macedonian man. He stood imploring Paul: "Come over to Macedonia and help us!" ¹⁰Because of this vision, we, convinced that God had called us to preach the good news to the Macedonians, immediately set about finding a way to get there.

Comments on the Story

The directional terms in our translation of Acts 16:7, above, are supplied so as to help the reader understand what is going on. But, in the end, our translator, Richard Pervo, comments, "The route of travel proposed all but defies rational analysis."[3] Modern maps may help, but we should keep in mind that Luke did not have access to them. Further, even if we can find his designations on maps, it is unclear whether he understood these terms—Phrygia, Galatia, Bithynia, Mysia—as denoting political entities or less well-defined ethnic locations. Probably the best we can say is that Paul and company were headed in a westerly direction and ended up in Troas. Beyond locating Paul's Macedonian vision in Troas, Luke makes no effort to call attention to the significance of the city and its associations with ancient Troy, known to readers from the Homeric epics.

The geographical notes may be perplexing, but the stress in these verses on the divine guidance given to Paul in the extension of his mission is abundantly clear. Luke suggests that the Holy Spirit (Acts 16:6) and the Spirit of Jesus (16:7) thwarted Paul's intentions to preach in Asia and Bithynia. Luke does not wish to tell us how these omens were revealed, but when he locates Paul in Troas, he tells of a vision: a Macedonian man appears to Paul and pleads for help (16:9). The negative directions given by the Holy Spirit and the Spirit of Jesus (which here must designate the same thing) finally give way to a positive calling, and the direction of the Pauline mission becomes clear: he is to cross the Aegean and go to Macedonia. From one perspective, this crossing is momentous in that it signifies a continental move from Asia to Europe. Although he must have regarded the entry into Macedonia as significant, Luke may not have seen it in terms that impress us moderns. In his day the political unity of the Greco-Roman world was manifest. Despite the ethnic diversity of the many locales that Paul might visit, he will nevertheless find Greek-speaking Jews and Gentiles in Macedonia, as well as in Greece and Italy.

In Acts 16:10 the narration suddenly changes from third person to first person. Here is the first of the so-called "we"-passages (16:10–17; see also 20:5–16; 21:1–18; and 27:1–28:16). The vision of the Macedonian man appears only to Paul, but its interpretation is not left to him alone. "We" decide on its meaning. Just who is included among the interpreters is not clear. Paul and the narrator must be among them, but the total number is never stated, and the identity of the narrator is never provided. The we-passages in Acts constitute a notorious problem. See more on this issue below and in the cameo essay, "We-Passages in the Acts of the Apostles," p. 191, by Dennis MacDonald.

In Search of History

This text is clearly embedded in the Lukan theme of divine guidance for all major events in the story, most notably the Gentile mission. In keeping with that theme, here it is divine guidance that intervenes in two forms, one in which the missionaries are hindered from going where they had planned to go and another communicated in a dream/vision, a favorite device of ancient storytelling. It is also a favorite device of generic religious myths of origins and other stories of divine guidance in relation to travel narratives.[4]

All that being said, there still remains the choice of Troas as the location of the vision—presumably it could have happened anywhere on the journey to this point. But, as MacDonald explains in his cameo essay, Troas is a good choice because of its literary baggage. Troas, which was known as the site of ancient Troy, was the starting point for the journeys of one of the best known literary characters in the ancient world, Odysseus. Just as Odysseus often used the first person in the narrative of his journeys, so also here, in what is apparently self-conscious imitation, Luke uses the first person in his narration of the voyage from Troas to Macedonia.

The story is steeped in literary formulas and imbued with Luke's plot and theology. There is nothing here that qualifies as potentially historical.

The we-passages appear and disappear abruptly at various points throughout the latter half of Acts and do not lend themselves to any one simple explanation. The Fellows found that the most persuasive explanations were those that identified these enigmatic passages as literary motifs used in imitation of ancient literary models, and so they voted red, or "probable", on several representative literary proposals. One such motif was the use of the first person when narrating a sea voyage, which the Fellows affirmed as a cogent explanation for this motif in Acts; however, they were not willing to designate the *Odyssey* as the only such source, thus giving it a pink vote. As a literary motif, the use of the first person in these passages represents an authorial pseudo-identity as a companion of Paul. This device allowed the author to identify himself and his community with the mission of Paul, and, in the process, connect the mission of Paul, who is very specifically not an apostle in Acts, with a post-apostolic period. While it is possible that the author used "Luke" as his pseudonym, the Fellows were only willing to give this proposal a gray vote. Conversely the Fellows found arguments that propose the we-passages to be markers of an eyewitness account to be unconvincing and voted black, or "improbable", on a collection of representative proposals.

The Votes of the Fellows

Red/Probable
- The narrator of Acts intends the reader to connect the first-person narratives with the narrator.
- The narrator of Acts assumed a pseudo-identity as a companion on Paul's sea voyages.
- The literary function of the we-passages in Acts strongly suggests that Acts was not composed by a close associate of Paul.
- The use of the we-passages in Acts fits well within an early second-century context.

Pink/Possible
- The first-person narrative of the sea voyage from Troas in Acts 16:10–18 is written in imitation of first-person narratives of sea voyages in Homer's *Odyssey*.

Gray/Doubtful
- Luke-Acts was originally composed under the pseudonym of Luke.

Black/Improbable
- The we-passages in Acts provide evidence for a first-century date of Acts.
- The narrator of Acts was a companion on Paul's sea voyages.
- It is likely that one of Paul's traveling co-missionaries would have portrayed himself or herself as post-apostolic.

Conversion of Lydia in Philippi

16 ¹¹We sailed from Troas on a straight course to Samothrace and came to Neapolis the next day. ¹²From Neapolis we went to Philippi, a city of the first district of Macedonia and a Roman colony. We spent several days in that city. ¹³On the Sabbath we went beyond the city gate to the riverside, where we thought there would be a place for prayer. There we sat and began to converse with the women who had assembled. ¹⁴One of them, a devout woman named Lydia, who was a dealer in purple cloth from Thyatira, began to take interest. The Lord opened her heart, so that she paid close attention to Paul's words. ¹⁵When Lydia, together with her household, had been baptized, she urged, "Since you have concluded that I am a genuine believer in the Lord, come and stay in my house." We found her argument compelling.

Comments on the Story

The geographical notes become much clearer here, as the group sails from Troas, via Samothrace and Neapolis, to Philippi, presumably the destination called for by the Macedonian vision. Luke calls attention to the status of Philippi as a Roman colony and an important Macedonian city. Early readers would remember it as the place where Octavian, who became the Roman emperor Augustus, and Mark Antony defeated the assassins of Julius Caesar (42 BCE).

Of central importance here is the conversion of Lydia, the first convert in Europe. Paul and his group go outside Philippi to the river, where they assume that they will find a place of prayer. There they encounter a group of women who have assembled on the Sabbath, and they speak to them about Jesus. One woman, Lydia, listens attentively, accepts baptism, and becomes hostess for the visiting group.

In one sense this narrative serves as a counterpart to the conversion of Cornelius in Acts 10:1–11:18. Luke stresses the devotion of both Cornelius and Lydia, and he notes that in both cases the entire household was baptized along with the principal. Despite the parallels, Cornelius receives far more attention than Lydia. In addition, while every detail in the Cornelius narrative is guided by divine initiative, for Lydia it is said only that the Lord opened her heart (16:14).

The parallelism with the Cornelius story may suggest that Lydia is a Gentile Godfearer, but this is not so clear from the narrative itself. In Acts 16:14 Luke uses a word to describe her—*sebomenē* (devout)—that he uses to describe other Gentile adherents of synagogues (see 13:43; 17:17), but he also uses this term for persons who are probably (13:50) or certainly (17:4) not associated with Jews. Cornelius, in 10:2, is described as a fearer of God (*phoboumenos*), a similar but not identical expression. Further, it is not clear what kind of service is going on at the riverside outside Philippi. If it is a Jewish observance, we would expect a reference to a synagogue, since Luke uses this term at almost every appropriate opportunity (see, e.g., 9:20; 13:5, 14; 14:1; 17:1, 10, 17; 18:4, 19; 19:8). But in 16:13 (and 16:16), we find a word that appears nowhere else in Acts—*proseuchē*—a place of prayer. The absence of men is also an intriguing aspect of the narrative. Might Luke intend for us to think of a place where Gentile women customarily came to pray to their own gods? Two matters make it more likely that we are to think of a Jewish observance. For one thing, Luke sets the incident on a Sabbath day (16:13). For another, the Christian missionaries in Acts do not elsewhere interfere with an explicitly Gentile religious observance. They speak in public places that may not be devoid of religious significance (e. g., Acts 17:16–34), but, as good Jews, they avoid contact with "pagan" religious observances. We should, therefore, think of an open-air Jewish observance occurring at a spot outside Philippi, near the river.

Lydia, then, would be a Gentile who, like Cornelius, was attracted to Judaism. Luke, however, was not only interested in her religious attachment but in her social position. He described her in terms of her profession and origin: she was a dealer of purple clothing from Thyatira in Asia Minor. She was an immigrant and a businesswoman, socially marginal but upwardly mobile. We also learn that she had a domicile that could house her own household and was sufficient also for Paul and his entourage. The description places Lydia in an ambiguous position. The production end of her business would tend to depress her social standing, since it involved "the filthy, 'sordid', smelly process of extracting dye from plants or mollusks and treating materials with animal urine."[5] The sales end, however, would put her in contact with wealthy elite persons and even with royalty and so would raise her status. Perhaps Luke intended for readers to think of the socially ambiguous situation for Lydia, but the fact that he mentions only her dealing in purple clothing and not her association with its production makes it likely that he wants to present her as among the wealthy elite.

The significance of women in the narrative of Acts has frequently been noted, and here we have a prime example: Lydia is a Godfearer who worshipped with a group of women. She is the first Pauline convert in Europe, and she becomes prominent as the hostess for the group of missionaries and perhaps the leader of the local church at Philippi. If the story of Cornelius is a counterpart to that of Lydia, it is notable that we learn nothing about Cornelius' role after his baptism. Lydia, however, is important as providing a base for Paul and company in Macedonia. Some readers may be led to contrast the story of Lydia with that of Timothy in Acts 16:1–3. Luke tells us that, when Paul found Timothy, he invited him to accompany him on his future journeys. Lydia receives no such invitation. Her role, although significant, is more domestic, more in line with the traditional roles of ancient Mediterranean women. The fact that Luke frequently highlights the roles of women is notable, but we must not forget that in Acts there are no women among the leading characters. There are no female apostles or travelling missionaries (see also the cameo essay, "Women in Acts," p. 193). The glass ceiling in Acts is palpable.

In Search of History

After having been guided so carefully by divine direction, the missionaries arrive at Philippi, which, according to the logic of the narrative, is exactly where God wanted them to go. The narrative of their stay in Philippi is therefore framed as exemplary for Paul's missionary endeavors in a new mission field. It is an extensive story, encompassing verses 11–40, and includes many adventures that follow characteristic narrative patterns of Acts. It is clear that the entire set of episodes in Philippi is set up to correlate with established themes of the overall story of Acts. If any historical data has been used, it has been buried in a narrative frame that is demonstrably nonhistorical, as will be seen in the discussion below.

The story of Lydia is the first narrative segment. The overall construction of this narrative segment is framed as a report by an unnamed "we," which, as argued above, is a narrative device used by the author to lend narrative credibility to the story. The change from third person to "we" happens abruptly at verse 10, at the point where a sea voyage began. The first person "we" continues to be used after the voyage ends and the stay in Philippi begins. The Lydia story throughout is told by a "we" narrative voice. This voice continues until the beginning of the next episode at verse 16, the story of the slave woman, and then abruptly drops out in verse 19, when Paul and Silas are apprehended. The use of this device marks this entire section of narrative as nonhistorical, at least in regard to its framing.

The story itself also follows standard patterns of the author. Paul first goes to a Jewish worship site, in this case a *proseuchē* or "place for prayer," which, as a narrative device, corresponds to a synagogue. Changing the location perhaps allows the author to introduce a feature that would not be common at synagogues, namely that it is a place of prayer for women. This device then allows the author to introduce a prominent woman into his story of Christian beginnings, a preference he has shown elsewhere in Luke-Acts.

Lydia is defined as an ideal disciple according to Lukan themes. She is a Gentile, probably a "Godfearer," like Cornelius. She offers her home as a place of hospitality for the missionaries, as do other characters in Luke-Acts. Nevertheless, Luke stops well short of portraying Lydia in a role beyond the cultural limitations on the social roles of women, as pointed out in the cameo essay, "Women in Acts" (p. 193). She is also described as a dealer in purple cloth from Thyatira, a city associated with the purple cloth trade, details which lend verisimilitude to the story. Luke shows himself to be a master of such verisimilar details in other stories in Luke-Acts. All in all, the story functions so well as a component of Luke's narrative program that it is highly unlikely that any of its details were derived from historical data.

References

Phillips, "Post-Apostolic Consciousness"
MacDonald, "And So We Left Troy-Troas"

We-Passages in the Acts of the Apostles
A Cameo Essay by Dennis R. MacDonald

The original title of Luke-Acts is lost, a lamentable reality which has led to speculations concerning the identity of the author: Does the present title retain the author's name, that of Paul's associate Luke? Was the two-volume work originally anonymous? Did the author write under a pseudonym and foist his work on Luke? This much is clear: the "me" in the opening verses refers to the author.

> Since many have attempted to set in order an exposition of the matters that have come to fruition among us, [2]as those who became from the beginning firsthand observers and assistants of the message handed on to us [their expositions], [3]it seemed good to me, too, having followed them all thoroughly, to write [an exposition] precisely in sequence for you, most excellent Theophilus, [4]so that you may recognize the certainty of sayings about which you have been instructed. (Luke 1:1–4; MacDonald's translation)

The preface to the Acts of the Apostles indicates that it was written by the same author and to the same recipient: "I composed my first account, Theophilus, about everything that Jesus began both to do and to teach up to the day he was taken up" (1:1–2a). The author never speaks in the first person from Luke 1:5–Acts 16:9, but at Acts 16:10 he seems to introduce himself into the narrative: "Because Paul had seen the vision, *we* immediately sought to leave for Macedonia, inferring that God had called *us* to proclaim the good news to them." The author resumes the first-person-plural voice again in 20:5–15; 21:1–18; and 27:1–28:16.

The origin and function of these passages has been one of the most controversial topics in the interpretation of Luke-Acts. Conservative commentators are prone to view them as evidence that the author of Acts actually accompanied Paul on these journeys, but nowhere does the text otherwise identify him as a participant in the events. Source critics often have seen in these passages evidence of a personal travelogue that the author of Acts used without attribution, but surely he was capable of shifting the first-person source to his own third-person voice. Furthermore, the we-passages display the same vocabulary and style as the rest of the work, evidence either that he composed them himself, or that he thoroughly revised whatever source he may have used. Some critics thus have proposed that the author of Acts used the first-person voice to claim the historical veracity of an eyewitness. Others have taken these passages as expressions of solidarity with Paul and his churches.[6]

The author's models for these "we-voyages" may have come from Homer's *Odyssey*, where several characters narrate their returns (*nostoi*) home after the Trojan War, none more extensively or dramatically than Odysseus himself.[7] The hero began his account as follows:

> Let me describe my disastrous *nostos*
> that Zeus laid upon me as I traveled from Troy.
> The wind carried me from Ilium and brought me to the Cicones
> at Ismarus.[8]

Throughout books 9–12 of the *Odyssey* the narrator switches gracefully among the first-person plural, the first-person singular, and the third person.

It is worth noting that after Odysseus left the Troad his first stop was Ismarus, which scholars usually locate in southern Thrace, opposite Samothrace. According to the *Aeneid*, the Trojans built their fleet at Antandros and sailed to the shore of Thrace, where they founded the city Aeneadae, facing Samothrace (Vergil, *Aeneid* 3.1–18). Paul's first voyage nearly retraces the first leg of Odysseus' *nostos* and Aeneas' flight: "We sailed from Troas [related in antiquity to ancient Troy] on a straight course to Samothrace and came to Neapolis the next day" (Acts 16:11–12). Luke apparently expected his readers to be jarred by the change in the narrator's voice and to view Paul's first voyage to Europe as a Christian *nostos*.

But what connections do these first-person-plural passages have, if any, to the first-person-singular preface? Christian texts contemporaneous with the author linked Paul intimately with an associate named Luke. It would be natural for readers of Acts to look for the identity of the author among Paul's associates who are not named, and "Luke" is not found there. The name appears inconspicuously in Phlm 24, but as Paul's "beloved physician" in Col 4:14. According to 2 Tim 4:11 only Luke was with Paul in Rome on the eve of his execution. Regardless of who the actual author was, it is reasonable to speculate that the title of the two-volume work identified him as Luke and advertised that this account of Christian origins would have a Pauline slant.

Women in Acts
A Cameo Essay by Shelly Matthews

Because he mentions so many of them, the author of Acts is sometimes considered a friend of women. But careful consideration of how women characters function in this narrative suggests that the overarching rhetorical aim of this author is not to demonstrate friendliness toward women, but rather to circumscribe women within limited social and ecclesiastical roles.

To be sure, there are adversaries of women more hostile than the author of Acts in the early second century. The author of the Pastoral Epistles, who pronounces that women should have no teaching authority and offers women salvation only through childbearing (1 Tim 2:15), might have written a narrative of the emerging Jesus movement less friendly than Acts. The words attributed to Peter in the Gospel of Thomas 114, "Make Mary leave us, for females are not worthy of life," could also be judged as more misogynist than anything Acts asserts. Acts, in contradistinction to these texts, does allow glimpses of women with agency in the early Jesus movement. Paul is hosted in Philippi by Lydia, a female head of household (Acts 16:11–15, 40); Priscilla, as well as Aquila, are acknowledged as Paul's co-workers (18:1–4), and both of these missionaries instruct Apollos in the Way (18:26); Acts allows that Phillip had four prophesying daughters (21:9).

But comparing Acts to other texts which feature the involvement of women in the early Jesus movement demonstrates this text's overarching androcentrism. Consider the narrative of the replacement of Judas among the Twelve taken up in 1:21–23. One could imagine that a true survey of Jesus' followers about which of those who accompanied him, from the beginning until the day he was taken from them, would be best suited for leadership, might produce the name of Mary Magdalene. Other traditions of crucifixion and resurrection events regard Mary as much more faithful than Peter himself (compare their respective roles in the Gospels of Mark, John, and Mary). But Acts adds a gender requirement that renders ineligible the woman whom other traditions name as primary witness both to the crucifixion and the resurrection. Luke goes so far as to obliterate Mary Magdalene from his historical record of the post-ascension church, mentioning women only as unnamed companions to the men in the upper room (1:14).

Peter's Pentecost speech includes the intriguing, if indirect, acknowledgement that women, both free and slave, might have been among those who uttered prophecy in the movement, through his citation of Joel's utopian vision in Acts 2:17–18. But this glimpse of a relatively utopian prophetic movement is framed by an emphasis on the masculine space in which Peter speaks. Peter addresses his audience with gender specific references to "men" and "brothers" and, aside from the reference to Joel, gives no indication of women either among those speaking in tongues or those receiving the speech. In spite of the promise of Acts 2:17–18, no prophetic speech of a female Jesus follower (or of a male slave) is recorded in subsequent narratives.

Acts' circumscribing tendency can be traced in many other passages. The widows are mentioned as a source of dissension in 6:1 but not, as in other church traditions, as church leaders. Lydia hosts Paul in Acts 16, but she does not spar with him over theological issues, as Euodia and Syntyche apparently do in Philippians (cf. Phil 4:2). Philip has prophesying daughters, but what they prophesy is of no consequence to this author. Prisca is the only one of Paul's female co-workers known from Romans 16 who is acknowledged in Acts, and readers receive no clue of how precisely she risked her neck for Paul's sake (Rom 16:4). We are left only to imagine what stories could have been told of Phoebe (Rom 16:1–2), Mary (Rom 16:6), Junia (Rom 16:7), Tryphena and Tryphosa (Rom 16:12), Julia (Rom 16:15), or the mother of Rufus (Rom 16:13), if an author more generous than Luke had penned an account of women's agency in the early church.

A Prison Break in Philippi

16 ¹⁶While we were on the way to the place of prayer, a slave woman with a prophetic spirit who made plenty of money for her owners by issuing oracles encountered us. ¹⁷As she trailed along behind Paul and us, she kept on shouting: "These people are slaves of the Most High God! They commend to you a means of deliverance." ¹⁸She kept this up day after day, until Paul became so irritated that he turned around and addressed her spirit, "I hereby command you in the name of Jesus Christ to leave her." It left her right away.

¹⁹Her owners realized that their expectation of income had also left. They apprehended Paul and Silas and hauled them to the authorities in the city center. ²⁰When they had brought them before the chief magistrates, they said, "These fellows are convulsing the city! They are Jews ²¹and commend practices that we Romans can neither accept nor follow." ²²The crowd pitched in against them, so the chief magistrates tore off the clothes of the accused and ordered a flogging. ²³After many blows with the rod, the officials tossed them in jail, directing the jailer to secure them carefully. ²⁴In obedience to these instructions, he put them in the innermost cell and shackled their feet in stocks.

²⁵Sometime in the middle of the night, as Paul and Silas were praying and praising God in song while the other prisoners listened to them, ²⁶there was suddenly an earthquake so powerful that the foundations of the prison were rocked. All the doors popped open, and the chains of all the prisoners came loose. ²⁷The jailer awakened, saw the doors of the prison wide open, and, presuming that the inmates had escaped, pulled out his sword with the intention of killing himself. ²⁸But Paul shouted very loudly: "Don't harm yourself. We're all here!" ²⁹The jailer called for

illumination, rushed in, and fell trembling before Paul and Silas. ³⁰After bringing them out, he asked, "Milords, what must I do to be saved?"

³¹"Believe in the Lord Jesus and you will be saved, together with your household." ³²They thereupon told the jailer and all in his home the message about the Lord. ³³Late as it was, the jailer took them where he could cleanse their wounds. He and all of his people were then baptized without delay. ³⁴He then escorted them to his own home, where a meal was set before them. The household was ebullient because each and all had come to faith in God.

³⁵The next morning the chief magistrates sent their police escort with the message, "Let those people go." ³⁶The jailer gave Paul the word: "The chief magistrates have sent orders that you two are to be released. All right, then, come on out and be happily on your way!" ³⁷"They give us," said Paul, "a public beating, us, Roman citizens convicted of no crime, then toss us into jail, and now they want to kick us out of town secretly? Not a chance! Let them come in person and remove us from jail."

³⁸The police reported this to the chief magistrates, who were terrified to learn that their victims were Roman citizens. ³⁹The magistrates came with reassuring words, took them out of jail, and requested that they leave town. ⁴⁰After their release Paul and Silas went to see Lydia. They provided the believers with spiritual nurture and then left Philippi.

Comments on the Story

Paul and his associates remain in Philippi for several days after the conversion of Lydia. In the course of their mission, they meet up with a slave woman who seems to offer support for them, but Paul finally exorcises her prophetic spirit. The slave's owners, recognizing that a source of their income has been compromised, bring charges against Paul and Silas, who are summarily cast into prison. At midnight, however, a powerful earthquake destroys the prison and loosens the prisoners' shackles. Fearing that he will be held accountable for the prisoners' escape, the guard attempts suicide, but Paul stops him, assures him that all the prisoners have been accounted for, and the guard is converted to the Jesus movement. The following morning, the city authorities determine to release Paul and Silas, but Paul objects. He claims Roman citizenship for both, maintains that they were illegally arrested and punished, and demands a public release. Finally, the authorities comply: the prisoners are released and advised to leave Philippi.

This complex narrative begins with a story of a slave woman and her proclamation about Paul and his associates (Acts 16:16–18). Luke tells us that she constantly followed the Pauline group and shouted, "These people are slaves of the Most High God! They commend to you a means of deliverance [or salvation]" (16:17). Her proclamation appears to be supportive of the Pauline mission and so Paul's toleration of her is understandable. Commentators frequently point to the story of Jesus' exorcism of the Gerasene demoniac in Luke 8:26–39 as bearing similarities to the narrative in Acts 16. The demoniac in Luke shouts, "What do you want with me, Jesus, you son of the most high God?" (Luke 8:28). The demoniac recognizes who Jesus is, and he speaks of the divine in language like that of the slave woman in Acts 16. The parallels are not exact: the Gerasene does damage to himself, but the slave woman does nothing more than proclaim something about Paul and his entourage. But if readers of Acts are to understand the slave woman's proclamation as stating the truth, we must ask why Paul finally disavows her support and expels the spirit that inspired her utterance. In Luke 8, Jesus exorcised the demon from the Gerasene to relieve the victim's self-torment, but Paul seems to be motivated only by annoyance at the constant shouting (Acts 16:18), and the exorcism leaves the slave woman—now unemployed—in worse condition than before.

There are, however, good reasons to think that Paul's annoyance had a sound basis and was directed, not at the woman's habitual activity, but at the message itself. The key is in the initial description of the woman in Acts 16:16. The usual translations do not reveal the fact that the Greek text actually says that she had a "Python" spirit (here translated as "a prophetic spirit;" 16:16). The term "Python" would associate the slave woman with the priestess at the temple of Apollo in Delphi, who was called the Pythia. Inspired by Apollo, she delivered oracles whose meanings were notoriously uncertain. Perhaps in Acts 16:16–18 we are to think of a local counterpart to the oracle of Delphi, who likewise delivers ambiguous utterances inspired by Apollo. She proclaims that Paul and company are slaves of "the Most High God" and that they show a way of salvation (16:17). Her proclamation may seem to support the Pauline message, and yet the phrase, "Most High God" is problematic. The term is familiar in the LXX, and in the third gospel Luke frequently uses it, or a variation of it, to designate the one God of Jewish and Christian faith. In Acts 7:48 he has Stephen use a similar phrase, and the context makes it clear that the reference is to the OT deity. But the phrase, or a variant of it, is also found in Greek literature and in a number of inscriptions, where it designates Zeus or another god in the Greek pantheon. The superlative does not rule out belief in other gods, and so it is appropriate in a polytheistic setting. To determine the meaning we must attend to the context.

What might the phrase suggest in the mouth of a Gentile woman with a Python spirit? The key probably lies in the very ambiguity of the message, since ambiguity was the characteristic feature of the Delphic oracles. Misinterpretations frequently led to tragedy. Paul, however, is not victimized by the uncertain meaning of the slave woman's oracle. It takes him several days to determine its meaning, but when he does he acts decisively: in the name of Jesus he casts out the Python spirit (16:18). Under this interpretation, we are not dealing with Paul's psychology, but with the competition of major religions. In the exorcism we are led to see the victory of the Lord Jesus over the Lord Apollo.

The victory of Jesus over Apollo has serious consequences: beneath the theological level of this incident lies the economic. Since the owners of the slave woman had made considerable sums from displaying her fortune-telling abilities and since these were now lost, they attempt to retaliate against Paul and Silas for depriving them of their just profits. They haul the two missionaries before the city authorities, who immediately throw them into jail.

It is notable that, in one major respect, Luke departs from his usual formula in narrating the exploits of Paul in Philippi. In so many of the stories we find that Paul goes first to a synagogue. After limited success there he meets up with opposition from unconverted Jews and then turns to Gentiles, who are very receptive to his message (see, e.g., Acts 13:13–52; 17:1–15). In Philippi, however, the Pauline group meets with Jews at the river outside the city, and one notable woman becomes a believer (16:11–15). But instead of opposition arising from Jews who did not accept the Lordship of Jesus, it comes from Gentiles whose incomes have been reduced by the action of Jesus' missionaries. Indeed, Paul and Silas are thought to be Jews, who advocate a non-Roman morality (16:20–21).

Luke's narrative includes a number of details about Paul's Philippian mission, but the niceties of the legal situation remain somewhat obscure. Although he and Silas are not the only ones involved in the mission, it is only they who are charged with introducing an inappropriate morality. The narrative reads more like a mob lynching than responsible Roman legal procedure, what with the vague charges against the accused and the crowd joining in (16:22–23). On hearing accusations against the two, the authorities strip and beat them harshly and then order them to a maximum security prison, but—without citing a cause—order their release the following morning (16:35). Although it would be hard to ignore an earthquake that occurred the previous night, Luke does not say that the guard reported it to the city authorities. In any event, Paul refuses to accept a secret release and claims that his (and Silas') rights as Roman citizens have been violated (16:37). The historicity of Paul's citizenship and rights will be discussed below in Chapter Five, but it seems reasonable to think that Luke's second-century audience would understand that Roman citizens could expect less harsh treatment from colonial authorities than could the natives. Nevertheless, at the level of the story, Paul's claim of Roman citizenship so unnerves the authorities that they come to the jail, release the prisoners, and persuade them to leave town. Paul and his group comply, but not before a final visit to the home of Lydia (16:40).

The entire story of imprisonment and earthquake prepares us for the conversion of the guard. His story may be compared with those about the conversions of Cornelius and Lydia, both of whom may be thought of as Godfearers. Cornelius previously had a close contact with the synagogue (Acts 10:2), and Lydia met with other Jewish women at the river outside Philippi (16:13–14). Both were converted along with their households. But the unnamed prison guard at Philippi has no Jewish connections, at least none cited by Luke. He, along with his entire family, would then be a symbol for those Gentiles who had no Jewish connections. The Philippian guard is a "pure Gentile," not a Godfearer.

Further, the circumstances of his conversion contrast with those of Cornelius and Lydia. Cornelius was directed by a vision to seek out and listen to Peter (Acts 10:1–6). Lydia was led by God to listen to the preaching of Paul (16:14). The motivation of the Philippian jailer appears to be sheer terror. He survived an earthquake only to realize that he would be held responsible for the prisoners he thought had escaped. After Paul stops him from committing suicide, it is only natural that he would ask, "What must I do to be saved?" (16:30). Luke here plays on the multiple connotations of salvation. In context, the guard's question would probably mean, "What must I do to escape the inevitable punishment from my superiors?" Paul's response is, at one level, a counsel to trust the Lord

Jesus for a resolution of the present situation, but at another level a statement about the guard's ultimate fate. We, of course, do not learn anything about the guard's ultimate salvation, but it is notable that he suffers no retribution from the authorities in Philippi.

Dennis R. MacDonald and others maintain that Luke's story of Paul and Silas in prison was influenced by Euripides' play, the *Bacchae*, and there is much to be said for the resemblances between the two accounts. For more information, see his cameo essay, "Prison Breaks in Luke's Literary World," p. 72.

Finally, we should note that the author has subtly switched from first-person to third-person narration after Acts 16:17. The next we-passage will be found in 20:5.

In Search of History

The heart of this story is the miraculous prison break, and it follows a model well known in ancient literature and used more than once in Acts. The case for this being an imitation of an ancient literary motif is outlined in the cameo essay, "Prison Breaks in Luke's Literary World" (p. 72). The Fellows were convinced by these arguments and voted red on the propositions that this story is a Lukan fiction and that it shows signs of conscious imitation of a similar story in Euripides.

The Votes of the Fellows

Red/Probable

- Acts 16:13–40 is written to emulate the prison break of Dionysus in Euripides.
- Acts 16:13–40 is a Lukan fiction.

One could still ask whether bits of data in the story may qualify as historical. However, there are other components of the narrative that betray the author's hand.

Luke used a similar story earlier at a similarly pivotal point in the plot. In the previous case, in Acts 13:4–12, it is a Jewish magician who is silenced by Paul's ability to perform miracles; this takes place as the event which defines Saul as Paul, missionary to the Gentiles. In this case, it is a slave woman who is silenced by a miracle performed by Paul, and it takes place as one of two introductory events to a new phase in Paul's mission work. Of course, the story is also marked as a composition of the author by the fact that it is a miracle story, which is a literary form in Acts that lacks historical credibility. Another Lukan theme in the narrative is the description of the jailer's conversion. Like characters in other conversion stories in Acts, the jailer confesses belief and is baptized. Like Lydia, his entire household is baptized with him. Also like Lydia, he exhibits his true discipleship by immediately providing hospitality to the missionaries in his house. These two stories, coming as they do at the very beginning of Paul's work in this new region, establish Luke's version of a model for leadership in early Christian house churches.

Oddly, after hosting the missionaries at his home, he apparently escorts them back to the prison so that their prison term can end on a dramatic note. Then, before departing, Paul and Silas enjoy Lydia's hospitality once more, thus ending their stay in Philippi by affirming that they are leaving behind an established Christian house church.

The story of Paul's stay in Philippi is tightly woven with favorite literary themes of Luke. Its function is to affirm that this new mission endeavor in the heart of Gentile country is imbued with the presence and power of God. It is an evangelistic message, not an historical account.

Thessalonica and Beroea

17 After leaving Philippi, Paul and Silas took the road through Amphipolis and Apollonia and came to Thessalonica, where there was a Jewish synagogue. ²As was his normal practice, Paul visited the congregation. For three Sabbaths he lectured on the Scriptures, ³showing by interpretation that the Messiah had to suffer and rise from the dead. "This is the Messiah, Jesus, the one about whom I am telling you." ⁴Some of them were convinced and attached themselves to Paul and Silas, as did a large number of devout gentiles and quite a few prominent women. ⁵These conversions aroused the envy of the Jews, who collected some of the worthless loafers that loitered around the city center into a mob and thereby aroused the entire populace. This mob converged upon the house of Jason with the intent of hauling Paul and Silas before the assembly. ⁶Since they couldn't find those two, they dragged Jason and some believers to the magistrates, shouting: "These people who are fomenting rebellion everywhere are in our midst! ⁷Jason is harboring them. In opposition to the decrees of Caesar they want to set up another emperor, claiming that Jesus rules." ⁸When they heard these charges, the mob and the officials became thoroughly agitated. ⁹Jason and the others were not released until they had paid a bond. ¹⁰As soon as darkness fell, the believers sent Paul and Silas on to Beroea. When they got to Beroea, they entered the synagogue.

¹¹Now the Jews there were of a better quality than those at Thessalonica. They applied themselves eagerly to the message and engaged in daily scrutiny of the Scriptures to discover whether the claims might be true. ¹²Many, in fact, came to believe, including a substantial number of upper-crust Greek women and quite a few men. ¹³Once the Jews of Thessalonica had learned that Paul had also proclaimed the message of God in Beroea, they showed up there as well and threw the masses into disorder by their agitation.

¹⁴The believers immediately sent Paul to the seacoast, while Silas and Timothy remained behind. ¹⁵After those who were conducting Paul had got him to Athens, they returned with instructions for the other two to join him as soon as possible.

Comments on the Story

In this section Paul and his associates visit two Macedonian locations, Thessalonica and Beroea. The narratives about these locations are governed by a formula that we have previously noted, and Luke even calls attention to it in Acts 17:2. He writes that, "as was his normal practice," Paul went first to a synagogue in Thessalonica and sought the conversion of Jews and Godfearers. He met with some success, but Jewish opposition arose, and Paul was forced to leave town. He then went to Beroea, where much the same things happened.

The opposition that arose in Thessalonica is said to have been caused by Jewish envy at Paul's success. The word in Acts 17:5 that is translated "envy" also designates one's zeal or earnest desire, and this may be the intended connotation of the word here. We may think of Jews as avidly adhering to their faith or as envious that Paul made converts from their midst, or both. In any event, these Jews are able to find support from questionable sources among the Gentile population, and together they foment a great disturbance. Their actions, however, result in less trouble for Paul than for his host, Jason, and other believers. Unable to find Paul or Silas, the crowd captures their host and takes him before the city authorities, alleging that he has extended hospitality to politically suspect persons. Jason is required to post bail, apparently agreeing to withhold further hospitality from these dissidents. Paul's supporters recognize that he is in danger, and so they sneak him out of town by night.

The burden of Paul's preaching in Thessalonica relates to the interpretation of the Hebrew Scriptures. It is said that he met with people in the synagogue there for three Sabbaths (Acts 17:2), that is, for a period of three weeks. His message was that, according to the Scriptures, it was necessary for the Messiah to suffer and that Jesus is the Messiah. That the Scriptures affirm the necessity for the Messiah to suffer is an important theme in Luke-Acts (see, e.g., Luke 24:44–49). It is notable, however, that, although he frequently cites specific OT passages to support various points that are made, Luke never does so in connection with the death of the Messiah. He seems convinced that this theme is present in the Hebrew Scriptures but is either unable or unwilling to refer to a specific text.

But the Jews who heard Paul's preaching do not speak of these contentions when they—now supported by a crowd of Gentiles—confront the city authorities. Neither the identity of Jesus as Messiah nor the necessity of his suffering is cited in Acts 17:7. Rather it is alleged that Paul's preaching is political and treasonous: he is said to proclaim that Jesus, not Caesar, is emperor. Although Luke frequently refers to the kingdom of God, he rarely links kingship with Jesus (but see Luke 22:30; 23:2). It seems likely that Luke intends to imply that the allegation in Acts 17:7 is false, but he includes no specific denial of it, unless his characterization of Paul's synagogue preaching in 17:2–3 is meant to do so. In any event, it is of interest to note the ways in which Luke deals with the understanding of Messiahship in different communities. For Jews, the term needs no explanation, but it is clear that the crucifixion of Jesus is a severe impediment to their accepting claims about him. For Romans, the proclamation of Jesus' Messiahship would appear to be a claim of rival imperial power and thus a threat to the peace and well-being of the political order. Our author shows sensitivity in his awareness of these different implications of early Christian preaching.

The episode in Beroea is similar to that in Thessalonica but with less detail. The narrator calls attention to a difference in character between the Jews in Thessalonica and those in Beroea: the latter, he says, "were of a better quality" (Acts 17:11). This means that they were more willing to give Paul a fair hearing, although we should not forget that some in Thessalonica joined up with Paul and Silas

(17:4). This is a rare positive note about Jews. Robert Tannehill comments, "The description of the Beroean Jews shows that the narrator has not completely stereotyped Diaspora Jews. Despite the repeated emphasis on Jewish opposition, the narrator here inserts a contrasting picture, preserving a sense of local variety of response."[9] Perhaps, but the seemingly positive comment about the Beroean Jews is more than offset by the image of Thessalonian Jews, who go out of their way to oppose the Christian message (17:13). Things apparently would have been quite peaceful in Beroea had it not been for Thessalonian Jews who came to stir up trouble. The episode here is similar to that in 14:19, when opposing Jews from Iconium and Antioch appeared in Lystra to press their case against Paul.

We should also note Luke's stress on elite Gentile converts (Acts 17:4, 12). Our author does not wish to portray Gentile converts as members of the lower classes, but rather as people of influence. Our unnamed leading male and female citizens in Thessalonica and Beroea now join company with Cornelius (10:1–11:18), Lydia (16:11–15), and others of a relatively high social class.

Paul's associates always play a subsidiary role in Acts, but it is important to keep up with them. Silas was with Paul in prison in Philippi (Acts 16:25–40) and accompanied him on the trip from there to Thessalonica (17:1–9) and Beroea (17:10–15). But as Paul is leaving Beroea, we suddenly learn that Timothy is also there (17:14). There is also an indefinite number of unnamed supporters who conduct Paul from Beroea to Athens (17:14–15). The narrator notes that Paul is alone in Athens but that he has left instructions for Timothy and Silas to join him as soon as possible. They do not catch up with him, however, until 18:5, by which time he has left Athens for Corinth.

In Search of History

Acts assumes an itinerary in which Paul travels into Greece by the northern route through Macedonia, the route Paul himself chose for his second trip to the region (1 Cor 16:5). According to Acts, after making converts in Philippi, Paul then traveled to Thessalonica before turning south toward Athens, passing through Beroea on the way. This route was probably constructed out of comments in Paul's letters. He wrote to the Thessalonians that he had already been in Philippi, and had been shamefully treated there, before arriving in Thessalonica (1 Thess 2:1–2). His next stop was Athens (1 Thess 3:1). Luke simply adds other cities to the route that Paul does not mention. The road from Philippi to Thessalonica is the Via Egnatia, and any traveler on that road would pass through Amphipolis and Apollonia. To go south, however, one would have to leave the Via Egnatia and travel to Athens either by a sea route or by a coastal road. Luke prefers the coastal road option, and this allows him to create a stop in Beroea.

Nothing about the rest of Luke's narrative in this segment of Paul's journey matches anything from Paul's letters. According to Paul, the opposition he met was in Philippi, not Thessalonica. His letter to the Thessalonians assumes a Gentile community with whom he had built a close relationship (1 Thess 1:6–10); there is no hint of trouble there except for 1 Thess 1:14–16, which many scholars consider to be an addition to Paul's letter by a later editor. Furthermore, there is no mention of Beroea in Paul's letters, or anywhere else in the NT for that matter.

On the other hand, Luke's narrative is constructed out of favorite themes found elsewhere in his story of Paul. As is common in Acts but not in Paul's letters, Paul begins his preaching in the synagogue, both in Thessalonica and Beroea. He faces fierce opposition from Jews in Thessalonica, is carried before the magistrates by an unruly mob, and has to leave under duress. In this case, the Jewish response is all Luke wants to talk about. Though he mentions that there were Greek converts, there is little information about them. According to Paul, the community of believers in Thessalonica became renowned throughout Macedonia and Achaia. According to the story in Acts, it was the Jewish opposition that became renowned. The Acts version, since it is built out of favorite narrative themes of Luke, is simply not credible as history.

The entire sojourn in Beroea seems to have been created by Luke to expand on the adventure tale he is constructing. The escape by night is a favorite device of Luke (see, for example, Acts 9:23–25). Beroea is handy as the nearby city to which he could escape. In Beroea, Paul followed standard practice according to Acts and preached in the synagogue. Luke's emphasis that the Jews were friendlier in Beroea fits the contrast that the narrative needs; that is, Beroea functions best narratively as an escape route if in fact Paul is safe there. And he *is* safe, at least until the rabid Jews from Thessalonica pursue him there. Then Paul has to escape surreptitiously again. According to the Acts story, Paul could hardly have had time to catch his breath. How could he have overlooked saying something about those events in his letter to the Thessalonians? The answer is, because they never happened. Luke made them up.

Are there components of the story that could have derived from tradition (other than 1 Thessalonians), perhaps even historical tradition, out of which Luke constructed his made-up story? The itinerary of Paul's travels, as we have seen, can be created from Paul's letters; there is no need to posit an itinerary source (see the cameo essay, "The Itinerary of Paul," p. 206). The mention of a local convert named Jason fits the author's practice of creating names to give verisimilitude to his story. Further supporting this as a made-up name is the fact that he is pivotal to a made-up story. There is nothing about the Beroea story that suggests there was a Beroea source. In short, there is nothing in this Acts segment that qualifies as historical data to supplement what we know from Paul's first letter to the Thessalonians.

The Itinerary of Paul

A Cameo Essay by Dennis E. Smith and Joseph B. Tyson

Acts has long been used as a resource for reconstructing the itinerary of Paul. Such usage is supported by the presupposition that the author of Acts did not use the collection of Paul's letters as a source. Building on this presupposition, many scholars have concluded that the author of Acts had an independent "itinerary source," which he used to provide a basic framework for telling the story of Paul. The Acts Seminar, however, is convinced that the author of Acts *did* have access to Paul's letters and made use of them as major resources. This means that the burden of proof has shifted, particularly in regard to hypotheses about proposed sources of Acts. When one works from the perspective that the author had access to the itinerary data in Paul's letters, the evidence for a separate itinerary source is not only seriously undermined, it evaporates.

Acts sometimes follows the Pauline letters rather closely and sometimes diverges from or supplements what the letters contain. For example, in 1 Thessalonians Paul recalls that he came to Thessalonica after the visit to Philippi (1 Thess 2:2) and that he travelled to Athens after leaving Thessalonica (3:1). This is the same sequence of locales in Acts 16:11–17:34, but with significant variations. Acts 17:10–15 reports a mission in Beroea, a place Paul never mentions. Acts 17:14 says that Silas and Timothy did not accompany Paul to Athens, but in 1 Thess 3:1–6 Paul tells of sending Timothy from Athens back to Thessalonica to learn of the situation there and of receiving good news upon his return. Nothing is said about Silas, although a Silvanus joins Paul and Timothy in writing the letter (1 Thess 1:1). Assuming that Luke had access to Paul's letters, he would have learned about the Philippi-Thessalonica-Athens sequence, but he obviously felt free to adapt this information as he saw fit.

The disagreements in respect to Paul's itinerary are frequently explained as due to the author's use of additional historical data contained in an itinerary source. We propose, however, that he was creatively adapting the story of Paul to fit the agenda of Acts. We see his hand at work especially in the way he frames the itinerary. Many readers of Acts see a portrayal of Paul's career in terms of three missionary journeys (Acts 13:1–14:28; 15:36–18:21; 18:23–21:14), but the letters of Paul show no awareness of such a pattern. John Knox aptly remarked, "If you had stopped Paul on the streets of Ephesus and said to him, 'Paul, which of your missionary journeys are you on now?' he would have looked at you blankly without the remotest idea of what was in your mind."[10] Luke's organization of Paul's missionary career in terms of three journeys is dictated by his own agenda, in which he focuses major attention on Jerusalem and apostolic leadership. This agenda requires Paul to pay periodic visits to Jerusalem. Acts has five such visits (Acts 9:26–27; 11:29–12:25; 15:1–29; 18:22; 21:15–23:30), while only three are mentioned in the Pauline letters (Gal 1:18–21; Gal 2:1–10; Rom 15:25–32).[11] Luke has an interest in portraying Paul as closely linked to the Jerusalem apostles, and so he has him go there as frequently as possible.

An unbiased search for history is guided by the principle that primary sources—in this case the letters of Paul—are to be preferred to secondary sources—in this case the Acts of the Apostles. Thus, there are solid grounds for distrusting the historical reliability of Paul's itinerary in Acts both in terms of its overall framework and its many individual narratives. Agreements between Acts and Paul are due to the use of the letters by the author of Acts; disagreements are due to Luke's literary creativity. In this volume, when we discuss specific episodes, we attempt to "look over the shoulder" of our author at work. We trace how he drew data from Paul's letters, analyze those points where he differs, and suggest reasons why he made such changes.

Paul Preaches in Athens

17 [16]While Paul awaited the arrival of Timothy and Silas, he investigated the sights. He found the abundance of idols quite disturbing. [17]So he began to address Jews and devout gentiles in the synagogue and, on weekdays, whoever happened to be present in the city center. [18]Among those who encountered Paul were Epicurean and Stoic philosophers. "What point is this dilettante trying to make?" some asked, while others said, "He seems to be a herald of alien gods." (This is because he was preaching about Jesus and the resurrection.) [19]So they apprehended Paul and led him to the Council of the Areopagus, asking, "May we learn what this novel doctrine you are talking about is? [20]Since you are propounding alien ideas, we certainly wish to know just what point you are trying to make." ([21]All Athenians, whether native or immigrants, delight in nothing so much as to hear or speak about anything that is quite novel.)

[22]Whereupon Paul, standing in the middle of the council, said: "Gentlemen of Athens. I observe that you are in every way quite devout. [23]While I was walking about and examining your devotional monuments, I even found an altar bearing the inscription 'To an unknown god.' What you thus revere in ignorance is what I am proclaiming to you.

[24]"The God who fashioned the universe and all that is does not, as sovereign over heaven and earth, inhabit temples of human manufacture, [25]nor does the One who bestows life and breath and everything else require the ministration of human hands, as if God had needs! [26]From one person God fashioned every race and nation to occupy the entire surface of the earth, having established times of dominion and boundaries of habitation. [27]Humankind was fashioned so that it would strive after God, in the hope that it might apprehend God, as it were, and achieve the object of its quest. God is not, in fact, distant from any one of us, [28]for 'In God we live, thrive, and exist.' This is how some of our poets put it: 'For we are God's offspring.'

[29]"Since we have sprung from God, we ought not imagine that the Deity resembles gold or silver or stone, the products of human thought and mortal craft! [30]God will overlook past failures that were due to ignorance. For the present, God invites all people everywhere to change their lives, [31]for God has set a time at which he intends to judge the world justly by a man he has selected, in proof whereof God has raised this man from the dead."

³²Some engaged in ridicule when they heard about resurrection of the dead, but others said, "We shall listen to more of what you have to say about this subject on another occasion." ³³At that Paul left the council. ³⁴Some people did become pupils of Paul and come to believe. These included, among others, Dionysius, a member of the Areopagus, and a woman named Damaris.

Comments on the Story

The focus of this narrative is Paul's speech (Acts 17:22–31). The verses leading up to it set the scene and prepare us to hear and understand points in the speech (17:16–21). The verses that follow it let us know how the speech was received (17:32–34).

The Setting (Acts 17:16–21)

We first learn that, while Paul waits in Athens for his companions to arrive from Beroea, he examines the many religious objects in the city and becomes quite agitated (Acts 17:16). He is no casual tourist; rather he spends his time in dialogue with Jews and Godfearers in synagogues and with Gentiles in the agora (the marketplace or city center, 17:17). Among the interested auditors are certain Stoic and Epicurean philosophers, some of whom think that he is empty-headed and others who suspect that he is talking about foreign deities (17:18). To inquire further, they take him to the Areopagus and give him a chance to explain his ideas more extensively (17:19).

Ancient readers would think of Athens as the center of enlightened philosophical activity, and so the presence of Stoic and Epicurean philosophers is only to be expected. These schools would have been well represented in Athens. The image of Paul speaking to passersby in the agora would remind them of Socrates, whose dialogues were recorded by Plato. Luke is not Paul's Plato, but he rather pointedly shows that his hero engaged in dialogue as did Socrates. In Acts 17:17, the word here translated as "addressed" may more literally be read as "dialogued." Moreover, readers would be aware that in 399 BCE Socrates was executed in Athens on the charges of corrupting the youth and a lack of proper concern for the gods. Paul was suspected of doing something equally wrong, namely introducing foreign deities.

Luke's image of Athens is, however, a city characterized not by enlightened reason, but of unenlightened religion. As Luke describes it, its citizens worship a multitude of deities (Acts 17:16), are obsessed with novelty (17:21), and suspect foreignness (17:18, 20). In Acts 17:18, Luke explains the Athenian suspicion of Paul, perhaps suggesting that they thought that when he proclaimed Jesus and Resurrection (*Iesous* and *Anastasis*) that he was introducing two new gods. But is Luke's description coherent? If Athens is so full of gods, why would the citizens be wary of two more? If Athenians are obsessed with novelty, why would they be suspicious to hear a proclamation of new gods? How can Luke conceive of Athenians as, on the one hand, constantly seeking for something new and, on the other, wary of foreign ideas? To be sure, a desire for novelty and xenophobia are not incompatible ("we like new ideas but only from our own"). But Luke's portrayal here seems to suggest a tension between reception and resistance, and the tension is not resolved.

When Paul is taken to the Areopagus, it is not clear if he is under arrest or simply being given an opportunity to expand on his dialogues in the agora. In other words, when Luke writes of the Areopagus, is he thinking of the place of that name or of the judicial body that met there? Scholars have long debated this issue, but if we examine this narrative in the light of the many other episodes in Acts, it is likely that it is the judicial council that Luke has in mind. Recall how often we have seen this pattern at work: Paul enters a city and speaks with Jews, some of whom accept and others reject his message. Then he speaks to Gentiles, who receive him positively. Later he gets into trouble with the city authorities, who arrest him and/or punish him. Finally Paul is forced to leave. In Athens, there is no suggestion that Paul was punished, but, unless there is a complete departure from the usual Lukan pattern, the incident at the Areopagus should be seen as an interrogation before the city authorities. There is no violence as there is in most of the other narratives, but there is a suggestion of arrest in 17:19 in the verb translated as "apprehended." To be sure, the situation seems restrained and polite, but it is more likely, as Luke presents it, that the local authorities grilled Paul than that he had a friendly discussion with fellow philosophers.

The Speech (Acts 17:22–31)

The first time Luke recorded a speech of Paul to Gentiles who were not associated with synagogues was in Acts 14:15–17. In Acts 17 we have the second, a more fully developed speech. It is clearly important for Luke to focus on the occasion when his hero had an opportunity to speak in the city renowned for its culture and intellect. In previous speeches to Jews and Godfearers the Lukan Paul could count on acquaintance with a common body of sacred literature, but how can he approach those who do not share this heritage and approach the divine in a quite different way? The speech of Paul before the Areopagus is Luke's answer.

In the speech Paul makes a number of points, which can be enumerated as follows:

You Athenians are very religious. Paul begins his speech with what appears to be a compliment to the Athenians: "I observe that you are in every way quite devout" (Acts 17:22). There is, however, a nuance to the word translated "devout" that may not be so complimentary. It suggests an overdone kind of piety and sometimes is best translated as "superstitious." Although this is a possible reading of 17:22, it does not cohere well with the tone of the speech to this point. The verse leads up to the Pauline statement about the altar to an unknown God (17:23). The idea is that the Athenians worship, among others, an unknown God; they are so religious that they do not wish to leave any God un-worshipped. Paul does not condemn them for this worship, but rather fastens on it to proclaim this God as the creator.

Athenians unknowingly worship the creator. The unknown God whom Athenians worship is, Paul claims, the creator of all things and Lord of heaven and earth. Paul's words to the Gentiles in Acts 14:15–17 made a similar point, but there we saw a clearer proclamation of monotheism than here in Acts 17. Paul called upon the people of Lystra to abandon their worship of the traditional gods and turn to the one living God (14:15). In the Areopagus address, Paul does not explicitly call for the exclusive worship of the creator God, although he implies that his auditors must abandon their traditional religion (see 17:30–31). In 17:24–25 he contrasts the traditional Greek gods with the creator, who does not live in shrines and does not need sacrifices. But Luke must have been aware that some Athenians may well have thought that Paul was talking about one god among many. Indeed, even in some forms of Christian thought at the time of Acts, the creator is not the high God, and for Marcion the creator God is not the God and father of Jesus Christ. Clearly Luke opposes these theologies, but many readers would expect a more vigorous endorsement of monotheism on Paul's part than we have here.

We must, however, pay attention to the function of this speech within its Acts context. Luke has told us that Paul had been suspected of trying to introduce new gods to the Athenians. The identification of the creator God with the unknown God is a clever strategy to support a denial of this charge. We should understand Paul as saying that he is not introducing new, foreign, or strange deities; he is rather revealing the true nature of the God already worshipped in Athens.

God created all humans, whose purpose is to seek God. At Acts 17:26 Luke's Paul turns to the creation of human beings. Drawing on Genesis, he claims that all humans came from the one person and that the creator God determined times and boundaries, apparently meaning historical epochs and national borders. The purpose of humanity, he says, is to seek and perhaps find God, who is not far from any of us. On the one hand, since God is not far from us, we should have little difficulty in finding God. On the other hand, the finding is expressed in tentative terms ("in the hope that it might apprehend God, as it were, and achieve the object of its quest," 17:27).

God and humans are related; idolatry is condemned. Paul draws on Greek poets to make the point that human beings exist in God and are actually related to God. The quotation in Acts 17:28 is from the poet Aratus. Paul then argues that, since we are related to God, we should not imagine the divine as composed of gold or silver, or as the product of human art.

Repent, for the day of judgment is coming. Finally, Paul says that God has overlooked the times of ignorance but now requires repentance from all people in preparation for the day of judgment (Acts 17:30–31). The mention of ignorance in verse 30 recalls verse 23 at the beginning of the speech. Related Greek words—*agnostos; agnoia*, signifying a lack of knowledge—appear in both verses. The connection suggests that the past worship of the unknown God will, as due to ignorance, be overlooked. From now on repentance is required, and in this light it becomes clear what repentance involves: for the people of Athens, and indeed for all people, it means the abandonment of their traditional worship—with idols, shrines, and sacrifices. The time for repentance is limited, since God has designated a day on which the risen one will judge in righteousness (17:31).

It is striking to note the various elements that make up the Areopagus speech. First, concepts about creation appear to be drawn from the Hebrew Scriptures, even if the concept is known also in Greek thought. Even some of the language in the speech echoes that of Genesis: one God created all that is, creating humans from one original (Gen 2:7) and setting boundaries of time and space (Gen 1:14). The need to search for God and the concept that God is near are both found in the OT (see Deut 4:29; Isa 55:6; Ps 145:18; Jer 23:23), although divine nearness is also a Stoic idea. The condemnation of idolatry is fundamental in much of the OT and Jewish thought. Second, there are some elements that seem to be closely related to Greek thought and literature. Acts 17:28 commends a kind of pantheism that would have been foreign to the OT and Jewish thought. There is a probable allusion to literature about Epimenides and a quotation from Aratus' *Phaenomena*. Third, specifically Christian elements appear only at the end of the speech, when Paul warns about a coming day of judgment. It is notable, however, that even here the name of Jesus does not appear (although it does in 17:18), nothing is said about his death, and christological ideas are absent.

Just how these elements cohere is difficult to discern. It is surprising to hear Paul condemn idolatry but identify the Athenian worship of the unknown God as covert acknowledgement of the creator. And how can he bring together the doctrine of creation, which he vigorously affirms, with the pantheistic tendencies he also expresses? Teaching about creation tends to distance humans from the divine; pantheism brings them close together. These issues are troublesome, but we should keep in mind the fact that Luke, the probable author of the speech, was not a systematic theologian and so not greatly concerned to fit together the fine points of the speech. Perhaps it is the melding of distinct and intriguing concepts that is the speech's attraction.

The Result (Acts 17:32–34)

Luke reports three responses to Paul's speech: some ridiculed the speaker; others said they would hear Paul again at a later date; still others joined the Pauline movement. The first group reacted against Paul's claim about resurrection in Acts 17:31. It is interesting to note that Luke focused on resurrection as the point of ridicule. This should not be interpreted to mean that the Athenians accepted Paul's other contentions, such as the identity of the unknown God. But Luke tends to lift up the doctrine of resurrection as the major factor in Pauline teaching, and we shall see how this theme operates as a deterrent not only for Gentiles but also for Jews. The response of the second group is sometimes taken to be a polite rejection of Paul, but we should probably understand it as straightforward. C. K. Barrett probably captures Luke's meaning in the following paraphrase: "This is interesting; we do not come to decisions quickly, but there is a *prima facie* case and we should like to hear the argument again."[12] The third group includes those who accepted Paul's message and joined up with him. Some commentators conclude from Acts 17:34 that Luke means to stress the meagerness of the positive response to Paul, but this is probably not Luke's intention. It is true that only two names are recorded, but one of them—Dionysius—is a member of the very council that interrogated Paul, and Luke adds that there were others. Moreover, we might compare the response here with that at Philippi, where there is only one named convert—Lydia (16:14–15). The harvest did not seem meager there, and there is no reason to think it so in Athens.

In Search of History

The detail that Paul visited Athens is historically accurate. Paul tells us that himself. It is part of his travel itinerary during his first trip to Greece. After leaving Thessalonica, after a "short time" he sent Timothy back to visit the Thessalonians while Paul waited in Athens (1 Thess 2:17; 3:1–2). After Timothy reported back, Paul wrote them the letter we know as 1 Thessalonians (1 Thess 3:6). By that time, Paul may have been in Corinth, the next stop in his travel itinerary. Luke's source for a visit to Athens is clearly 1 Thessalonians, especially since Luke repeats the odd detail that Paul was in Athens without Timothy. However, Luke chooses to change the details about Paul's co-workers. According to Acts 17:15, Paul arrived in Athens after fleeing in haste from Beroea, but Silas and Timothy remained behind, intending to join him later. They only catch up with him in Corinth (18:5). Luke leaves out the detail that Timothy was dispatched by Paul from Athens to check up on the Thessalonians (1 Thess 3:2). Such an intentional omission must have a reason. Perhaps Luke wished to avoid any detail that might suggest, even obliquely, that Paul wrote letters, a detail about the historical Paul that Luke carefully avoids, even though Paul was famous as a letter writer in his own lifetime (2 Cor 10:10).

It is not entirely unlikely that Paul preached in some form while in Athens, but, if so, he himself makes no mention of it. In fact, in his recounting of his itinerary, Athens seems to be no more than a stopover for him. In any case, the story in Acts is entirely fictional. The centerpiece, a speech by Paul to the Athenians, is part of the collection of speeches found throughout Acts, all of which are identified as creations of the author of Acts (see the cameo essay, "Speeches in Acts," p. 45). Like the others, this speech represents what the author thinks would have been appropriate for Paul to say on this occasion. But the Paul who speaks in Athens is the Paul of Acts, not the historical Paul, and the content of the speech represents Luke literally putting words in Paul's mouth; this speech in no way can serve to represent Paul's ideas. The story setting up the speech draws on a theme emphasized elsewhere in Acts, that the apostles preached in a manner comparable to the philosophers (see the cameo essay, "When Apostles Become Philosophers," p. 60). This is clearly a Lukan motif. Also, as pointed out in the commentary above, the idea that "resurrection of the dead" was the point of controversy for the audience is a major theme of the plot of Acts.

Two people are named as converts in Athens, "Dionysius, a member of the Areopagus, and a woman named Damaris" along with unnamed "others" (Acts 17:34). Scholars routinely give credence to the listing of proper names in Acts, thinking they are likely to be historical residue. In this book, we argue that Luke, in fact, creates names as a way of lending verisimilitude to his story (see cameo essay, "Names in Acts," p. 22). This verse may be "exhibit A" for that argument. From Paul we learn that his first converts in Achaea were the members of the household of Stephanas in Corinth (1 Cor 16:15; see also 1 Cor 1:16). Luke, however, is entrapped by his own created story of Paul's preaching in Athens. The story carries the aura of the gospel being preached in the center of ancient philosophical learning. Luke needs the speech to be successful; thus, he creates a list of converts in Athens, one of which is named as a member of the city council itself.

Paul Preaches in Corinth

18 After his encounter with the Areopagus, Paul left Athens for Corinth, ²where he came upon a Jew, Aquila, from Pontus, and his wife Priscilla, who had recently arrived from Italy because the Emperor Claudius had ordered all Jews out of Rome. Paul presented himself to this couple ³and came to live with them because they, like him, crafted with fabrics. So Paul went to work.

⁴Every Sabbath he lectured in the synagogue, trying to persuade both Jews and gentiles. ⁵When, however, Silas and Timothy arrived from Macedonia, Paul devoted

himself fully to the mission, declaring to the Jews that the Messiah was Jesus. ⁶When they impiously opposed him, Paul shook out his clothes in a symbolic gesture and announced: "You are responsible for your own fate. Don't blame me. Henceforth I shall apply myself to the gentiles."

⁷He transferred his mission from the synagogue to the adjacent house of the devout Titius Justus. ⁸The leader of the synagogue, Crispus, came to faith in the Lord, as did his entire household. Learning of this, many Corinthians embraced the faith and received baptism.

⁹The Lord addressed Paul in a nocturnal vision: "Have no fear. Continue to speak and do not desist, ¹⁰for I am with you. No one will be able to attack you successfully, for my people are numerous in this city." ¹¹Paul settled there for eighteen months, teaching the word of God.

¹²Now while Gallio was governing the province of Achaea, the Jews converged upon Paul *en masse* and brought him before the bench. ¹³"This man is trying to persuade people to worship God unlawfully," they charged. ¹⁴Just as Paul was about to reply, Gallio addressed the Jews: "If there had been an actual injury or any serious misbehavior, my dear Jews, I should have quite properly entertained your claims, ¹⁵but, since these are quibbles about mere language, titles, and your own regulations, please see to the matter yourselves. I have no desire to pronounce judgments on these issues." ¹⁶Gallio then had the Jews removed from his court, but not before everybody mobbed Sosthenes, the leader of the synagogue, and gave him a beating in court. ¹⁷Gallio showed no interest in any of this.

Comments on the Story

Paul apparently travels alone from Athens to Corinth, a distance of about thirty-seven miles. He dialogues with Jews and Godfearers in the synagogue, obtains a divided response, and then turns to present his message to Gentiles. He meets up with Aquila and Priscilla, who had been expelled from Rome in a recent pogrom and who will play significant roles in later narratives. After Silas and Timothy arrive from Macedonia, Paul intensifies his mission to the Jews, but most of them reject his message. Paul then repeats an announcement he had made in Pisidian Antioch to the effect that, because of Jewish rejection, his mission hereafter will be to

Gentiles. Despite the announcement, Luke notes that Paul made an important Jewish convert, Crispus, who bore the title "leader of the synagogue" (*archisynagogos*), and that many others followed his lead. In any event Paul changes the base of his operations to the house of Titius Justus, which is next door to the synagogue. One night he receives a vision in which the Lord appears to him and encourages him to continue his mission in Corinth, and Luke notes that Paul stays there for eighteen months, an unusual length of time for episodes in Acts. But at some point during this time the Jews unite in opposition to Paul and bring him before the Roman proconsul, Gallio. They charge him with inducing people to worship God in ways contrary to the law. Gallio, however, judges that the matter is an inner Jewish affair and irrelevant to Roman law. He therefore dismisses the case, and the crowd beats Sosthenes, the new leader of the synagogue.

The episode in Corinth follows the basic Lukan pattern, which has Paul first present his message to Jews and then go to Gentiles when Jewish opposition arises. But there are significant variations. Here Luke mentions the names of some of the converts from among Jews and Godfearers, even noting the influence of a converted leader of the synagogue. Also in Corinth the Jewish opposition leads to legal action against Paul and his cohorts, an action that turns against the accusers. The case against Paul is dismissed, and the leading accuser is attacked.

Acts 18:6 is the second of three statements in which Paul announces that he no longer intends to evangelize Jews but will hereafter go to Gentiles. The first of the three statements was in 13:46–47; the final one is in 28:25–28. The statement here is accompanied with a gesture—shaking out clothes—and a curse: "Your blood on your own heads. I am clean;" or, in our translation, "You are responsible for your own fate. Don't blame me" (18:6). Despite this solemn announcement, Paul will meet again with Jews in Ephesus (18:19; 19:8, 10) and Rome (28:17–28), just as he did after the announcement in 13:46–47. On one level, each of the three announcements is meant for the locality in which it is proclaimed. Acts 13:46–47 means that Paul and Barnabas ceased their efforts among Jews in Pisidian Antioch and turned to the Gentiles in that area. Acts 18:6 means the same for Corinth, and 28:25–28 for Rome. But the announcements are probably not merely local statements. They remind the reader of the pattern that governs almost all of the episodes Luke reports for Paul's missions: he goes first to the Jews and then after their rejection turns to the Gentiles. The use of this pattern in descriptions of Paul's activity in Thessalonica, Iconium, Beroea, and Corinth repeats in sharp focus what the announcements proclaim for the ministry as a whole. Thus we have the anomaly of Paul visiting synagogues even after he has disowned a mission to Jews. Within the individual narratives the announcements appear to be intended for Pisidian Antioch, Corinth, and Rome, or more broadly for Asia, Greece, and Italy. But taken together they function as powerful summaries of Paul's mission as a whole: *Jews have heard but rejected the message, which is accepted by Gentiles.*

It is notable, however, that not all the details of Luke's narratives support this general thesis. Here in Corinth there are Jews who accept Paul's message, for example, the synagogue leader, Crispus (Acts 18:8). He was so influential that many others followed along with him. Actually, almost all of the episodes that Luke recounts tell of Jewish conversions. But, apparently due to the rejection by the larger number of Jews, Paul is able to pronounce a judgment on Jews as a whole. In the Corinth episode the blood curse is particularly prominent. It means that Paul is no longer responsible for whatever might happen to Jews, since they have heard and rejected his message (18:6). The reader will recall that at Thessalonica, although some of the Jews joined Paul and Silas, "these conversions aroused the envy of the Jews" (17:5), who stirred up the crowd against the Christian missionaries. Likewise, in Corinth Paul converted the leader of the synagogue and numerous others, but Luke says that "the Jews" resisted (18:6) and accused him before Gallio (18:13). The juxtaposition of Jewish acceptance and rejection is remarkable. We might expect our narrator to praise the accepting Jews and condemn the rejecters. Instead Luke ultimately neglects the former group and characteristically refers to the opponents simply as "the Jews" (see also 13:45, 50; 14:4; 17:5; 18:12, 14, 28; 20:3, 19). The rhetorical effect of this strategy is to lead readers to de-emphasize the accepting group and to think of "the Jews" only in their role as opponents of Paul and the Christian message.

Luke's strategy regarding Jews is also apparent in the incident before Gallio (Acts 18:12–17). Jews present a united front in bringing charges against Paul before the Roman proconsul. They say that he is "trying to persuade people to worship God unlawfully" (18:13). The reader may recall the charges that were brought in Thessalonica (17:7) and Athens (17:18). These charges, however, were those of Gentiles. In Corinth it is Jews who charge Paul with teaching "unlawful" worship. What law is intended here, Roman or Jewish? Since the case comes before a Roman official, we might expect that Paul is being charged with a violation of Roman law, but the context requires that the plaintiffs are speaking of Torah, and the remarks of Gallio make it clear that Roman law is not in the picture. Indeed, Gallio is able to dismiss the case because it does not deal with "an actual injury or any serious misbehavior" but with "quibbles about mere language, titles, and your own regulations." (18:14–15). His verdict, addressed to the Jews ("see to the matter yourselves," 18:15), may suggest that matters relating to Paul's message are intramural Jewish affairs. But this is not likely to have been Luke's intention. His focus is on Jewish objections to Paul's message, and the implication is that these are not serious. Even so, the contrast between Jewish and Roman law that Gallio draws would leave readers with the impression that Roman law deals with important matters that are necessary for the social good but that Jewish law deals with minor matters, such as the meaning of names and words. Furthermore, the plaintiffs in this case are made to appear quite foolish in thinking that cases involving Jewish law can be adjudicated in a Roman court. To add injury to insult, the new leader of the synagogue, Sosthenes, is attacked and beaten, although it is not clear who is involved in the assault (18:17). Perhaps we are to think of Jews attacking their leader for losing the case against Paul, and, if so, Luke must have intended to characterize Jews as brutally contentious with one another. But if the attackers are Gentiles, Gallio's tolerance suggests that such attacks are not only to be expected but also justified. In either case we can see Luke's rhetorical strategy at work against Jews and Judaism.

The vision to Paul in Acts 18:9–10 calls for little comment. Paul is told not to fear because the Lord is with him and he will not be harmed. The Lord adds that many of his people are in this city. The words are probably intended to be predictive: if Paul will continue the mission in Corinth, many are destined to become the Lord's people.

Finally, we should take note of some of the minor characters who appear in Corinth. Timothy and Silas had been with Paul in Macedonia, and apparently Paul expected them to meet him in Athens (Acts 17:16). Their failure to appear there is not explained, but their arrival in Corinth (18:5) allows Paul to intensify his operations. Aquila and Priscilla appear for the first time in 18:2, where Luke says they were Jews who, though originally from Pontus, had been deported from Rome by the Emperor Claudius (see below on the possible historical aspects of this reference). Paul went to live and work with them in Corinth. At this point it is not stated that Priscilla and Aquila are followers of Jesus, but their close association with the Pauline mission becomes clearer in subsequent references. In 18:18–19 they accompany him on the trip from Corinth to Ephesus, and in 18:26 they instruct Apollos in Christian doctrine. We hear nothing further of Crispus or Titius Justus, to say nothing of Gallio or Sosthenes.

In Search of History

In verses 5–17, Luke tells a story that, except for the names and the places, he has told before and will tell again. It contains plot devices that are patently Lukan.

1. After arriving in a city, Paul preaches first to Jews in the synagogue (18:5; see also 9:20; 13:5, 14; 14:1; 17:1–4, 10; 18:19; 19:8).
2. Invariably, the Jews in the synagogue oppose him with such vehemence that he is forced to leave (18:6; see also 13:45–51; 14:2; 17:5–9, 13; 19:9). Here in 18:6 Paul also makes an official statement that he is now turning to Gentiles, a device Luke uses elsewhere (see also 13:46; 28:28).
3. He continues his preaching in another venue where he is very successful, primarily among Gentiles (18:7–11; see also 13:48–49; 19:9).
4. The Jews attack Paul more violently and take him to trial before the local Roman official (18:12–17), a theme that dominates the story of Paul's arrest and various trials in 21:27–26:32. In 19:23–41, there is a variant in this pattern in that it is Gentile silversmiths who take Paul to court. In some cases, Paul and his companions are driven out of the city (see also 9:23–25; 13:50; 14:5, 19; 17:10, 14).
5. A Roman official judges Paul innocent in a process that regularly involves a speech by the official (18:14–17; see also 19:35–41; 21:27–26:32).

Even though the story is clearly Lukan, it has been widely considered historically credible, based on the fact that Gallio was a historical character. However, as the cameo essay, "The Gallio Episode," points out, this bit of historical data is not sufficient to make the entire story historical. As a result of these arguments, the Seminar voted against the historical reliability of 18:5–17.

The Votes of the Fellows
Red/Probable
- The story of Paul's hearing before Gallio is a Lukan creation.
- The story of Paul's hearing before Gallio should be read in accordance with Lukan theology and themes.

Gray/Doubtful
- Paul was in Corinth when Gallio was proconsul of Corinth.

Black/Improbable
- The story of Paul's hearing before Gallio is a source for historical data about Paul.

As for Aquila and Priscilla, Paul's letters affirm that they were historical characters. The question is whether additional data in Acts is credible. After reviewing the arguments summarized in the cameo essay "Priscilla and Aquila" (p. 223), the Fellows drew the following conclusions:

The Votes of the Fellows
Red/Probable
- Aquila and Priscilla were actual historical characters.
- Aquila and Priscilla were a married couple.
- Aquila and Priscilla at one time lived in Ephesus.
- Aquila and Priscilla were, at one time, associated with Paul in Ephesus.

Pink/Possible
- Aquila and Priscilla at one time lived in Corinth.
- Aquila and Priscilla were associated with Paul in Corinth.
- Priscilla was regarded as, in some sense, the more important of the two.
- Priscilla's actual name was Prisca, but the author of Acts, for whatever reason, changed this to the diminutive form.

Gray/Doubtful
- Aquila and Priscilla were "tentmakers" by trade.
- Aquila and Priscilla lived at one time in Rome but left because of Claudius' edict banishing all Jews from Rome.

- Aquila, at least, was Jewish.
- Aquila, at least, was originally from Pontus in Asia Minor.

References

White, "Paul, Gallio, and the Bema at Corinth"
Walker, "The Portrayal of Aquila and Priscilla"

The Gallio Episode
A Cameo Essay by Dennis E. Smith

According to Acts 18:12–16, Paul was taken before the proconsul Gallio for judgment at the Corinthian tribunal (Greek: *bema*; our translation: "the bench"). This incident has become an important cornerstone for all reconstructions of Pauline chronology. This is because the proconsulship of Gallio can be verified, and because we have now excavated the tribunal at Corinth. Because of such independent evidence confirming details of the story, the Acts story is widely considered to be historically reliable.

The proconsulship of Gallio has been confirmed by an honorific inscription found at Delphi that was originally set up in the temple of Apollo. The inscription transcribes a letter to the citizens of Delphi by Emperor Tiberius that makes a reference to Gallio as proconsul of Corinth. Because the letter refers to the twenty-sixth acclamation of Tiberius as Emperor, a datable event, it allows one to interpret the proconsulship of Gallio to have taken place sometime between the years 49 to 54. Thus, as many scholars conclude, Paul would most likely have appeared before Gallio in about the year 52, that is, if one accepts this story as credible.[13]

In an unpublished paper presented to the Acts Seminar in March 2007, L. Michael White argued against the historical probability of this incident.[14] He pointed out that the excavated tribunal was originally dated to the mid-first century CE by using Acts as a reliable historical resource documenting its existence during the time of Paul. More recent excavation work at Corinth, however, has begun to re-examine the dating of a number of monuments in the Forum, including the tribunal, by using more rigorous methods than had been applied before. White argued in his paper that it is quite likely that the tribunal did not exist as such until late in the first century; it was thus not there in the time of Paul but had been constructed by the time Acts was written.

In regard to the Gallio inscription, White pointed out that it is characteristic of the author of Luke-Acts to make references to local rulers based on his research into existing historical records. Sometimes he gets his data wrong, however, as in the case of the census under Quirinius (Luke 2:1–2) which was actually a much smaller event than Luke claims, and would have taken place after Quirinius became provincial governor in 6 CE, which was well after the birth of Jesus. White proposed that the reference to Gallio in Acts is based on Luke's practicing the method of "autopsy," a method of research also practiced by his contemporary, Plutarch, in his series of biographies about famous historical figures. That is, Luke had seen the Gallio inscription in Delphi and used the data it contained in his story about Paul in Corinth. White concludes that even though the proconsulship of Gallio was historical, in itself it does not confirm the Acts story to be historical.

Priscilla and Aquila
A Cameo Essay by William O. Walker, Jr.

Priscilla and Aquila appear three times in Acts (18:1–3, 18–19, and 24–26), and Prisca and Aquila—clearly the same couple ("Priscilla" is simply the diminutive form of "Prisca")—are mentioned three times in the Pauline corpus (1 Cor 16:19b; Rom 16:3–5a; and 2 Tim 4:19a). Acts presents considerably more information regarding the pair than does the Pauline corpus, but recent scholarship suggests that the portrayal in Acts is based on material in the Pauline corpus that has simply been adapted and embellished in the service of Luke's own theological/apologetic and literary agendas.[15] Thus, the transformation of "Prisca" into the diminutive "Priscilla" is consistent with Luke's general denigration of the role of women in the early Jesus movement. Further, the identification of her as Aquila's wife simply makes explicit what is clearly implied by Paul, and the couple's move from Rome to Corinth serves as a literary device to bring them into association with him. In addition, the apparently irrelevant identification of Aquila as both a Jew and a native of Pontus may reflect Luke's desire to draw a clear distinction between this Jewish companion of Paul and the "heretic" Marcion, who also was from Pontus but sought to separate Christianity from Judaism. Finally, the portrayal of Priscilla and Aquila, Paul's associates, as correctors of Apollos' "heresy," suggests that Paul also was an opponent of (Marcionite?) "heresy." In short, Acts offers little if any independent historical information regarding the couple in question, but its portrayal does reflect important aspects of the author's own agenda.

Depending solely on Paul's references to the couple, only the following can be said regarding Priscilla and Aquila: (1) the woman's name was actually "Prisca," not "Priscilla." (2) Prisca and Aquila are always mentioned as a pair, never separately, and the order in which the two names appear varies, thus suggesting that they were regarded as of equal status and importance in the Jesus movement. (3) There was a "church" in their house in one city, probably Ephesus, and perhaps in another, Rome. (4) The couple was with Paul, probably in Ephesus, when he wrote 1 Cor 16:19b. (5) They were known to the Corinthian church, which suggests that they may, at one time, have resided in Corinth. (6) If Romans 16 is an original part of Paul's letter to Rome, the couple was in Rome when he wrote the letter. (7) Paul expresses high esteem for the couple as his "fellow-workers" who "risked their necks to save [his] life" (Rom 16:4). (8) Paul notes the gratitude of "all the Anointed's communities of the nations" (Rom 16:4) to the couple, and this, though surely hyperbolic, suggests that they may have traveled rather widely in the Gentile world. In short, Prisca and Aquila appear to have been highly regarded within the circle of the Pauline churches.

What Luke has done, then, is to adapt and embellish Paul's references to Prisca and Aquila in such a way as to serve his own theological/apologetic and literary agendas. For the most part, however, his portrayal of the couple is essentially consistent with, if not identical to, that in the Pauline letters.

Paul Returns to Antioch

18 ¹⁸Paul stayed on for a number of days before saying his farewells to the believers and sailing off to Syria with Priscilla and Aquila. At the Corinthian port of Cenchreae he had his hair cut off, because he had undertaken a vow.

¹⁹When they reached Ephesus, Paul separated from the couple. He himself went to the synagogue and engaged the Jews. ²⁰They asked that he spend more time, but he could not agree, ²¹and bade them farewell, promising, "God willing, I shall come back to you at another time." Leaving Ephesus by ship, ²²Paul arrived in Caesarea and went from there to *Jerusalem*, where he paid his respects to the church before continuing on to Antioch. ²³He spent some time there and then set out again, moving through Galatian territory and Phrygia, strengthening all the believers in each community as he traveled.

Comments on the Story

The translation above makes the course of travel in this section reasonably comprehensible. The Greek that lies behind the translation is not, however, so clear on some details. For example, Acts 18:19 seems to say that Paul left Priscilla and Aquila in Ephesus, but then we find that he remained in Ephesus, dialoguing with Jews in the synagogue. Apparently Luke means to locate all three characters in Ephesus but to confine synagogue preaching to Paul. What Priscilla and Aquila did during this time is not indicated here, but we will learn in the next section that they were quite active in the synagogue (see 18:26). Moreover, in 18:22, Paul lands at Caesarea and goes up to greet the church. The Greek text does not tell us where this church is located, but Pervo's translation is based on the assumption that it is in Jerusalem. A literal translation of 18:22 would read, "After arriving in Caesarea and going up and greeting the church, he went down to Antioch." We might surmise that the church in question is in Caesarea, and we could imagine Paul going up from the harbor into the city. But many scholars have asked why, if Paul was headed for Syria, as 18:18 says, he landed in Caesarea, rather than in the port of Antioch (see 13:4). Arriving at Caesarea would seem to be appropriate only if Paul intended to go to Jerusalem. Thus, Luke seems to be saying that Paul left from Corinth, spent a short time in Ephesus, then sailed to Caesarea, went up to Jerusalem and then to Antioch.

In Acts 18:18 Luke takes note of a vow that compelled the cutting of hair. The language allows us to understand that it was Aquila who made the vow, but it is more likely that, because of his primary interest in Paul, it is he that is intended. Luke does not explain the nature of the vow, but most scholars understand it to be something like a Nazirite vow, the stipulations for which are based on Num 6:1–21. In Numbers a person who undertakes a Nazirite vow abstains from all grape products, including wine, and allows his hair to grow long. The vow appears to be a lifetime dedication to an especially devout life, but it is possible that some persons took it for a specific time and under special circumstances. If this is the case with Paul, the cutting of his hair in 18:18 would signify the conclusion of the vow. We will see that many people in Jerusalem believed that Paul taught his followers to abandon Torah (see 21:20–21). Luke intends to show that this is a false charge, and the taking of a vow of special devotion is probably intended to support the image of Paul as a faithful Jew.

The response from Jews in Ephesus (Acts 18:20–21) is surprising in light of the previous narratives in which Paul receives at most a divided response. Here the Jews invite Paul to remain with them in Ephesus, but he declines, promising to return. Luke treats this episode as preliminary to the more extensive narrative of Paul's mission in Ephesus (see 19:1–40).

After Paul visited Antioch he returned to the mission field in Galatia and Phrygia (Acts 18:23). This verse is frequently understood to signify the beginning of a new missionary journey on Paul's part. In this construction, the first journey would encompass Acts 13–14, the second 15:36–18:22, and the third 18:23–21:16. Some scholars have, however, raised questions about this construction, arguing that the Acts narrative cannot so easily be outlined. Note here, for example, that no incidents are recorded about the mission in Galatia and Phrygia and that everything in this section centers on Ephesus.

In Search of History

After Paul's lengthy and significant stay in Corinth, Luke inserts a convoluted, brief travel narrative prior to what will be a lengthy and significant stay in Ephesus (chapter 19). He already knows Ephesus is in the future; he gets that from 1 Cor 16:8. So he has Paul travel directly to Ephesus, but on this first visit Paul does not stay there. Instead he takes a long, seemingly inconsequential detour that takes him to Jerusalem and Antioch before he finally arrives once more in Ephesus for a longer stay (Acts 19:1). To better discern why Luke tells his story in this way, we need to reconstruct what he started with.

Luke starts with three pieces of data, all of which he gets from 1 Corinthians. First, 1 Cor 16:8 tells him that Ephesus was visited after Paul left Corinth. Second, 1 Cor 16:19 tells him that Priscilla and Aquila settled in Ephesus. Third, 1 Cor 3:6 tells him that Apollos arrived in Corinth after Paul had left. With these building blocks, Luke creates the travel narrative in Acts 18:18–28.

Luke's fingerprints on this narrative can be seen in the underlying purpose for all of the details. First, Paul stops in Cenchreae, the port city of Corinth and a necessary component of a journey to Ephesus. It did not have to be mentioned; after all, Luke is regularly vague about how Paul gets from place to place. Luke could have learned from Rom 16:1–2 that Paul had made converts in Cenchreae, one of which was a prominent woman, Phoebe. However, he did not use this information. Rather, Luke's reason for the stop in Cenchreae is to insert the note that Paul shaved his head for a vow. The alert reader would recognize that this is a Jewish vow. Second, when he arrives in Ephesus, Paul goes directly to the synagogue, by now a practice easily recognizable as a mark of Lukan creativity. Third, he makes an unlikely stop in Caesarea and visits a Christian group there, followed by a quick visit to Jerusalem, which is likely to be the only reason for such a roundabout detour. Fourth, he next goes to Antioch. After that, he makes an unremarkable overland trip back to Ephesus. The vow and the synagogue visit reiterate Paul's Jewish bona fides. The visits to Jerusalem and Antioch remind of Paul's subservience to these two cities and their leadership. These are themes distinct to Acts. Adding these details at this point in Luke's story is simply a way to reinforce such ongoing themes.

Certainly one can propose that Luke is using here an independent travel itinerary for Paul, but, if so, one can only reconstruct from such a source the raw data that Paul traveled from A to B. What happened on the journey from A to B is clearly attributable to Luke's own narrative interests. But the existence of such an itinerary without any accompanying narrative is highly unlikely, and the pertinent information is readily available in 1 Corinthians. On the other hand, using such plausible geographical details as a context for creating new stories about Paul is a recognizable mark of Luke's attention to verisimilitude. Consequently, nothing contained in the entire travel narrative in Acts 18:18–28 qualifies as historical data (see also the cameo essay, "The Itinerary of Paul," p. 206). Further evidence regarding 18:24–28 will be discussed in the next section.

The Preaching of Apollos

18 ^{24}An Alexandrian Jew by the name of Apollos came to Ephesus. Apollos was an eloquent fellow who knew how to make effective use of the scriptures. ^{25}He had received instruction in the way of the Lord, could speak with spiritual ardor, and propound the story of Jesus with precision, but he was aware only of the baptism proclaimed by John. ^{26}Apollos launched a vigorous preaching mission in the synagogue. After Priscilla and Aquila had heard him, they took him aside and expounded the Movement more fully. ^{27}When Apollos expressed a desire to go to Achaea, he received support from the believers, who wrote to encourage the disciples there to receive him. After his arrival he was of considerable value to those who had come to believe through grace, ²⁸for he decisively routed the Jews in public debate, demonstrating from the scriptures that the Messiah is Jesus.

Comments on the Story

Apollos, an Alexandrian Jew, arrives in Ephesus and begins a vigorous preaching campaign. Luke says that Apollos is eloquent, learned, and powerful in his knowledge of the Scriptures. He accurately teaches the way of Jesus but is only aware of the baptism of John. After further instruction from Priscilla and Aquila and with the encouragement of the believers in Ephesus, he goes to Achaea (probably Corinth), helps the believers, and refutes the Jews there.

Many questions arise about this paragraph. Luke seems to stress the positive features of Apollos—his eloquence, his learning, his spiritual power. He has an accurate knowledge of the "story of Jesus," but there is obviously a deficiency in that he knows *only* the baptism of John. Priscilla and Aquila provide him with further knowledge about "the Way," and he becomes fully acceptable to the believing community. What does it mean that he knew only the baptism of John? The attentive reader would naturally think of the words of the risen Jesus in Acts 1:5: "John baptized with water. Before many days have passed you will be baptized with Holy Spirit." Baptism with Holy Spirit then was described in the Pentecost episode in Acts 2. But the book of Acts does not make it clear how the two baptisms are related. In Peter's speech at Pentecost he calls upon the audience to repent and be baptized in the name of Jesus, and he promises that they will receive the Holy Spirit (2:38). His comment about the household of Cornelius reverses the order but implies that both baptisms are necessary. After these Gentiles experienced the phenomenon of glossolalia, Peter announced, "There is no reason why these people, who have received the Holy Spirit just as we did, cannot be baptized with water, is there?" (10:47; see also 11:16). On another occasion, water baptism seems to be sufficient (see 8:36).

Despite the disparity, it seems clear that, in Luke's judgment, Apollos' awareness only of John's baptism constitutes a deficiency on his part. Why then does he not receive a spiritual baptism? Instead he receives further instruction from Priscilla and Aquila. What further information would they supply? We may find an answer to this question if we compare two summaries of Apollos' preaching, one before his conference with Priscilla and Aquila (18:25) and the other afterward (18:28). In the former he was able to recount the data about Jesus, while in the latter he identified the Messiah as Jesus. The comparison would suggest that what Apollos lacked was the belief in Jesus' Messiahship and that this doctrine was what Priscilla and Aquila taught him.

The question of Apollos' spiritual baptism is still troubling. If Apollos' theology was insufficient, Priscilla and Aquila helped him correct it. But, despite the fact that he knew only the baptism of John, no additional baptism was required. This issue becomes even more vexing when we examine the next paragraph about some twelve disciples who, like Apollos, had received only the baptism of John but who, unlike Apollos, were required to be baptized in the name of Jesus (see below on Acts 19:1–10).

In Search of History

Luke is here expanding on a character, Apollos, who is given a cameo role in 1 Corinthians. He is mentioned there as if a competitor to Paul, since there is a split between those who follow Paul and those who follow Apollos (1 Cor 1:12). The issue is apparently related to baptism (1 Cor 1:13–17). But in 1 Cor 3:6 he is identified as a co-worker who arrives after Paul ("I planted") and supports Paul's work ("Apollos watered"). With this bit of information from 1 Corinthians, Luke takes the story of Apollos in a direction never implied by Paul but important for Luke's story. He makes Apollos into an example of an inadequate doctrine associated with "the baptism proclaimed by John" (Acts 18:25). In doing so, he draws on data from the Gospel of Luke, in which John is defined as one who proclaims "the way of the Lord" and a "baptism and a change of heart" (Luke 3:3–4). The story of Apollos serves to set up the more extended analysis of the issues surrounding "the baptism proclaimed by John" in the next section, 19:1–10.

The term "the Way" occurs in both v. 25 and v. 26, but our translator, Richard Pervo, prefers to translate the term differently in these two instances, choosing "the way of the Lord" in verse 25 and "the Movement" in verse 26. He therefore considers the term to be used differently in these instances. It seems more likely that the usage is the same in both instances. The term is distinctive to Acts as a descriptive, almost technical, term for the movement Acts is describing (Acts 9:1–2; 19:9, 23; 22:4; 24:14).

Also distinctive to Acts is the concept of "the baptism proclaimed by John" as a problematic doctrine and practice (Acts 1:5; 19:1–7). As Pervo points out, it is best understood as "a Lucan cipher for inadequate doctrine and rite."[16] It is not false teaching, just inadequate. Thus Apollos knows "the way of The Lord" but must be instructed more fully by Priscilla and Aquila.

The story follows themes distinctive to Luke: "the baptism proclaimed by John" as problematic, teaching in the synagogue, and "routing the Jews in public debate" when Apollos arrives in Corinth (Acts 18:28). The detail that Priscilla and Aquila instruct Apollos in correct doctrine means that Luke has painted him as subordinate to Paul. The details of the story serve multiple interests particular to Luke, thus ruling out the probability that any of these details, other than those derived from Paul, qualify as historical (see also the cameo essay, "Priscilla and Aquila," pp. 223).

The Votes of the Fellows
Black/Improbable
- Aquila and Priscilla corrected Apollos' defective version of the gospel.

Paul in Ephesus

19 While Apollos was in Corinth, Paul made his way by the inland route to Ephesus, where he came upon some disciples. ²He asked them, "Did you receive the Holy Spirit when you came to believe?" "No," they answered, "We did not even hear that there is a Holy Spirit." ³"What sort of baptism did you receive, then?" "John's baptism." ⁴"John's baptism dealt with repentance," explained Paul. "He told the people about one who would come after him, in whom they were to believe. Jesus is the one of whom he spoke." ⁵Once they had learned this, they received baptism in the name of the Lord Jesus. ⁶After Paul had laid hands on them, the Holy Spirit descended upon them, and they began to speak in tongues and utter prophecies. ⁷This group numbered about twelve men altogether.

⁸Paul devoted the next three months to preaching in the synagogue, where he vigorously sought to persuade people about the nature of God's dominion. ⁹Since some of his hearers stubbornly refused to be convinced and publicly maligned the Movement, he withdrew, and, taking the followers with him, continued his daily presentations in the facility of Tyrannus. ¹⁰This lasted for two years, with the result that everyone in Asia, Jews and Greeks alike, heard the message about the Lord.

Comments on the Story

After Apollos goes to Corinth, Paul returns, as promised, to Ephesus. There he finds some twelve disciples who have received John's baptism but have not heard that there is a Holy Spirit. Paul then explains that John's message is really about his successor, Jesus. The disciples are then baptized in the name of Jesus, and, when Paul lays hands on them, they receive the Spirit, speak in tongues, and prophesy. Paul speaks for some time in the synagogue, until some deride his message, and he, with his followers, leaves and sets up new headquarters in a public meeting hall, where he continues to speak for two more years. As a result, Luke comments, all Jews and Greeks in Asia hear the word of the Lord.

Some aspects of this section do not surprise readers. Acts 19:8–10 is governed by a familiar motif: Paul speaks in a synagogue but departs from it after some Jews rise up in opposition. We have seen this theme in almost all the narratives dealing with the Pauline mission, but the closest parallel is the one about Corinth (18:1–17). After opposition from synagogue members, Paul moves to the house of Titius Justus in Corinth (18:7) and to the hall of Tyrannus in Ephesus (19:9). He remains in Ephesus, says Luke, for three years altogether, a longer period than he spent even in Corinth, and during that time all Asia hears the word (19:10). This statement is surely an exaggeration, but it is worth noting that Luke does not say that Paul personally preached to all these people. We may well imagine that followers of Paul spread out to deliver the message, although Luke does not specifically say that this is what happened. Readers may recall that in 16:6 the Pauline group was forbidden by the Holy Spirit to speak the word in Asia. Presumably that prohibition has now been lifted. Luke also stresses that the auditors in Asia included Jews as well as Gentiles (19:10), effectively affirming that, despite Paul's vow in 18:6, the mission to Jews is not over.

In a major respect the narrative about the twelve disciples mirrors the previous one about Apollos. In both cases we have characters who know only the baptism of John. In the case of Apollos, Luke does not explain the meaning of this deficiency, although it seems that it involved an essential theological doctrine. In the case of the disciples, the lack is explained: they not only lacked a spiritual baptism, but they had not even heard that there was such a thing as the Holy Spirit (19:2–3). This explanation reflects the words of Jesus in 1:5, which distinguish between two baptisms: "John baptized with water. Before many days have passed you will be baptized with Holy Spirit." It appears that Luke uses the same phrase to designate different but related deficiencies. For Apollos, to "know only the baptism of John" is to be unaware of the Messiahship of Jesus. For the twelve, to "know only the baptism of John" is to be unaware of the Holy Spirit. Apollos becomes an effective Christian preacher after receiving instruction from Priscilla and Aquila, and the twelve exhibit charismatic gifts after receiving spiritual baptism and the laying on of hands.

Interpretation of this section rests partly on an understanding of the word *disciples* in Acts 19:1. Some scholars insist that the word must designate Christians, because elsewhere in Acts the word always refers to Jesus-believers. In this case Luke would be referring to an aberrant group of Christians who only know the baptism of John. Other scholars think that Luke means to call attention to followers of John the Baptist, presumably a sect distinct from believers in Jesus. Still others suggest that *disciples* in this context would likely designate followers of Apollos, that is, Apollos before he received instruction from Priscilla and Aquila. It is impossible to be certain about Luke's meaning, but if the word should designate Baptist followers of Apollos (i.e., a combination of the second and third alternatives above), the narratives have a certain coherence. Note that Luke first observes that Apollos, who knew only the baptism of John, preached successfully in the Ephesian synagogue (18:24–26). Then he reports that there were some disciples in that same church, disciples who, like him, knew only the baptism of John. Perhaps we should call the disciples Apollonian Baptists.

However we understand Apollos and the twelve, we must not miss the significance of an important Lukan theme that is at work here: *no group can be truly Christian except under apostolic leadership*. That theme was evident in the story of Philip and the Samaritans (Acts 8:4–25). Although Philip, one of the seven, had converted and baptized the people of Samaria, things were not complete until Peter and John came down to lay hands on them. Then they received the Spirit. So here, Aquila and Priscilla, who acted as Pauline surrogates, must approve Apollos, and Paul himself must approve the twelve. Although Paul is not, according to Luke, an apostle, he here acts as the successor of the authentic Twelve. For Luke, who in Acts 19 reveals his awareness of aberrant groups, the only church is the church of the apostles.

Readers who find the sections on Apollos and the twelve disciples difficult to understand are in good company. Ernst Käsemann once wrote that "Taken as an isolated passage, Acts 19.1–7 is the despair of the exegete. Almost every sentence presents its own difficulties and the whole section gives the impression of being contradictory and untrustworthy."[17] Actually, the difficulties are compounded when the section is not taken in isolation but paired with Acts 18:24–28. In these paragraphs two very similar characters are treated quite differently. Apollos is accepted after his theological views are corrected. The disciples not only require instruction about John the Baptist but also a second baptism and the laying on of hands. Luke seems not to regard perfect consistency as a literary virtue.

In Search of History

In Acts 19, Ephesus emerges as a major center of the Pauline mission, which is remarkable since Paul only mentions Ephesus twice in all of his letters, both of which are in 1 Corinthians. It is the location from which he writes 1 Corinthians and where Aquila and Prisca have settled down (1 Cor 16:8, 19), and it is a location where he had a trying experience that he describes metaphorically as having fought "wild beasts" (15:32). Paul provides little information about a mission in Ephesus, but Acts provides a great deal. As a result, the stories in Acts about Ephesus have been highly influential in most reconstructions of Paul's mission.

Certainly Ephesus emerged as a center of Paulinism in the years after the death of Paul. This is evidenced especially in the pseudo-Pauline letter that we call "Ephesians," a writing that most scholars consider to be made up of segments taken from other letters attributed to Paul, most notably Colossians. Our question is whether any of the details about the Ephesian mission in Acts may be considered historical.

Richard Pervo points out that Acts includes a significant set of details about Ephesus that do not derive from the letters of Paul: "the 'Hall of Tyrannus' (19:9); a civic assembly that meets in a theater (19:29); the cult of Artemis, whose image is of divine origin; the title 'Neocoros,' the 'Executive Secretary' (19:35); and an organization of silversmiths (19:25)."[18] He concludes that the author had "intimate local knowledge" of the city. Coupled with the emphasis on the importance of Ephesus in the story of Acts, this leads Pervo to conclude that Acts was written in Ephesus.[19] This is a credible hypothesis and a good explanation for the details about Ephesus that are contained in Acts. What remains, then, is to analyze each story individually to see if any might contain historical data.

In this text, we have a well-constructed example of the storyteller's art, with the use of back-and-forth dialogue. The structure of the story, therefore, is a creation of the author. The major detail about "disciples" in Ephesus who knew only the baptism of John and were unfamiliar with the Holy Spirit represents a theme distinctive to Acts. Even if one were to propose that such groups existed in Paul's day, Paul's response to them in Acts does not pass historical muster, since the response shows a familiarity with the story of John as found in Luke's Gospel. Paul's own writings do not demonstrate such familiarity. Furthermore, the story has striking parallels with a story in Acts 8:14–17, in which it is necessary for the apostles Peter and John to impart the Holy Spirit by the laying on of hands. For Acts, the Holy Spirit is especially connected with apostolic authority, which, in this case, is an authority Paul shares as well.

The details in Acts 19:8–9 are also distinctive themes in Acts: Paul preached in the synagogue first; then, because of opposition there, he moved to another location. What is unusual here is the location, the "facility of Tyrannus." This latter detail pictures Paul in the guise of a philosopher giving lectures at a public venue. It is characteristic of Acts to picture the apostles as philosophers (see the cameo essay, "When Apostles Become Philosophers," p. 60).

In conclusion, both the story and the details in this text derive from the author. There is no data here—other than the bare fact that Paul spent time in Ephesus—that qualifies as historical.

The Sons of Sceva

19 [11]Moreover, God began to perform remarkable miracles through Paul's hands. [12]Indeed, even the handkerchiefs and work clothes that had touched his skin were taken to the suffering, resulting in the removal of their illnesses and the expulsion of evil spirits.

[13]Some itinerant Jewish exorcists endeavored to employ the name of the Lord Jesus in their work with those possessed by evil spirits. They used this formula: "I adjure you by the name of that Jesus whom Paul proclaims." [14]Among those attempting to follow this technique were seven sons of Sceva, a Jewish high priest. [15]In response the evil spirit said to them, "I am familiar with the name of Jesus and know that of Paul, but who are you people?" [16]The pos-

sessed person then leapt at them and was able to overpower the entire group. They ended up running away from that house wounded and nude. [17]Word of this incident spread among all the Jews and Greeks living in Ephesus. All were filled with awe and praised the name of the Lord Jesus.

[18]Those who had become believers began to come forward in large numbers to confess and disclose their improper practices, [19]and many persons who had engaged in magic collected their texts and burned them in public. The value of these items was calculated at 50,000 pieces of silver. [20]In such ways proclamation of the Lord's message grew mightily and went from strength to strength.

Comments on the Story

Through Paul, the word of the Lord reached more and more people, not only by his speaking but also his deeds. In this paragraph, attention focuses on the doing: many cases of healing and exorcism occurred through Paul. And he had imitators. Luke gives us a striking incident involving an attempted exorcism by seven sons of a Jewish high priest by the name of Sceva. Their attempt is a humiliating failure: the evil spirit turns on the would-be exorcists, who flee the scene wounded and naked. Word of this incident impresses the townspeople, including a number of believers, who confess their practice of magic. These bring forward and burn their books of magic in public.

Some modern readers may experience discomfort when reading of this incident. Those of us who live on this side of the Age of Enlightenment probably prefer stories in which Paul bests his opponents by the strength of his arguments to those in which he defeats them by divine power. But we should bear in mind the fact that Luke was part of the culture of his own time, a prescientific time when, for many, exorcists and healers were the major providers of health and well being. Luke undoubtedly recognized this, and so "these ten verses indicate what people desired: power over the misfortunes of life, exemplified and symbolized in disease and demon possession."[20]

Some elements in this section recall earlier incidents. People are healed by clothing that has previously come in contact with Paul's body (Acts 19:12); people were also healed by Peter's shadow (5:15). The sons of Sceva attempt to imitate Paul's beneficial activity

(19:14–16); Simon Magus wanted to dispense the Holy Spirit as Peter and John did (8:18–19). Luke used these and other parallels to stress the harmony that, in his view, existed between Paul and the apostles.

The sons of Sceva were dramatically unsuccessful, and the incident resulted in two reactions. Citizens of Ephesus, apparently non-believers, were so amazed that they began to praise the Lord Jesus (Acts 19:17). Believers were so impressed that they brought out their books of magic spells and burned them publicly (19:18–19). It is surprising to learn that some of Paul's Ephesian converts continued to practice magic even after their conversions. If magic were a bad thing, why would its practice not be abandoned at conversion? But Luke is not altogether clear on the morality of this situation, nor does he clearly distinguish between magic and the miraculous powers of Paul. There seems to be very little difference between the use of magical spells and healings by way of contact with Paul's clothing. In terms of the text at hand, two incidental notes may be helpful. First, Luke does not say that the powerful deeds were done by Paul but by God, who "began to perform remarkable miracles through Paul's hands" (19:11). Second, in 19:19, there is a calculation of the value of the books that were burned. C. K. Barrett suggests, "That Luke puts a price on them [the books of magic] may reflect his strong dislike of the money-making side of magic and his clear rejection of it from the Christian side; cf. his treatment of Simon Magus (8.4–25)."[21] To many readers these explanations will seem overly subtle, and it would not be amiss to conclude that the distinction is in the eye of the beholder: for Luke, a divine miracle is something attributed to Paul, while magic is attributed to others, including believers and opponents.

The characters who come off most negatively in this narrative are Jews, but this is not surprising, since Jews have been Paul's most intrepid opponents throughout Acts. So here we have a narrative in which they appear laughably inept. Note that, after the failure of the sons of Sceva to exorcize the evil spirit, Paul does nothing to help the unfortunate victim. This tells us that this is not a story that is meant to illustrate the compassionate qualities of the Christian message. It is a story of power. Those who want to imitate Paul have been laughed out of court, and the incident results in the growth of his mission. The narrative of the sons of Sceva is yet another occasion for Luke to engage in anti-Jewish rhetoric and to focus attention on what he takes to be the inferiority and malice of Jews.

In Search of History

The story of Paul as a healer follows a pattern found elsewhere in miracle stories and therefore presents Paul in rather conventional terms as a miracle worker. All of the miracle stories in Acts are conventional and have been judged by the Acts Seminar to be non-historical (see discussions of 3:1–26; 9:32–43; 14:8–20). This story also follows fairly closely the model of another such story from an earlier chapter in Acts. In chapter 8, Philip's ministry includes healings and exorcisms (8:6–7) like Paul's ministry here (19:11–12). This creates a competition with a local practitioner of magic in which the evangelist emerges as the winner (8:9–12; 19:18–19). This leads the pagan practitioners to attempt to copy the magic formula of the evangelists (8:18–19; 19:13). They fail at this, but the believers, who have not yet received the Holy Spirit, are blessed by the apostolic laying on of hands (8:14–17; 19:7). As noted in the commentary above, this parallelism functioned to solidify Paul's connection with the apostolic leadership that preceded him in the Acts story.

The story of the sons of Sceva is cast as a story about Judaism gone bad, in a fashion typical of Luke. The story itself is rather burlesque in style and thereby exhibits a connection with themes found in ancient novels and other similar literary forms, a stylistic resource on which Luke frequently relied. Pervo points to a similar story in Plautus' *Casina* 758–954.[22]

As part of his enhancement of Paul's mission in Ephesus, Luke seems to be pulling out all the stops. These themes fit Luke's apologetic interests and do not contain any details that can be proposed as historical.

Riot of the Silversmiths

19 [21]In the wake of these accomplishments Paul resolved, with the guidance of the Spirit, to travel through Macedonia and Achaea and then on to Jerusalem. "After I have been there," he said, "I must see Rome as well." [22]He sent two of his assistants, Timothy and Erastus, on to Macedonia, but he himself spent some more time in Asia.

[23]The Movement was the subject of a major disturbance at about that time. [24]There was a silversmith named Demetrius, who was engaged in the manufacture of silver shrines of Artemis, a trade that turned a pretty profit for

the artisans. ²⁵Demetrius called a meeting of those artisans and workers in affiliated trades.

"Gentlemen," he began, "you are well aware that our prosperity depends on this craft. ²⁶Your own eyes and ears have made you aware that this creature Paul has persuasively seduced a vast number, not only here in Ephesus but in nearly all Asia as well, into believing that manufactured gods are not genuine. ²⁷This threatens not simply to discredit our line of business. Even worse, it threatens to bring the temple of the great goddess Artemis into utter disrepute! The hour draws near when she whom all Asia, indeed the entire civilized world, worships will see her majesty slipping away!" ²⁸In response they were filled with rage and began to chant: "Great is Artemis of the Ephesians!"

²⁹Confusion gripped the city. Two of Paul's traveling companions, Gaius and Aristarchus (both from Macedonia) were seized, and the populace rushed into the theater *en masse*. ³⁰Paul wanted to appear before the People, but the followers would not permit him to do so. ³¹Moreover, some of the Asiarchs, who were well disposed toward Paul, sent word urging him not to risk going to the theater.

³²The Assembly was in an uproar, with various people shouting different things, few of them knowing why they were there. ³³Some of the crowd hurled suggestions at Alexander, whom the Jews had sent forward, but, after he indicated that he wished to offer a defense before the People, ³⁴they realized that he was a Jew, and broke into their unison chant, "Great is Artemis of the Ephesians!" This went on for about two hours.

³⁵Once he had got the crowd calmed down, the People's secretary said:

"Gentlemen of Ephesus. Who could possibly be unaware that Ephesus has honorary custody of the Great Artemis and of the image that has come down from heaven? ³⁶Since these claims are unimpeachable, you simply must remain calm and avoid any rash action. ³⁷These men whom you have brought here have neither harmed the temple nor defamed our goddess. ³⁸So then, if Demetrius and his associated artisans have charges to lodge against anyone, there are regular court sessions as well as governors before whom they may argue their cases. ³⁹Any addi-

tional disputes should be resolved by the regular assembly. ⁴⁰The fact is that it is *we* who are liable to be accused of fomenting a riot over what has happened today, since we can provide no explanation to justify this disturbance."
⁴¹He thereupon dissolved the assembly.

Comments on the Story

While Paul plans for future missions, a silversmith named Demetrius foments a riot in Ephesus. He convinces his peers that Paul's preaching is a threat to the worship of the goddess Artemis and that their own livelihoods are consequently in jeopardy. The disturbance caused by Demetrius grows into a full-fledged riot when just about everybody in town rushes to the theater, along the way seizing Gaius and Aristarchus, associates of Paul. Paul himself wants to go to the theater but is restrained by his own disciples and some leading citizens known as Asiarchs. In the theater confusion reigns. The Jews put forward one Alexander as a spokesperson, but he is not allowed to speak. The crowd shouts out for two hours and is only quieted when the People's secretary appears and speaks. The gist of his speech is that no harm has come from the missionaries, that the temple of Artemis has not been attacked, and that the role of Ephesians as guardians of the temple has not been compromised. He advises that, if Demetrius and his associates want to pursue their charges, there are constituted venues for doing so, and he warns that, if the riot continues, citizens of Ephesus are in danger of committing a serious crime against Roman authority. His calming words have the desired effect, and the disturbance is over.

The narrative is marked by a good deal of local color. The temple of Artemis at Ephesus was known as one of the seven wonders of the ancient world. The theater was a famous feature of the city. Asiarchs were prominent political and social leaders in Asian cities, as were the People's secretaries and provincial governors (literally proconsuls).

Despite the attractive local color, the story itself is somewhat tangled. Demetrius and the People's secretary do not see eye to eye about Paul's impact. Demetrius' complaint is that Paul has been very successful in his attacks on the traditional religion of Ephesus. He summarizes Paul's teaching as the claim that gods made by human hands are not really gods (Acts 19:26), and he warns that, if Paul and his cohorts are not restrained, the glory of the goddess Artemis will fade (19:27). The secretary, on the other hand, asserts that no harm has been done to the temple and that the missionaries have done nothing to diminish the glory of Artemis (19:37). It must have been Luke's intention to oppose the figures of Demetrius and the Ephesian town clerk. The effect is to show that, despite opposition that springs from crass motives, judicious civic leaders act to protect the Christian missionaries. And yet, the reader knows that Demetrius is closer to the truth than is the secretary. Paul had indeed asserted that gods made by human hands are not gods at all (see 17:29), and we learned earlier that his message has spread throughout Asia (19:10). If denying the divinity of Artemis is not defaming to her, it is difficult to know what might be.

The narrative tells us very little about the characters involved in it. We are given some information about Demetrius, but almost nothing about the others. Gaius and Aristarchus are said to be Macedonians, but a few verses later it is only Aristarchus who is from Thessalonica in Macedonia, while Gaius is said to be from Derbe in Galatia (Acts 20:4). We are told nothing about the Asiarchs who were Paul's friends (19:31) or about the People's secretary who quelled the riot (19:35–40). Luke uncharacteristically leaves these persons nameless. Most perplexing is a named character, Alexander (19:33), about whom we are told only that he is a Jew.

And why does Luke even mention Jews in this narrative? Why are they involved? The speech of Demetrius has only implicated Paul (Acts 19:26), although attacks on idols might also be part of a diaspora Jewish agenda. Perhaps Luke intended to suggest that, in this respect, Jews and Christians stand side by side. But unfortunately Alexander, appointed to defend allegations against Jews, is never given a chance to speak (19:33–34). The only role he plays is one that illustrates the low regard in which the citizens of Ephesus held Jews. Christian readers learn from this that, when challenged by Gentiles, they will not receive support from Jews. More importantly, the few words about Alexander demonstrate Jewish ineptitude and lack of respect and so serve to reinforce Luke's anti-Jewish rhetoric.

Despite the problems, the narrative about the riot of the silversmiths advances Luke's theme of Pauline triumphalism. Paul himself is offstage throughout the episode, and even his surrogates are silent. But, as he did in the narrative about Philippi (Acts16:16–21), Luke makes it clear that opposition to Paul's message springs from low commercial motives and that the opponents are blundering and ineffective. Even Demetrius' religious concerns are ultimately based on his fear of losing business. Paul's defenders may not fully grasp his message, but they are nevertheless effective. Ernst

Haenchen's comment on the shouting crowd is germane: the two-hour shout, "Great is Artemis of the Ephesians!" (19:34) "reveals that in final analysis the only thing heathenism can do against Paul is to shout itself hoarse."[23]

In Search of History

The itinerary data presented in Acts 19:21–22 allow us to look over the author's shoulder and see how he works (see also the cameo essay, "The Itinerary of Paul," p. 206). Once again, his primary source is 1 Corinthians 16. At the time of the writing of the letter, Paul is in Ephesus (1 Cor 16:8) but plans to go to Jerusalem with the collection (16:3), a journey that will take him first to Macedonia, then Corinth (16:5). Luke also used Romans 15–16, from which he got the rest of his itinerary data. Here Paul adds the detail that he will travel to Rome after he has visited Jerusalem, using a phrase that is repeated almost verbatim in Acts. Compare "I hope to see you [the Christians in Rome] while I am passing through. . . . However, before I come to see you, I am going to Jerusalem" (Rom 15:24–25) with "After I have been there [Jerusalem], . . . I must see Rome as well" (Acts 19:21). This is one of the few times Luke puts words in Paul's mouth that actually came from Paul. Finally, while Luke was delving into Romans for itinerary data, he likely picked up the names "Erastus" (Rom 16:23; Acts 19:22) and "Gaius" (Rom 16:23; Acts 19:29), although he created a different identity for each of them.

If Luke starts with any historical data in his story about the riot of the silversmiths, it is found in the details about the cult of Artemis, the city government of Ephesus, and the existence there of a guild of silversmiths. As already noted above (see under Acts 19:1–10), these details represent the author's close familiarity with Ephesus, such that it is highly likely that Acts was written in Ephesus. He adds these details to give the story verisimilitude; they do not in themselves constitute historical data about specific interactions in the time of Paul. The story also includes two long speeches, a literary form that has already been shown to be a creation of the author. Finally, the plot itself contains components that have been used and reused throughout Acts: an unruly mob opposes Paul and brings him before the government officials; the officials judge Paul innocent and command the crowd to disperse.

The story functions to enhance the apologetic themes presented throughout Acts 19. Luke has promoted Ephesus as the site of healings, the defeat of magic, success over against the great goddess

Artemis, and friendly judgment, almost endorsement, by the city officials. There should be no doubt at this point in Luke's story that Ephesus has emerged as the pinnacle of the Pauline mission. And just in time, for it is the last major missionary endeavor of Paul in Acts. From this point on, he will be on a journey that will end with his imprisonment in Rome.

Artemis of Ephesus
A Cameo Essay by Christine R. Shea

Far from the tomboyish huntress of modern representations, this "Lady of the Wild Animals" is closer to the ferocious mother goddesses of the Near East (Cybele or Ishtar-Astarte) or Egypt (Hathor or Isis). As two stone versions of her cult statue in the Archaeological Museum of Ephesus, one of the first, the other of the second century CE, reveal, "Great Artemis of the Ephesians" is more a symbol of unfettered animal fertility than of pure and remote virginity. These statues show the goddess with a mural crown (symbol of the city perhaps?), a zodiac design on the neck or upper chest, and a torso covered with largish egg-shaped projections, once thought to be breasts or udders or even bulls' testicles. Recent excavations have revealed these projections to be replicas of the amber jewelry that decorated the Geometric-era statue. The goddess' robe is covered with griffins, lions, bulls, leopards, and goats. Her pose is static, with lower body confined by her robe.

In the geographer Strabo's (64/63 BCE–at least 21 CE) sketch of the Ephesian foundation myth, Hera, enraged because Zeus had impregnated Leto, harried the Titaness all over the Mediterranean, until Leto came to rest at Ortygia, a cypress grove a little above the sea near Ephesus. Here she gave birth to Artemis, while a band of young men, the Kuretes, clashed their arms on Mount Solmissos and frightened off Hera, who was lurking nearby. Leto then crossed to the island of Delos where Artemis helped her give birth to her twin, Apollo.

Worship of the goddess centered on the great temple at Ephesus, dubbed one of the "Seven Wonders of the World." The Roman encyclopedist Pliny the Elder (23–79 CE) describes the temple of his time as 425 by 220 feet (130 by 67 meters), with 127 columns. By comparison, the Parthenon in Athens is 220 by 101 feet (69.5 by 30.9 meters) with 69 columns.

The prestige of Ephesus rose with this tale of the birth of an Olympian god. Civic rituals featured the acting out of elements of the birth tale: annually on Artemis' birthday an elaborate parade traveled through town, led by prominent citizens dressed as Kuretes. A priestly college of Kuretes served civic functions as well.

In the early Empire, Romans and philo-Roman Ephesians transformed the city. There was a wealth of architectural projects from the time of the emperor Augustus (who ruled from 27 BCE to 14 CE) through the reign of Domitian (who ruled from 81 to 96 CE), many of which aimed at reorienting sacred sites to reflect the Roman imperial cult. Thus, for example, a temple to Domitian was constructed, featuring a colossus of the emperor, estimated to be either sixteen feet (sitting) or twenty-three feet high (standing).

In the Roman period, as Ephesus grew to a megalopolis (estimated population 250,000), the city was flooded with newcomers of diverse ethnic and religious backgrounds. It has been suggested that, to avoid just such conflicts as Acts 19 describes, the Ephesians came to emphasize the birth of Artemis as a trans-historical event, which could bond the population and overshadow the Roman imperial cult.

Acts 19 is the only ancient testimony for the cult statue as fallen from the sky, (i.e., probably made of a meteorite). The second-century *Acts of John* has the temple split in half by the power of the apostle at the birthday festival. This may be a reminiscence of the earthquake of 17 CE, which did extensive damage.

The Journey of Paul to Rome According to Acts

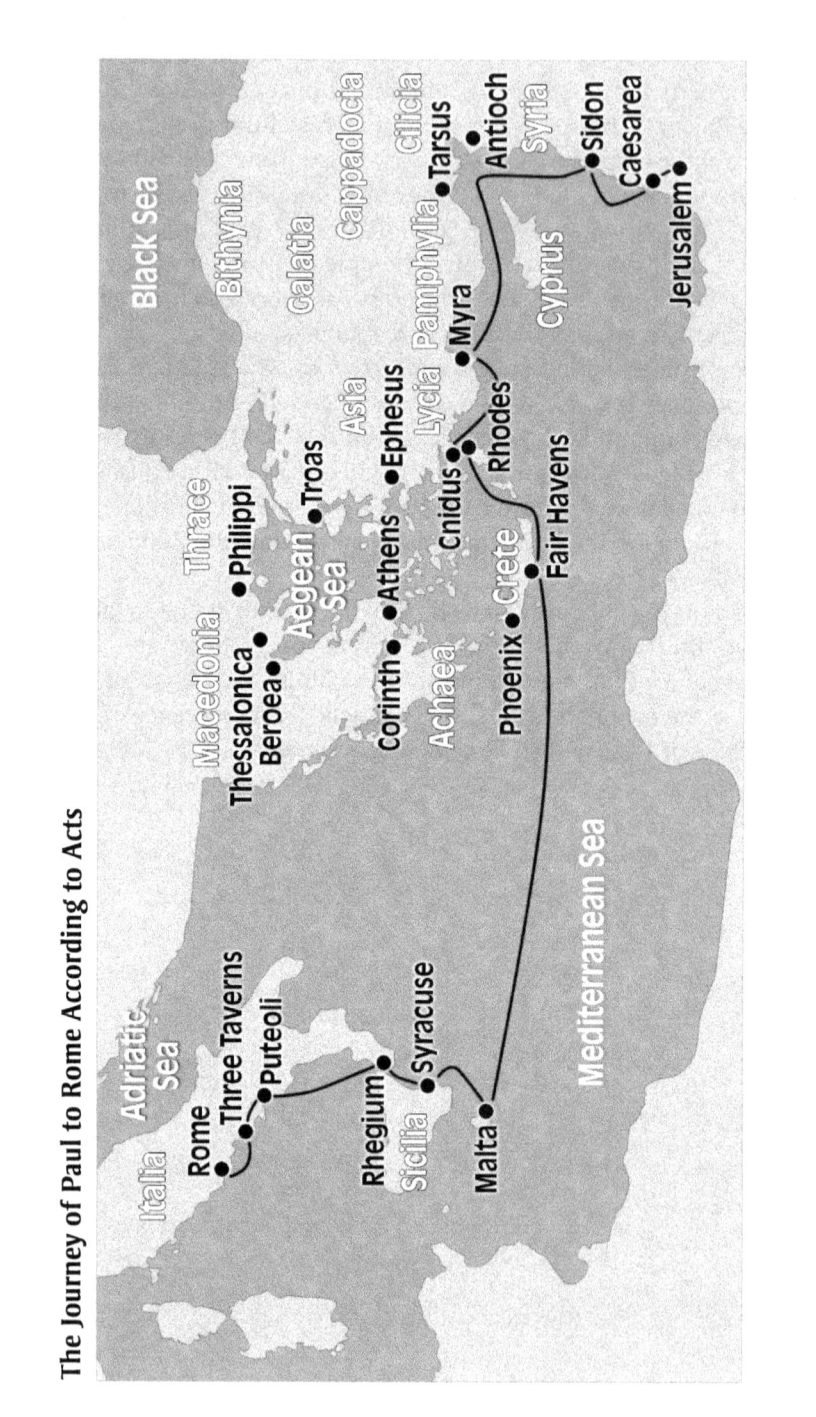

5
To the Ends of the Earth
Acts 20:1–28:31

Paul to Macedonia and Greece

20 Once the uproar had died down, Paul summoned the followers for an uplifting farewell speech before setting out for Macedonia. ²He traveled through those regions, delivering many an uplifting message, arriving eventually in Greece, ³where he spent three months. As he was about to take ship for Syria, a Jewish plot against him led to a change of plans, and he returned by way of Macedonia. ⁴Associated with him were Sopater the son of Pyrrhus, from Beroea; Aristarchus and Secundus, both Thessalonians; Gaius of Derbe; Timothy; and the Asians Tychicus and Trophimus. ⁵They had gone ahead and were awaiting us in Troas. ⁶We sailed from Philippi after the Days of Unleavened Bread and joined them in Troas five days later. There we remained for a week.

Comments on the Story

These verses are totally dedicated to Paul's itinerary. The reader must recall the plans laid out in Acts 19:21, when Paul was still in Ephesus. Luke told us there that Paul intended to go to Macedonia and Greece, then to Jerusalem and finally Rome. As expected, 20:1–2 tells of the first leg of this journey, but in 20:3 we learn of a change of plans. Paul travels through Macedonia and spends three months in Greece (presumably Corinth), but then, because of a Jewish plot, he decides to return to Macedonia (presumably Philippi). He does so, accompanied by several companions, some of whom go on to Troas. Paul and others later depart from Macedonia and rejoin their associates in Troas, where they remain for a week.

The Jewish plot alluded to in Acts 20:3 is not detailed, but it is a familiar theme in Acts. Jewish opposition to Paul continues unabated and increases as Paul nears Jerusalem, where it comes to a head. The reader's sense of Jewish opposition is sharpened by

Luke's use of another important theme, namely Paul's fidelity to Jewish traditions. Although he plans to sail from Philippi to rejoin his companions, he postpones the trip until after Passover (20:6). He observes the "Days of Unleavened Bread" before embarking for Troas.

In Acts 20:4 we learn that Paul is accompanied by seven named companions, some of whom are also mentioned elsewhere in Acts. Timothy was first introduced in 16:1–3, and the reader will recall that Paul had him circumcised and drafted him as a fellow traveler. He was from Lystra and joined Paul in the mission to Beroea (17:14–15) and later Corinth (18:5) and Ephesus (19:22), whence Paul sent him, with one Erastus, on a further mission to Macedonia. Aristarchus is presumably the person who was captured during the riot in Ephesus (see 19:29). Only this note informs us that he had survived and escaped. A man named Gaius was also captured during the riot, but there he was identified as a Macedonian and here he is said to be from Derbe, one of the Galatian cities (see 19:29). We should think of two persons of the same name. Trophimus will reappear in 21:29, where Paul is accused of taking him into the Jerusalem temple. None of the others—Sopater, Secundus, Tychicus—is mentioned again in Acts, although these or similar names come up in letters of Paul and/or letters attributed to him.[1] The local identifications of these companions are of interest in suggesting the widespread results of Paul's mission or, perhaps, in suggesting that they are delegates of some sort. We know from the Pauline correspondence that Paul intended to return to Jerusalem with representatives of his churches bearing a collection for the church there (see 1 Cor 16:1–4). Nothing is mentioned in Acts about a collection, but, as noted below, the Pauline letters may have influenced our author at this point. The list of churches includes Beroea, Thessalonica, Derbe, Asia (probably meaning Ephesus), and by implication Lystra. Notably absent are Corinth and Philippi.

In this paragraph the author returns to the use of "we" (Acts 20:5–6). If readers follow the geographical references carefully, they learn that the person who speaks in the first person plural seems to be associated with Troas and Philippi. The previous we-passage brought the Pauline party from Troas to Philippi (16:10–17), and here we encounter the "we" narration again on a return trip. However we account for the use of "we" in these passages, we should observe the literary effect. Robert Tannehill described it as enfolding the reader into the narration: "A first-person narrator is a focalizing channel through whom the story is experienced.

Our experience of events is limited to the experience of the first-person narrator, and this common perspective creates a bond of identification."[2]

In Search of History

We are now in the midst of a narrative arc created by Luke that will take us to the end of Acts. From chapter 20 to the end of Acts, Paul is on a farewell journey which will eventually take him to Jerusalem and then to Rome. The plot and story motifs are Luke's. The only questions to consider will be whether there are details of the story that qualify for consideration as history.

As we noted in the discussion of 19:21–23, Luke has derived from Paul's letters the building blocks of the itinerary he is following for this journey. Paul himself envisioned this as a farewell journey, since he planned the trip to Jerusalem with the collection for the Gentile churches (1 Cor 16:3) to be followed by a trip to Rome, from which he planned to embark to Spain (Rom 15:23–29). What Luke does not get from Paul is the story of an arrest and imprisonment in Jerusalem, with the result that, according to Acts, Paul will arrive in Rome as a prisoner. What remains to be seen is whether any of the additional narratives Luke attaches to Paul's planned itinerary are historical.

Luke's primary source for Acts 20:1–4 is 1 Cor 16:5, in which Paul tells the Corinthians that he is on his way to visit them after passing through Macedonia. This is Luke's cryptic version of that journey. In the process, he keeps his own plot on the front burner, especially by inserting an undefined "Jewish plot" into the narrative. The idea that Paul delivers a "farewell speech" is one of many such texts in the remainder of Acts that foreshadow the upcoming end of the story.

The names of various individuals accompanying Paul at this point represent a device by the author to lend verisimilitude to the story. Since the source for the journey is Paul, the detail that seven co-workers were accompanying him seems unlikely to have been derived from an independent source. Such a large entourage is highly unusual for Paul in Acts. Notice how the collection of individuals here is distinguished primarily by how they represent different key cities in Luke's narrative. It is clear that this is Luke's creation and not a list he picked up from a "source" when we notice that some of the cities represented here only emerge as important in the Acts story, not in Paul's letters, most especially Beroea and Derbe. The author has created this cast of characters to support the theme he is developing here that this is Paul's last journey to these regions. That is their only significance; they, and the cities they represent, get no further treatment in this brief summary of a journey that takes Paul down the length of Greece and back again.

This text forms a bridge to a we-passage, which, like the other such passages in Acts, is a story about a sea voyage. In the cameo essay "We-Passages in the Acts of the Apostles" (p. 191), Dennis MacDonald has addressed the collection of sea voyage stories in Acts that incorporate the genre of first-person narration. He shows how this style of narrative is typical of sea journey stories in Greek and Latin epic literature, especially sea voyage narratives in Homer's *Odyssey*. The Fellows found his arguments convincing for epic literature in general, but were hesitant about the argument that Homer's *Odyssey* was the only source.

The Votes of the Fellows

Pink/Possible

- The first-person narrative of the sea voyage from Troas in Acts 20:5–15 is written in imitation of first-person narratives of sea voyages in Homer's *Odyssey*.

Paul's Farewell Visit to Troas

20 [7]While we were gathered on the first day of the week for the breaking of bread, Paul addressed them. Since he intended to leave the next day, he extended his sermon until midnight. [8]The lamps in the upper room where we were meeting were numerous, [9]and a young man named Eutychus, who was sitting on the windowsill, got more and more drowsy as Paul talked on and on. Eventually he fell sound asleep and plunged three floors to the ground. When picked up he was found to be dead, [10]but Paul descended, threw himself upon him, and embraced him. "Stop your fuss," he said, "He's alive." [11]Paul went back upstairs to break the bread, eat, and continue conversing at length until daybreak, at which time he left. [12]To the immense relief of everyone, they took the boy away alive.

Comments on the Story

This episode, set in Troas, involves a long sermon by Paul and the death and resurrection of a young man named Eutychus (on the name, see the cameo essay, "Names in Acts," p. 22). It is a narrative that differs from most of the others in Acts in that there is no attempt by Paul to preach to Jews, no rejection by them, and no conflict with authorities. These differences have led some scholars to conclude that Luke assimilated an earlier source into his own account at this point. The setting shows Paul preaching to believers, who have gathered for the explicit purpose of breaking bread and dialoguing with him. Although it is not clear what time of day it was when Paul began to speak, the author tells us that he prolonged his sermon until midnight, since he planned to leave town the next day. The young man Eutychus is overcome with sleep, falls from the third-floor window, and is pronounced dead. Paul, however, embraces the young man and announces that his spirit is still in him. Then Paul continues his sermon until dawn, when he leaves.

The primary question that faces us in this narrative is whether we should think of it as a resurrection from the dead. Some interpreters suggest that what we have is a difference in diagnoses between those unnamed persons who pick Eutychus up in Acts 20:9 and that of Paul in 20:10. In this case we would regard the statement that the young man had died as incorrect. Paul discovered something about him that indicated that he was still alive. But this reading of the story ignores the wording of 20:9: it is not characters within the story who pronounce Eutychus dead but the narrator. It is not that he is thought to be dead but that he is, in fact, dead. It seems probable that Luke intended the readers to understand this as a resurrection miracle performed by Paul. In this case, however, it is remarkable that so little is made of it in the narrative itself. At the end we have only the statement that the believers were relieved, but nothing expressing marvel or wonder (20:12).

Luke does not make clear what kind of gathering this is. The narrative is set on a Sunday, the day that became sacred to Christians. It is unclear when Sunday took the place of the Sabbath as the holy day for Christians, but the reference here seems to indicate that the observance had, by the time of the composition of Acts, begun to take hold. Paul makes a reference to the first day of the week (1 Cor 16:2), but it is not clear that he means to refer to a gathering of believers. Luke portrays the meeting in Acts as an occasion for the breaking of bread and a sermon, not a bad characterization of a Christian observance. It is notable, however, that on this occasion the breaking of bread occurs midway through the sermon and after midnight (20:11). It is not likely that Luke is reflecting a typical service of worship at this point. The demands of the narrative take precedence over a reflection of actual practice.

The setting in Troas, within the context of Acts, is surprising. We recall that Paul had earlier passed through Troas, from where he was challenged to go to Macedonia (Acts 16:8–11). Luke had not reported an evangelistic mission of Paul in Troas, but now we learn that there were believers there (20:7). Those present at this gathering consisted of "we" and "them." The "we" continues the first-person narration that we observed in 20:5–6 and probably now includes the seven associates named in 20:4. The "them" would appear to designate natives of Troas who are followers of Jesus. They probably are not Pauline converts, and the origin of the Troas community remains unknown.

The narrative is set in an "upper room" (Acts 20:8), a location reminiscent of an early meeting place in 1:13 and of another raising from the dead in 9:36–43. Indeed, the episode of Paul and Eutychus in 20:7–12 resembles the story of Peter and Tabitha in 9:36–43.

Many commentators have pondered the meaning of the numerous lamps that Luke mentions in 20:8. Does the heat from the lamps contribute to Eutychus' drowsiness? Or does Luke mention the lamps in an attempt to counter a charge that the Christians were engaging in lewd activities? We know that such charges were made, and it may be that Luke wants his readers to understand that intense light would make such activity impossible. Although both interpretations are possible, it is more likely that Luke mentions the lamps simply to make the all-night meeting more credible to his readers. Night meetings would probably appear unusual to most second-century readers, so Luke would want to stress that such events occurred in full light.

In Search of History

In the discussion of Acts 16:6–10, it was pointed out that the we-passages in Acts, which are concentrated in sea-voyage narratives, provide a literary means for the author to identify himself and his community with the mission of Paul. These texts therefore form a literary bridge between the time of the Acts story and the time of the community to which it is being told. That theme is especially important in this, the farewell journey of Paul. Here the we-passages enable the community to imagine itself as the generation to whom Paul is passing the baton. Theirs is not a comprehensive view of the historical gap between Paul's day and their own. Rather, the tone of Acts impresses the readers with the idea that these events took place just yesterday.

Consequently, the scene in the upper room is meant to be one which the readers are assumed to recognize as a normal church service in their own time. The scene is in a private house and centers on a communal meal ("breaking of bread") and a sermonic exhortation. The reference to an "upper room" is programmatic for meetings in Acts (1:13; 9:37, 39). Pervo defines the imagined space as "the third floor of a Roman tenement," and notes how such a space would have been quite small; thus it would not take very many people to overcrowd the meeting. He suggests it was "a worship setting familiar to Luke and his readers."[3] The term "breaking of bread" is Luke's characteristic term for the community gathered for worship at the meal table (Luke 24:35; Acts 2:42).

The story itself idealizes the community gathering by inserting an entertaining story full of comedy and miracle. It has features reminiscent of motifs in Greco-Roman literature and in other contexts in Luke-Acts. For example, like the road to Emmaus resurrection narrative (Luke 24:13–35), a resurrection experience takes place during the "breaking of the bread" gathering. It works well as a symbolic narrative, but lacks historical credibility.[4]

References

Phillips, "The Post-Apostolic Consciousness in Acts"

Paul's Farewell to Ephesus

20 [13]We, meanwhile, had gone ahead to the ship and sailed for Assos, where we intended to take Paul on board, for he had told us to do so, intending to travel by land, himself. [14]He did meet us at Assos, so we took him aboard and went on to Mitylene. [15]From there we sailed on the following day to a point opposite Chios, and on the next we crossed to Samos, arriving in Miletus the day after, [16]for Paul had decided to sail past Ephesus, so that, if the possibility permitted, he would not spend too much time in Asia. He was in a hurry to be in Jerusalem at Pentecost, if that were at all possible. [17]He did, however, send a message from Miletus to Ephesus, directing the presbyters of that church to report to him. [18]When they had arrived, he addressed them:

"You know well how I spent my time while I was with you, from the very first day that I set foot in Asia, [19]how I served the Lord without asserting my privileges, in misfortunes that make grown men cry and the frustrations brought about by Jewish machinations, [20]how I never avoided saying whatever was beneficial for you or from teaching both in public and in private. [21]I urged Jews and Greeks alike to redirect their lives Godward and to place their trust in our Lord Jesus.

[22]"Now, as to what lies before us. Firstly, the Spirit compels me to go to Jerusalem. What might happen to me there I do not know. [23]What I do know is that in city after city the Holy Spirit discloses that arrest and afflictions loom before me. [24]But continued existence has no value for me beyond completing my task, which is the ministry that I received from the Lord Jesus: to make God's gracious message manifest.

[25]"Secondly, I am aware that not one of you among whom I went about proclaiming God's reign will ever see my face again. [26]I therefore swear to you on this very day that I am not responsible for the loss of anyone, [27]for I have proclaimed to you, with no reservation or qualification, the entirety of God's will. [28]Be attentive to yourselves and attend to all the flock in which the Holy Spirit has placed you as 'bishops' charged to shepherd the church of God, which was acquired by the death of God's own. [29]I know that after my departure vicious wolves will fall upon you. They will show no mercy to the flock. [30]Moreover, from your very midst will arise some who will distort the message in an attempt to get the followers to accept their leadership. [31]You must therefore maintain constant vigilance. Keep my example in mind, how for three years I constantly and tearfully issued warnings to all.

[32]"Finally, I entrust you to the gracious message of God, which has the power to build you up and give you what is in store for all of God's own. [33]I have had no designs upon anyone's money or personal property. [34]You well know that I have met all of my own needs and those of my companions with these very hands. [35]I have served as an example of how we are to care for those who require assistance: by hard work. Remember what the Lord Jesus said: 'Giving brings more happiness than does receiving.'"

[36]When Paul had finished, he knelt and prayed with the entire group. [37]They all wept without restraint and em-

braced him with repeated kisses, ³⁸terribly grieved because he had said that they would never see him again. They then escorted him to the ship.

Comments on the Story

The first part of this section consists of detailed information about the travels of Paul and his party (Acts 20:13–16). Paul travels by land from Troas to Assos and there joins his associates. The group then sails south along the coast of Asia Minor, calling at Mitylene, on the isle of Lesbos, then Chios and Samos. The proximate destination is Miletus, a coastal city some thirty-five miles, as the crow flies, from Ephesus. Luke calls particular attention to Paul's intention to avoid Ephesus and explains that he was in a hurry to get to Jerusalem in time for Pentecost. Scholars have, however, calculated that little or no time would be saved by this procedure. Paul would have sent emissaries from Miletus to Ephesus and then waited for the Ephesians to return. No more time would have been required for Paul himself to visit Ephesus. Further, Luke pretty much drops the Pentecost deadline after this reference, and we are not told if Paul arrived in Jerusalem in time for the observance or not. An examination of Paul's letters might show that he had other reasons to avoid Ephesus, but Luke is not interested in them (see, e.g., 1 Cor 15:32). Instead he takes the opportunity to employ a by-now familiar theme—Paul's fidelity to Jewish traditions.

In any event, our author has set the scene for a poignant speech in which Paul says farewell to the Ephesian presbyters and bids them to guard the teachings he has delivered to them and to protect the people under their care (Acts 20:18–35). The speech of Paul at Miletus is actually the only recorded Pauline speech delivered to believers. In the previous section Paul preached a long sermon to believers in Troas, but Luke did not tell us what he said (20:7–12). Here, however, we have the words that Luke reckoned Paul to have spoken.

The speech, surely composed by Luke, is not easy to analyze, because it does not seem to move from one discrete point to another and has a number of repetitions and overlapping statements. Rather than discussing it in terms of a supposed structure, it seems better simply to call attention to its major points. As a farewell to the presbyters from Ephesus, the speech looks both backward and forward, and so some of it is concerned with Paul's previous mission in Ephesus, while other parts of it deal with his future and that of the community.

In Acts 20:18–21, Paul reminds the audience of his great difficulties in Ephesus and how he preached to both Jews and Greeks about repentance and faith. He calls attention both to his public and his private preaching and to the fact that he never asserted his own privileges. In 20:27, he insists that he withheld nothing from the congregation, and in 20:33–34 says that he never desired material things but supported himself and his colleagues with his own labor. These points give us information that was not supplied earlier but does not surprise the reader.

But there are some discrepancies between the speech and the earlier narratives about Paul in Ephesus. A minor variance is to be seen in the extent of time that Paul spent in Ephesus. In the Miletus speech he claims that he preached there for three years (Acts 20:31), but in the narrative about Ephesus the total time was two years and three months (19:8, 10). A more significant disparity appears in the reference in the speech to "Jewish machinations" (20:19), something that has no support in the earlier narratives about Ephesus. On Paul's first visit there he spoke to Jews in the synagogue, and relations appear to have been amicable (18:19–21). He was invited to stay longer, but he declined the invitation and promised to return. When Paul did return to Ephesus he spoke in the synagogue, where there was opposition that forced him to retire to the "facility of Tyrannus" (19:8–9), but there is no reference to a plot. The incident with the sons of Sceva (19:13–20), though something of a contretemps, could hardly be called a Jewish plot against Paul. The riot, from which the city leaders personally protected Paul, was not precipitated by Jews but by Gentile artisans (19:23–40). Although no specific incident can be cited to support the contention about Jewish plots in 20:19, the charge fits very well with Luke's theme of Jewish opposition to the Jesus movement, which he has employed in numerous other incidents.

The speech not only recollects the past but also looks to the future. The Lukan Paul insists that he must complete his ministry by going to Jerusalem, despite spiritual warnings he has received about imprisonment and punishment that await him there (Acts 20:22–24). Paul exhibits a sense of mission with bravery not unlike that of Jesus as described in the Gospel of Luke (see, e.g., Luke 18:31–32). He regards the preservation of his own life as of less importance than the preaching of the gospel. Some readers may be surprised to learn that Paul had received these premonitions "in city after city" (Acts 20:23), since Luke has not previously alluded to them. Apparently he preferred to hold back on such communications and have Paul tell about them in this farewell speech. Following these dire predictions, Paul makes the solemn announcement that the Ephesian presbyters will never "see my face again" (20:25). It is well known that Luke does not include a narrative specifically telling about Paul's death. But 20:25 leaves the reader with no uncertainty: Paul will go to Jerusalem (and Rome) but will not return to the scene of his major missionary activity. Martin Dibelius rightly captures Luke's literary intentions: Paul "has reached the end of his public work in the chief theatres of activity and, since the author does not intend to tell about his martyrdom, Luke does to some extent press the crown of martyrdom upon his head, giving a retrospect of his life and making him direct a warning to the whole Church."[5] By substituting Paul's own prediction of his death for a narrative about it, Luke imparts to the reader a sense of divine necessity along with expressions of human grief and poignancy.

The speech also expresses concern for the mission and the future of the community. The Lukan Paul warns that, after his departure (probably meaning after his death), "heretics" will come from both outside and inside the community (Acts 20:29–31), and he calls upon the leaders to be alert to these dangers. He reminds them that he had issued these warnings while in Ephesus, although Luke did not record them in the narratives about Ephesus. The Pastoral letter 2 Timothy asserts that, after Paul left from there, the community turned against him (see 2 Tim 1:15). Indeed, the Miletus speech displays a number of conceptual relationships with the Pastoral Epistles, and these relationships tend to support a dating of the composition of Acts in the second century, the time of the Pastorals.

The references to "vicious wolves" from outside the community and distorters within clearly suggest the rise of "heresies" (Acts 20:29–30). Although the speech does not specify the beliefs of these distorters, surely Luke himself is looking at the situation from the perspective of his own time, and he knows of various groups contending for influence in the Christian community, some of which—Marcionites, for example—made use of the Pauline letters to support their claims. There is a hint in 20:20 that reflects a claim that may have been made by some of the "heretics." In that verse the Lukan Paul maintains that he withheld nothing and spoke both in public and in private. The verse seems intended to forestall an attempt to claim the authority of Paul on the basis of secret sayings. How better to counter the claims of these "heretical" groups than to have Paul himself warn his contemporaries about them?

The leaders of the Ephesian church, who form Paul's audience at Miletus, are called presbyters or elders (Acts 20:17), and bishops (20:28), terminology that, with the exception of Phil 1:1 ("bishops and deacons"), is foreign to the letters of Paul. Interpreters of Paul tend to think that the reference in Philippians is not to be taken in the sense of formal ecclesiastical offices. The SV, for example, translates the phrase, "leaders and their assistants."[6] Here in Acts 20, however, the terms appear to designate formal offices, as they do in the Pastorals and General Epistles (see 1 Tim 3:2; 5:17, 19; Titus 1:5, 7; Jas 5:14; 1 Pet 2:25; 5:1; 2 John 1:1; 3 John 1:1). Readers of Acts have met presbyters before (see Acts 11:30; 14:23; 15:2, 6, 18, 20, 23), but the term for bishops appears in Acts only in 20:28. Although some translators prefer the term "guardians" to "bishops"—a legitimate translation—the context of the speech suggests that formal ecclesiastical offices are in the author's mind. Even so, it appears that, for Luke, the two terms are interchangeable: the same "presbyters" addressed in Acts 20:17 are the "bishops" of 20:28. Apparently Luke applies to the time of Paul something from his own time, when ecclesiastical offices are beginning to be formalized but do not yet define discrete roles. Luke, employing the voice and authority of Paul, is probably addressing these words to his own second-century church, warning about "heresy" and encouraging the leaders to guard against it.

In the process of warning the leaders about his future and that of the church, the Lukan Paul, almost incidentally, speaks about the ethical heart of the Christian mission. He encourages his listeners to follow his own example of self-giving, and to care for the needy. And, he cites a saying of Jesus to support this imperative: "Giving brings more happiness than does receiving" (Acts 20:35). In substance, the quotation is similar to the tenor of Jesus' sayings in Luke and the other Synoptic Gospels, but in wording it appears nowhere else. It may have been a saying left over from Luke's sources for the Gospel, and he used it here as a fitting summary of Jesus' sayings.

Despite its structural problems, the speech is moving and effective. It is Paul's farewell to the mission field. It warns the reader of the dangerous situation that awaits him and provides an unmistakable signal of his doom. It skillfully claims the authority of Paul for beliefs that oppose those of the "heretics." It situates the church's leaders as the authentic heirs of Paul. Above all, it shows Paul to be a true hero, who is willing to sacrifice his own life for a divinely inspired mission.

In Search of History

This text is the primary farewell speech of Paul in Acts. That it is to leaders of the church in Ephesus is significant since Paul's mission in Ephesus is given special attention in Acts. This leads Pervo to propose that Acts was written in Ephesus.[7] The reference to "presbyters" at Ephesus is a bridge to Luke's own day. Paul does not refer to such an office in an established form in his day, but by the time of Acts and the Pastorals, such officers had become common. The speech, like all such speeches in Acts, is composed by the author. Furthermore, Paul's emotional parting would have special resonance for Luke's community, if, in fact, that community was located in Ephesus.

Portions of Luke's story are built directly out of 1 Cor 16:8–9, where Paul details his travel plans on his way to Jerusalem: "I'm going to stay in Ephesus until Pentecost, because a large and promising door is open to me even though we have many opponents." Paul's trip from Ephesus through Macedonia to Corinth and then on to Jerusalem (1 Cor 16:1–4) is the basis for Luke's creative elaboration in Acts 20:1–16, as discussed above under 20:1–12. Here in 20:16 the narrator makes use of the reference to Pentecost, but changes it from the date when Paul departed from Ephesus to the date he planned to arrive in Jerusalem. This change fits Luke's narrative agenda, in which Paul's Jewish identity and tensions with Judaism are to be heightened when Paul gets to Jerusalem.

The reference to "many opponents" is utilized by Luke in Acts 20:29–30, where he has Paul prophesy to the Ephesian *presbyteroi* that "after my departure . . . from your midst will arise some who will distort the message in an attempt to get the followers to accept their leadership." Robert Price proposed that the "other leadership" mentioned here was actually a reference to a second-century competition in Ephesus between the Paul tradition and the John tradition.[8] The Fellows found his proposals plausible.

References
Price, "Paulus Absconditus"

The Votes of the Fellows
Red/Probable
- Paul's "prediction" that opponents of the truth would arise in Ephesus (Acts 20:29–30) reflects tensions in Ephesus at the time Acts was written.

Pink/Possible
- The Ephesian narrative in Acts 19–20 was written to claim Paul for the author's preferred version of Christianity.
- Acts 19–20 reflects the supplanting of the legacy of Paul in Ephesus by the John tradition as represented in the *Acts of John*.
- The defense of the legacy of Paul in Acts 19–20 is intended to rescue Paul from the heretics and reconcile him with the early Catholic tradition represented by the legacy of John.

Paul's Journey to Jerusalem

21 When we were able to tear ourselves away from them, we set out on a straight run to Cos, reaching Rhodes the next day and then Patara. ²We located a ship that was crossing to Phoenicia, boarded it, and set sail. ³We came within sight of Cyprus, which we passed on the right and continued on to Syria, landing at Tyre, where the ship was to offload its cargo. ⁴We looked up the believers and stayed there with them for a week. Moved by the Spirit, they tried to tell Paul to abandon his plan to visit Jerusalem. ⁵When the time came to leave them and travel on, they all—women and children included—escorted us outside of town, where we knelt down to pray on the beach. ⁶Then we said farewell to one another, and we boarded the ship while they returned home.

⁷Resuming the voyage, we traveled from Tyre to Ptolemais, where we visited the believers and spent a day with them. ⁸We left on the next day and reached Caesarea, where we went to the house of Philip the Evangelist, one of the Seven, and stayed with him. ⁹Philip had four unmarried daughters endowed with the gift of prophecy. ¹⁰After we had been there for quite a number of days, there arrived from Judea a prophet named Agabus, ¹¹who approached us and grasped Paul's belt, with which he bound his own hands and feet. "Thus says the Holy Spirit," he announced. "Just as I have bound myself, so will the Jews bind the man who owns this belt and will deliver him to the gentiles." ¹²After hearing this, both we and those who lived there implored him to break off his trip to Jerusalem. ¹³Paul said, "Why are you breaking my heart with these tears? For the Name of the Lord Jesus I am not only ready to be arrested

in Jerusalem; I am even prepared to die there." ¹⁴Since we could not dissuade him, we said, "The Lord's will be done" and dropped the subject.

¹⁵When our stay came to an end, we got ready for travel and set out for Jerusalem. ¹⁶Some of the believers from Caesarea accompanied us as guides to the home of one Mnason from Cyprus, a believer of long standing, with whom we lodged. ¹⁷When we got to Jerusalem, we were warmly welcomed by the believers.

Comments on the Story

The narrative pace picks up considerably in this section, as Paul and his party cover a great distance in just a few verses. After the speech at Miletus, the group, including the narrator, travels toward Jerusalem, stopping at Cos and Rhodes, islands just off the coast of Asia Minor, and Patara, on the Southwest coast. From there they board another ship headed for Tyre, in Phoenicia, and then head south to Jerusalem, stopping at Ptolemais (the present Acre, Israel) and Caesarea along the way.

In Paul's speech to the presbyters in Miletus, he said that, "in city after city," the spirit had warned him about his fate in Jerusalem (Acts 20:23). Those warnings, not explicitly noted in previous narratives, now come from believers in Tyre (21:4) and the prophet Agabus in Caesarea (21:11). The warnings lead those associated with Paul to plead with him not to go to Jerusalem, but he insists that he is ready even to give up his life for the sake of the name of the Lord Jesus (21:13).

We may well wonder why Jerusalem has become so dangerous for Paul. He had been there on other occasions, when there was controversy but not enemy attacks (see Acts 15:1–35). The fact is that Luke gives us no clue but rather employs this sequence of narratives to build up the sense of doom that began with the Miletus speech. Readers of Paul's letters learn that he had organized a group of his adherents to take a special collection to the church in Jerusalem (see 1 Cor 16:1–4; 2 Cor 8:1–9:15; Rom 15:25–28), but there is nothing about this in Acts.

Luke had told his readers that Paul wanted to arrive in Jerusalem before Pentecost (Acts 20:16), but that desire has disappeared in the present section, where the sense of urgency seems diminished. We note that Paul and his party stayed in Tyre for a week (21:4), in Ptolemais for one day (21:7), and in Caesarea for several more (21:10). This leg of the journey may not seem leisurely, but there is little sense of urgency. And there is nothing to tell us if Paul arrived in Jerusalem in time for Pentecost or not. We have only the note that the brothers there received the group warmly (21:17).

Two characters who appeared in earlier narratives in Acts reappear here: Philip and Agabus. We first met Philip in Acts 6:5, where he was listed as a member of the Seven, who addressed the problem of the neglected widows. Later Philip took the gospel to Samaria (8:4–25), and in Judea he converted the eunuch from Ethiopia (8:26–40). It should be noted that, according to 8:40, he ended up in Caesarea, so his location in the present section is consistent with that reference. In 21:8, Luke recalls Philip's membership among the Seven, but he denominates him as "the Evangelist," possibly recalling his other roles in Samaria and Judea. The reference to Philip's four unmarried (or virgin) daughters who prophesied is curious (21:9). In view of the other prophetic warnings that Paul received, we might expect another to come from these daughters, but it does not. They serve to add texture to the character of Philip but play no role in the narrative.

Agabus also appeared earlier. He, along with other Judean prophets, came to Antioch and predicted a worldwide famine (Acts 11:28). Luke chooses to introduce him here as if for the first time, not counting on readers to remember the earlier reference. His enacted prophecy may remind readers of similar incidents reported in the OT (see, e.g., Jer 13:1–11), but it doesn't foretell Paul's fate exactly as Luke will describe it. Agabus says that the Jews will capture Paul and turn him over to the Romans, but, as we shall see, it is Roman authorities who arrest him in the attempt to rescue him from the Jewish mob (see 21:27–36). On the other hand, Agabus' prophecy does fit the situation of the Lukan Jesus, and our author surely intends readers to see the story of Paul as a parallel to that of Jesus (see Luke 22:47–23:5).

In this section Luke is building a portrait of Paul as heroically dedicated to the mission of Jesus. Despite ominous warnings from friends and supporters, who emotionally plead with him, he is unwavering in his decision to go to Jerusalem and endure his dire fate.

In Search of History

This story is made up of an imaginary, but geographically plausible, continuation of the sea journey which takes Paul to Jerusalem. It is imaginary because it is a we-passage (see the cameo essay,

"We-Passages in the Acts of the Apostles," p. 191) and because all of the narrative elaborations on the journey are embedded in the specifics of Luke's narrative. Thus Paul continues with his emotional farewells to believers in various locations. To this theme are added explicit references to the trials that await Paul in Jerusalem along with Paul's vow that he will readily accept whatever lies ahead. These references foreshadow the specific details of Luke's plot and represent literary creations of the author.

The Votes of the Fellows

Pink/Possible
- The first-person narrative of the sea voyage in Acts 21:1–18 is written in imitation of first-person narratives of sea voyages in Homer's *Odyssey*.

Paul's Temple Piety

21 [18]The next day Paul and the rest of us went to see James. All of the elders were present. [19]Following the initial greetings Paul set out in full detail all that God had accomplished through his ministry to the gentiles.

[20]His report brought repeated praise of God, after which they said: "You see, brother, how many myriads of Judeans have become believers. All of them are ardent observers of Torah. [21]About you, however, they have been informed that you teach all Diaspora Jews to renounce the Law of Moses, telling them that they should stop circumcising their sons or observe our practices. [22]What about this? They will doubtless learn that you have arrived. [23]You must therefore do what we tell you. Four of our number have placed themselves under a vow. [24]Take responsibility for them, get yourself purified, and pay their expenses so that they may get their heads shaved. Everyone will then know that what they have heard about you is quite false and that you live an observant life. [25]Now regarding the gentile converts, *we* have determined, and have so advised them in writing, that they should take care to avoid food that has been offered to idols or contains blood or has been killed by strangling, as well as from prohibited sexual relationships."

[26]So Paul took charge of those men and went with them on the following day to undergo purification. He entered

the temple to give notice of when the vow would be discharged, at which time the prescribed offering would be made for each of them.

Comments on the Story

The previous section ended with Paul and his party receiving warm greetings from the Jerusalem believers. The present section begins with a more official-sounding reception by James and the elders, who glorify God because of Paul's mission among the Gentiles. But suddenly a more ominous threat shows itself, as James informs Paul of certain suspicions about him, namely that he has been teaching Jewish believers to cease circumcising their sons and observing Torah. James also proposes a way for Paul to prove his fidelity to Torah, by supporting four members who are under a vow. Paul readily accepts this remedy, undergoes a ritual of purification, and goes to the temple to give notice about the completion of the vow.

The way in which this section is introduced suggests that Paul is now reporting to someone in authority. He goes in to meet James, who is surrounded by elders (Acts 21:18). We have noted the significance of James before. In 12:17 Peter directed other believers to tell James about his miraculous release from prison in Jerusalem. Later it was James who determined the policies toward Gentile believers (15:1–35). So readers may not be surprised to find James in a dominant role when, in Acts 21, Paul arrives in Jerusalem for the last time. But, when set over against Luke's own prescriptions for church leadership (see 1:22), it is astonishing. In dealing with Acts 15:1–35, we observed that James had become the authoritative spokesperson for the church, a position formerly occupied by the apostle Peter. We further suggested that the ascendancy of James reflects a probable clash that Luke wanted to conceal. His concepts of apostolic leadership and total harmony in the believing community prevented him from narrating the circumstances that surrounded the change from Peter to James. In any event, the change that we saw in Acts 15 is confirmed in Acts 21, where the non-apostolic James appears to be in full control at the Jerusalem church. In both passages the reader has difficulty suppressing a suspicion that there is more going on than Luke wishes to tell. See below for more on the probable historical aspects of this narrative.

Readers of Paul's letters may understand why suspicions about him have arisen, but Acts actually provides no basis for the charges in 21:21. It is clear from 15:1–36 that Paul firmly believed that circumcision was not to be required of Gentile believers, but there is nothing to support the contention that he advised Jewish believers to dispense with it. Indeed, Acts 16:3 is probably intended to show, preemptively, that the suspicions of 21:21 are false, for there Paul had Timothy, whose mother was Jewish, circumcised. When he undertook a vow in 18:18, we are to understand the depth of Paul's fidelity to Jewish traditions. Further, apart from those Pharisaic believers with whom Paul and Barnabas debated (15:1–2), Luke did not stress any differences between Paul and other Jewish believers. But here, in a city where the believers are all said to be Torah-observant, Paul is under suspicion. Luke does not immediately identify the source of the charges against Paul; rather he saves that for the next section, where the hostility of Asian Jews leads to Paul's arrest by the Romans (see 21:27–28). In any event, it is clear that Luke wants the reader to understand that the suspicions have no basis. James does not believe them, and he proposes a way to disprove them (21:23–24). His remedy is intended to show everyone that Paul, like the other Jerusalem Christians, is Torah-observant and that there is nothing to the charges against him.

The remedy that James suggests (Acts 21:23–24) may have been clear to Jewish believers, but Gentiles would probably have difficulty understanding it. It seems to reflect the Nazirite vow that we encountered when Paul left Corinth (see Acts 18:18 and the comments on p. 225, above). If this is the case, we have to do with four Jewish Christians who have undertaken the Nazirite vow, and Paul is advised to pay their expenses. The expenses would be related to a sacrifice that concludes the period of the vow. Paul is also told to purify himself, apparently to clean himself from the presumed contamination that came from his contact with Gentiles. If the details are unsure, the purpose of the proposed remedy is clear: Paul is to show that he is faithful to Jewish traditions. Paul's fidelity to Moses and Jewish traditions is a major theme throughout Acts, and so Luke has him readily participating in the proposed rituals. Without hesitation, Paul goes to the temple to announce the fulfillment of the vow by the four Jerusalemites, and this turns out to be a fateful decision on his part.

Readers will observe that, in his comments to Paul, James reminds him of the policy toward Gentile believers, who must "avoid food that has been offered to idols or contains blood or has been killed by strangling, as well as from prohibited sexual relationships" (Acts 21:25). His words repeat those of the Apostolic Decree in 15:20, 29, although in a slightly briefer version. The Lukan Paul would have known of this decree, since he was present at the session when it was adopted (see Acts 15:2, 12) and was one of the delegates commissioned to deliver the decision to churches in the North (see 15:30). Although directed to Paul, James's words are intended for the reader, who may not remember things exactly.

In Search of History

According to Paul, the purpose of his trip to Jerusalem was to carry the collection from the Gentile churches to the Jerusalem community (1 Cor 16:1–4; Rom 16:25–28). In Acts, the only reference to the collection is in a defense speech of Paul before Felix (Acts 24:17), but it is never referred to as the reason Paul travels to Jerusalem. Rather Paul seems to be compelled to travel to Jerusalem by fate or divine necessity, following a narrative format much like that of Greek tragedy. As he says in his speech to the Ephesian *presbyteroi*, "The Spirit compels me to go to Jerusalem. What might happen to me there I do not know" (20:22). In Paul's version, which would therefore be the historical version, Paul is on his way to Jerusalem with a gift for the Jerusalem community. It is implausible to think it would have been rejected, yet scholars have proposed exactly that.[9] They do this primarily on the basis of the Acts story, which emphasizes tensions with the Jerusalem community which will result in Paul's arrest. Yet, since Acts omits the collection from its narrative, it seems unwise to use Acts to draw conclusions about the historical fate of the collection in Jerusalem. Luke does, however, make use of Paul's trepidation about the trip, which he expressed to the Romans:

> Join me in your prayers before God that I may be delivered from those in Judea who refuse to accept [God's world-transforming message], that the good will and support that I am conveying for the Jerusalem community will be well-received by the Anointed's people there. (Rom 15:30–31)

Luke builds his own story out of this data. In the Acts version, the themes of Jewish opposition to Paul come to a head, despite Paul's allegiance to Jewish traditions. Luke has once more manipulated the data he has from Paul in order to make the story fit his agenda. Although Paul expressed trepidation about the trip, we never hear from him how it all turned out. Luke's story is insufficiently reliable to provide any details of Paul's reception in Jerusalem.

Paul Arrested in the Temple

21 ²⁷Just as the seven-day period of purification was about to end, the Asian Jews saw Paul in the temple. They tried to seize him and incite a general riot by ²⁸shouting: "To the rescue, men of Israel! This is the fellow who is teaching against the People, the Torah, and this Place to everyone everywhere! Now he has had the temerity to bring Greeks into the temple and profane this Holy Place!" ²⁹(They made this accusation because they had seen the Ephesian Trophimus in the city with Paul and supposed that Paul had brought him into the temple.) ³⁰The entire city was thrown into an uproar. A mob rushed in, nabbed Paul, and dragged him outside of the temple. The gates were immediately slammed shut.

³¹While the mob occupied itself with trying to murder Paul, the military tribune commanding the cohort received word that Jerusalem was in an uproar. ³²Accompanied by soldiers and centurions, he immediately set out on the double toward the scene of the action. When the crowd caught sight of the tribune and the soldiers, they stopped pummeling Paul. ³³Once he got there, the tribune had Paul taken into custody and ordered that he be shackled with two chains. He then asked who this person might be and what he had done. ³⁴Since the responses were so many and varied, he directed that Paul be taken to the barracks, as the tumult made it impossible to learn what was actually going on. ³⁵Once they reached the stairs, the force of the crowd made it necessary to have Paul carried by the soldiers, ³⁶for the mob kept pressing upon them with shouts of "Away with him!"

Comments on the Story

The attempt to quell rumors about Paul fails miserably. Jews from Asia spot him in the temple and, thinking that the Gentile Trophimus is with him, seize Paul, drag him outside, and incite a riot in the city. Hearing news of the disturbance, the Roman tribune, with a military escort, arrests Paul and conducts him to the barracks. The Jewish accusers follow with shouts of "Away with him."

The narrative may remind readers of the riot in Ephesus (Acts 19:21–40). In both, charges are brought against Paul, and the accusations lead to a full-fledged riot, which is controlled only by official intervention. In Ephesus, however, no direct action was taken against Paul himself, while in Jerusalem he is in mortal danger. In Ephesus, the People's secretary was able to calm the crowd with his carefully chosen words. But here, it is the speedy action of a Roman official that prevents Paul from being massacred, and the narrative ends with Paul under arrest. Luke portrays Jerusalem as a place of increasing violence and impending doom.

Luke probably intends to point to the Asian Jews as the source of suspicions against Paul. In the previous section James told Paul about these suspicions: that he was teaching diaspora Jews to forsake circumcision and Torah observance (Acts 21:21). Now we learn that Asian Jews are charging Paul with similar errors: everywhere he goes he teaches against the people, the Torah, and the temple (21:28). In addition, they accuse him of defiling the temple by bringing in a Gentile (21:28–29). A common point is the suspicion that he teaches against Torah. Although the phrasing is not exact, the similarity between the two expressions is sufficient to convey the implication that it was the Asian Jews who had been spreading the rumors and continue to do so.

Who are the Asian Jews? We do not learn from Acts whether they were visitors to Jerusalem or long-term residents. But when we recall earlier references to Jewish opposition to Paul and plots against him (see especially Acts 20:3, 19; 21:11), it becomes plausible to think of them as those who had come to Jerusalem from Ephesus for the express purpose of bringing a halt to his activities.

A specific charge of the Asian Jews is that Paul took a Greek into the temple, an act that was regarded as sacrilege. Luke identifies the suspected Greek as Trophimus, whom we have met before. He was listed in Acts 20:4 as one of the associates of Paul who preceded him from Philippi to Troas. He was there identified as being from Asia, presumably Ephesus, and so Jews from there could have recognized him. Luke does not explicitly deny that Paul took Trophimus into the temple, but he strongly suggests that the suspicion was in error. He had only been seen in the city, not in the temple, and, to express the basis for their suspicion, Luke uses a word (*nomizō* "supposed") that he frequently uses in contexts where doubt is possible (see Luke 3:23; Acts 16:13) or to indicate a mistaken idea (see Luke 2:44; Acts 7:25; 8:20; 14:19; 16:27; 17:29). He means to claim that the Asian Jews only supposed that Trophimus was in the temple and that their supposition was wrong. Note also that no action is taken against Trophimus, who disappears from Acts after 21:29.

The Asian Jews have little trouble inciting the crowd in Jerusalem to come to a fever pitch and almost kill Paul. Where are the "myriads" of Judean believers now (Acts 21:20)? Are we to think that, although Paul has followed James's advice to support the four men under a vow (21:23), the Torah-observant Christians in Jerusalem continue to be suspicious of him? Certainly Luke does not want us to think of them as part of the group that seized Paul in the temple, but it is notable that they hold essentially the same suspicions about him as do the Jews from Asia and that they do nothing to protect him from the violence of the rest of the population. The distinction between believing and non-believing Jews in Jerusalem has become blurred. Luke's negative images of Jewish people are so powerful that they rub off even on those Jews who follow Jesus.

The Roman tribune, later identified as Claudius Lysias (see Acts 23:26), arrests Paul, seemingly to determine the cause of the disturbance circulating around him. One may wonder why he did not arrest the ringleaders of the opposition—the Asian Jews—who were about to kill Paul (21:31–32). Instead he arrests Paul in an effort to interrogate those present. Since he was unable to learn anything because of the unruly crowd, he has Paul taken to the Roman barracks. Luke holds back in defining the tribune's suspicions about Paul until 21:39 (on which see below). The tribune is not motivated by a concern for the victim in this incident, but his action does serve to preserve Paul's life. The main point, however, is that Paul is now in Roman hands, and the prediction of Agabus is, to some extent, fulfilled (see 21:11). Jews did not turn Paul over to the Romans, as they did Jesus (see Luke 23:1), but their violent opposition to Paul had that result.

In Acts 21:30, after Paul had been attacked in the temple and dragged outside, Luke announces that "the gates [of the temple] were immediately slammed shut." Perhaps we are to understand that the gates were closed to prevent further damage to the sacred area, but the closing of the gates also has powerful significance at this point in Acts. After this no follower of Jesus enters the temple, nor does it function in any way in the following narratives. It seems that the closing of the temple gates serves to symbolize for Luke the irreparable break between Jews and Christians.

In Search of History

Here Luke creates a narrative that parallels the story of the riot in Ephesus (Acts 19:21–40), as pointed out in the comments above. It contains the now-familiar plot devices of Acts: Jewish opposition, mob rule, capture of Paul with intent to harm him, and his rescue by Roman authorities. Now that the Jewish opposition motif is coming to a head, Luke makes his agenda clear by including the reference to the closing of the gates to the temple. This is meant to symbolize the estrangement of Christianity from official Judaism (see further in the comments above). The story and all of its details function as devices to further Luke's plot. There are no details here that qualify to be considered historical.

The Jews according to Acts

A Cameo Essay by Shelly Matthews

Acts' perspective on Jews and Judaism is best explained by its overarching concern with respect to its Roman imperial context. Romans, as a rule, despised new religions as superstitions whose mere existence might do harm to the state. Gentile followers of Christ situated around the Aegean were ripe for the charge of superstition, as their claims to be heirs of Israelite culture were belied by their disregard for common Jewish ritual observances relating to food and circumcision—to say nothing of the fact that their ethnic origins were not obviously Jewish/Judean. This author's treatment of Jews and Judaism, then, may be understood as his attempt to carve out a legitimate place for his largely (if not exclusively) Gentile community in the face of accusations that these Jesus followers constituted a new and thus potentially subversive religion.

He does so by appropriating "things Jewish" for his own group, insisting that Jewish Scriptures and worship, when properly understood, should lead to the confession that Jesus is Lord. He also underscores that the leadership of the movement of those who confess Jesus as Lord is Jewish and Jerusalem-centered. Thus, the ancient Scriptures of Israel, which signify the antiquity of the movement, are repeatedly invoked, most often as proof that the events surrounding Jesus' death, resurrection, and the subsequent apostolic mission were foretold by the prophets of old. Pious Jewish practices and institutions such as prayer, alms-giving, Pharisaic erudition, the temple, and the law, are most often depicted favorably as signs of the movement's antiquity and stability (see below for exceptions). The apostles witness the resurrected Jesus in Jerusalem; James, the Jerusalem-centered brother of Jesus, takes a key authorizing role; Jewish converts to the movement are celebrated (e.g., Acts 21:20); Paul is depicted as an exceedingly pious practitioner of Jewish ritual (e.g., 21:26; 22:17; 26:4–7). The insistence that his group constitutes the "true Israel" is accompanied, unfortunately, with the counter-claim that non-confessing Jews have forfeited their claim to this Israelite heritage. This denigration of non-believing Jews involves frequent depictions of them as unruly inhabitants of the empire, who are blind to the wisdom of their ancestral traditions and prone to riot. The author frequently reminds readers that these Jews killed Jesus (e.g., Acts 2:22–23, 36; 3:12–15a; 4:8b–10a; 5:30; 7:51–52; 10:39; 13:27–28), killed Stephen, and desire and/or plot to kill subsequent leaders of the Jesus movement (e.g., 5:27–33; 9:23–24, 29; 12:3, 11; 14:2–4; 20:2–3; 21:27–31; 22:22; 23:12, 14, 21). Thus, Acts may be understood to lay the foundations for subsequent Christian supersessionist claims: Christians, because they accepted the Messiah rejected by the Jews, have surpassed the Jews as the chosen people of God. Because he writes somewhat earlier than the Christian apologists, before the category of Christianity as something distinct from Judaism became firmly fixed, the terms of his supersessionist argument are sometimes slippery. This slipperiness might be best captured through consideration of passages such as Acts 18:24–28, where "an Alexandrian Jew by the name of Apollos," is noted as one who powerfully and publicly "routed the Jews" by proving that Jesus is Christ. It could be said that the rupture enacted by "the Jew" upon "the Jews" in this particular passage captures precisely both the split Acts asserts, and the confusion the narrative has in naming it. Acts is a book in which individual Jews—Stephen, Apollos, Peter, and quintessentially Paul—vehemently refute the Jews, through confessing Christ (cf. Acts 9:22).

Such slipperiness of terminology also helps to clarify why Luke's assessment of "things Jewish" is not perfectly consistent. Scholars note, for instance, that sometimes the temple is depicted as a positive institution, and sometimes negatively. If we understand that Acts attempts a distinction between "true Jews=Christ believers" and "blind Jews" the inconsistency is ameliorated. In Luke's judgment, followers of the Way employ Jewish traditions correctly, and hence, when they pray in the temple or follow prescriptions for purification observances, Jewish institutions are rightly observed.

Non-believing Jews employ Jewish traditions incorrectly, and thus, for instance, when they occupy the temple it becomes "a den of robbers."

Paul's Defense before the Roman Tribune

21 ³⁷On the verge of being taken into the barracks, Paul said to the tribune, "May I have a word with you?"

"You speak Greek," he exclaimed! ³⁸"So you're not the Egyptian who once started a revolution and led four thousand terrorists out into the wilderness?"

³⁹"I am a Jew," replied Paul, "from Tarsus in Cilicia, and a citizen of that renowned metropolis. Would you be so kind as to allow me to address the people?"

⁴⁰His request approved, Paul took a place upon the steps and gestured for the crowd's attention. After they had become quite still, he began to speak to them in Aramaic.

22 "Elders and gentlemen, please listen now to my defense." ²When they realized that he was speaking in their own language, they became even quieter.

³"I am a Jew. Although born at Tarsus in Cilicia, I was reared in this very city and received under Gamaliel an education based upon the strict interpretation of our ancestral code. As a fervent partisan of God, like you today, ⁴I persecuted this movement, promoting the death penalty and delivering shackled prisoners—women no less than men—into custody. ⁵The high priest and the entire Sanhedrin can support me on this matter. After obtaining written authorization from them to our coreligionists in Damascus, I set out for that place, intending to bring the local followers of the movement back to Jerusalem in shackles, for punishment.

⁶"When, in the course of my journey, I was getting near to Damascus, an enormous light from above suddenly engulfed me—at noon! ⁷I fell to the ground and heard a voice speaking to me: 'Saul, Saul, why are you persecuting me?' ⁸"'Who are you, Lord?'

"'I am Jesus the Nazoraean, whom you are persecuting.' (⁹My companions saw the light but did not hear the voice of the one who was addressing me.)

¹⁰"'What shall I do, Lord?' I said.

"'Go right now to Damascus. There you will be told about all that has been arranged for you to do.'

¹¹"Since I couldn't see because of the brightness of that light, I had to make my entry into Damascus guided by my companions.

¹²"One Ananias, a very observant man well thought of by the local Jews, ¹³came to visit me, 'Brother Saul,' he said, 'regain your sight.' At that very moment I glanced up at him, and I had regained my sight!

¹⁴"'Our ancestral God,' he said, 'has selected you to experience his will, to see the Just One and to receive a message from his very lips. ¹⁵For you will be a witness for him to everyone, a witness of what you have seen and heard. ¹⁶What are you waiting for? Get yourself baptized right away and be cleansed of your sins by calling upon his name.'

¹⁷"On one occasion after my return to Jerusalem, while I was praying in the temple, I fell into a trance ¹⁸and saw Jesus. 'Get out of Jerusalem as quickly as you can,' he said, 'because they will not accept your witness about me.'

¹⁹"'Well, lord,' I replied, 'they are quite aware that I used to lock up people who believed in you and have them flogged in one synagogue after another. ²⁰While the blood of your witness Stephen was gushing out, I stood right there approving of the business and guarding the coats of his murderers.'

²¹"'Get going, for I am sending you far away, to the gentiles.'"

²²The crowd kept listening until he said "gentiles," but then raised a loud shout: "Wipe this creature from the face of the earth! He does not deserve to live!" ²³Since they kept on shrieking, tossing their coats around and kicking up dust, ²⁴the military tribune directed that Paul should be taken within the compound and interrogated under the whip to learn why the crowd was denouncing him. ²⁵Just when they had stretched him out to be whipped, Paul asked the attending centurion, "Are you authorized to flog a Roman citizen who has not been found guilty?"

²⁶At this the centurion went to the tribune and said: "This fellow is a Roman citizen! What are you going to do about *that*?"

²⁷The tribune went to Paul and said: "Tell me, are you a Roman citizen?"

"Yes."

²⁸"It cost me an arm and a leg to achieve that status."

"I was born to it."

²⁹The soldiers delegated to interrogate him quickly got out of the way. The tribune was also alarmed at the realization that he had put a Roman citizen in bonds.

Comments on the Story

This section begins a long series of trials and gives our author the opportunity to compose a number of defensive speeches for his hero. Paul's speech here to the Jewish crowd is of major interest, but some preliminary matters will be treated first.

Paul respectfully requests permission to speak to the tribune and then to the crowd. Permission is granted, and Paul speaks, including some autobiographical comments and focusing on his conversion experience. The crowd listens quietly up to the point where Paul tells of his commission to go to the Gentiles but then engages in a dramatic demonstration, calling for Paul's death. After the outbreak, the tribune sends Paul back to the Roman barracks and orders him to be beaten and questioned. Just as the beating is about to start, Paul asks if it is legal to beat an unconvicted Roman citizen, and when this is reported, the fearful tribune orders the beating to be aborted.

When Paul requests permission to speak, the tribune seems surprised to learn that his captive speaks Greek (Acts 21:37). His surprise may be due to an assumption that those involved in the melee near the temple would only be able to speak their native language. It is more likely, however, that it is due to his assumption that Paul is Egyptian. Luke is careful about language at this point and calls attention to the languages that are appropriate for each situation that he describes. Paul speaks Greek in addressing the Roman official (21:37), but Aramaic when addressing the Jewish crowd (21:40; 22:2). In subtle ways, these notes contribute to the characterization of Paul as an educated Jew who is able to move in various social contexts.

Actually, the tribune thinks that he has captured an important at-large outlaw—an Egyptian terrorist (Acts 21:38). Paul's use of Greek appears to disabuse him of this assumption, but his reaction is not really explained, since some Egyptians also used Greek. In any event, the reference is to a character described by Josephus, an Egyptian who led a large number of followers out of the desert and to the Mount of Olives with the intention of capturing Jerusalem.[10] Felix (Governor of Judea, ca. 52–58 CE) had repulsed most of his forces, but he had escaped, so it is likely that Roman officials would have continued to search for him. Paul's defense before the Roman tribune begins with his assertion that he is a Jew from Tarsus, not from Egypt (21:39).

After the speech and the mob disturbance, Paul is able to escape Roman punishment by calling on his Roman citizenship (Acts 22:25). The incident will remind readers of a similar episode in Philippi, when Paul used the same trump card to demand an apology from the authorities (16:37). In 22:28 Luke takes the opportunity to suggest the social and political superiority of Paul to his captor: the tribune bought citizenship at a high price, but Paul was born to it.

Our chief interest naturally is in Paul's speech and, more particularly, in that section in which he tells of his conversion. The main purpose of the speech is to affirm Paul's fidelity to Torah and Jewish traditions, a major Lukan theme. Paul's listeners are told of his birth in Tarsus and his education in Jerusalem under Gamaliel (Acts 22:3). Readers will remember Gamaliel and his moderate advice about the Jesus movement in 5:34–39. Paul maintains that his zeal for Torah led him to persecute the followers of Jesus (22:3–4). Evidently, he did not learn, or did not accept, from Gamaliel the moderate position that his teacher proclaimed.

Paul then tells of his experience near Damascus. This is, of course, the same episode that we read about in Acts 9:1–31. There Luke wrote in the third person, and now Paul tells it in the first, but that is not the only difference between the two narratives. Similarities between the two accounts are sufficient to leave no doubt that the author is referring to the same incident. In both accounts Paul has letters authorizing the arrest of believers (9:1–2; 22:5); in both he is approaching Damascus when he sees a bright light and falls to the ground (9:3–4; 22:6–7); in both a voice asks "Why are you persecuting me?" (9:4; 22:7) and identifies the speaker as Jesus (9:5), or Jesus the Nazorean (22:8); in both Saul is told to go to Damascus where he will be told what to do (9:6; 22:10); in both Ananias plays a major role (9:10–17; 22:12–16); and in both Saul is led by the hand into Damascus (9:8; 22:11).

But between the two accounts, there are striking and puzzling differences. In Acts 9:4, Luke wrote that Saul's travelling companions heard the voice but saw no one, but in 22:9, Paul said that the others saw the light but did not hear the voice. It is difficult to account for this contradiction. Luke may have been drawing on different traditions about Paul's conversion, but even so it would appear that a careful writer would iron out such glaring disparities. Moreover, Ananias is differently described. In 9:10, it is clear that he is a believer, but in chapter 22 this is not so clear. He is a loyal and respected Jew in 22:12, but in 22:16 he orders Saul to get baptized. Nothing is said in chapter 22 of Ananias' vision (9:10) or of Saul's vision of him (9:12), although in both he is shown to be the agency of Saul's recovery from blindness (9:17–18; 22:13). In 9:13–14 he is reluctant to visit Saul because of his reputation as a persecutor, but in 22:12 he comes uninvited to visit Saul. In chapter 9, Saul spent some time in Damascus after his conversion and escaped from there in a basket (9:19–25), but nothing is said of this mission in chapter 22. Instead he goes straight to Jerusalem, where he receives a second vision while praying in the temple (22:17–22). Chapter 9 had also contained an episode of Saul in Jerusalem, where he encountered opposition from Hellenists and was spirited away to Tarsus by other followers. In chapter 22, no mission is described, but Paul is told to leave Jerusalem because his testimony will not be believed (22:18), and he is sent to Gentiles far away (22:21).

Other differences, many of them minor, may also be observed by attentive readers, but enough have been mentioned to raise questions about the author's literary procedures. Some disparities may be explained by Luke's aim to create literary variation. Others, in particular the note about what Saul's companions heard on the road to Damascus (Acts 9:4; 22:9), may suggest the use of different traditions. But still others, such as the differences in the characterization of Ananias and Paul's vision in the temple, support the author's intention in recording this speech, namely to stress Paul's fidelity and alignment with Jewish traditions. The narration as a whole says to readers that Paul's conversion was not *from* but *within* Judaism. Thus the characterization of Ananias as a loyal Jew (22:12) and the setting of Paul's vision in the temple (22:17–21) create a strong association with Jewish life.

Paul's ecstatic experiences will be narrated once more in yet another Pauline speech in Acts 26, and there we will again need to examine the similarities and differences and explore Luke's probable intent.

In Search of History

This story contains the first in a series of speeches by Paul delivered while he was a prisoner. It contains the speech proper (Acts 22:1–21) framed by incidents which include back-and-forth dialogue of the characters, both of which are characteristics of Luke's creative activity (see the cameo essay, "Speeches in Acts," p. 45). The content of the speech is the second of three recountings of Luke's version of Paul's conversion (see the cameo essay, "Comparing Paul and Luke on Paul's Conversion," p. 114). The plot itself is built around standard motifs in Acts: the Jewish mob tries to harm Paul but Roman authorities rescue him.

Paul's adventures as a prisoner will dominate the latter portions of Acts, from Paul's arrest in 21:33 to the end of Acts. It takes up a significant portion of Acts and demonstrates Luke at his storytelling best. Here Luke is following a tried and true method found in adventure tales of the day, ranging from ancient Roman fiction to early Christian Apocryphal Acts. What these contemporary writings have in common is the use of plot devices in which the heroes and heroines face continuous perils, including being attacked by mobs, rescued in the nick of time, arrested, and brought to trial.[11]

Luke pictures Paul as an idealized prisoner, often directing events himself and capable of speaking eloquently and persuasively both to Jewish crowds and Roman officials.[12] Here Paul first impresses the Roman tribune with his command of Greek, then is allowed to address the crowd, then has such a commanding presence that he can, with a gesture, silence a crowd that had moments before been an unruly mob (21:37–40).

Luke has once more done his homework in order to gather credible details to enhance his narrative. The tribune had confused Paul with a notorious "Egyptian." This is most likely a reference Luke derived from an account in Josephus.[13]

After his speech, Paul is saved from a flogging in the nick of time by informing his Roman captors that he is a Roman citizen. This becomes a significant plot device throughout the rest of the narrative, propelling the story from hearing to hearing and eventuating in Paul's being sent as a prisoner to Rome. The details presented here, that Paul was from Tarsus and was a Roman citizen, have been considered basic historical details about Paul throughout Christian history, but neither detail is found in Paul's letters. There is no credible source behind the story itself; it is clearly a creation of

Luke, and the citizenship detail is an essential part of the plot Luke has created. What has to be proposed is that Luke had access to bits of historical data about Paul that he was able to use in a fortuitous way in his story. How credible is this as history? The point has been argued frequently, but, as Pervo points out, the best proponents can argue is the possibility that Paul was a Roman citizen.[14] But it fails the probability test. Roman citizenship was based on wealth and status, of a level that is highly improbable for Paul, even the Paul of Acts, who is pictured as a craftsman. Furthermore, Luke's plot device, that his citizenship saved Paul from a flogging, was unknown to Paul himself, who referred to three beatings he had received at various times in his ministry (2 Cor 11:25). Because Roman citizenship for Paul is so firmly embedded in Luke's plot, and because it was not derived from an identifiably reliable source, and because it is historically improbable, we therefore conclude that it cannot be affirmed as reliable history.

What about the detail that Paul was from Tarsus? Once again, this is not verified in Paul's own letters. Acts uses this as a means for Paul to claim citizenship, so it's veracity as a detail on its own merits is shaky. Furthermore, Acts here undermines the idea that Paul was a citizen of Tarsus by claiming, at the same time, that he was raised and educated in Jerusalem (22:3). Tarsus as Paul's hometown is therefore historically questionable.[15]

Paul's Defense before the Jewish Council

22 [30]The very next day, determined to learn exactly what accusations the Jews were making against Paul, the tribune took him out of confinement and directed the high priests and the entire Sanhedrin to assemble. He then brought Paul into their presence.

23 Paul looked directly at the Sanhedrin and said, "My fellow believers, all my life I have served God with an entirely clear conscience." [2]At this the high priest, Ananias, ordered those who were near Paul to strike him on the mouth. [3]Paul responded, "God will strike you, you old phony. Here you sit, judging me in accordance with the same law you flout by having me struck." [4]Those who had been told to strike him exclaimed: "How dare you revile God's own high priest?" [5]"I was not aware, my brothers, that this person was the high priest," he replied. "As Scripture says: 'Do not defame a ruler of your people.'" ⁶Realizing that some were Sadducees and the rest Pharisees, Paul shouted: "Fellow believers, I am a Pharisee, as was my family before me. I am on trial because of my hope in the resurrection of the dead."

⁷These words provoked a conflict between the Pharisees and the Sadducees, leading to a sharp division in the body, ⁸since Sadducees say that there is no resurrection, neither angel nor spirit, whereas Pharisees affirm them. ⁹Loud shouting erupted, and some scribes of the Pharisaic faction took the floor to join the fray with these words: "We find no fault in this person. Perhaps a spirit or an angel has spoken to him!" ¹⁰The disruption became so violent that the tribune began to fear that they would tear Paul to pieces; he ordered the military to go down and rescue Paul from them and then return him to the fort. ¹¹The Lord appeared to him the next night, saying: "Don't falter, for just as you have given testimony for my cause in Jerusalem, so also must you testify in Rome."

Comments on the Story

The Roman tribune has still not determined the cause of the disturbance at the temple, so he sends Paul to be examined by the Jewish Sanhedrin. After an initial run-in with the high priest, Paul plays the division in the council to his advantage, claiming to be a Pharisee. He goes on to say that he has been charged with holding beliefs that are characteristic of Pharisees, and some scribes support him. A violent dissension ensues, and Paul is in great danger, avoided only when the tribune sends soldiers to rescue him and return him to the Roman barracks.

It is helpful to approach this section as made up of two major subsections, followed by a vision. The first subsection, Acts 23:1–5, appears to be a kind of verbal jousting between Paul and representatives of Ananias, the high priest. In the second subsection, 23:6–10, Paul seizes on the division within the Sanhedrin between Pharisees and Sadducees and causes a near riot. In the vision (23:11), Paul is told that he must bear witness to the Lord in Rome, as he has in Jerusalem.

The first subsection is among the most bewildering scenes in the book of Acts. Paul begins to defend himself but is struck on orders of the high priest (Acts 23:1–2). Luke gives the reader no clue as to the reason for Ananias' action. Paul has not said anything approaching blasphemy, nor has he insulted the high priest. But Paul's outburst in 23:3 appears to be over the top. In it he accuses the high priest of violating the law, although no law is cited. But these questions pale into insignificance when compared with Paul's statement in 23:5. When told that he has cursed the high priest, Paul says that he did not know the presiding officer at the Sanhedrin was the high priest. He issues something short of an apology, quoting Scripture to condemn his own actions. It is difficult to accept Paul's denial about the high priest. We learned in 9:1–2 that he had been commissioned by the high priest to search out Jesus believers, and in just the previous speech he claimed that the high priest, and indeed the entire Jewish council, could support the fact that he once persecuted these believers (see 22:5). Of course some time has passed between the persecuting activity of Paul and the present hearing, and it is possible that Luke understands that the present occupant of this office is a different one. But this is not noted in the text (see also 4:6, where the high priest is given a similar name—Annas). There have been numerous attempts to illuminate this passage, but the problems remain. Some commentators suppose that Paul was blind (see Gal 4:15; 6:11), and others say that the situation was so confused that Paul could not recognize the participants. Needless to say, the text provides no help in solving this problem.

Although the subsection is mystifying, it nevertheless seems to be intended to support two major Lukan themes—Paul's fidelity to Jewish traditions; and the faults of the Jewish people. We first hear Paul proclaiming that he has a clear conscience when it comes to his adherence to Torah (Acts 23:1). Then at the end of the subsection, he lets us know that he would not knowingly disobey a command of Scripture (23:5). We may not believe his denial that he did not know the high priest, but his quotation from Exod 22:28 must be intended to illustrate his claim in Acts 23:1 and to show that Paul is loyal to Torah.

The faults of the Jewish people are illustrated in Luke's characterization of Ananias. Although named, the high priest is a shadowy figure. He has no speaking parts, and he does not act directly. Given the place that Paul occupies in Luke's narrative, the reader is likely to take his judgment against Ananias in Acts 23:3 seriously. Paul is a reliable character in Acts, and his judgment provides us with an image of a major leader of the Jewish people who disobeys Torah and is unqualified to be a judge. The narrative presents us with a striking anomaly: believers in Jesus are the most faithful Jews; deniers are disobedient to Torah.

The same two themes drive the second subsection (Acts 23:6–10). The fidelity of Paul to Jewish traditions is affirmed in his self-identification as a Pharisee (23:6). Indeed, he affirms that his core beliefs are Pharisaic and that he is being judged for these beliefs. Readers should not miss the force of the present tense verb in 23:6: Paul claims that he *is* a Pharisee. It is startling to hear Paul identify himself this way so late in the narrative of Acts. In his letter to the Philippians he seems to think of his adherence to Pharisaism as a thing of the past (see Phil 3:5–8). Luke too had included a number of negative images of Pharisees in his gospel. But in Acts 5:34–39, the Pharisee Gamaliel called for a moderating policy toward the Jesus believers, and Acts 15:5 called attention to Pharisaic Christians, albeit opponents of Paul. In the present section, there is such a close relationship between the beliefs of Christians and Pharisees that Paul can be called by either name.

The faults of the Jews come out strongly in this subsection. We see here an image of a judicial body in disarray. The Sanhedrin is fractious and contentious. The deep division within the council prevents it from taking action in Paul's case and leads to violence and rioting, limited only by the swift action of an alert Roman tribune.

The night vision (Acts 23:11), in which the Lord (probably meaning Jesus) encourages Paul, is interesting in comparison with 22:18. In the earlier verse Paul tells of a vision in the temple in which he was directed to leave Jerusalem because his testimony would not be accepted there. By returning to Jerusalem, was Paul disobedient to this vision? Luke never touches on this topic, but in 23:11 he records that the Lord acknowledged Paul's witness in Jerusalem, and the accompanying narratives provide abundant evidence that he was not accepted. Then the reader is reminded that Paul's ultimate goal is Rome.

In Search of History

This story is embedded in a narrative created by Luke and is an elaboration of standard themes in Acts as well as an echo of Jesus' trial before the high priest in Luke 22:63–71. Luke also uses data about Paul that he apparently derived from Phil 3:5–6, where Paul identified himself as having been a Pharisee, as in Acts 23:6, and "in regard to the requirements of the law, I was flawless," which corresponds to Paul's claim here that "all my life I have served God with an entirely clear conscience" (Acts 23:1). Thus, these are historical claims of Paul. But the context in which they are placed in Acts is not historical. Here when Paul proclaims his clear conscience, he is struck (compare Luke 22:63–64). When he strategically claims his Pharisaic identity, it functions to create a division in the Sanhedrin which causes the meeting to devolve into a virtual brawl. In Phil 3:7–8, Paul devalued his Jewish credentials in comparison with his new status in relation to "God's Anointed" (3:7–8). Here in Acts there is a different script; here Paul's claims of faithful Jewish piety serve to identify him as more pious than the members of the Sanhedrin, who are incapable of rational behavior. In the end, in contrast to the Jewish leaders, Paul is affirmed directly by a visionary message from God, a favorite literary device in Acts. As in other instances in Acts where these messages occur, here the Lord assures Paul that everything that is happening to him is according to God's purpose and will eventuate in his going to Rome.

A Plot and Escape to Caesarea

23 [12]When day came the Jews concocted a plot, solemnly vowing neither to eat nor to drink until they had killed Paul. [13]More than forty entered into this conspiracy. [14]They approached the high priest and the elders with this message: "We have vowed with the utmost solemnity to taste nothing until we have killed Paul.

[15]"Now you people must, together with the Sanhedrin, advise the tribune that he is to bring Paul back before you on the grounds that you wish to make a more thorough and decisive inquiry into his situation. We shall be ready to kill him before he can get there."

[16]Paul's sister's son caught wind of the proposed ambush and went to the fort to inform his uncle. [17]Paul summoned a centurion and said, "Take this young man to the tribune, as he has some information to give him." [18]The centurion accompanied the youth to the tribune, and said, "The prisoner Paul summoned me and asked that I convey this lad to you because he has information for you." [19]The tribune took him by the hand to a spot where they could speak privately and asked, "What is it that you wish to tell me?"

[20]"The Jews have arranged to request that you send Paul to the Sanhedrin tomorrow on the grounds of making

a more thorough inquiry. ²¹Don't let them convince you, for they are going to ambush him. More than forty of them have vowed neither to eat nor to drink until they have assassinated him. They are already prepared and merely waiting for your consent."

²²The tribune sent the young man away, warning him to tell no one "what you have disclosed to me." ²³He summoned two particular centurions and said: "Make preparations for two hundred infantry, seventy cavalry and two hundred of other arms to proceed toward Caesarea beginning at 2100 [9:00 p.m.]." ²⁴He also ordered them to provide mounts for Paul, whom they were to deliver safely to Governor Felix.

²⁵He prepared the following letter:

"Claudius Lysias to Governor Felix, Your Excellency. ²⁷This man was caught by the Jews, who were about to kill him. I arrived with a detachment and extracted him when I found out that he was a Roman citizen. ²⁸As I was determined to discover the grounds behind their accusation, I brought him before their Sanhedrin. ²⁹It transpired that they were charging him on matters pertinent to their law, but not of any capital offense or of some crime demanding incarceration. ³⁰When it came to my attention that there was a plot against his life, I determined that I should send him to you forthwith. I have also instructed his accusers to lay their charges regarding him before you."

³¹In accordance with their orders, the soldiers took Paul to Antipatris, traveling by night. ³²The next day the infantry returned to their fort, leaving the cavalry to escort him. ³³The latter went on to Caesarea, where they delivered the letter to the governor and brought Paul before him. ³⁴After reading the communication, Felix asked Paul for his province of residence and learned that it was Cilicia. ³⁵"I shall hear your case when your accusers arrive," he said, and then directed that Paul be detained in Herod's palace.

Comments on the Story

Paul remains Luke's hero, but in this section he is the object rather than the subject of action. The actors include some forty conspirators, Paul's nephew, the Roman tribune, numerous military personnel, and the provincial governor. Although the action centers on Paul, he has only one line.

Luke begins the section by describing the details of a plot on Paul's life: some forty Jews have taken an oath neither to eat nor to drink until they have killed Paul. They have devised a plan to ambush him as he is being conducted from the Roman barracks to the Sanhedrin. The high priest and the elders are implicated in the plot, which requires that they request the Roman tribune to bring him to the Sanhedrin for further interrogation. But the plot is foiled when Paul's nephew learns of it and reveals it to Paul, who arranges for the young man to have an interview with the tribune. When the tribune learns of it, he orders Paul to be conducted from Jerusalem to Caesarea, escorted by a large contingent of infantry, cavalry, and auxiliary soldiers, and to have a hearing under the governor, Felix. The tribune, finally named as Claudius Lysias, drafts a letter to the governor explaining the case so far. Felix reads the letter and grants Paul a hearing.

Comments on this section will consider three aspects of the narrative: the plot against Paul; the treatment of Paul; and the tribune's letter.

The Plot against Paul

Luke meticulously provides the details of the plot against Paul. Although he notes that some forty people are involved in it, the rhetorical force of the narrative would lead the reader to think that almost all Jews are included. He first writes that *the Jews* made a plot (Acts 23:12) before telling us that only forty or so were actually involved in it (23:13). Even so, this is a large conspiracy, and readers may ask how secrecy could be maintained among so many. We learn later that it wasn't. The image we derive from these verses is that of a group of fiercely dedicated people who are willing to make drastic sacrifices to achieve their goal. Nothing is said, however, of the reasons for such hatred. Are we to recall that Paul had initially been charged with taking a Gentile into an area of the temple that was off limits (see 21:28–29)? That charge has not been repeated or maintained in subsequent episodes, and it is likely that Luke means to be intentionally vague on the charges. We shall see that this is the case throughout the following trials. The vagueness adds to the portrait of Jews that Luke paints: they are ferocious in their opposition to Paul, but not for good reasons. Here is another example of Luke's anti-Judaism, a major emphasis in Acts.

The plot against Paul is of interest for a number of reasons. Paul's nephew suddenly and conveniently pops up, but Luke has no interest in explaining how he learned of the plot (Acts 23:16).

Was he initially involved in it? Did he know one or more of the conspirators? Perhaps this is asking too much of our author, but Luke has spared little in describing the details of the plot, and it would not be inappropriate for him to explain the nature of the nephew's connection to it.

The timing of the plot is also of interest. Recall that the tribune had already sent Paul to the Sanhedrin in order to determine the nature of the charges against him (see Acts 22:30–23:11). Now the conspirators demand a repeat. Would it not have been better for Luke to have placed the story of the plot against Paul before his narrative of the Sanhedrin hearing? In its present location the conspirators appear to be clumsy, asking the high priest and elders to do it again. Why would they think the tribune would agree to a re-hearing when the first one ended inconclusively and with a near riot? But the probable fact is that Luke intended to call attention to the ineptitude of the opposition to Paul.

Moreover, the Sanhedrin now seems to be united in opposition to Paul, whereas, as we have seen, in Acts 23:6–10 there was a deep division between Pharisaic and Sadducaic members. One suspects that Luke has suppressed this point here, since it would not serve him well in the present episode.

The Treatment of Paul

Already we have seen that the tribune's treatment of Paul, motivated by the claim of Roman citizenship, has been loose if not friendly. In the present section there seems to be no limitation on access to him. There is no doubt that he is a prisoner, but his nephew encounters no difficulty in visiting him (Acts 23:16). He is able to convince one of the centurions to arrange a meeting between the tribune and the nephew (23:17–18). The tribune, without investigation, accepts the young man's testimony and acts immediately on it (23:22–24). Brian Rapske sees this point clearly: Paul's "freedom to summon a centurion and tell him to take his nephew to the Tribune (apparently without resistance or questioning; Acts 23:17f.) suggests that the officers have orders to accommodate him and grant his reasonable requests."[16]

The haste with which the tribune arranges for Paul's transfer to Caesarea is impressive. So is the military escort that Paul has for the trip. He himself is mounted on horseback and accompanied by some 470 troops (Acts 23:23–24). Is such a force necessary against a group of 40 inept Jews, who are not yet aware that their plot has been discovered? We must recognize here something about Luke's literary intent. He wants to contrast the fairness and force of Roman justice with the malice and maladroitness of Jews, even if he has to exaggerate to do so. So he shows how well the Romans in authority treated Paul. Further we should recall that the tribune was frightened when Paul claimed his Roman citizenship (22:25). So when he learned of the conspiracy, he felt the obligation to protect his prisoner at all costs. If the plot had been successful, it would have constituted a serious threat against Roman justice and authority, and that could not be allowed. In terms of the narrative that Luke constructs, if not of history, the tribune's attempt to protect Paul and dispatch him safely to the governor's jurisdiction is reasonable.

The Tribune's Letter

To accompany the prisoner, the tribune composes a letter for Governor Felix. In it he summarizes Paul's case, reviews the history of his treatment of him, and comments on the charges against him. It is of special interest to observe that his summary does not precisely cohere with the previous narrative. Recall that it was only when Paul was about to be tortured under orders from the tribune that he played his trump card, revealing his Roman citizenship (Acts 22:25). In his letter to Felix, however, the tribune claimed that he learned of Paul's citizenship earlier, before he rescued him from his Jewish assailants (23:27), and he makes no reference to his order to have Paul tortured. It is not unlikely that a person in the tribune's position would tweak history to his own advantage. Certainly he does not want to call Felix's attention to his errors in handling Paul's case, and the tribune would not be the first or last public figure to polish his image before his superiors. It is, however, worth noting Luke's subtlety in composing this narrative. He is able to tell the story as he intends for his readers to see it, but he is able also to tell it credibly from the perspective of one of his characters.

The tribune also notes that the charges against Paul related to Jewish law and that neither imprisonment nor death is an appropriate penalty (Acts 23:29). This judgment will remind readers of that of Gallio in 18:14–15, who dismissed the case against Paul. The meaning must be that Claudius Lysias also recommended that the case be dismissed as not actionable in a Roman court. So far as Roman law is concerned, Paul has done nothing deserving imprisonment or death. Presumably we are to conclude that he is now a prisoner only for his own protection. Luke once again stresses the contrast between the fairness of Roman justice and the chaos of unfounded Jewish malevolence.

In the last verses of this section, we see Paul before Felix, who grants him a hearing to begin when the accusers arrive (Acts 23:33–35). We are now prepared for a climactic trial of Paul before the highest-ranking Roman authority in Judea.

In Search of History

This section includes quoted dialogue and quoted contents of a letter, both of which are narrative devices already discredited in this study. The heart of the story is a Jewish conspiracy against Paul, which is the last in a long line of Jewish plots against Paul in Acts and serves to reinforce the idea of the intransigence of the Jews. These stories of Jewish opposition have been shown throughout this study to be creations of the author to fit his narrative agenda.

The story includes a surprising amount of detail. First there is a description of a conspiracy among the Jews. Not only does the narrator know exactly how many there were but also he is able to quote their plan in their own words. Then the narrator introduces a character otherwise unknown who comes onstage just for this moment: Paul's nephew. The nephew is apparently quite skilled at spy craft since he is able not only to learn about the conspiracy but also able to report the exact details: "More than forty of them have vowed not to eat nor to drink until they have assassinated him" (Acts 23:21), which is exactly what the narrator had told us in describing the plot moments before (23:13–14). It is as if the nephew had read the description in Acts. Both Paul and the nephew are also pictured as quite skilled at diplomacy, since the soldiers and the tribune both condescend to give them special favors and a private audience. The story lacks credulity from beginning to end, but it is a rip-roaring adventure tale.

Richard Pervo considers this story to be based on two probable historical details, namely the arrest of Paul in Jerusalem and his transfer under guard to Caesarea.[17] If that was the case, clearly Luke has told his own version of how that happened, a version that in all of the rest of its details lacks historical credibility.

Paul's Defense before Felix at Caesarea

24 Five days after Paul had been conveyed to Caesarea Ananias the high priest came down from Jerusalem.

With him were some members of the Sanhedrin and one Tertullus, a professional advocate. They pressed charges against Paul to the governor. ²Bidden to speak, Tertullus presented the opening statement for the prosecution:

"Your Excellency, Felix, through your attentive care we enjoy substantial peace, and this country has welcomed numerous improvements through your administration, ³always and everywhere. For this we remain fully grateful.

⁴"I have no desire to drag this out. Please listen, with your accustomed courtesy, to this brief summary of the facts. ⁵We have discovered that this creature is a pest. A ringleader of the Nazorean faction, he foments rebellions among all Jews throughout the empire. ⁶He even attempted to defile the temple, at which point we put him under arrest. ⁸You need only interrogate him to verify all of our allegations."

⁹The Jews then pitched in to affirm that matters were as he had stated. ¹⁰When the governor gave him leave, Paul spoke:

"Since I know that you have served this nation in a judicial capacity for many years, I shall cheerfully speak in my own defense. ¹¹You can establish that I arrived in Jerusalem on pilgrimage no more than twelve days ago. ¹²No one ever found me engaging in individual discussions or collecting crowds in temple, synagogue, or anywhere else in the city, ¹³nor can they substantiate their present accusations against me.

¹⁴"But one thing I <u>will</u> admit to you: I do revere our ancestral God and believe all that is commanded in the Law and written in the Prophets. ¹⁵My hope in God is also that of those who accuse me: we look forward to a coming resurrection of both the good and the wicked. I serve God by following the Movement, which they denominate a 'faction.' ¹⁶In this service I likewise strive ardently at all times to be free from any conscious offense to God and to mortals. ¹⁷After an absence of many years I came here to bring funds to my people and to offer sacrifices. ¹⁸They found me engaged in these rites, in a state of ritual purity. There was no crowd, no agitation, ¹⁹but there were some Jews from Asia—if they really had any accusations to make against me, they would have to be present. ²⁰Well, they aren't here, so, let these people who are here speak for themselves

about what I did wrong while I was standing before the Sanhedrin. ²¹Maybe this is it: that one sentence I shouted while in their midst, 'The issue about which I am arraigned before you this day is the resurrection of the dead.'"

²²Felix, now fairly well informed about the Movement, halted the proceedings with the announcement: "I shall reach a decision on these matters when Tribune Lysias puts in an appearance." ²³He ordered the centurion to retain Paul in custody but not in maximum security. There were to be no restrictions upon the efforts of his friends to attend to his needs.

²⁴Some days later Felix, while with his Jewish wife, Drusilla, had Paul brought in and listened to his presentation of belief in Christ Jesus. ²⁵When he began to speak about proper behavior, self-control, and the future judgment, Felix became uncomfortable. "That's enough for now," he said, "I shall summon you again, as my schedule permits." ²⁶He did, in fact, summon Paul quite often and engage in conversation with him, because he was also hoping for a personal consideration from Paul.

²⁷After two years had elapsed, Porcius Festus succeeded Felix, who had left Paul in custody in the hope that it would improve his standing with the Jews.

Comments on the Story

In this section Luke gives us a summary of a formal judicial session. At least, it appears to be a formal trial, with the prosecution presenting charges against Paul and Paul defending himself. The prosecution has hired a professional spokesperson, one Tertullus, who is described as a *rhetor* and who functions as a prosecuting attorney. Paul has no attorney but adequately presents his own defense. After the two brief statements of Tertullus and Paul, the governor, Felix, postpones a decision but occasionally meets with Paul to hear his presentation of the Christian message and in hopes of receiving a bribe. When his term as governor is over, Felix leaves Paul imprisoned, expecting to curry favor with the Jews.

Luke probably had the trial of Jesus in mind when he composed this long section about Paul. The trials of Jesus in the Gospel of Luke and the trials of Paul in Acts display a basic structural parallelism: both Jesus and Paul were subjected to a hearing before the Sanhedrin (Luke 22:66–71; Acts 22:30–23:11); both appeared before a Roman governor (Luke 23:1–5, 13–25; Acts 24:1–27; 25:1–12); both appeared before a Herodian (Luke 23:6–12; Acts 25:23–26:32). But there are striking differences that should not be overlooked: the entire process relating to Jesus is much briefer in Luke than that of Paul in Acts. Jesus offers nothing in his own defense, but Paul presents his case in speeches before two governors and a king. Jesus appears before one Roman authority, while Paul argues his case before two governors and one tribune. It seems likely that Luke had a basic structural pattern that he used for both Jesus and Paul but felt free to heighten the dramatic force of the trials in Acts by greatly extending the narratives about Paul.

The comments that follow will focus on three aspects of Paul's trial before Felix: the prosecution, the defense, and the outcome.

The Prosecution

Tertullus' prosecution properly begins with flattering words addressed to the judge (Acts 24:2–3). This tactic, known as a *captatio benevolentiae*, was generally accepted in Roman times, and Luke's early audiences would have recognized but tolerated the exaggerations and misleading statements. Note that Paul also engages in the flattery of Felix (24:10).

Tertullus' task is to present the charges against Paul and the evidence supporting them. There are four charges. (1) In a section that purports to be the record of a formal trial, Luke may have intended a certain irony in reporting that (in our translation) Tertullus' first charge is that Paul is a pest (Acts 24:5). The charge is, however, more serious than it might at first appear. Think of a pestilence that profoundly disturbs a community. The Lukan Tertullus means to suggest that the cause of such a danger should be eliminated. (2) Tertullus continues to explain that Paul is a ringleader of a sect of Nazoreans (24:5). Several times in Acts Luke has referred to Jesus "of Nazareth" or Jesus "the Nazorean" (see 2:22; 3:6; 4:10; 6:14; 22:8; 26:9), but it is only here that he allows one of his characters to use the term "Nazorean" to designate Jesus' followers. It is not Luke's preferred designation for the movement. That term is "the Way" (see especially Paul's counterclaim in 24:14; also 9:2; 19:23; 18:25, 26; 19:9; 22:4; 24:22). Nor is Luke averse to using the term, "Christian" (see 11:26; 26:28). "Nazoreans," especially when coupled with the term, "sect" (*hairesis*), has a pejorative ring, as if this is the word that the movement's opponents might use to refer to it. Note also that a derivative of the word *hairesis* is "heresy," the term that later Christian groups frequently hurled at each other. (3) Tertullus adds that not only is Paul a ringleader of the movement, but he has also caused rebellions among Jews throughout the empire (24:5). (4) Finally, Tertullus charges Paul with attempting to defile the temple (24:6), reflecting the charge made by Asian Jews against Paul in 21:28. Note here that the prosecutor departs from the Lukan narrative: he claims that "we put him under arrest" (24:6). The phrase suggests an orderly seizure of a prisoner by those whom Tertullus represents—the high priest and elders of the Sanhedrin—rather than the chaotic and violent attack upon Paul described in 21:27–30. Tertullus presents no evidence for the charges but claims that Felix can discover it by interrogating Paul (24:8).

It is questionable if Tertullus' charges against Paul would have been applicable in a Roman court of law. Calling Paul a pest or plague has rhetorical weight but lacks specificity. The charge that Paul is a ringleader of Nazoreans is more of a theological than a civil grievance. The original charge of the Asian Jews in Acts 21:28 would be taken seriously in a Roman court, but in Tertullus' formulation it appears to be a matter pertaining only to internal Jewish concerns. The third charge, however, might well get Felix's attention: "he foments rebellions among all Jews throughout the empire" (24:5). Acts, of course, provides no evidence that Paul stirred up Jewish rebellions against Rome, only that his message brought about reactions against him and, on some occasions, internal dissension. The Lukan Tertullus, however, intends for Felix to understand the charge as political. The word translated "rebellions" is, in Greek, *stasis*, a word used to designate civil disturbance or unrest (see 19:40; 23:7, 10), and Roman authorities characteristically took the charge very seriously. If Tertullus is right, Felix would be required to see Paul as a threat to Roman society and government.

The Defense

Like Tertullus' prosecution, Paul's defense begins with a *captatio benevolentiae*, words intended to elicit the governor's favorable response, or at least to avoid offending him at the outset. The defense does not address each of Tertullus' charges in turn, but focuses explicitly on the third and alludes to the others. Paul's speech accomplishes two things: (a) it calls attention to the lack of witnesses to the alleged misdoings; and (b) it removes the political aspects of the charges against him and re-characterizes them as religious.

Paul dismisses any thought that he could be associated with *stasis* by claiming a lack of evidence. He says that no one can testify that he stirred up crowds while in Jerusalem (Acts 24:12, 18). One purpose of Paul's speech is to deny the factual basis of Tertullus' third charge. But the language stresses the lack of witnesses: "No one ever found me engaging in individual discussions or collecting crowds," (24:12); "nor can they substantiate their present accusations against me," (24:13). Then follows an incomplete thought: "but there were some Jews from Asia—if they really had any accusations to make against me, they would have to be present" (24:19). The idea seems to be that, although no one can prove their allegations, some Jews from Asia brought charges. This would connect with 21:27–28, where Asian Jews charged Paul with taking a Gentile into the temple. The Lukan Paul's point is that if the Asian Jews really had any verifiable accusations to make against me, they would be here in Caesarea. Since they are not, there can be no testimony that I did anything illegal.

A major emphasis in Paul's defense before Felix is his fidelity to Judaism, a key theme in Acts. Paul calls attention to the fulfillment of his religious duties in Jerusalem and to the funds he brought for his people (Acts 24:17). In 11:27–30 there was a reference to famine relief that was carried to Jerusalem by Barnabas and Saul. Apparently those funds had been delivered long ago, and a pending famine was not the occasion for Paul's contribution at this time. We know from Paul's letters that he had spent considerable energy in collecting money from the churches he established and that these funds were to be presented to the leaders of the church in Jerusalem (1 Cor 16:1–4; 2 Cor 8:1–15; Rom 15:25–33). But Luke makes no reference to such a collection elsewhere in Acts. Only here do we have a hint of it. And in the present context it is likely that Luke intends us to understand that the fund was meant for the Jewish people and not restricted to believers in Jesus. If it had been the latter, we would expect Paul to have presented it when he first met with James in Acts 21:18–19. Luke has Paul mention the contribution here to support his characterization of him as a faithful Jew, a claim that the Lukan Paul makes specific in 24:14–15. He stresses his belief in the ancestral God, the Scriptures, and resurrection.

Paul's defense is a subtle and brilliant attempt to shift the nature of the charges against him, so that they are no longer applicable in a Roman court. Paul first claims that no witnesses can testify that he is guilty of *stasis*. Then he shows that, if he bears any guilt, it resides in his religious beliefs, which he shares with other Jews. He states this pointedly in Acts 24:20–21, saying that if there is any guilt, it is his proclamation in the Sanhedrin: "that one sentence I shouted while in their midst, 'The issue about which I am arraigned before you this day is the resurrection of the dead.'" Here the point is not that belief in the resurrection is a Jewish belief—although that claim has not faded from view (see 24:15)—but that the issue basic to the accusations against Paul is a religious one, not a political one. Paul's defense is that the case should be dismissed not only due to a lack of evidence but also because the charges are not appropriate in a Roman court of law.

The Outcome

Readers may be disappointed with the outcome of the hearing before Felix. They have been led to expect some conclusion to the procedures against Luke's hero, but instead the governor adjourns the hearing and postpones his decision (Acts 24:22). The character of Felix is ambiguous in this narrative. Luke's previous narratives featuring Roman authorities should lead readers to expect Felix to be fair and reasonable in his judgments. But what if no judgment is given? Ostensibly, Felix intends only to await the arrival of Claudius Lysias and to resume the trial when the tribune comes down from Jerusalem. In the meantime the governor treats Paul well (24:23) and converses with him about religion (24:24–25). But he leaves Paul languishing in prison until the end of his term in hopes of securing funds for his release and leaves him imprisoned in order to placate the Jews (24:26–27). Although he appears to be open to Paul's message, Felix's venality finally wins out over his better nature.

In Search of History

This segment is made up of two long speeches, one by the advocate presenting the case against Paul and the other by Paul himself. The trial scenes and speeches in Acts have already been discredited as narrative devices of the author. The question that remains is whether there is any information within this created story that can qualify as historical data.

The governor before whom Paul makes his defense is Felix, an official whom Luke would have known about from Josephus, and from whom he learned the name and background of Felix's wife, Drusilla.[18] The connection of Felix with Paul, however, is Luke's own creation, following a pattern in Luke-Acts to introduce named Roman officials at key parts of the story to lend verisimilitude to the narrative (see also the discussion of Gallio in Corinth, p. 222). Luke's addition of Drusilla to the story is a motif derived from Mark's story of the involvement of Herodias in the death of John the Baptist (Mark 6:18–20). Felix, like the proconsul in Acts 13:12, finds what Paul says to be intriguing and invites him back on several occasions to hear him speak. Paul's power as a philosopher/preacher is thereby enhanced, and his positive reception among the Roman officials is further contrasted with the rejection by the Jews.

The details of the story provide a backdrop for the narrative agenda of Luke. They do not have historical credibility on their own. Even the connection of Paul with Felix lacks credibility, since the dates of Felix are not known[19] and since his function in the story simply provides another means for Luke to develop his narrative agenda. For that reason, and because the meanings of the names "Felix" and "Porcius Festus" would seem too good for Luke to pass up when trolling for data to add to his story, the Fellows found the existence of both Felix and Festus in the narrative to be highly suspicious (see also the cameo essay, "Names in Acts," p. 22).

The Votes of the Fellows

Gray/Doubtful
- Felix ("Happy") and Porcius ("Porky") Festus were the names of the actual Roman governors at the trials of Paul in Acts 23:24–26:32.

Paul's Defense before Festus

25 Two days after setting foot in his province Festus went from Caesarea to Jerusalem, ²where the chief priests and the Jewish leaders put their case against Paul before him. ³They urged Festus to do them a favor, to Paul's disadvantage: that he have him transported to Jerusalem. This was because they intended to set an ambush and kill Paul en route. ⁴To this Festus replied that Paul was in custody in Caesarea, whither he himself would presently be returning. ⁵"Your preeminent people may accompany me and, if there are any grounds for it, make their case against him there." ⁶After spending no more than eight or ten days with them in Jerusalem, he returned to Caesarea. The next day he took his place on the bench and directed that Paul be brought in. ⁷Once he was there, the Jews from Jerusalem ganged up on him and made a number of quite grave charges that they were unable to support. ⁸In his defense Paul contended "I have done absolutely nothing wrong, either regarding

Jewish law, or the temple, or Caesar." ⁹Since Festus wished to ingratiate himself with the Jews, he asked Paul, "Are you willing to go to Jerusalem and be tried there by me on these charges?" ¹⁰Paul replied, "I am standing in Caesar's court. This is the proper venue. I have committed no offense against the Jews, as you well know. ¹¹If, however, I am in violation and am guilty of a capital crime, I shall not attempt to evade dying, but if there is no substance in the charges they are making, no one has the authority to surrender me to these people. I appeal to Caesar!" ¹²After conferring with his staff, Festus announced: "You have appealed to Caesar. To Caesar you shall go."

Comments on the Story

Festus, the new governor, acts speedily in dealing with Paul. He first confers with Jewish leaders in Jerusalem but denies their request to bring Paul there for trial. Luke tells us that these Jews, like the conspirators in Acts 23:12–22, plan to ambush and kill Paul on his way from Caesarea to Jerusalem. As an alternative, Festus invites the Jewish leaders to accompany him to Caesarea, where the trial is to be held. At the trial, the Jerusalem contingent brings serious but unsubstantiated charges against Paul, who maintains his innocence. Without reaching a verdict, the governor asks Paul if he would be willing to be tried in Jerusalem, and Paul vigorously rejects the suggestion, insisting that he should be tried in a Roman court. He appeals to Caesar, and Festus agrees to send him on to Rome.

At first glance this section appears to do little to advance the action. A new governor comes into the province, promising speedy action but reaching no verdict in Paul's case. Jews devise another plot to ambush and kill Paul as he is being transferred from one venue to another, but it is foiled. Unproven charges are brought, and Paul denies them. Festus exhibits no greater integrity than his predecessor, first denying a Jewish request but finally caving in, so as to ingratiate himself with his subjects. Luke seems here to be recycling old material rather than moving the narrative toward a conclusion.

But there are aspects of the narrative that portend that something more is going on. It is not difficult to see that something of importance is involved in the controversy about a venue for Paul's trial. Should it be in Caesarea, the Roman governor's headquarters, or in Jerusalem, the center of Judaism? The Jewish leaders argue for Jerusalem because Paul's transfer provides them a chance for an ambush (Acts 25:3). Paul's objection may be based on his fear of assassination, but his words indicate that there is a different reason. He says that he must be tried in Caesar's court, since he has done nothing against the Jews (25:10). This is a puzzling statement, because, although Paul denies his guilt, he had previously maintained that the charges against him were internal to Judaism and not actionable in a Roman court (see 24:11–21). In 25:8 he declares his innocence of any crimes against law, temple, or Caesar; that is, he is guilty of no crimes against either Jews or Romans. In 25:10–11, he repeats his claim of innocence in respect to Jewish concerns but insists that he should be tried in a Roman court. The reader is left to infer what these charges are (*stasis*?) but is disposed to accept Paul's declaration of innocence.

A further difficulty is that Governor Festus has not proposed to turn Paul over to Jews for trial, but only to hold the Roman trial in Jerusalem. His question to Paul is, "Are you willing to go to Jerusalem and be tried there *by me* on these charges" (Acts 25:9)? In Paul's mind, however, the alternatives are: (a) to be tried in Caesarea for alleged crimes against the Roman state; or (b) to be tried in Jerusalem for crimes against Torah or temple. A change of venue for him means a change of jurisdiction. So he can say to Festus: If the Roman charges against me are invalid, you cannot turn me over to the Jews. Thus, he appeals to Caesar (25:11).

Since the governor has handed down no verdict, Paul's appeal cannot be against an adverse decision. He is appealing for the trial to be heard by the emperor himself, rather than by one of his subordinates. It is difficult to tell, from an examination of the relevant texts, if this kind of appeal was permitted in Roman law, although some scholars maintain that it was. But the issue for us is not whether the appeal makes sense in terms of Roman law but whether it makes sense within the Lukan narrative. The difficulties noted above show that the Lukan narrative is not altogether lucid at this point.

But we need to examine this issue within a larger framework. Not all that Luke wants to convey to the reader occurs on the level of courts, trials, and human judgments. Readers should recall the vision in which it was revealed to Paul that he must go to Rome (Acts 23:11; see also 19:21). Divine revelations carry a great deal of weight in Acts and ultimately drive the narrative. For Luke, if God says that Paul must (Greek, *dei*) go to Rome, nothing can prevent him from doing so. However convoluted the course of action may be that takes him to his destination, it is incumbent on Paul to get to Rome. He must, therefore, reject both Jerusalem and Caesarea as venues for his trial, which can only take place in the city of Rome. We learn later that he even sacrifices his legal innocence and personal freedom by appealing to Caesar (26:32). Nothing may preclude his getting to Rome: not trials, not his own innocence, not storm, shipwreck, or snake bite (see 27:1–28:10). Festus' proclamation at the end of this section has the effect of reiterating and confirming the divine order of 23:11: "You have appealed to Caesar. To Caesar you shall go" (25:12).

In Search of History

This story functions to allow Paul a hearing before still another Roman governor and to foil still another Jewish attempt to kill him. Once again, the Roman official is pictured as treating Paul fairly, and the Jews are pictured as being intractable foes.

The story also functions to define how Paul, who was arrested in Jerusalem, gets to Rome. After all, there is no reason to send him to Rome in order for him to get a Roman trial. The device Luke uses is Paul's appeal to Caesar. It was not unusual for Roman citizens to be remanded to Rome for trial. Here, however, the appeal to Rome functions as a narrative device, and it depends on the purported Roman citizenship of Paul. These details are found only in Acts and, as shown above in the discussion of Paul's citizenship (p. 275–76), are not entirely consistent with Paul's own representation of himself. Luke began Paul's journeys upon leaving Greece with a reference to Paul's plans to visit Jerusalem and then go to Rome, details that were derived from Paul's own expressed plans (Rom 15:23–29). Paul intended to take the collection to Jerusalem and then travel to Rome to secure support for a planned mission trip to Spain. Luke keeps the itinerary but changes the details; his version has Paul arrested in Jerusalem and conveyed to Rome as a prisoner. The Acts version, rich in stories of Jewish opposition, multiple trials, benevolent Roman officials, and multiple defense speeches of Paul, fits Luke's narrative agenda. But he needs a device to get Paul to Rome, and citizenship and appeal to Rome serve that purpose. These details fit well as devices within Luke's created plot. Since there is no external evidence supporting historicity, it is highly unlikely that these are historical details.

Festus Consults King Agrippa

25 ¹³Not long thereafter King Agrippa and Bernice arrived in Caesarea and gave Festus an official welcome. ¹⁴Some days into their visit Festus brought the case of Paul to the king's attention.

"There is a man left in custody by Felix. ¹⁵When I was in Jerusalem, the Jewish high priests and elders brought the case to my attention, demanding that I find him guilty. ¹⁶I explained to them that it is contrary to Roman practice to execute a sentence upon an accused person before that individual has had opportunity to confront the accusers and offer a defense against the charge.

¹⁷"When they came here, I took my seat on the bench without delay—the very next day, in fact—and had the man brought in. ¹⁸When the accusers arose to make their case, however, they did not allege any of the crimes about which I had expected to hear. ¹⁹Instead, they took up with him some controversies involving particular religious matters, as well as questions about a certain deceased Jesus, whom Paul claimed to be alive. ²⁰Since *I* had no idea how to adjudicate matters of this sort, I asked whether he would like to go to Jerusalem and stand trial there on these issues. ²¹Because, however, Paul appealed to be retained for a decision by His Majesty, I ordered him to be kept in custody until I could remand him to Caesar."

²²Agrippa said, "I really should like to hear this man."

"Tomorrow you will have your opportunity," replied Festus.

Comments on the Story

A welcoming visit by Agrippa and his sister provides Festus an opportunity to consult with the Jewish king about Paul's case. He summarizes matters so far, pleads ignorance about the charges brought against the prisoner, and arranges for Agrippa to interview Paul the following day.

The previous section has probably led most readers to expect to find Paul finally on his way to Rome. But, just as the hearings under Felix and Festus were inconclusive, so here justice is delayed. Before he can leave Caesarea Paul must undergo yet another hearing, this time under Agrippa, regarded by Luke as a king. It is a hearing that serves Luke's purposes in a number of ways. First, the narrative escalates Paul's case and introduces a perspective that is Jewish but not that of Paul's accusers. Of course, Agrippa does not hear the case in an official capacity, but it is presumed that he is knowledgeable about things Jewish and unbiased. He is in a position to provide important information for a perplexed Roman governor, and his status as king carries weight even if he is only a consultant in the case. Second, the introduction of Agrippa serves as a fulfillment of the divine word in Acts 9:15, which announced that Paul would appear before "Gentiles, monarchs and Israelites." In Acts Paul has frequently spoken to Gentiles and Israelites, but Agrippa is the only monarch before whom he appears. Third, it serves to fill out the parallelism between the trials of Jesus in Luke and those of Paul in Acts. Both appeared before the Jewish Sanhedrin (Luke 22:66–71; Acts 22:30–23:11) and Roman governor(s) (Luke 23:1–5, 13–25; Acts 24:1–27; 25:1–12). Both also appeared before a Herod (Antipas in the case of Jesus, Luke 23:6–12; Agrippa in that of Paul, Acts 25:23–26:32). Thus we should observe that the introduction of Agrippa here not only serves to escalate the case of Paul to a very high level, but also to fulfill prophecy and to underscore the parallelism between Paul and Jesus.

Festus wastes no time in bringing Paul's case to Agrippa's attention. He fills the king in on the case, but there are discrepancies between his report and the events as described in Luke's narrative, and it becomes apparent that "Festus' account is partly a whitewash. He attempts to make his own handling of Paul's case look better than it was."[20] Luke's characterization of Festus fits comfortably with that of another Roman official. In Acts 23:26–30 we observed the tribune Claudius Lysias spinning the record in his own favor, so Festus' summary to Agrippa should come as no surprise.

Some of Festus' summary coheres with the preceding Lukan narrative: he spoke with Jewish leaders in Jerusalem about Paul (Acts 25:1–3); he rejected their request to move Paul from Caesarea to Jerusalem (25:4); he held a trial in Caesarea (25:6–8); he asked Paul if he would be willing to be tried in Jerusalem (25:9); and Paul appealed to the emperor (25:11).

But in the Lukan narrative the Jews in Jerusalem did not ask Festus to find Paul guilty; instead they asked him to send Paul to Jerusalem for trial and formed a plot to ambush him along the way(Acts 25:3). Festus did not explain Roman legal procedure to the Jewish leaders; instead he maintained that Paul was a prisoner in Caesarea and invited the accusers to appear at the trial to be held there (25:4-5). The most serious variation appears in Festus' account of his question to Paul about being tried in Jerusalem. In the narrative he asked if Paul would be willing to go to Jerusalem but made it clear that he, Festus, would be the judge (25:9). In speaking to Agrippa, Festus says that he asked if Paul would be willing to go to Jerusalem and be tried *"on these issues"* (25:20). The reference is to issues that Festus admittedly does not understand and characterizes as "controversies involving particular religious matters, as well as questions about a certain deceased Jesus, whom Paul claimed to be alive" (25:19). In Luke's narrative the proposed Jerusalem trial is Roman, but in Festus' reprise it is Jewish.

Festus' statement to Agrippa is one that attempts to put the speaker in the best possible light. But it also adds a Roman perspective to the legal situation. In the hearing before Felix, Paul argued that the charges against him were inappropriate in a Roman court, but, before Festus, he pleaded innocent on all charges, insisted on a Roman trial, and appealed to the emperor. Now Festus admits that, as governor, he is unequipped to handle the case, which involves Jewish religious matters. So we eagerly await further enlightenment about Paul's legal situation that may come from yet another perspective, that of the Jewish king, Agrippa.

In Search of History

As noted in the comments above, the parallelism between the trial of Jesus in the Gospel of Luke and the trials of Paul in Acts represents a clear intention to parallel Paul's trials with those of Jesus. But there is another phenomenon to notice: that one-fourth of Acts is devoted to these trial scenes of Paul. The amount of space given to these stories is intentional and must be considered an important component of Luke's narrative apologetic.[21]

Here Luke uses a standard device, a speech. It seems excessive to present the contents of a speech of Festus to Agrippa, but it lends support to Luke's purpose in picturing Roman officials as personally involved in all matters pertaining to Paul. This supports the reader's impression that Paul's importance and presence as a philosopher/orator could not go unnoticed.

Paul's Defense before Agrippa

25 [23]The next day Agrippa and Bernice arrived in considerable splendor and entered the audience chamber with tribunes and the local notables. At Festus' direction Paul was brought in.

²⁴"King Agrippa and all you ladies and gentlemen. You see this man. The entire Jewish community has appealed to me, both here and in Jerusalem, clamoring that he must be put to death directly. ²⁵In my view, however, he has done nothing deserving death, but, because he appealed to His Majesty, I decided to send him *to Rome*. ²⁶I have nothing definite to transmit to our Sovereign concerning him. I have therefore brought him before you all, and particularly you, King Agrippa, so that, upon the completion of an inquiry, I might have something to communicate. ²⁷For it makes no sense to me to transfer a prisoner without also stipulating the charges against him."

26 Agrippa advised Paul, "You may now state your case." Making the appropriate gesture, Paul began his defense.

²"King Agrippa, I regard myself as fortunate to have this opportunity to defend myself today against all the charges lodged against me by Jews, ³particularly because you are an expert about all Jewish customs and controversies. Please lend me a patient ear. ⁴Every Jew knows my manner of life from my early youth, because I lived among my people in Jerusalem. ⁵They have long been well aware—and could so testify if they wished to—that I have followed the rule of life of the most punctilious group our way of worship has to offer. I am a Pharisee. ⁶I am now on trial because of my hope for fulfillment of the promise God made to our forebears, ⁷that for which our twelve tribes yearn, with continuous and heartfelt devotion, to experience. Your Majesty, the Jews are accusing me of having this hope! ⁸Why do you people think it incredible that God might raise the dead? ⁹My own view was that I was obliged to do a great deal against the name of Jesus the Nazorean, ¹⁰and I did so. Authorized by the high priests, I locked up many of God's people in Jerusalem and cast my vote for their subsequent execution. ¹¹No synagogue escaped my attention. I frequently sought to torture them into committing blasphemy. In a fury verging upon insanity I extended my pursuit to other cities. ¹²While so engaged I was en route to Damascus with the permission and authorization of the high priests, ¹³when, while traveling at midday I saw, Your

Majesty, a light from above, brighter than the sun, sweep over me and my companions. [14]We all fell to the ground. I heard a voice, which said to me, in Aramaic,

'Saul, Saul, why are you persecuting me? You can't swim against the flood.'

[15]"'Who are you, Lord?'

"'I am Jesus whom you are persecuting. [16]On your feet, now! I have appeared to you to appoint you as an agent and witness of what you have seen and what I shall show you. [17]I shall rescue you from your own people and from the gentiles to whom I am sending you, [18]to open their eyes, so that they may turn from darkness to light and from the power of Satan to God and receive forgiveness of sins with a place among those who have been made holy by their trust in me.'

[19]"Therefore, Your Majesty, I obeyed that apparition from on high. [20]In consequence I began to urge people, in Damascus first, then in Jerusalem, then to both Jews and gentiles in every region, to change their ways and turn to God, demonstrating this change by appropriate actions. [21]This was why the Jews apprehended me while I was in the temple and attempted to murder me. [22]With God's help I am still able to maintain my views, testifying to those of high degree and low nothing other than what the prophets and Moses said would take place: [23]that the Messiah would suffer, be the first to rise from the dead, and, by rising, be a herald of light to my people and the gentiles alike."

[24]At this point Festus loudly interrupted: "Paul, you are crazy! All this research is driving you over the brink!"

[25]"I am not insane, Your Excellency. What I declare is the sober truth. [26]His Majesty is well informed about these matters, and it is to him that I am speaking without equivocation. I am certain that none of these matters has eluded his attention, since this is no storefront mission! [27]Do you believe the prophets, Your Majesty? Of course you believe them!"

[28]Agrippa replied, "Are you trying to make me a Christian in such short order?"

[29]"I would to God that, by one word or many, not just you, but everyone listening to me today could share what I now have—apart, of course, from these shackles."

³⁰At this point the king stood up, followed by the governor, Bernice, and all who were present. ³¹On their way out people commented to one another, "This fellow is engaged in nothing that deserves execution or incarceration." ³²Agrippa said to Festus, "If he had not appealed to Caesar he could have been discharged."

Comments on the Story

Paul gives his final defensive speech before King Agrippa, with the king's sister, the Roman governor, and other dignitaries in attendance. Festus introduces Paul to Agrippa, noting that the entire Jewish community called for his death. Since, says Festus, Paul appealed to the emperor, it is necessary to send along with him a bill of particulars, listing the charges against him. He requests that Agrippa interview Paul and fill him in on these charges, which, being Jewish, are beyond Festus' competence.

Paul's defense begins with the usual *captatio benevolentiae*, stressing the king's familiarity with Jewish traditions. Paul claims that he has always observed a Jewish life and belongs to the most strictly observant Jewish party, the Pharisees. The charge against him, says Paul, is that he believes the promise that God gave Israel, namely the expectation of resurrection. He then tells, for the third time, of his persecution of Jesus' followers, his conversion on the road to Damascus, and his divine commission to preach to Jews and Gentiles. He adds that, since the time of this experience, he has preached only what the prophets predicted—that the Christ must suffer and rise from the dead—but the Jews tried to kill him. Festus interrupts, saying that Paul has gone mad, and Paul turns to the king, who suspects a conversion attempt. As the king and the other attendees get up to leave, there is talk that Paul has done nothing deserving death, and Agrippa says to Festus that Paul could have been released had he not appealed to the emperor.

The comments Festus makes in introducing Paul to Agrippa continue from the previous section, where, as we saw, he took some liberties in narrating his own actions. The narrative told us that chief priests and Jewish leaders in Jerusalem brought charges against Paul (see Acts 25:2), but now Festus says that the entire Jewish community demanded Paul's death (25:24). When he tells Agrippa that he considers Paul innocent but needs something to write to the emperor, we hear again the contention that a Roman court is not the appropriate venue for Paul's case (25:25–27).

Paul's speech (Acts 26:2–29), the centerpiece of this section, is just about what most readers would expect. His defense stresses his fidelity to Jewish ways of life, his belief in resurrection, and the prophetic background of this belief. In the hearing before the Sanhedrin Paul had claimed to be a Pharisee (23:6), and he repeats that claim here (26:5). His interpretation of the charge against him as his belief in the resurrection came out strongly in the Sanhedrin trial (23:6), and that understanding shows up here as well (26:6–7). He told of his conversion experience in chapter 22 and tells of it again here, where the details vary from those in both of the other versions (9:1–31; 22:1–29). In this third telling, Paul's persecution of believers is more vigorous and includes his punishment of them in synagogues, his attempts to get them to blaspheme, and his pursuit of them to foreign cities (26:10–11). The light that shined on the road to Damascus was brighter than the sun (26:13); not just Paul, but he and his fellow travelers *all* fell to the ground (26:14). In this third telling there is no reference to Paul's blindness (see 9:8; 22:11), and no mention of Ananias (see 9:10–18; 22:12–16).

In all three stories the commission to Paul is stressed, but it is differently conceived. In all three the commission, which makes Paul a missionary to Jews and Gentiles, is given by the Lord (probably meaning Jesus), but in Acts 9:15 the Lord communicates it to Ananias, while in 22:15 Ananias gives the charge to Paul. In the second version, there is an added vision that makes the commission more specific. Paul says that he was in the temple and that Jesus appeared to him to send him far away to Gentiles (22:21). In the third version the commission is given on the road to Damascus and directly to Paul (26:16). The effect is that, in this third telling, there are no intermediaries: the Lord speaks directly to Paul and appoints him as his witness to Jews and Gentiles.

That the conversion narrative is important to Luke is obvious. Triple repetition is sufficient evidence of its significance. Paul's use of it in his defense speeches is intended to highlight the power that motivates him. His persecution of the early believers is cited as an example of his adherence to Jewish traditions, and his radical change from opposing to embracing the religion of Jesus is intended to confirm the rightness of his new life: it was not just a change of mind or belief but a conversion driven by the divine. We may never know why certain details vary in the three versions of the story. Perhaps Luke wanted to avoid rigid repetition; perhaps he was drawing on different sources; perhaps he did not remember exactly what he had written in the earlier narratives. The last supposition will appear inappropriate to those who regard Luke as an infallible writer. But if we think of him as human and fallible, we will be able to think of him as similar to most of his readers, ancient and modern, who tend to overlook these variations in detail.

In Acts 26:22–23 the Lukan Paul claims prophetic backing for the belief that the Messiah must suffer and rise from the dead. Notably, however, he does not cite a single passage from the prophets. Readers of Luke's gospel will recall something similar there. In Luke 24:25–27 the risen Jesus, speaking to two disciples on the road to Emmaus, rebukes them for not believing the prophets. He then explains to them the prophetic writings that predict the Messiah's death and resurrection. But no Scripture is cited (see also Acts 17:3). This lack is surprising in view of the fact that, elsewhere, Luke is not reluctant to cite and quote those Scriptures that support his contentions. Certainly the death and resurrection of the Messiah was a central belief that Luke embraced. Further, a major theme in Acts is that the believers in Jesus, notably Paul, were faithful Jews, believing everything in Scripture and the prophets (see 24:14). So the lack of a single citation foretelling the death and resurrection of the Messiah is striking.

At the end of this section Agrippa says to Festus that Paul could have been released if he had not appealed to the emperor (Acts 26:32). Agrippa thus adds his own verdict of innocence to those of Claudius Lysias and Festus (see 23:29; 25:25). His privately communicated verdict seems to be based on the conviction that an appeal to the emperor is irrevocable and that no one of lower rank has the authority to impede the proceedings. This means that, legally, nothing that Luke reports after Acts 25:11 has any bearing on Paul's case. Nor has the interview with Agrippa clarified the charges against Paul. Luke may leave the legal aspects of Paul's trials quite murky, but we should not overlook the rhetorical force of his narrative. He has told a story that progressively mounts in excitement and apprehension as Paul moves from one trial to another. The appeal, though not successful in releasing him, gets him out of the hands of the Jews, his constant enemies, and under the jurisdiction of the Romans, who, though imperfect, have so far treated him fairly. Will he be treated fairly in Rome or will the Jews be able to press their case against him? Without tipping his hand about the outcome of Paul's trial in Rome, Luke leads the reader to continue to attend the story with high anticipation.

In Search of History

There is high drama to this story. The king enters with a flourish, along with other important officials and his sister, Bernice. Festus then plays the role of master of ceremonies by introducing Paul to the gathered number. Agrippa gives leave for Paul to speak and, with a practiced skill in formal rhetoric worthy of the occasion, Paul delivers what, to the reader, would be understood to be a masterful speech. It includes the third version in Acts of Paul's conversion (see the cameo essay, "Comparing Paul and Luke on Paul's Conversion," pp. 114). Agrippa is impressed, so much so that he raises the possibility that he could be persuaded to be a Christian. He then dismisses Paul and, as they are leaving, he and the other distinguished guests decide in private conversation that Paul appears clearly to be innocent. In a final aside to Festus, Agrippa opines that Paul could have been released on the spot if he had not appealed to Caesar. It is a scene with dramatic action worthy of Hollywood. But it lacks historical credibility.

Luke would have learned of Porcius Festus and his friendship with Agrippa from Josephus.[22] However, the dates of Festus are just as obscure as those of Felix, so a connection with Paul cannot be determined from external sources. Agrippa II was the king of Chalcis, located in modern day Syria, which he inherited as part of the Herodian legacy. Acts brings him to Caesarea on a diplomatic mission to welcome the arrival of Porcius Festus as the new governor. This provides Luke with the pretext to bring Paul before a Herodian and thus complete the parallelism of trials of Jesus and Paul.

Paul Sails for Rome

27 Once it had been determined that we were to sail to Italy, they transferred custody of Paul and some other prisoners to a centurion of an Imperial Cohort named Julius.

²We boarded a ship of Adramyttium that was going to stop at ports along the Asian coast and set out. Aristarchus, a Macedonian from Thessalonica, was with us. ³We put in at Sidon the subsequent day, where Julius very kindly permitted Paul to visit friends and receive attention from them. ⁴After we departed from Sidon contrary winds compelled us to keep to the sheltered side of Cyprus. ⁵We then crossed the open water along the coast of Cilicia and Pamphylia

and arrived at Myra in Lycia. ⁶There the centurion located an Alexandrian ship destined for Italy and put us aboard it. ⁷Many days of slow and labored sailing got us no farther than the vicinity of Cnidus, where, unable to make headway, we sailed for Crete, off Salmone, ⁸and hugged the coast with some difficulty until we reached a place called Fair Havens, which is near the city of Lasaea.

⁹As some time had passed and navigation had become risky because even Yom Kippur had come and gone, Paul advised them, ¹⁰"Gentlemen, I envision that the voyage will be attended with a great deal of damage and loss—loss not only of cargo and the vessel but even loss of our very lives." ¹¹The centurion, however, found the arguments of the owner and the master more convincing than those of Paul. ¹²Since Fair Havens was unsuitable for wintering, the majority preferred to sail on so that, if possible, they might reach Phoenix, a Cretan harbor exposed to winds from both the northwest and the southwest.

Comments on the Story

Paul is finally on his way to Rome, but before his arrival there Luke inserts a long story of the voyage from Caesarea. Paul has engaged in a number of trips before this, but none gets the attention that the trip to Rome does except perhaps the voyage from Philippi to Caesarea (Acts 20:6–21:8). Here is a narrative that consumes forty verses, amounting to about 6 percent of the entire book of Acts. It is an exciting story of a dangerous sea voyage that goes into great detail about ships and storms but has little to do with Paul's evangelistic mission or his legal situation. It is tempting to think that the entire section, Acts 27:1–28:16, is an interpolation that was added after the rest of the book was completed or an importation from another source. We know that, from the time of Homer, stories of seagoing adventures were very popular in the ancient world, and it is not surprising that such a story would be told of Paul. Resemblances to the epic tradition have frequently been noted, and the narrative has surely been influenced by this literature. But, within the plot structure of Acts, the narrative seems to serve no purpose other than to get Paul to Rome, and Luke could have told about this in far fewer words.

Luke probably would not agree that his story of Paul's trip to Rome contributed little to his plot. Similarities between his stories of Jesus and Paul may give us a hint about his intentions in devoting so much space to it. We have previously noted a number of parallels between these stories. These parallels became quite prominent in the chapters of Acts that dealt with Paul's trials. Indeed, the trials of Paul before the Sanhedrin, Roman governors, and the Herodian Agrippa appear to be modeled on the Lukan narrative of Jesus' passion. As such, they lead the reader to expect that the story of Paul will end in some way similar to that of Jesus. Luke does not write that Paul was crucified and resurrected, but he nevertheless tells the story of his sea voyage as a kind of passion narrative. Paul does not die and rise from the dead, but he faces and overcomes almost certain death on more than one occasion.

First-person narration resumes in these sections, going from Acts 27:1–28:16. This feature, together with the details about ports of call, winds, and ships has led many interpreters to conclude that the sea voyage from Caesarea to Rome was drawn from a source written by an eye witness or that Luke himself was the eye witness. Fellows of the Acts Seminar have concluded, however, that first-person narration was a characteristic of such tales and not an indication of authenticity. Although some readers find profit in reading Acts 27:1–28:16 as an account of an actual journey, such a reading may overlook the narrative's significance as an adventure story with deep symbolism. As Luke's hero, Paul must persevere in obedience to the will of God, undergo suffering, and overcome it, as did Jesus. The tale of the voyage to Rome narrates this.

In Acts 27:1–12 we have the first leg of a long journey. Paul and the other prisoners are transferred to the custody of a centurion named Julius, and the group departs on a boat registered in Adramyttium. They call first at Sidon and then sail around Cyprus. When they arrive at Myra in Lycia, they board a second ship, this one from Alexandria, bound for Italy. Opposing winds create sailing difficulties, and the captain seeks good harbors on Crete, docking first at Fair Havens and then sailing on to Phoenix, where they plan to spend the winter.

In our translation of Acts 27:9, there is a reference to Yom Kippur. The Greek texts refer more generally to "the fast." The point of the verse is that the trip had already consumed a great deal of time and that it was becoming risky to travel any farther. This must mean that winter is near, since it is generally agreed that travel on the Mediterranean was risky to impossible after a certain time in the autumn. It is not unreasonable to think that the reference in 27:9 is to Yom Kippur, the only fast in the Jewish calendar.

Occurring in September or October, it could well signify the end of good weather sailing.

In Acts 27:10–12 Luke tells of a controversy between Paul and those responsible for operating the ship. The ship has docked at Fair Havens, in Crete, and Paul seems to take the position that any travel beyond that point will incur a risk of the loss not only of the ship and its cargo, but of lives. Those responsible for the ship and a majority of the sailors, however, decide that it is better to move on to a better harbor in Phoenix. It is not clear that a decision was made at this point to proceed beyond Crete, although this is what happened (see 27:13–17). It seems unlikely that a prisoner would be in a position to advise experienced mariners, but the Paul of Acts is knowledgeable and prescient. In these verses Luke is preparing the reader for his hero's later role in the wreck of the ship (27:21–26), when everybody on board learns that they should have listened to Paul.

In Search of History

Like earlier sea voyage stories in Acts, this story is made up of an imaginary, but geographically plausible, voyage. As was the case in earlier sea voyage stories, it is imaginary because it is a we-passage (see the cameo essay, "We-Passages in the Acts of the Apostles," p. 191). Sea voyages were common devices in adventure tales from the time of Homer, as mentioned in the comments above. Our author is a clever storyteller, so he makes the story credible by proposing a realistic itinerary for the voyage. But, given the date of composition of Acts and the literary nature of the story, it can by no means be an actual first-person account. It makes for a good tale, but it is not history.

Storm and Shipwreck

27 ¹³The appearance of a light southerly breeze seemed to satisfy their requirements, so they weighed anchor and hugged closely to the coast of Crete. ¹⁴But shortly thereafter a violent wind, known as the Euraquilo, came roaring down from Crete ¹⁵and overpowered the ship. Since no headway could be made, we let ourselves be carried along. ¹⁶When we passed under the protection of an island called Cauda, we managed, with considerable difficulty, to get control of the ship's boat. ¹⁷They hoisted it in and then deployed some materials to strengthen the ship. Fearing that they might be wrecked on the Libyan coast, the crew loosed the sails and let the ship have its own way.

[18] Since the storm continued to pound us fiercely, they began to jettison material on the next day. [19] The day after that they began to heave gear overboard by hand. [20] Since neither sun by day nor stars by night had been seen for many days and the terrible storm raged unabated, any hope that we might be rescued finally began to fade.

[21] No one had received any nourishment for a long time when Paul stood in their midst and said: "Gentlemen, you really should have done what I said and not left Crete. Then we should not have experienced this damage and loss. [22] Now I am urging that you keep your spirits up, for not one of you will be lost; only the ship is doomed. [23] Last night there appeared to me a messenger of the god to whom I belong and whom I serve. [24] 'Do not be afraid, Paul,' he said. 'You must appear before Caesar. God has granted you all those who are making this voyage with you.' [25] Cheer up, then, gentlemen, for I trust God and that things will turn out as I was told. [26] We shall, however, have to run aground on an island."

[27] In the middle of the fourteenth night, as we were still being driven over the Mediterranean, the sailors began to suspect that land was near. [28] They took soundings and found twenty fathoms. A bit later they cast again and found fifteen. [29] Anxious that we might be dashed against a rocky shore, they cast four anchors from the stern and began to long for dawn.

[30] When the sailors attempted to desert the ship by lowering the boat on the pretext of dropping anchors from the bow, [31] Paul protested to the centurion and his detachment, "If they do not remain in the ship, you won't have a chance of being rescued!" [32] In response the soldiers cut the lines of the boat and let it fall away.

[33] When day was about to break, Paul started urging everyone to take some nourishment: "This is the fourteenth day you have lived in suspense, going hungry and receiving no meals. [34] I therefore urge you to take some nourishment, for your own good. None of you will lose even a single hair from your heads." [35] He then took some bread, gave public thanks to God, broke it, and began to eat. [36] All felt better, and they, too, had something to eat. [37] There were

276 of us aboard that ship. ³⁸After they had taken their fill, they set about lightening the ship by heaving the grain overboard.

³⁹When day arrived, they were not able to recognize the place, but they noticed a bay with a beach onto which they planned to run the ship aground, if possible. ⁴⁰So they slipped the anchors and left them in the sea, while also loosing the ropes that had secured the rudders and hoisting the foresail to catch the wind and make for the beach. ⁴¹But they ran the ship onto a shoal, so that the bow jammed fast and wouldn't move, while the stern started to break up under pressure.

⁴²The soldiers decided to kill the prisoners to prevent any from swimming ashore and escaping, ⁴³but the centurion put a stop to this idea because he wished to save Paul. He ordered that those who could swim should leap overboard and make for shore first, ⁴⁴while the rest would fasten on to planks or cling to other people from the ship. By those means all came ashore safely.

Comments on the Story

Contrary to Paul's advice, the captain orders the ship to sail on beyond Fair Havens, and a moderate south wind seems to have confirmed the wisdom of this decision. The intention is to hug the southern coast of Crete, but soon a violent northeast wind blows the ship far off course and toward the coast of North Africa. The ship's boat, the only lifeboat, which usually trails the ship, is in danger of doing damage to both, so the crew hoists it on board. Experienced sailors are afraid of running aground on a shoal known as Syrtis, off the coast of Libya, so they drop anchor and allow the ship to drift. The storm becomes ever more violent, and so they begin to jettison the cargo and then some of the ship's tackle. For several days they see neither sun nor stars and so are unable to navigate. At this point Paul reminds all on board that they should have listened to him and not left Crete, that is, Fair Havens. But, contrary to his earlier warning, Paul promises that there will be no loss of life. After fourteen days at sea, the crew becomes aware that land is near, and they take soundings to confirm it. The first sounding shows a depth of 120 feet (20 fathoms), and the second 90 feet (15 fathoms), and so they drop anchors to prevent the ship from running aground. Confusion abounds during the night. The sailors lower the lifeboat in an attempt to jump ship, but Paul tells the centurion about it, and his soldiers then cut the lifeboat loose. Paul seems to have taken charge of things, encouraging the men to take nourishment, presiding at a meal, and promising that all will be saved. The crew readies the ship for running aground on the beach, but before they reach land the bow gets stuck on a shoal and the stern begins to break up. Soldiers plan to kill the prisoners to prevent their escape, but the centurion stops this plan and orders everybody to get to shore the best way they can, either by swimming or grabbing a plank. In this way all passengers and crew survive, 276 in all.

If the author of this account simply meant to tell a gripping tale of danger at sea, he or she has succeeded. This is a story that can cause readers to sense the harrowing situation of ancient Mediterranean mariners in a helpless ship, desperately trying to keep it afloat and survive. But why has Luke included this narrative as part of his own story of Jesus-believers in a hostile world?

The key to understanding Luke's intent at this point must somehow be sought in the characterization and role of Paul. Note how improbable his role is. He is a prisoner, probably in chains and incarcerated below deck, but he has a friend in the centurion Julius, who allows him to visit friends in Sidon (Acts 27:3) and listens to his advice (27:10, 31). Julius' friendship with Paul is given as the reason he stopped his soldiers from killing Paul and the other prisoners to prevent their escape (27:43). And, as improbable as it seems, Paul is allowed to address all on board (27:21–26; 33–34). It is difficult to imagine him trying to maintain his balance and speaking against a howling wind to rapt listeners, but Luke has Paul encouraging the crew, promising that all will survive, and presiding at something that resembles a Christian Eucharist.

At one point Paul's action prevents one disaster but leads to another. He reveals to the centurion that sailors are lowering the lifeboat in an apparent attempt to desert the ship (Acts 27:31). He rightly maintains that the survival of the ship depends on the sailors remaining on board, but the centurion's decision to cut the lifeboat loose puts survival in serious jeopardy (27:32). If the lifeboat had been available at the critical moment, passengers and crew could have made land with little difficulty.

But Paul is not merely an advisor on things nautical; his major role is that of foretelling the future and encouraging passengers and crew. Luke's stress on these aspects of his characterization of Paul suggests that the narrative has theological overtones. It has frequently been noted that the word "to save" or a related term appears several times in the narrative (see Acts 27:20, 31, 34, 43, 44). At one level it signifies survival in a life-threatening situation. In 27:31, for example, Paul warns that the salvation (or "rescue" in our translation) of passengers and crew depends on the sailors remaining on board. Acts 27:44 reports that all 276 persons on board were saved; that is, they reached shore safely. An audience of second-century Christians, however, might well see the term as embracing eternal salvation in a religious sense. In this sense, Paul becomes an agent of salvation for all on board, and the basis of their salvation is the divine necessity for him to reach Rome.

In this respect, the remarkable point is the stress in the narrative on the salvation of *all*. Luke could have told of the death of 275 persons on board the ill-fated ship and focused totally on Paul as the sole survivor, but he did not. Is Paul then the agent of something we could call universal salvation?

Just before dawn on the ship's last day, Paul holds a gathering that has the ring of a Christian Eucharist. He takes bread, gives thanks, breaks it, and begins to eat, as others join in (Acts 27:35). Again, it would be easy for early Christian readers of Acts to think of the connotations of this description and read the incident as a Eucharist. The wording closely resembles the words of Jesus at the Last Supper with his disciples (see Luke 22:19).

These overtones should not, however, be overly stressed. The meal aboard ship is, after all, a meal, not a religious rite. It is true that Acts 27:35 resembles the words of Jesus in Luke 22:19, but there is no reference in Acts to wine, nor any suggestion that bread and wine signified Jesus' body and blood. The narrative of the storm and shipwreck graphically calls attention to the fragility of life and attributes survival as due to Paul. But if Paul is an agent of eternal salvation, it is remarkable that nothing is said about repentance or belief in Jesus. If this is a story about eternal salvation, Luke has seriously compromised the earlier apostolic (see Acts 2:38; 3:19; 5:31; 8:22) and Pauline (see 17:30; 20:21; 26:20) teaching about the need for repentance and the doctrine that Paul and Silas announced to the Philippian jailer, "Believe in the Lord Jesus and you will be saved" (16:31). It is doubtful that such a drastic alteration in the Lukan concept of salvation was intended.

Interpreters have frequently noted resemblances between the story in Acts 27 and the book of Jonah. Both feature a character on board a ship during a violent storm. But Jonah and Paul are in fact polar opposites. Jonah received a divine order to go and preach in Nineveh, and he boarded the ship to escape from this duty (Jonah 1:1–3). Paul had a divine directive to go to Rome, and, although a prisoner, he is on board the ship in the act of fulfilling this command (Acts 27:24). Those on the ship with Jonah threw him overboard in order to appease his God, and they were saved when the storm ceased (Jonah 1:15). Those on the ship with Paul are saved *because* he is there, carrying out the will of his God (Acts 27:24). Those on the way to Nineveh survive only *without* Jonah; those on the way to Rome survive only *with* Paul. These considerations suggest that Luke includes Acts 27 to stress the irresistibility of the will of God and the good that results from obedience to it.

In Search of History

Once again demonstrating how well-read he is in ancient literature, and how accomplished he is as a storyteller, Luke resorts to a tried and true theme for adventure stories: he weaves a tale of a shipwreck. Such tales were common in ancient narrative and as such were satirized by Lucian. He described the pattern commonly followed, in which, after detailing the "tempests, headlands, strandings, masts carried away, rudders broken," the storyteller would insert into the story the appearance of a divine being who "sat on the masthead or stood at the helm and steered the ship to a soft beach where she might break up gradually and slowly and they themselves get ashore safely by the grace and favor of the god."[23]

As pointed out in the cameo essay, "Shipwrecks in Luke's Literary World" (pp. 313), shipwrecks were common and Paul even mentions having experienced three shipwrecks, none of which could have been the one described in our text since, when Paul wrote this, he had not yet been to Jerusalem (1 Cor 11:25–26). Of course, there could have been a shipwreck on Paul's voyage to Rome. But even if that was the case, this cannot be the story of what happened nor even a story that can be used to confirm that one did happen. That is because from beginning to end it is a literary construct, following the standards of this type of story. In addition, it is told in the guise of a first-person narrative, a motif that has already been discredited as an indication of historical reliability (see the cameo essay, "We-Passages in the Acts of the Apostles," p. 191). Because this story follows so closely the standard literary model, the Fellows voted that it is not historically reliable in any of its details. They also affirmed that it most likely followed an epic model and likely copied details from shipwreck narratives in both Homer's *Odyssey* Book 5 (see the cameo essay, "Shipwrecks in Luke's Literary World, p. 313) and Vergil's *Aeneid* Book 1, as argued by Christine Shea.[24] They were also convinced by Shea's argument that the naming of a character as "Julius" is an intentional echo of the *Aeneid* and its mythologizing of the Julio-Claudian family of Roman emperors.

References
Shea, "Pieces of Epic."
Bonz, *The Past as Legacy*

The Votes of the Fellows

Red/Probable
- The shipwreck narrative in Acts 27:1–44 is created out of motifs from the epic tradition.
- By imitating epic tradition, the author of Acts is promoting an "epic" view of Christian history, which culminates, on the model of the *Aeneid*, with the hero arriving in Rome to become the founder of a great people.

Pink/Possible
- The first-person narrative of the sea voyage and shipwreck in Acts 27:1–28:16 is written in imitation of first-person narratives of sea voyages in Homer's *Odyssey*.
- The character of "Julius" is based on the character of "Iulus" in Vergil's *Aeneid*.

Black/Improbable
- The character of "Julius" is based on historical reminiscence.

Shipwrecks in Luke's Literary World
A Cameo Essay by Dennis R. MacDonald

"Writing the storm" was a routine exercise in ancient literary education, and such stories found their way into many ancient narratives, from epics, to histories, to biographies, and to novels. Actual shipwrecks took place, of course, and Paul claims to have suffered three of them (2 Cor 11:25–26), though obviously not the one narrated in Acts 27. This is the last of several "we"-voyages in Acts (see the cameo essay on p. 191 for various explanations of this distinctive phenomenon), and the first-person-plural voice has led many interpreters to conclude that the account is a historical reminiscence, perhaps taken from a diary of one of Paul's travel companions. What concerns us here is not the historicity of the event or Luke's use of a "we"-source, but his literary models for this famous narrative.

The typical literary storm follows this pattern: Someone begins a journey by launching with favorable winds and a calm sea. When land fades from view, waves swell and darkness falls, prohibiting navigation, and the winds contend with each other such that the crew must furl the sails. As the storm builds, those on board pray for safety, and the crew may have to lower the anchors and jettison the cargo to let the vessel ride higher. No one can eat or sleep, and the passengers pray for divine assistance. Then a god (or nature) may come to the rescue, preventing the loss of ship and souls. On the other hand, a huge wave also might crush the ship, or a rocky coastline may turn it to splinters. Some of the travelers drown while others swim or ride planks to terra firma, invariably at an unintended destination, where they will be at the mercy of local residents, who may show themselves to be either hostile or hospitable.[25]

The paragraph above might suffice also as a summary of Acts 27:1–28:10, but it may be possible to pinpoint Luke's literary model more precisely. No shipwreck was more generative of literary imitations than Odysseus' shipwreck in the fifth book of the *Odyssey*, where Poseidon sends a storm against him as he sails his raft alone from the island of Calypso to that of the Phaeacians. Virtually all of the narrative elements listed in the preceding paragraph appear here as well, but there is another element that appears in no other ancient storm narrative except for the one in Acts 27!

> As the tempest drove Odysseus' boat, a goddess appeared.
> She [Ino] took pity on wandering Odysseus with such woes;
> she emerged from the sea like a flying gull,
> sat on the firmly bound boat, and spoke,

> "Surely Poseidon will not utterly destroy you, even though he is bent on doing so.

> Strip off these clothes and leave your boat to be driven by the winds
> and try to reach the land of the Phaeacians by swimming with your arms,
> for it is your fate there to escape.
> Here, stretch this immortal headscarf under your chest.
> You are in no danger of suffering or perishing"[26]

As Paul's ship drifts out of control, an angel appears to him, just as Ino appears to Odysseus. This is what Paul tells the weary sailors:

"Last night there appeared to me a messenger of the god to whom I belong and whom I serve. 'Do not be afraid, Paul,' he said. 'You must appear before Caesar. God has granted you all those who are making this voyage with you.' Cheer up, then, gentlemen, for I trust God and that things will turn out as I was told. We shall, however, have to run aground on an island." (Acts 27:23–26)

Just as Ino has pity on Odysseus, God takes pity on Paul and the other passengers. In both cases the hero learns that it is his fate to survive, but he will lose the ship.

More distinctively Homeric is the expression in Acts 27:41 "ran the ship into a shoal." Luke here calls Paul's ship a *naus*, a word that appears nowhere else in the NT. In addition, the verb Luke uses for grounding the ship is *epikellein*, which appears nowhere in the LXX nor anywhere else in the NT. "Little else except a reminiscence of the *Odyssey* would explain the only appearance of *epikellein* and *naus* in the New Testament."[27]

Paul on Malta

28 After we were safely ashore, we recognized that the island is called Malta. ²The natives were uncommonly kind to all of us. Because of the rain that had begun to fall and the chill, they kindled a bonfire and brought all of us to it. ³Paul had gathered some sticks into a bundle and was tossing it onto the fire when a viper, roused by the warmth, came out and fastened itself to his hand with its fangs. ⁴When the natives saw the creature dangling from his arm, they reassured one another, "This fellow must be a murderer for sure. No sooner had he escaped from the sea than the goddess Justice did him in." ⁵Paul, however, shook the creature into the fire and suffered no harm. ⁶They kept waiting for him to swell up or suddenly drop dead, but, after waiting for some time without seeing him show any negative reaction, they revised their opinion and began to declare that he was a god.

⁷Publius, the island's leading citizen, had an estate in the vicinity. He took us in and gave us quite cordial hospitality for three days. ⁸His father lay afflicted with fever and dysentery. Paul visited him, prayed, and laid hands upon him.

He became well. ⁹At that all the sick on the island began to come to Paul, and they were cured. ¹⁰They responded by providing us with many gifts and, on our departure, supplied us with what we required.

Comments on the Story

As it was observed in the cameo essay, "Shipwrecks in Luke's Literary World," (p. 313), stories of shipwrecks are frequent in ancient literature. In such narratives, those who greet the survivors may be hostile or hospitable. Fortunately for our hero, the natives of Malta are of the latter type. Readers approach the narrative of Acts 28 with a sense of relief; the long ordeal at sea is over, and Paul and his companions may now unwind. Well, not quite. While handling kindling for a fire, Paul suffers an apparently fatal snakebite. The Maltese natives expect him to fall over dead, but he exhibits nothing malignant. The chief man of the island, one Publius, extends them an invitation to lodge with him, which they do for three days. During his stay on Malta, Paul heals Publius' father and other townspeople.

The narrative is unusual in two respects. First, there is nothing in it that would characterize Paul as a prisoner. Of course, the reader who has engaged the narrative of Acts up to this point knows that he is on his way to Rome to stand trial before the emperor, but Acts 28:1–10 gives us no hint of his legal situation. Missing in action now are Julius and his soldiers, as well as the ship's captain and crew. It was important that 276 people survive the shipwreck, but once on Malta, Luke seems to have no literary use for them.

Second, Paul does not preach to the Maltese in an attempt to convert them to belief in Jesus. He has a perfect opportunity when the natives change their views about him. Thinking at first that he is a murderer whom the goddess Dike (Justice) has finally brought to justice, the inhabitants of Malta conclude that he must be a god, since he survived the bite of a poisonous snake (Acts 28:6). Readers of Acts will recall that, when Paul and Barnabas were in Lystra, something similar happened and the missionaries were thought to be gods. On that occasion the missionaries quickly corrected the misconception and used it as an occasion to preach about belief in the one God (see 14:14–18). But here there is no such attempt. Further, in 28:8–9 Paul willingly heals all comers, but he does so with no mention of Jesus. The narrative contributes to the characterization of Paul as a hero with special powers and divine protection, but not as a Christian missionary.

A key concept in the narrative is that of kindness. Luke uses two related Greek terms (*philanthrōpia; philofronōs*) to express the kindness of the natives in welcoming Paul and his group (Acts 28:2) and that of Publius in inviting them to stay with him (28:7). We are also reminded of Julius, who treated Paul kindly (*philanthrōpōs*) at the beginning of the trip (27:3). These terms do not appear elsewhere in Luke-Acts, and it is of interest that our author is able to think of pagan Gentiles in such positive terms, terms that he never uses for non-believing Jews. Note only the tepid expression in 17:11.

Our translation uses the term, "natives," to designate the inhabitants of Malta (Acts 28:2, 4). The Greek word here may literally be translated, "barbarians," and several modern translations use this term. It is found rarely in the NT: Luke has it only here; Paul uses it twice (Rom 1:14; 1 Cor 14:11), and it appears also in Col 3:11. It was generally used to designate those persons who did not speak Greek, but cultural distinctions may be secondary among its meanings. It is doubtful, however, if Luke intends to convey a sense of cultural difference in this passage. The brief glimpse he gives us of Maltese piety tells us that they hold a traditional belief in the power of the goddess Dike (Acts 28:4). It seems that they may not be distinguished from other Greeks except in terms of their speech; thus "natives" or "foreigners" conveys the meaning in English better than the more literal "barbarians."

In Search of History

Initially, this story would seem to lack historical credibility simply because it takes place as part of a shipwreck narrative that has already been judged unreliable. Its inclusion with the shipwreck narrative is also common to that literary device. Furthermore, the narrative includes two miracle stories of Paul, a device that has earlier been discredited; that is to say, whereas Paul may have been a healer, the stories in Acts are not historical evidence for that datum since they follow standard literary models of miracle stories. Embedded in this story is the character of Publius, but, as has already been pointed out before, Luke regularly creates names for his characters to lend verisimilitude to his story (see the cameo essay, "Names in Acts," p. 22). Therefore it is highly unlikely that the Publius of this story was a historical character. The story exhibits Luke's exceptional skill as a storyteller; consequently it is one of the more popular stories about Paul in Christian lore. Alas, it lacks historical credibility.

Paul in Rome

28 [11]We set out three months later on an Alexandrian vessel that had wintered at the island. Its figurehead was the Dioscuri. [12]We put in at Syracuse and spent three days there [13]and then sailed up to Rhegium. The next day a south wind sprang up, so we reached Puteoli within two days. [14]There we found some believers, who urged us to stay with them for a week.

This is how we got to Rome: [15]The believers there heard the news about us and came to the Market of Appius and Three Taverns to welcome us. When he saw them, Paul gave thanks to God and plucked up his courage. [16]When we reached Rome, Paul received permission to live on his own with the soldier who guarded him.

[17]Three days after arriving, Paul called a meeting of the local Jewish leaders. "My fellow believers," he said after they were in place, "I am here as a prisoner from Jerusalem. Although I had done nothing against the people or the ancestral practices, I was surrendered to the Romans. [18]After investigating the case, they wished to release me, since I had committed no capital crime, [19]but, because the Jews said otherwise, I was compelled to appeal to Caesar. Please do not think that I have any accusations to make against my nation. [20]This is why I have asked to meet you and address you: I wear this shackle for the sake of the hope of Israel."

[21]They replied, "We have received no correspondence about you from Judea, nor have any of our people who have come here reported or said anything damaging about you. [22]We should be pleased to hear from you what you think, for we do know that this sect is the subject of universal opposition."

Comments on the Story

The speed of the narrative picks up considerably at this point, as Paul and his party travel from Malta to Rome in about two weeks. The trip is without incident, except for meetings with believers from Puteoli and Rome. Roman Christians come to meet him, some traveling thirty-three miles to Three Taverns and others forty-three miles to the Market of Appius. These groups not only form a welcoming party for Paul but also constitute an escort for his triumphal entry into Rome. Soon after his arrival Paul calls together a group of leading Roman Jews and introduces himself as a prisoner from Jerusalem. He insists that he has done nothing against the Jewish people and has violated none of their customs, but maintains that the Jews handed him over to the Romans and prevented his subsequent release. The leaders respond that they have received neither written nor oral reports about him but that they are interested in hearing from him as one representing a sect that is universally condemned.

The meeting of Paul with the Roman Jews is the first of two, and we shall examine the second below. The first (Acts 28:17–22) is cordial and free of contention. The Jews of Rome seem to be quite distant, not only geographically but also ideologically, from those in the East. They are removed from the controversies and opposition that Paul met in his previous travels. They know nothing about him, although they have heard of the Jesus movement. Presumably, Luke describes the Roman Jews in this way in order to prepare the way for the second meeting (28:23–28). They seem ready to give Paul a fair hearing and to make a judgment about him in an unbiased way.

Paul uses this occasion to explain his legal situation, but it is notable that his summary in Acts 28:17–20 is not fully consistent with the earlier Lukan description of the events. He maintains in 28:17 that the Jews surrendered him to the Romans, but in 21:31–33 the Roman tribune rescued him from a violent Jewish mob. In 28:18–19, Paul says that the Roman authorities wanted to release him but that the Jews objected and he was then forced to appeal to Caesar. But in the earlier narrative the appeal to Caesar came during Paul's trial before Festus when he was given the alternative to be tried in Jerusalem rather than in Caesarea (25:9–12). It was at a later hearing that Agrippa expressed the judgment that Paul was innocent (26:31–32). The main lines of the summary in Acts 28 are, however, consistent in expressing the relatively benevolent attitude of Roman authorities and the constant Jewish opposition to Paul. Paul is also consistent in maintaining that he has suffered for the hope of Israel, that is, for his belief in resurrection (28:20; cf. 23:6; 24:15; 26:6, 7).

It is significant that, in dealing with the Roman ministry, the only incident that Luke wants to report is one that tells of Paul's relationships with Jews. The meeting is the culmination of a long narrative in which the mission of Paul to Jews has been a matter of deep concern. This meeting is not, however, an evangelistic occasion. Paul uses it to introduce himself and to stress his fidelity to traditional Jewish beliefs and practices. It is in the second meeting that Paul will present his message about the dominion of God and Jesus.

We must not undervalue the dramatic force of this section of Acts, which centers upon Paul's arrival in Rome. Readers have anticipated this moment for some time, as Luke foretells it and characterizes it as a divine vocation (see Acts 19:21; 23:11; also 25:11, 12; 27:24). It is because Paul must go to Rome that all the passengers and crew survived the shipwreck on Malta (see 27:24). Even the bite of a poisonous snake could not prevent Paul from arriving in Rome (see 28:3–6). In 28:14 he finally arrives. In fact, although the language is somewhat smoothed out in our translation above, Luke has him arrive twice: "and so we came to Rome" (28:14); "when we arrived in Rome" (28:16). The double mention of Paul's arrival in Rome adds dramatic emphasis to an event of great theological importance.

In Search of History

This text is embedded in a narrative that has been creatively crafted by Luke from beginning to end. Luke started with the data, derived from Paul, that he intended to travel to Jerusalem and from there to Rome (Rom 15:24–29). Luke's story gets Paul from A to B to C, but the story he weaves is his own and follows his own narrative agenda. Thus, when Paul finally gets to Rome in the Acts story, it is under the circumstances and narrative agenda already created by Luke. Paul is a prisoner (because of Jewish opposition); he gets to Rome because he appealed to Caesar; thus he arrives in Rome as a prisoner, but once there he is primarily interested in finishing his business with the Jews.

The travel details in Acts 28:11–16 are once more presented in a first-person narrative, and upon arrival in Rome the first-person narrative ceases abruptly. This is the pattern found throughout Acts for sea voyages. The itinerary itself may be geographically credible, but the story is entirely Luke's; there is no reason to assume a source at this point.

After arriving, Paul meets up briefly with members of the Christian community there, fulfilling in quite cryptic terms Paul's stated plans in Romans. But, while Luke used Paul's letter to the Romans for this bit of data about a Christian community already being there, what he does with it is entirely his own creation, put together to fit Luke's created version of Paul's arrival in Rome. To fulfill his own narrative purpose, therefore, he completely suppresses the desires of the historical Paul to spend some quality time with the Christian community there (Rom 15:24).

Luke has also created a less-than-credible account of Paul's conditions as a prisoner in Rome. He lives as if under "house arrest" with only one guard. He is completely free to communicate at will with outsiders. He can even bend his opponents, "the local Jewish leadership," to his will by summoning them to meet with him. He converses with them as someone who has status in their eyes and to whom they feel an obligation to listen. This scene fulfills a larger narrative theme in Luke: namely that everything happens according to the manipulation of God. Paul had received a divine vision more than once that he would make it to Rome and be a witness there (Acts 23:11; 27:23–24). Note also that the form of his witnessing follows Lukan priorities: the main concern of Paul in Rome is to settle affairs with the Jews, affairs that the historical Paul did not mention at all in his letter to the Romans but that the plot of Luke demands.

Since the story derives from bits and pieces of data from Paul but in its essence and details is Lukan, there is little, if any, historical value to the Acts story of Paul's arrival in Rome.

References
Lüdemann, "Historical Issues"

The Votes of the Fellows
Gray/Doubtful
- Acts 28:1–16 is historically accurate in reporting that Paul was transported from Malta via Syracuse, Rhegium, and Puteoli to Rome.
- Paul was guarded by one soldier (Acts 28:16).
- Paul practiced his craft and underwrote the expense of his guard.

Black/Improbable
- Paul met Jewish leaders in Rome.

Paul's Last Words in Rome
28 ²³On the day arranged for this purpose a considerable crowd came to his lodgings to hear Paul. He spoke from dawn to dusk, setting forth his convictions about the dominion of God and seeking to convince them about Jesus

by appeal to the Law of Moses and to the Prophets. ²⁴Some found his arguments appealing, but others remained skeptical.

²⁵As they were on their way out without having reached any general agreement, Paul had one more statement: "Aptly did the Holy Spirit say to your forebears through the prophet Isaiah: ²⁶'Go to this people and say: "You will certainly hear but by no means understand, and you will certainly look but by no means perceive, ²⁷for the heart of this people cannot feel. They are hard of hearing and have shut their eyes. They do not want to use those eyes for seeing, those ears for hearing, and those hearts for understanding because they do not wish to change their ways so that I may make them well."' ²⁸Therefore, be assured of this: God's salvation has been offered to the gentiles. They shall listen."

³⁰Paul remained in his rented quarters for two full years. He received all who came to see him, ³¹proclaiming the dominion of God and telling the story of the Lord Jesus Christ, with full freedom and without any impediment.

Comments on the Story

Roman Jews assemble, and Paul speaks to them about the dominion of God and Jesus. Some respond positively to Paul's message but others do not believe, and as they are leaving Paul quotes to them words from Isa 6:9–10. The quotation is intended to explain Jewish rejection of the gospel, and Paul concludes with the announcement that God's salvation has been sent to the Gentiles, who will listen. The book of Acts ends with a summary statement about Paul's remaining years in Rome.

The second meeting of Paul with the Jews of Rome is the occasion for him to present his gospel and, citing the Scriptures, attempt to convert them. What is the Jewish response? Acts 28:24 says that there is both a positive and a negative response on the part of those who listen to Paul. The Greek verb that Luke uses to designate the positive side may actually signify a variety of responses. Are these Jews favorably impressed by Paul? Are they persuaded by his arguments? Do they become believers? Our translation suggests a somewhat weak response: "Some found his arguments appealing." The NRSV translation is stronger: "Some were convinced by what he said." In any case, Luke tells readers that there is a divided response to Paul on the part of the Roman Jews, just as there was in earlier episodes (see 13:13–52; 14:1–7; 17:1–15). For example, Acts 13:13–52 reports that Paul and Barnabas met with Jews in Pisidian Antioch and came away with a divided response. In neither Acts 13 nor Acts 28 do Jews accept repentance and undergo baptism, but there is no question that, in both, Luke notes a positive response on the part of some Jews.

Despite the partial acceptance in Pisidian Antioch and Rome, Paul quotes words from Isaiah to explain Jewish rejection and announces that salvation has been sent to Gentiles (Acts 13:46–47; 28:25–28). In Acts 28 the quotation from Isa 6:9–10, together with an application, claims that Jews are unhearing, unperceptive, and unreceptive of God's messenger. In a quite literal sense, these remarks are inappropriate to the situation that Luke has described. Although some Jews, not only in Rome but throughout the East, have accepted Paul's message, he applies Isaiah's condemnation to Jews generally. The application in 28:28 implicitly contrasts the receptiveness of Gentiles with the lack of understanding and perception found among Jews.

Luke's attitude toward Jews as demonstrated in Acts is complex. He goes to great pains to convince readers that Paul is a faithful Jew and that belief in Jesus agrees with the Hebrew Scriptures. Yet, writing in the second century, he must deal with the fact that, as a whole, Israel has not accepted the gospel and that there has been a "parting of the ways" between Jews and Christians. His bias against non-believing Jews has frequently been noted. In the last speech in the book, the Lukan Paul makes strenuous efforts to convert Roman Jews and comes away with only partial success. Luke cannot blame Paul and his fellow believers for this failure. The fault, in his judgment, lies in the people, and the Scriptures confirm this. He cannot regard Paul's partial success as something to be celebrated, since, for him, what is demanded is the conversion of *Israel*. He is not hesitant to report that some of Paul's Jewish hearers responded positively, nor is he reluctant to condemn Jews as a whole for their rejection of the message. The goal of the Lukan Paul is the wholesale repentance of the Jewish people and their turning to accept Jesus as the Christ sent for them, and so the positive response of individual Jews is insufficient. Wholesale acceptance has not been forthcoming, so the mission to the Jews must be declared a failure, and it is terminated in favor of a successful mission to Gentiles.

But is the mission to Jews terminated? After all, Paul twice before announced a shift from a Jewish to a Gentile mission (see Acts 13:46; 18:6), and after each of these he attempted to convert Jews (see, e.g., 14:1; 17:1-4; 18:19-21). And even in Rome, Paul welcomes all who come to him, and there is no sign that Jews are excluded (28:30). Now, however, we are at the end of the book, and the statement in 28:28 carries special narrative weight. It functions as the culminating announcement, justification for which draws not only on Paul's immediate experience in Rome, but also on all those previous occasions of Jewish rejection. The announcements in Acts 13 and 18 are anticipations of this final proclamation of the termination of the Pauline mission to the Jews. The note in 28:30 does not speak of a renewed mission to Jews, but rather of openness to those individuals who take the initiative to come to Paul.

In Acts 28:30-31 Luke reports that Paul remained in Rome for two years and was not hindered in his preaching and teaching. He is still a prisoner of the Roman government, but Luke's stress is on his liberty. This theme is consistent with the portrayal throughout the last several chapters of Acts, as Romans have been remarkably permissive in respect to Paul.

Readers will want to know what happened after the two years of Acts 28:30, but Luke does not reveal this. He has devoted a good deal of space providing details of a trial that has no outcome. A number of suggestions have been made to account for the peculiarities of the end of Acts, but none has been convincing. Some say that Luke wrote before the imperial trial was held, others that he intended to write more but died before he could. Still others suggest that Luke had no need to narrate the final outcome since his readers knew full well what happened. In view of the different indications we have previously encountered, it is not possible to say what Luke intended for readers to understand about the outcome of Paul's trial. On the one hand, there are warnings of a negative outcome. In the farewell speech to the elders of Ephesus Paul told them they would never see his face again, and they grieved at this word (Acts 20:25). Ernst Haenchen rightly observed that "Anyone who writes thus knows nothing of Paul's deliverance and return to the East, but rather of his death in Rome (see v. 38)."[28] The prediction of Agabus also foretells a tragic fate for Paul (see 21:10-11). On the other hand, we cannot overlook the inconclusive nature of the hearings before Felix, Festus, and Agrippa (chapters 24-26). Indeed, since Paul has been treated fairly in these episodes, it would be reasonable to expect that he would also receive a favorable hearing before the emperor. Luke has given conflicting grounds for an expectation of the outcome of Paul's trial, and it is not possible to say what he expected to convey to readers about it.

Focusing on Acts as we have it, what can we say about the way it concludes? First, the final chapter shows how important are Paul's relations with the Jewish people. These relationships have been important throughout the final chapters, as Luke has stressed Paul's fidelity to Judaism on the one hand and Jewish opposition on the other. When he arrives in Rome, Paul has a final opportunity to address Jews with the gospel, and the meetings provide the basis for a shift of attention to Gentiles.

Second, Acts 28 stresses the arrival of Paul in Rome as the fulfillment of his divine commission. Despite the obstacles that would have prevented it—opposition of Jews, storm, shipwreck, and snakebite—he has come to Rome, where he is able to preach without interference. His long voyage from Jerusalem/Caesarea to Rome symbolizes the passage of the Christian gospel from its Jewish origins to its arrival in the capital of the world. Although Luke knows that Christians preceded Paul to Rome, he minimizes their significance and treats Paul as God's instrument for this major transition, which was portended by the divine command in 23:11: "Just as you have given testimony for my cause in Jerusalem, so also must you testify in Rome." The arrival in Rome is of such significance that it eclipses the ultimate fate of Paul himself.

In Search of History

This section forms Luke's conclusion to his narrative and, to our ears, it is a surprising conclusion. We want to know what finally happened to Paul. Luke had a different purpose in mind. Paul's main activity in Rome is to settle the question of the Jews. As we have noted throughout this analysis, they played a major role in his story. By concluding the story as he does, Luke reminds us that this is actually a major theme for the entire book. He closes with a last speech of Paul, the purpose of which is to state, with finality, the theme that has been stated twice before: the Jews will not listen, so now we turn to Gentiles (see comments above). Luke-Acts began with a strong emphasis on the Gentile mission as the theme of the ministry of Jesus (Luke 4:16–30).[29] Luke carried that theme into the plot of Acts and made it central to its focus, as seen especially in the importance given to the Cornelius narrative (Acts 10–11). For Luke, however, that theme cannot be proclaimed without including the rejection of the Jews. At the root of Luke's theology is an incipient anti-Judaism. Its necessity to his perception of the legitimacy of the Gentile mission is seen in how he concludes with Paul's final speech.

There is another theme underlying this last scene, namely the ambivalent nature of Luke's view toward Roman authority. For much of the story, official Jewish opposition has been contrasted with official Roman benign acceptance of the legal legitimacy of the Christian mission. Thus, even though Paul becomes a Roman prisoner in Jerusalem and arrives in Rome as a prisoner, Luke has taken pains to paint Jewish opposition as the cause and Roman imprisonment as the action that saves Paul from Jewish violence. That is the essence of the case as Paul summarizes it in his first speech to the Jews in Rome (Acts 28:17–19).

The appeal to Caesar is what gets Paul to Rome, and getting to Rome was the divine plan. So insistent was God in making sure Paul got to Rome that God intervened during the storm at sea to make sure neither Paul nor the crew would be harmed. Now that Paul is in Rome and has divested himself and, by implication, all Christians thereafter, of any responsibility for the Jews, what next? The narrative arc implies that the preliminary judgments of Roman officials leading up to this point will finally reach fulfillment, and Paul would be pronounced innocent and released. One would think that Luke has set up the story to conclude in exactly that way. He even seems to imply as much with his incredibly positive view of Paul's continued imprisonment. The last words in Acts, fulfilling the will of God, tell us that Paul continued to preach in Rome "with full freedom and without any impediment" (Acts 28:31). Yet Luke leaves it there, with Paul still a prisoner, and with a termination date two years hence. Why does Luke neglect to follow his own narrative arc and tell the story of Paul's release? Scholars have long concluded that the likely reason was that Paul's execution by Roman authorities while in Rome was well known to Luke's readers. Yet it is only by reading between the lines in this last scene in Acts, and adding allusions to Paul's death earlier in Acts (see the comments above), that we can draw a tentative conclusion about the death of Paul as a Roman execution. These earlier allusions lead the reader to expect the story of Paul's death once he is a prisoner in Rome. Yet it is a story Acts refuses to tell, even though it has been implicitly promised. Ironically, in this case Acts in its final scene becomes a potentially reliable historical source based on what it does not say.

References
>   Lüdemann, "Historical Issues"
>   Tyson, "Paul's Speeches to the Jews

The Votes of the Fellows
Red/Probable
- Acts tells us nothing of historical value about early Christian communities in northern Palestine and Rome.
- The speeches of Paul in Acts 28:17–31 are Lukan compositions.
- Luke purposely omits any mention of Paul's death not only to finesse Rome's undoubted responsibility, but also to avoid sullying his picture of the Apostle's triumphant life with the report of a gory end.

Pink/Possible
- Paul was imprisoned in Rome.
- Paul was executed by imperial authority in Rome.

Black/Improbable
- Paul engaged in unhindered preaching in Rome.
- The speeches of Paul in Acts 28:17–31 contain historical information about Paul's communication with the Jews in Rome.

Conclusion

At this point, the reader may be wondering whether any positive results have come from the Acts Seminar project. The obvious answer, of course, is that any study that clarifies how we can reconstruct history more accurately is a positive result. We began this decade-long project with a profound regard for the importance of understanding early Christian history and the sources we use to reconstruct it. We think the project has made significant contributions to that effort. In this chapter we summarize the most important of those contributions.

Why Does This Study Make Such a Severe Break with Previous Scholarship?

Many of our colleagues in New Testament studies will disagree with our conclusions, primarily because we have departed so radically from previous interpretations of Acts. We reached these conclusions, however, because we developed a different set of working hypotheses, as outlined in the Introduction. Our conclusions are based on our view that Acts was written in the early second century and that it used the letters of Paul as a primary source. Much of the previous scholarship had assumed that Acts was written in ca. 85 CE, did not use the letters of Paul, and could possibly have had access to eyewitness sources. With a methodology based on these presuppositions, previous scholarship often found Acts to be a mostly reliable historical resource. In contrast, our presuppositions tend to rule out all previous methods for analyzing Acts as history. Once one understands Acts as a second-century document, the methodology and the burden of proof completely change. From this perspective, we now consider Acts to be unreliable unless proven otherwise.

The Acts Seminar, therefore, is the product of a paradigm shift that is taking place in scholarship. No longer can scholarly consensus assume a first-century date for Acts. The arguments for dating Acts in the second century are substantial and compelling. What we have accomplished in the Acts Seminar project is a complete and systematic re-reading of Acts according to the new paradigm.

In broad terms, once we factor in the letters of Paul as a source for Acts, all other previously proposed source theories are undermined. Instead, we have found that, if there is any reliable history in Acts, it is because it is derived from Paul's letters. Acts offers no reliable supplement to the letters of Paul. Furthermore, its use of data from Paul's letters has been so reworked that Acts emerges as a patently unreliable historical resource. In sum, the story Acts tells provides virtually no reliable historical data except for what can be verified in Paul's letters.

On Jerusalem Origins

The Luke-Acts version of Christian origins has long been distrusted in many of its details, but the basic template has nevertheless been accepted as a foundation for virtually all reconstructions of Christian beginnings. The standard story was based on the story Acts tells: after the death of Jesus, the apostles gathered in Jerusalem and organized the first Christian community. Christianity then spread from Jerusalem following the pattern outlined in Acts.

Our reconstruction starts with Luke's sources. The two sources from which he worked were Paul's Letter to the Galatians and, perhaps, a vaguely defined source called "The Gentile Mission Source." This latter source is thought to have derived from Antioch and to have contained a story about the origins of Jesus communities in Jerusalem and Antioch as told from the perspective of Antioch. However, it defies significant reconstruction and, in any case, cannot be assumed to be historical. Nevertheless, it may have provided a model for how Luke tells his version of the story.[1]

Another source that lies in the background for the beginning of Acts is the Gospel of Mark. The first version of Luke's resurrection and ascension story is found at the end of the Gospel of Luke and is constructed out of the empty tomb story of Mark. Luke, however, radically retells the Mark story in such a way as to set up resurrection appearances not in Galilee, as Mark presumes, but in Jerusalem and only in Jerusalem. Acts retells the resurrection/ascension story and shapes it into the foundation for the theme that Jerusalem is where it all began.

Luke learned from Paul that, at the time of his "conversion," which took place well after the death of Jesus, there were other apostles in Jerusalem (Gal 1:17). Paul also visited Peter and James there three years later (Gal 1:18), and fourteen years later he met there with the full community, whose leaders included Peter, James, and John (Gal 2:1–10).

From that data, Luke wove his story and created the template that has dominated most later reconstructions of Christian history. However, this template can no longer be considered reliable. First, his revision of Mark in creating his resurrection narrative shows that he is an unreliable resource; indeed, his is the only gospel story that assumes a coalescing of the apostles in Jerusalem. Second, his use of Paul's data about the Jerusalem community radically revises Paul's story. Whereas Paul argued for an independently authorized mission to Gentiles (though he attempted to smooth things over with Jerusalem; see Gal 1:15–20), Luke presents a Paul who is dominated by Jerusalem. Third, the template itself can be explained as a creation of Luke put together to fit Luke's apologetic program, namely, a beginning in Jerusalem and an orderly, divinely directed progression from there. Fourth, we now know there was a great deal of diversity in early Christianity that appears to date from its very origins. Acts not only cannot account for this diversity, it attempts to suppress it by telling a story that rules out such diversity.

To be sure, Paul does refer to an early community in Jerusalem that was very influential in the early years. But the historical account of that community cannot be written on the basis of Acts. Only when we have taken Acts off the table can we then write a history that does justice to the diversity of earliest Christianity.

On the Biography of Paul

There is hardly any biography of Paul that does not rely heavily on Acts.[2] This study has undermined the reliability of Acts as a source for the historical Paul and set the stage for writing a new Pauline biography.

Acts was written at a time when Paul was considered a hero of the faith and when his letters had just become widely available. Paul the hero spawned other stories of his miraculous activities, such as found in the mid-second century *Acts of Paul*. Paul the letter writer, however, was a problem. In the early to mid-second century, the writing we call 2 Peter highlighted the problem of Paul the letter writer: "There are some things in [Paul's letters] hard to understand, which the ignorant and unstable twist to their own destruction, as they do the other scriptures" (2 Pet 3:16, NRSV). Acts wrote of Paul the hero but squelched Paul the letter writer. As a result, his Paul fit perfectly into the Acts story.

Acts can be deceiving. Since authentic details about the life of Paul from the letters are filled out in more detail in Acts, we can be seduced into accepting the Acts version of events. However, it is unlikely that Paul would have recognized himself in the character created in Acts. Here are some of the key ways in which Acts has reshaped the Paul of the letters.

The Damascus Road Experience. Paul tells of his conversion (or call) experience in Gal 1:15–16 and supplemented it with his reference to a resurrection experience in 1 Cor 15:8. Paul's version is so cryptic that little of the underlying story can be reconstructed. Luke, however, knew how a conversion story should be told and created his own version. Luke's story became the standard account of Paul's conversion and defined for generations thereafter what a "conversion" experience should be. The Acts story has become the quintessential "Damascus road experience," but it rules out Paul's own characterization of his experience. Paul's version, cryptic though it may be, is the only reliable account we have for reconstructing his biography. According to his own description, Paul had a life-changing experience. It did not take place on the legendary "Damascus road" nor did it involve a light from heaven, a disembodied voice, a period of blindness, or instruction from one Ananias.[3]

Personal Details about Paul. The following details are found only in Acts: Paul was once called Saul, he was from Tarsus, he studied in Jerusalem under Gamaliel, he was a tentmaker, and he was a Roman citizen. None of these details can be verified in Paul's letters, some of them are at odds with Paul's own representation of his history (e.g., his Roman citizenship),[4] and all of them fit motifs emphasized by Luke. With varying degrees of certainty, we would have to exclude all of these details from an authorized biography of Paul.

Paul's Missionary Identity and Methodology. According to Acts, Paul was commissioned by the church at Antioch to be a missionary to the Gentiles (13:1–3). In contrast, we learn from Paul's letters that, even though he had been closely associated with the Antioch community, he consistently defined his commission as having come, not from any human being, but from God (as in Gal 1:11–17). While Paul's emphasis on a commissioning by God may be too self-serving to be wholly reliable, the Acts account is not a valid alternative since it is constructed to fit Luke's emphasis on the orderly succession of power under the overall leadership of the apostles.

According to Acts, Paul followed a regular pattern in his mission work. When he arrived in a new community, he would first preach in the synagogue. Invariably there would be trouble with the local Jewish population, causing him to leave the synagogue and concentrate on the Gentile population. He would then have success among the Gentiles, but the Jewish opposition would grow so fierce that he would have to flee for his life (see, for example, Acts 13:13–52). It is a story that is too firmly embedded in Luke's apologetic agenda to be considered reliable. Nor does it fit Paul's own version of his story as it can be derived from his letters. A historical description of Paul's mission methodology should not give any credence to the Acts characterization.

The Jerusalem Conference. Luke appears to have mined the letters for selective references to the biography of Paul, especially the Letter to the Galatians. The Jerusalem conference fit his agenda since it can be read as an attempt by Paul to seek authorization for his mission to the Gentiles (see Gal 2:1–10). Nevertheless, Luke chose not to tell the story as Paul wrote it (see Acts 15:1–29). For example, he toned down the underlying tension at the meeting as Paul described it. In Luke's version, the meeting is a model of concord. He also restructured it to fit his version of the origin of the Gentile mission. Whereas Paul in his letters consistently saw himself as uniquely commissioned to be the apostle to the Gentiles (as in Gal 1:16), Luke gives that divine charge to Peter (15:7). Paul understood Peter to be commissioned primarily as a missionary to the circumcised (Gal 2:8) and had to oppose Peter for not fully accepting the legitimacy of Gentile Christians (Gal 2:11–14). In contrast, Acts gives to Peter the most eloquent case for the Gentile mission (Acts 15:6–11). Paul specified that the only requirement made upon him was that he "remember the poor" (Gal 2:10). Acts leaves out that reference and substitutes instead a decree that Gentiles must follow a modified version of the Jewish dietary laws (15:19–29), a decree for which there is no evidence in the letters of Paul (see, for example, Rom 14:1–15:13).

The Acts version of the Jerusalem conference is so similar to Paul's version that it has to be the same event. It can readily be accounted for as having been derived from Paul. There are no grounds for presupposing that Luke had another reliable source for this event besides Paul. An authorized biography of Paul should therefore use only Paul's version of this conference; there is no reliable independent information to be derived from Acts.

The Itinerary of Paul. It has often been proposed that Acts had a reliable source for the itinerary of Paul. Consequently, since the Acts itinerary is more complete than what we find in Paul, it is heavily relied on for telling the story of Paul's journeys. However, when we factor in the use of Paul's letters as a source, we find that the Acts itinerary is primarily built out of the data found in Paul's letters. This data tends to be concentrated at the ends of Paul's letters where he discussed upcoming travel plans. Luke collected this data and then supplemented it with additional travel details he created out of a general knowledge of the geography of the region. Travel narratives were important plot devices in both Luke and Acts, and they exhibit the author at his storytelling best.

It is Acts that gives us the standard itinerary in which Paul took three journeys, all of which began from Antioch. The three-journey motif is a Lukan construct, and does not fit the pattern we can reconstruct from Paul. A corrected version of Paul's missionary method has been proposed by Helmut Koester. Koester lays out a pattern that fits Paul's own descriptive data quite well and provides a foundation for developing a new biography of Paul.[5]

According to the letters, such cities as Thessalonica, Corinth, and Ephesus were highlights of Paul's mission work. Sometimes the letters provide a bit of data about Paul's initial work in the city to which the letter was addressed, but for the most part such details are lacking. That is where Acts stepped in with stories to fit each location, and many more locations besides. Each of these stories has been analyzed individually in this volume. We have found them to derive primarily from the creative hand of the author, following his favorite themes, without recourse to any other source besides Paul's letters. On this point, Acts is perhaps most seductive to the historian. There is just enough correlation with the letters to make the Acts stories seem credible, but we have found them all to be unreliable. A new biography of Paul should tell the story of Paul's mission without supplementation from Acts.

The Theology of Paul. Luke was apparently familiar with the theology of Paul but, like others of his generation, such as the writers of 2 Peter, *Acts of Paul*, and the Pastoral Epistles, he suppressed it. Paul's sermons in Acts are creations of Luke and are not derivative from Paul's theology. Ironically, it is in the preaching of Peter where allusions to Paul's theology are found. At the Jerusalem conference, Peter presents a case for the Gentile mission utilizing theological themes from Paul (Acts 15:6–11). Here Peter has not only taken over Paul's role as primary apostle to the Gentiles but he also justifies it with themes cribbed from Paul.[6]

The Final Journey and Death of Paul. The final journey of Paul is laid out in the form of a prospective itinerary in Rom 15:22–29. Here Paul states his plans to visit Rome after he has traveled from

Ephesus to Jerusalem with the collection he has gathered from the Gentile communities. In 15:30–32, he further alludes to the possibility of tensions with the non-believers there and an uncertainty about whether the collection will be acceptable to the Jerusalem Jesus community. This is the only reliable data we have about the last journey of Paul. From this bit of data Luke constructs an elaborate and lengthy travel narrative. We have analyzed this narrative in detail in Chapter Five of this volume.

Since there is no other version of the end of Paul's life, the Acts version has been widely accepted as generally reliable. But closer study of the individual narrative units shows that they can be identified as elaborations of the author. These stories follow themes found throughout Acts. They tell of Jewish intrigue, numerous defense speeches of Paul before Roman leaders, Paul's appeal to Rome, his eventful journey to Rome, which includes a dramatic shipwreck, and his imprisonment in Rome under house arrest, which allows him to continue his mission. After ruling out the individual narrative units, we are left with a core set of data: Paul made a final trip to Jerusalem, he was arrested there, he was sent to Rome as a prisoner, and he died by Roman execution. None of these details can be affirmed directly from Acts. At best, they represent an assumption that a tradition about Paul's death may lie in the background of the elaborate story told by Acts. With so little to go on, this is the best we can do to reconstruct the ending of Paul's biography.

Acts in an Age of Uncertainty

We thus conclude that the significance of Acts does not rest on the historical reliability of the narratives its author tells. We need, however, to examine the time at which it was written and the contribution this book made to its own historical context.

There is no evidence that anyone had seen the book we know as the Acts of the Apostles before about 150 CE. The better evidence dates from a quarter-century later, when Irenaeus of Lyons used it as a fundamental text in opposing what he regarded as heresy. The usefulness of Acts in controversies against Marcionite Christianity and other forms of suspected thought is well known and well-documented. Irenaeus' arguments rested firmly on his claims that the faith he advocated was that of the apostles and that the apostolic tradition was transmitted to the church from Jesus through those whom he appointed. To make these claims Irenaeus depended heavily on the book of Acts.

The situation in the first half of the second century, when Acts probably appeared, was, however, very different. From the point of view of the still-fragile Christian communities, it would seem to be a time of exceptional uncertainty. Walter Bauer has led us to see this situation more clearly than we did before. Bauer maintained that, through much of the second century, there was great diversity among those who considered themselves Christians and that in many locations beliefs and practices associated with "unorthodoxy" prevailed. He maintained that in many areas the "unorthodox" were in fact dominant and so a conflict with the "orthodox" was not even necessary.[7] Discoveries since the publication of Bauer's study have only given us more confidence in this judgment.

Moreover, it is likely that Christian writers of the second century were creating rather than defending tradition. In a recent study, Daniel Boyarin used the metaphor of border lines to interpret the construction of both Christianity and Judaism.[8] He maintained that the separation of Judaism and Christianity was not a "natural-sounding" parting of the ways, but was rather the result of various attempts to establish border lines and thus to define the nature and limits of the two faiths. Calling those who wrote about and opposed the "unorthodox" "heresiologists," Boyarin wrote:

> "Heresiology"—the "science" of heresies—inscribes the border lines, and heresiologists are the inspectors of religious customs. Ancient heresiologists tried to police the boundaries so as to identify and interdict those who respected no borders, those smugglers of ideas and practices newly declared to be contraband, nomads who would not recognize the efforts to institute limits, to posit a separation between "two opposed places," and thus to clearly establish who was and who was not a "Christian," a "Jew."[9]

Boyarin stressed the role of the Christian heresiologists in this construction and claimed that these writers were more intent on providing theological assurance to their fellow believers than on keeping out the unorthodox. Boyarin did not include the Acts of the Apostles among the Christian heresiologists. Yet it would seem that its author, like the other Christian leaders, was also involved in the construction of religious boundaries. The author of Acts intended to define Christianity as a movement both distinct from and related to Judaism and under a corps of leaders of unquestionable authenticity. He attempted to provide assurance in the face of uncertainty on a number of fronts.

Although uncertainty faces almost every generation, there is evidence that the late first and early second centuries were particularly shaky times for the Christian churches. Earlier in this volume we called attention to the challenges that Marcion and his followers posed for other believers. The effect of Marcionite success was to question the leadership of the church and Paul's role therein. They maintained that the only legitimate apostle of Jesus was Paul and that Peter and the others were false apostles. They maintained further that Paul had preached that the role of Jesus was to redeem people from domination by the God who created the universe and required the observance of Torah. They defined Jews as people who lived under the domination of the creator-God and who continue to expect a politically oriented Messiah.

The author of 2 Peter, writing probably in the mid-second century, observed that Paul's letters were hard to understand and subject to diverse interpretations (see 2 Pet 3:16). This anonymous author reveals that the writings of Paul had become problematic for second-century Christians, but the writer's irritation is probably only the tip of the iceberg. Paul himself was clearly the subject of a good deal of controversy during his lifetime, and his death did little to resolve it. It has long been observed that the Deutero-Pauline letters serve to show that controversy about Paul continued for many decades.[10] His legacy was a matter of great concern for some time. Struggles for Pauline support and, hence, alternate interpretations of his significance, must have begun shortly after his death and continued for over a century afterward.

Christian literature from the turn of the century, though sparse, illustrates the problems with leadership. In ca. 95 CE, for example, there was a situation in Corinth that led to the ouster of some of the leaders in that church. We do not know what led to the disturbance, but an author we know as Clement, writing from Rome, considered the situation to be serious and wrote to the Corinthian church stressing the virtue of order. He underscored the concept of ecclesiastical order by stressing the role of the apostles. He traced the appointment of the apostles to Jesus and God and then connected the later leadership of the church to them. By so doing he claimed that the ousting of the elders at Corinth was tantamount to rebelling against God. It seems that Clement so vigorously stressed the authority of duly appointed elders in the church at Corinth precisely because the leadership of the church was not a settled issue.

Ignatius, Bishop of Antioch, writing a few decades later, reveals a similar viewpoint. Most notable is his insistence on the authority of the bishop. In a number of references he talks of seeing the entire congregation in the person of the bishop.[11] His image of the church appears to be that of a congregation gathered with the bishop, but also with the council of presbyters, and the deacons. One must be careful not to oppose the bishop,[12] believers must be subject to the bishop,[13] and, in respect to church practices, nothing can be done without the bishop.[14] William Schoedel is probably correct to observe that historically Ignatius represents a kind of church organization that may have been widespread but was not yet firmly established in all places. Schoedel further observes that Ignatius was so insistent on the authority of the bishop precisely because his own position had been threatened:

> We shall argue that the bishop's reactions to his situation reveal a person whose self-understanding had been threatened and who was seeking to reaffirm the value of his ministry by what he did and said as he was taken to Rome. One probable cause of Ignatius' self-doubts was his loss of control of the church in Antioch and the emergence of a group opposed to his authority.[15]

Ignatius vigorously insisted on the authority of the bishop precisely because the situation was fluid and the structure of church leadership uncertain.

In the middle of the second century, Justin Martyr composed a dialogue between himself and a Jewish leader. His *Dialogue with Trypho* is an extended debate that attempts to distinguish Christian from Jewish theologies. Justin's writing is evidence that believers in Jesus were uncertain about these theological differences and in need of assurance that their own tradition was the right one. Issues between Jews and Christians continued for some time and must have been of concern long before Justin wrote.

Surely, these and other issues deeply troubled believers in the early second century and revealed the need for a construction of Christianity that would remove as much uncertainty as possible. In this concluding essay we summarize the ways in which the author of Acts addressed three troubling issues: the leadership of the church; the significance of Paul; and relations to the Jews.

The Leadership of the Church. The author of Acts does not participate directly in the controversies that rocked Antioch and Corinth, since his narrative focus is on an earlier time. He nevertheless provides for these and other churches a sense of solid structure. For him there can be no doubt about the leaders of the church:

they are the apostles. And there is no doubt as to who they were: they were twelve men who were appointed by the historical Jesus and whose names are known. The most prominent is Peter. Even Paul, who became a successor to the apostles, was subject to apostolic review, and he happily harmonized his work with theirs. And in his farewell to Ephesus, Paul recognized the leadership of that church. It is true that the author of Acts does not spell out a rigid pattern of succession to the apostles, but he nevertheless provides a basis on which the doctrine of apostolic succession could comfortably be built.

Recall the role of the apostles in Acts. The composition of the group is carefully defined in the first chapter. Peter, as the spokesperson for them, defends the believers in Jerusalem through many trials. They appoint the Seven to resolve a problem between Hebrews and Hellenists. They follow up on Philip after he baptizes converts in Samaria. Peter extends the movement to Gentiles by converting Cornelius and his household, but even he is subject to the will of the apostolic group as a whole. Paul, although not an apostle himself, willingly submits to the authority of the Twelve. In all this Luke is participating in the process of creating Christian identity, so that second-century believers may conclude that a true Christian community is one that is led by those who have been authorized by the apostles.

The Significance of Paul. For the author of Acts, Paul was not an opponent of the Hebrew Scriptures and Jewish traditions. He did not declare Torah to be obsolete. Not only is he portrayed as adhering to the convictions and practices of the apostles, as shown above. His fidelity to the Scriptures, to Torah, and to Jewish practices is also stressed throughout the narrative. In Acts, Paul is a faithful Pharisaic Jew, believing everything in the Scriptures and devoutly adhering to the customs and requirements of his faith. He accepted and spread the decree that required Gentile believers to observe at least some minimal Torah requirements. Although he opposed the imposition of circumcision as a requirement for Gentile believers, he had Timothy circumcised. He repeatedly asserted that he was a Pharisee, and he stressed that his characteristic belief in resurrection was a major point of agreement with Pharisees. He took a Nazirite vow and supported others who did the same. He participated in worship at the temple in Jerusalem. In Acts Paul never hints at any critical attitude toward Torah. Only two verses may be cited as suggestions of Paul's views, and one of them was spoken by Peter rather than Paul (see Acts 13:38–39; 15:11).

Relations to the Jews. If, as Boyarin maintains, Christianity becomes defined in distinction from Judaism, Acts must be considered as playing a major role in this process. In the Acts narrative, Jews are those to whom the gospel was first preached, and the apostles and Paul made repeated efforts to present it to them, not only in Judea but also in the Diaspora. The author of Acts maintains that some Jews accepted the faith and joined with the other believers but that the vast majority rejected it. Furthermore, he shows that those who rejected the gospel violently opposed the apostles and Paul, bringing them to trial at every opportunity, even conspiring to kill them. The Lukan Paul would never have faced opposition from Roman authorities except that the Jews called for him to be tried and executed. The rhetorical effect of Acts is to persuade readers that Jews are the mortal enemies of Christians and that they are to be vigorously opposed, despised, and treated with contempt.

In the Introduction to this volume we claimed that Acts is a charter myth, a myth of origin. It is a literary construction of religious belief and practice in narrative form. Our studies have also convinced us that the author of Acts was influenced by well-known Greek and Latin epics and that, in many respects, his work resembles them. The Acts Seminar found precious little genuine history in the Acts narrative. Its author dealt with real persons and places but almost always shaped events to support his own agenda. If we read Acts to learn the history of the early Jesus communities, we will be sorely disappointed.

That Acts does not report reliable history does not mean, however, that the book is without significance. On the contrary, recognition of Acts as a charter myth or, in Boyarin's terms, an attempt to establish border lines, can lead to a more genuine appreciation of our author's work. It is true that, in the twenty-first century, we cannot applaud all that our author accomplished. In his presentation of Jews, he is culpable for contributing to the legacy of Christian anti-Judaism, which has had dreadful, catastrophic consequences. But in the second century, his insistence on apostolically based leadership was a potent element in the development of a firm structure of leadership for fledgling churches. Finally, we must recognize Luke's persistent affirmation of the identity of the God of Israel and the God of Jesus; his understanding of Paul undermines those who would sever the relationship between them. His stress on the importance of the Hebrew Scriptures for the followers of Jesus contributed to a history in which the OT became a constituent part of the Christian Bible. The retention of these Scriptures posed both possibilities and problems for the believers, since for the most part, they found it necessary to interpret them symbolically rather than literally. Nevertheless, those Christians whose lives were and are shaped by the myth of Acts cannot think of the revelation of Jesus without seeing it within the context of a long biblical history that began with Adam.

This brief chapter does not pretend to be an exhaustive summary of such a complex book as Acts. We hope, however, that our comments here and in the preceding chapters about the meaning of its story and its historical reliability will help readers to gain a heightened understanding of this important book.

Notes

Introduction

1. Based on Smith, "Top Ten Accomplishments."
2. See also Pervo, "Dating Acts" and *Dating Acts*.
3. See Josephus, *Antiquities* 20,267.
4. See also Tyson, "The Date of Acts," and *Marcion and Luke-Acts*.
5. See Irenaeus, *Against Heresies* 3,14:1.
6. See Irenaeus, *Against Heresies* 3,1:1.
7. See Harnack, *The Acts of the Apostles*.
8. See the cameo essay, "The Letters of Paul as Sources for Acts," p. 116; see also Walker, "Acts and the Pauline Corpus Revisited"; and Pervo, *Dating Acts*.
9. Psalm 110 in Hebrew.
10. Jer 9:26 in Hebrew.
11. See MacDonald, *Mimesis and Intertextuality*; see also the cameo essay, "Prison Breaks in Luke's Literary World," p. 72.
12. "D" is the designation given by textual scholars to Codex Bezae, a manuscript from the fifth or sixth century, containing the gospels and Acts. It was named for Theodore de Bèze, an associate of John Calvin, who owned the manuscript in the sixteenth century.
13. See also Tyson, "Acts: A Myth of Christian Origins."
14. Bultmann, *Jesus Christ and Mythology*, 15.
15. See Cameron and Miller, *Redescribing Christian Origins*.
16. Daniélou and Marrou, *The First Six Hundred Years*, 3.
17. Daniélou and Marrou, *The First Six Hundred Years*, 4.
18. See Frend, *The Rise of Christianity*.
19. Martin, "History, Historiography, and Christian Origins," 269–70.
20. Lüdemann, *The Acts of the Apostles*, 23.

Chapter 1: Beginning in Jerusalem (Acts 1:1–8:3)

1. Haenchen, *The Acts of the Apostles*, 145.
2. Parsons, *The Departure of Jesus in Luke-Acts*, 198; see further 189–99.
3. See Epp, *Junia*.
4. The title appears in Acts 14:4, 14, for Paul and Barnabas, but this does not compromise the concept of apostleship that governs Acts as a whole. See the notes on these verses.
5. Funk, *The Poetics of Biblical Narrative*, 135.
6. Haenchen, *The Acts of the Apostles*, 204.
7. See Funk and the Jesus Seminar, *The Acts of Jesus*, 530–31.
8. See Plato, *Apology* 19d, 38a.
9. Plato, *Apology* 24b, trans. Dupertuis.
10. Xenophon, *Memorabilia* 1.1.1, trans. Dupertuis.

11. See Plato, *Apology* 17a.
12. See Plato, *Apology* 41a–c.
13. See Bauer and Danker, *A Greek-English Lexicon*, s.v.
14. See Pervo, *Dating Acts*, 152–60.
15. Euripides, *Bacchae* 443–48, trans. MacDonald.
16. Euripides, *Bacchae* 635–36.
17. Euripides, *Bacchae* 659.
18. Euripides, *Bacchae* 794–95.
19. See Pervo, *Profit with Delight*, 18–24; Seaford, "Thunder, Lightning and Earthquake"; and Weaver, *Plots of Epiphany*.
20. See MacDonald, *Does the New Testament Imitate Homer?* 123–45.
21. Homer, *Iliad* 24.682–84 and 689–91, trans. MacDonald.
22. It is known as the Theodotus Inscription. Theodotus is named as the person who built the synagogue.
23. See Josephus, *Antiquities* 20.199–203.

Chapter 2: To Judea, Samaria, and Beyond (Acts 8:4–9:43)

1. See Irenaeus, *Against Heresies* 1,27:1; 3,4:3; 3,12:12.
2. See Justin, *First Apology* 26.
3. See Spencer, "A Waiter, A Magician, A Fisherman, and a Eunuch," 164–66.
4. Homer, *Odyssey* 1.23.
5. A. Smith, "Do You Understand?" 70.
6. See Pervo, *Acts*, 239.
7. See also Walker, "Acts and the Pauline Corpus Revisited," 77–86.
8. See Funk and the Jesus Seminar, *The Acts of Jesus*, 530–31.
9. See Spencer, "Women of 'the Cloth.'"
10. See Pervo, *Acts*, 254.

Chapter 3: Antioch and Jerusalem (Acts 10:1–15:35)

1. Cadbury, "The Hellenists," 68.
2. Cadbury, "The Hellenists," 66.
3. Pervo, *Acts*, 294–5.
4. The issues are discussed in Pervo, *Acts*, 303.
5. See Josephus, *Jewish Antiquities* 19,343–50.
6. Barrett, *Acts* 1:651.
7. In some manuscripts the term "apostle" appears also in Acts 14:14, but the text at this point is questionable.
8. See Ovid, *Metamorphoses* 8.611–724.
9. *Avodah Zarah* 8.4.
10. Translation taken from Segal, "Acts 15 as Jewish and Christian History," 69.

Chapter 4: Paul in Asia and Greece (Acts 15:36–19:41)

1. See Cohen, "Was Timothy Jewish (Acts 16:1–3)?"
2. Walker, "The Timothy-Titus Problem"; Pervo, *Dating Acts*, 86–88.
3. Pervo, *Acts*, 389.
4. Numerous examples are cited in Pervo, *Acts*, 391–92.
5. Spencer, "Women of 'the Cloth' in Acts," 148.

6. For an overview of the history of research, see Campbell, *The "We" Passages in the Acts of the Apostles*, 1–13; and, also by Campbell, "The Narrator as 'He,' 'Me,' and 'We.'"

7. See MacDonald, "The Shipwrecks of Odysseus and Paul."

8. Homer, *Odyssey* 9.37–40.

9. Tannehill, *The Narrative Unity of Luke-Acts*, 2:207.

10. Knox, *Chapters in a Life of Paul*, 26.

11. Rom 15:25–32 and 1 Cor 16:3–4 anticipate the same visit to Jerusalem, Paul's third.

12. Barrett, *Acts*, 2:854.

13. See Pervo, *Acts*, 447.

14. See White, "Paul, Gallio, and the Bema at Corinth (Acts 18:12–17)."

15. See Walker, "The Portrayal of Aquila and Priscilla in Acts."

16. Pervo, *Acts*, 459.

17. Käsemann, "The Disciples of John the Baptist in Ephesus," 136.

18. Pervo, *Acts*, 6.

19. Pervo, *Acts*, 5–7.

20. Pervo, *Acts*, 482.

21. Barrett, *Acts*, 2:914.

22. See Pervo, *Acts*, 478 n. 30.

23. Haenchen, *The Acts of the Apostles*, 578.

Chapter 5: To the Ends of the Earth (Acts 20:1–28:31)

1. For Sopater, see Sosipater in Rom 16:21; for Tychicus see Eph 6:21; Col 4:7. Secundus is not mentioned elsewhere in the NT.

2. Tannehill, *The Narrative Unity of Luke-Acts*, 2:247.

3. Pervo, *Acts*, 510.

4. For a full discussion of this story, its parallels, and its symbolism, see Pervo, *Acts*, 510–14.

5. Dibelius, *The Book of Acts*, 62.

6. Dewey et al., *The Authentic Letters of Paul*, 183.

7. See Pervo, *Acts*, 5–7.

8. Price, "Paulus Absconditus."

9. See Pervo, *Acts*, 546–47, for a discussion of these issues.

10. See Josephus, *Jewish War* 2,261–3; *Jewish Antiquities* 20,169–72.

11. See Pervo, *Profit with Delight*, 12–57.

12. See Pervo, *Acts*, 552–53.

13. See Josephus, *Jewish War* 2,254–63; *Antiquities* 20,161–71. See Pervo, *Acts*, 553; *Dating Acts*, 161–66.

14. See the full discussion of this issue in Pervo, *Acts*, 554–56.

15. See Pervo, *Acts*, 554.

16. Rapske, *The Book of Acts and Paul in Roman Custody*, 148.

17. See Pervo, *Acts*, 580.

18. See Josephus, *Antiquities* 20,141–47; see further Pervo, *Acts*, 587; *Dating Acts*, 42–43, 186–87.

19. See Pervo, *Acts*, 587.

20. Tannehill, *The Narrative Unity of Luke-Acts*, 2:311.

21. See Pervo, *Acts*, 592–93.

22. See Josephus, *Antiquities* 20,182–96; See Pervo, *Acts*, 608.
23. Lucian, *On Salaried Posts in Great Houses*, 1.
24. See Shea, "Pieces of Epic."
25. See Pervo, *Profit with Delight*, 50–57.
26. Homer, *Odyssey* 5.336–38, 341; 343–47, trans. MacDonald.
27. Praeder, "Acts 27:1–28:16: Sea Voyages in Ancient Literature and the Theology of Luke-Acts," 701. See also MacDonald, "The Shipwrecks of Odysseus and Paul."
28. Haenchen, *The Acts of the Apostles*, 592.
29. The importance of Luke 4 for understanding how Luke as a writer uses his sources is discussed further above, pp. 11–12.

Conclusion

1. Proposed by Richard Pervo; see the cameo essay, "The Gentile Mission Source," p. 99.
2. A notable exception is Knox, *Chapters in a Life of Paul*.
3. See further the cameo essay, "Comparing Paul and Luke on Paul's Conversion," p. 114.
4. See the discussion on pp. 275–76.
5. Koester, *History and Literature*, 103–4, 110. Note that Koester does rely on Acts for some of his reconstruction but disagrees with the "three missionary journeys" format of Acts.
6. See further the cameo essay, "The Letters of Paul as Sources for Acts," p. xxx.
7. See Bauer, *Orthodoxy and Heresy in Earliest Christianity*, 170.
8. See Boyarin, *Border Lines*.
9. Boyarin, *Border Lines*, 2.
10. See, e.g., Watson, "'In Whom Are Hid All the Treasures of Wisdom and Knowledge.'" See also, Babcock, *Paul and the Legacies of Paul*; Pervo, *The Making of Paul*.
11. E.g., Ignatius, *Ephesians* 1.3; *Magnesians* 2.1; *Trallians* 1.1.
12. See Ignatius, *Ephesians* 5.3.
13. See Ignatius, *Ephesians* 4.1; 6.1; 20.2; *Magnesians* 3.1, 4; 13.2; *Trallians* 13.2; *Polycarp* 6.1.
14. E.g., Ignatius, *Magnesians* 7.1; *Trallians* 2.2; 7.2; *Philadelphians* 7.2; *Smyrneans* 8.1–2; 9.1.
15. Schoedel, *Ignatius of Antioch*, 10.

Works Cited

Primary Sources

The Ante-Nicene Fathers. Ed. Alexander Roberts and James Donaldson. 1885–87. 10 vols. Repr. Peabody, MA: Hendrickson, 1994.

The Apostolic Fathers. Ed. and trans. Bart D. Ehrman. 2 vols. Loeb Classical Library. Cambridge: Harvard University Press, 2003.

Euripides. *Bacchae, Iphigenia at Aulis, Rhesus*. Ed. and trans. David Kovacs. Loeb Classical Library. Cambridge: Harvard University Press, 2003.

Homer. *Iliad*. Trans. A. T. Murray. Rev. ed. William F. Wyatt. 2 vols. Loeb Classical Library. Cambridge: Harvard University Press, 1924–25.

———. *Odyssey*. Trans. A. T. Murray. Rev. ed. George E. Dimock. 2 vols. Loeb Classical Library. Cambridge: Harvard University Press, 1919.

Irenaeus. *St. Irenaeus of Lyons against the Heresies*. Trans. Dominic J. Unger and John J. Dillon. Ancient Christian Writers 55. New York: Paulist Press, 1991.

Josephus. Trans. H. St. J. Thackeray et al. 10 vols. Loeb Classical Library. Cambridge: Harvard University Press, 1926–65.

Justin Martyr. *The First Apology*. Pp. 242–89 in *Early Christian Fathers*. Trans. Edward Rochie Hardy. The Library of Christian Classics 1. Philadelphia: Westminster Press, 1953.

———. *The Dialogue with Trypho*. Trans. Stephen B. Falls. *Saint Justin Martyr*. Fathers of the Church. New York: Christian Heritage, 1949.

Lucian. *The Dead Come to Life or The Fisherman*, et al. Trans. A. M. Harmon. Loeb Classical Library. Cambridge: Harvard University Press, 1921.

Ovid. *Metamorphoses*. Trans. Frank Miller. Rev. ed. G. P. Goold. 2 vols. Loeb Classical Library. Cambridge: Harvard University Press, 1916.

Plato. *Euthyphro, Apology, Crito, Phaedo, Phaedrus*. Trans. Harold North Fowler. Loeb Classical Library. Cambridge: Harvard University Press, 1914.

The Tosefta. Trans. Jacob Neusner. Peabody, MA: Hendrickson Publishers, 2002.

Vergil. *Aeneid*. Trans. H. Rushton Fairclough. Rev. ed. G. P. Goold. 2 vols. Loeb Classical Library. Cambridge: Harvard University Press, 1916, 1918.

Xenophon. *Memorabilia, Oeconomicus, Symposium, Apology*. Trans. E. C. Marchant. Loeb Classical Library. Cambridge: Harvard University Press, 1923.

Secondary Sources

Babcock, William S., ed. *Paul and the Legacies of Paul*. Dallas: Southern Methodist University Press, 1990.

Barrett, C. K. *A Critical and Exegetical Commentary on the Acts of the Apostles*. International Critical Commentary. 2 vols. Edinburgh: T & T Clark, 1994, 1998.

Bauer, Walter. *Orthodoxy and Heresy in Earliest Christianity*. Ed. Robert A. Kraft and Gerhard Krodel. Philadelphia: Fortress Press, 1971.

———. F. W. Danker, W. F. Arndt, and F. W. Gingrich. *A Greek-English Lexicon of the New Testament and Other Early Christian Literature*. 3d ed. Chicago: University of Chicago Press, 1999.

Bonz, Marianne Palmer. *The Past as Legacy: Luke-Acts and Ancient Epic*. Minneapolis: Fortress Press, 2000.

Boyarin, Daniel. *Border Lines: The Partition of Judaeo-Christianity*. Divinations: Rereading Late Ancient Religion. Philadelphia: University of Pennsylvania Press, 2004.

Bultmann, Rudolf. *Jesus Christ and Mythology*. New York: Charles Scribner's Sons, 1958.

Cadbury, Henry J. "The Hellenists." Pp. 59–74 in *The Beginnings of Christianity*. Ed. F. J. Foakes Jackson and Kirsopp Lake. Vol. 5. New York: Macmillan, 1920–33. Repr., Grand Rapids, MI: Baker Book House, 1979.

Cameron, Ron, and Merrill P. Miller, eds. *Redescribing Christian Origins*. Society of Biblical Literature Symposium Series 28. Atlanta: Society of Biblical Literature, 2004.

Campbell, William Sanger. "The Narrator as 'He,' 'Me,' and 'We': Grammatical Person in Ancient Histories and in the Acts of the Apostles." *Journal of Biblical Literature* 129 (2010) 385–407.

———. *The "We" Passages in the Acts of the Apostles: The Narrator as Narrative Character*. Studies in Biblical Literature 14. Atlanta: Society of Biblical Literature, 2007.

Cohen, Shaye J. D. "Was Timothy Jewish (Acts 16:1–3)? Patristic Exegesis, Rabbinic Law, and Matrilineal Descent." *Journal of Biblical Literature* 105 (1986) 251–68.

Daniélou, Jean, and Henri Marrou. *The First Six Hundred Years.* Trans. Vincent Cronin. The Christian Centuries 1. London: Darton, Longman and Todd, 1978.

Dewey, Arthur J., Roy W. Hoover, Lane C. McGaughy, and Daryl D. Schmidt, eds. *The Authentic Letters of Paul: A New Reading of Paul's Rhetoric and Meaning.* Salem, OR: Polebridge Press, 2010.

Dibelius, Martin. *The Book of Acts: Form, Style, and Theology.* Ed. K. C. Hanson. Minneapolis: Fortress Press, 2004.

Dupertuis, Rubén. "*Parrēsia,* Opposition, and Philosophical Imagery in Acts." Paper presented at the semi-annual meeting of the Westar Institute, Santa Rosa, CA, March 2008.

Epp, Eldon J. *Junia: The First Woman Apostle.* Minneapolis: Fortress Press, 2005.

Foakes Jackson, F. J., and Kirsopp Lake, eds. *The Beginnings of Christianity.* 5 vols. New York: Macmillan, 1920–33. Repr., Grand Rapids, Mich.: Baker Book House, 1979.

Frend, W. H. C. *The Rise of Christianity.* Philadelphia: Fortress Press, 1984.

Funk, Robert W. *The Poetics of Biblical Narrative.* Sonoma, CA: Polebridge Press, 1988.

_____. and the Jesus Seminar. *The Acts of Jesus: The Search for the Authentic Deeds of Jesus.* San Francisco: HarperSanFrancisco, 1998.

_____. and Roy W. Hoover, eds. *The Five Gospels: What Did Jesus Really Say? The Search for the Authentic Words of Jesus.* New York: Macmillan, 1993.

Haenchen, Ernst. *The Acts of the Apostles: A Commentary.* Trans. Bernard Noble and Gerald Shinn. Oxford: Basil Blackwell, 1971.

Harnack, Adolf. *The Acts of the Apostles.* Trans. J. R. Wilkinson. New Testament Studies 3. London: Williams & Norgate, 1909. Repr., Eugene, OR: Wipf & Stock, 2000.

Hills, Julian V. "Equal Justice under the (New) Law: The Story of Ananias and Sapphira in Acts 5." *Forum* 3 (2000) 105–20.

Käsemann, Ernst. "The Disciples of John the Baptist in Ephesus." Pp. 136–48 in *Essays on New Testament Themes.* Ed. Ernst Käsemann. Trans. W. J. Montague. Studies in Biblical Theology 41. Naperville, IL: Alec R. Allenson, 1964.

Kea, Perry V. "2 Corinthians 11:22–33 and Related Texts." *Forum* n.s. 7 (2004) 211–28.

_____. "The Hellenists and the Hebrews." Paper presented at the semi-annual meeting of the Westar Institute, Santa Rosa, CA, October 2007.

———. "Miscellaneous Saul Stories in Acts: Acts 8:1–3; 9:26–31; 13:13." Paper presented at the semi-annual meeting of the Westar Institute, Santa Rosa, CA, October 2008.

———. "The Septuagint as a Source for Acts 6:8–8:1." *Forum* 5 (2002) 95–104.

———. "Source Theories for the Acts of the Apostles." *Forum* 4 (2001) 7–26.

———. "The Speech of Stephen: Acts 7." Paper presented at the semi-annual meeting of the Westar Institute, Santa Rosa, CA, October 2003.

Knox, John. *Chapters in a Life of Paul*. Rev. ed. Ed. Douglas R. A. Hare. Macon, GA: Mercer University Press, 1987.

Koester, Helmut. *History and Literature of Early Christianity*. Volume two of *Introduction to the New Testament*. New York: Walter de Gruyter, 1982.

Livesey, Nina E. "Circumcision as a Means of Testing the Historicity of Acts 16:1–5." *Forum*, 3d series, 2 (2013).

Lüdemann, Gerd. *The Acts of the Apostles: What Really Happened in the Earliest Days of the Church*. Amherst, NY: Prometheus Books, 2005.

———. "Historical Issues in Acts 28:11–31." *Forum*, 3d series, 2 (2013).

MacDonald, Dennis R. "'And So We Left Troy/Troas': Pseudo-Luke's Imitation of the 'We-Voyages' in Homer's *Odyssey*." *Forum*, 3d series, 2 (2013).

———. *Does the New Testament Imitate Homer? Four Cases from the Acts of the Apostles*. New Haven: Yale University Press, 2003.

———. "Luke's Emulation of Homer: Acts 12:1–17 and *Iliad* 24." *Forum* 3 (2000) 9–29.

———. *Mimesis and Intertextuality in Antiquity and Christianity*. Harrisburg, PA: Trinity Press International, 2001.

———. "A Mimetic Interpretation of Prison Breaks in Acts." Paper presented at the semi-annual meeting of the Westar Institute, Santa Rosa, CA, October 2008.

———. "The Shipwrecks of Odysseus and Paul." *New Testament Studies* 45 (1999) 88–107.

Martin, Luther H. "History, Historiography, and Christian Origins: The Jerusalem Community." Pp. 263–73 in *Redescribing Christian Origins*. Ed. Ron Cameron and Merrill P. Miller. Atlanta: Society of Biblical Literature, 2004.

Matthews, Shelly. "Did Christianity Begin at Pentecost? Reflections on the Question." Paper presented at the semi-annual meeting

of the Westar Institute, Santa Rosa, CA, October 2006.
———. *Perfect Martyr: The Stoning of Stephen and the Construction of Christian Identity*. New York: Oxford University Press, 2010.
———. "The Stoning of Stephen and the Ethics of Historiography." Paper presented at the semi-annual meeting of the Westar Institute, Santa Rosa, CA, October 2007.
Moreland, Milton. "An Early Christian Idea of the New Jerusalem: Acts in the Context of 2nd Century Judaism." Paper presented at the semi-annual meeting of the Westar Institute, Santa Rosa, CA, October 2009.
———. "Reconstructing Jerusalem 'Christians': Archaeology and Acts." Paper presented at the semi-annual meeting of the Westar Institute, Miami, FL, March 2006.
Parsons, Mikeal C. *The Departure of Jesus in Luke-Acts: The Ascension Narratives in Context.* Journal for the Study of the New Testament Supplement Series 21. Sheffield: Journal for the Study of the Old Testament, 1987.
Penner, Todd. "Did Christianity Begin at Pentecost? Beginnings and the Ends Thereof." Paper presented at the semi-annual meeting of the Westar Institute, Santa Rosa, CA, October 2006.
Pervo, Richard I. *Acts: A Commentary*. Ed. Harold W. Attridge. Hermeneia—A Critical and Historical Commentary on the Bible. Minneapolis: Fortress Press, 2009.
———. "Converting Paul: The Call of the Apostle in Early Christian Literature." Paper presented at the semi-annual meeting of the Westar Institute, Santa Rosa, CA, October 2004.
———. "Dating Acts." *Forum* 5 (2002) 53–72.
———. *Dating Acts: Between the Evangelists and the Apologists*. Santa Rosa, CA: Polebridge Press, 2006.
———. "The Gates Have Been Closed (Acts 21:30): The Jews in Acts." *Journal of Historical Criticism* 11 (2005) 128–49.
———. "Is There a There There? Looking for Antioch in the Former Antioch Source." *Forum,* 3d series, 2 (2013).
———. *The Making of Paul: Constructions of the Apostle in Early Christianity*. Minneapolis: Fortress Press, 2010.
———. "Meet Right—and our Bounden Duty: Community Meetings in Acts." *Forum* 4 (2001) 45–62.
———. "My Happy Home: the Role of Jerusalem in Acts 1–7." *Forum* 3 (2000) 31–55.
———. *Profit with Delight: The Literary Genre of the Acts of the Apostles.* Philadelphia: Fortress Press, 1987.

Phillips, Thomas E. "The 'Post-Apostolic' Consciousness in Acts: The 'We'-Sections in Acts 16 and Beyond." Paper presented at the semi-annual meeting of the Westar Institute., Santa Rosa, CA, March 2009.

Praeder, Susan M. "Acts 27:1–28:16: Sea Voyages in Ancient Literature and the Theology of Luke-Acts." *Catholic Biblical Quarterly* 46 (1984) 683–706.

Price, Robert M. "Paulus Absconditus: Paul Versus John in Ephesian Tradition." *Forum* 5 (2002) 87–94.

Rapske, Brian. *The Book of Acts and Paul in Roman Custody.* Vol. 3 of *The Book of Acts in its First Century Setting.* Grand Rapids: William B. Eerdmans, 1994.

Schoedel, William R. *Ignatius of Antioch: A Commentary on the Letters of Ignatius of Antioch.* Ed. Helmut Koester. Hermeneia Commentaries. Philadelphia: Fortress Press, 1985.

Seaford, Richard. "Thunder, Lightning and Earthquake in the *Bacchae* and the Acts of the Apostles." Pp. 139–52 in *What Is a God? Studies in the Nature of Greek Divinity.* Ed. Alan B. Lloyd. London: Duckworth, 1997.

Segal, Alan F. "Acts 15 as Jewish and Christian History." *Forum* 4 (2001) 63–87.

Seim, Turid Karlsen. *The Double Message: Patterns of Gender in Luke-Acts.* Nashville: Abingdon, 1994.

Shea, Christine. "Names in Acts 2: Our Little Roman, Paul." Paper presented at the semi-annual meeting of the Westar Institute, Santa Rosa, CA, October 2008.

———. "Pieces of Epic in the Shipwreck in Acts 27." *Forum* 5 (2002) 73–86.

———. "What Isn't in a Name? Naming and the Mission of Acts." Paper presented at the semi-annual meeting of the Westar Institute, Santa Rosa, CA, October 2007.

Smith, Abraham. "'Do You Understand What You Are Reading?' A Literary Critical Reading of the Ethiopian (Kushite) Episode (Acts 8:26–40)." *Journal of the Interdenominational Theological Center* 22 (1994) 48–70.

Smith, Dennis E. "Religious Practices of Early Christian Converts According to Acts 2:41–47." *Forum,* 3d series, 2 (2013).

———. "Rethinking the Acts Story of Christian Beginnings: The Acts Seminar Report." Paper presented at the semi-annual meeting of the Westar Institute, Santa Rosa, CA, March 2010.

———. "The Top Ten Accomplishments of the Acts Seminar."

Paper presented at the semi-annual meeting of the Westar Institute, Salem, OR, March 2011.

———. "Two Speeches and a Letter: Acts 15." Paper presented at the semi-annual meeting of the Westar Institute, Santa Rosa, CA, October 2003.

———. "Was There a Jerusalem Church? Christian Origins According to Acts and Paul." *Forum* 3 (2000) 57–74.

Spencer, F. Scott. "A Waiter, a Magician, a Fisherman, and a Eunuch: The Pieces and Puzzles of Acts 8." *Forum* 3 (2000) 155–78.

———. "Women of 'the Cloth' in Acts: Sewing the Word." Pp. 134–54 in *A Feminist Companion to the Acts of the Apostles.* Ed. Amy-Jill Levine with Marianne Blickenstaff. Cleveland: Pilgrim Press, 2004.

Tannehill, Robert C. *The Narrative Unity of Luke-Acts: A Literary Interpretation.* Foundations and Facets. 2 vols. Minneapolis: Fortress Press, 1986, 1990.

Taussig, Hal. "Jerusalem as Occasion for Conversation: The Intersection of Acts 15 and Galatians 2." *Forum* 4 (2001) 89–104.

Tyson, Joseph B. "Acts: A Myth of Christian Origins." *Forum* 3d series 1 (2007) 171–89.

———. "The Date of Acts: A Reconsideration." *Forum* 5 (2002) 33–51.

———. "Guess Who's Coming to Dinner: Peter and Cornelius in Acts 10:1–11:18." *Forum* 3 (2000) 179–96.

———. *Marcion and Luke-Acts: A Defining Struggle.* Columbia: University of South Carolina Press, 2006.

———. "Paul's Speech to the Jews in Rome: Acts 28:17–31." Paper presented at the semi-annual meeting of the Westar Institute, Santa Rosa, CA, October 2003.

———. "Themes at the Crossroads: Acts 15 in its Lukan Setting." *Forum* 4 (2001) 105–24.

Walker, William O. "Acts and the Pauline Corpus Revisited: Peter's Speech at the Jerusalem Conference." Pp. 77–86 in *Literary Studies in Luke-Acts: Essays in Honor of Joseph B. Tyson.* Ed. Richard P. Thompson and Thomas E. Phillips. Macon, GA: Mercer University Press, 1998.

———. "Luke's Portrayal of Aquila and Priscilla and the Letters of the Pauline Corpus." Paper presented at the semi-annual meeting of the Westar Institute, Santa Rosa, CA, October 2007.

———. "The Portrayal of Aquila and Priscilla in Acts: The Question of Sources." *New Testament Studies* 54 (2008) 479–95.

———. "The Timothy-Titus Problem Reconsidered." *Expository Times* 92 (1980–81) 231–35.

Watson, Francis. "'In Whom Are Hid All the Treasures of Wisdom and Knowledge': Colossians and the Autonomy of the Gospel." Paper presented at the annual meeting of the Society for New Testament Studies, Halle, Germany, August 5, 2005.

Weaver, John B. *Plots of Epiphany: Prison-Escape in Acts of the Apostles*. Berlin and New York: Walter de Gruyter, 2004.

White, L. Michael. "The First Christians: What Did the Neighbors Think?" *Forum* 3 (2000) 9–29.

———. "Paul, Gallio, and the Bema at Corinth (Acts 18:12–17): Rethinking the Archaeological Evidence and the Literary Tradition." Paper presented at the semi-annual meeting of the Westar Institute. Miami, FL, March 2007.

———. "The Pentecost Event: Lukan Redaction and Themes in Acts 2." *Forum* 3 (2000) 75–103.

Wiest, Stephen R. "The Story of Stephen in Acts 6:1–8:4." *Forum* 3 (2000) 121–53.

Winter, Sara C. "Antioch in Acts and Maccoby's 'Two-Tiered' Christianity." *Forum* 4 (2001) 27–44.

Index of Ancient Sources

Hebrew Bible and Apocrypha

Genesis
  1:14   213
  2:7   213
  11:1–9   39
  18–19   162
Exodus
  19:16–19   39
  20:7   85
  20:13   169
  20:14   169
  23:16   39
  33:3   13
  33:5   13
Leviticus
  11   129, 130
  11:42   129
  17:7   176
  17:9   177
  17:10–15   176
  17:14   175, 177
  17:15   176
  18:6–20   176
  18:29   177
Numbers
  6:1–21   225
Deuteronomy
  4:29   213
  5:11   85
  16:10   39
  18:15   54
  23:1   103
1 Kings
  17:8–16   12
  21:8–13   90
2 Kings
  5:1–19   12
Psalms
  2   58
  2:1–2   58

  2:7   152
  15   12
  15:8–11   12
  16   12, 152
  16:8–11   40
  16:10   40, 152
  69:26   32
  109:1   12
  109:8   32, 33
  110   343
  110:1   41
  118:22   57
  145:18   213
Isaiah
  6:9–10   322, 323
  49:6   154
  55   152
  55:3   152
  55:6   213
  56:3–5   103
  56:7–8   103
  58:6   12
  61:1–2   12
Jeremiah
  9:25   13
  9:26   343
  13:1–11   260
  23:23   213
Joel
  2:28–32   12, 40
Amos
  5:25–27   13
  9:11   137, 168
  9:30   137
Jonah
  1:1–3   311
  1:15   312
4 Maccabees
  17:15   91

Other Jewish Literature

Josephus   3, 5, 45, 71, 92, 142, 273, 275, 291, 304, 343, 344, 345, 346, 347
  Antiquities of the Jews   5, 343, 344, 345, 346

Jewish War   345
Mishnah   89
Tosefta   176, 347

New Testament

Matthew		8:1–3	120
10:2–4	34	8:26–39	197
26:61	85	8:28	197
		8:41–42	119
27:3–10	32	8:49–56	119
28:1–4	72	8:51	40
28:16–20	25, 30	9:20	40
Mark		9:28–36	40
3:16–19	34	13:10–17	85
6:1–6	11, 12, 184	14:1–6	85
6:4	12	18:31–33	103
6:18–20	292	18:31–32	254
7:18–19	132	18:44–46	103
13:32	26	19:1–10	105
14:3–9	184	19:47–21:38	56
14:58	85	19:47–48	57
16:2–4	72	20:17	57
16:7	29	20:27	56
Luke		21:5–6	85
1–2	7	22:8	40
1:1–4	10, 21, 191	22:19	311
1:3	24	22:30	203
1:5	192	22:47–23:5	260
2:1–2	223	22:47–71	69
2:44	266	22:54–62	40
3	33	22:63–71	279
3:3–4	229	22:63–64	280
3:16	26	22:66–23:25	41, 139
3:23	266	22:66–71	287, 297
4	346	22:71	85
4:16–30	11, 151, 184, 325	23:1–5	287, 297
4:18–19	12	23:1	267
4:22	12	23:2	203
4:24–27	12, 13	23:4	54
4:28–30	12	23:6–12	139, 288, 297
5	33, 60	23:13–25	152, 287, 297
5:1–11	40	23:14	54
5:10	139	23:18–19	54
5:17–26	59	23:22	54
5:21	85	23:34	88
5:29–32	105	23:50–54	152
6:1–11	85	24	25
6:12–16	32	24:1–3	72
6:14–16	32, 34, 40	24:1	25
6:14	139	24:6–7	30
6:15	140	24:12	40
6:20–23	105	24:13–35	25, 251
6:31	169	24:13–32	104
7:11–17	119	24:13	25
7:22–23	105	24:25–27	103, 303
7:36–50	105, 184	24:27	103
8	197	24:33	25

24:35	251	2:9–11	39
24:36–49	25, 128	2:13	39
24:44–49	203	2:14–41	39
24:44–46	103	2:14–36	12
24:47	25	2:14–21	13
24:49	25, 26, 38	2:14	42
24:49b	30	2:17–21	12, 40
24:50–53	25	2:17–18	194
24:51	30	2:22–23	269
John		2:22	41, 42, 228
2:19	85	2:23–24	42
20:1	72	2:23	41
20:11–21:14	30	2:25–28	12, 40
Acts		2:27	40
1–15	10, 97	2:29	42, 59
1–7	3, 95, 108, 351	2:31–32	42
1–2	10	2:31	40
1	32, 38, 131, 158	2:32	40
1:1–2a	192	2:34–35	12, 41
1:1	24	2:36	41, 42, 269
1:3	25, 155	2:38	42, 64, 228, 311
1:4–5	38	2:39	41
1:4	25, 26, 30, 39	2:42–47	47, 53, 163
1:5	26, 228, 229, 231	2:42	251
1:6	26	2:43–47	65
1:7	26	2:44–45	63, 75
1:8	25, 26, 28, 38, 40, 94, 96, 102	2:44	63
		2:45	63, 65
1:9–11	26, 119	2:46	8, 32, 47, 55, 75, 168
1:9	30	2:47	8
1:11	26	3:1–5:16	10
1:13–14	42	3	54, 55
1:13	32, 34, 39, 40, 94, 139, 140, 157, 250, 251	3:1–26	60, 237
		3:1–11	53
		3:1–10	53, 58, 60, 159
1:14	46, 194	3:1–3	168
1:15–22	32, 35, 40	3:1	8, 168
1:15	42	3:2	8
1:16–20	141	3:3	8
1:18–19	34	3:6	288
1:21–23	194	3:8	8, 168
1:21–22	32, 140, 144	3:10	8, 168
1:21	111	3:11–26	59
1:22	157, 262	3:11	168
1:23	170	3:12–26	53, 54
1:24–25	58	3:12–15a	269
1:26	157	3:13–14	54
2	13, 26, 38, 39, 43, 54, 128, 129, 228, 354	3:13	54, 55
		3:15	54, 55
2:1–13	43, 100	3:17	54
2:1	39	3:18	54, 103
2:3	26	3:19–20	55, 64
2:5	39, 42	3:19	55, 311

Index of Ancient Sources 357

Acts

3:20	54	5:15	235
3:22–23	54	5:17–42	10, 138
3:22	54, 55	5:17–33	72
3:24	54	5:17–32	72, 141
3:25	55	5:17–26	13, 14, 68, 69
3:26	55	5:17	85
4	58, 69	5:20–22	168
4:1–22	59, 138	5:20	8
4:1–7	53, 56	5:21	8
4:1	8, 56, 85, 160, 168	5:22	8
4:2	57	5:24–26	168
4:4	42, 56, 59	5:24	8
4:6	56, 278	5:25	8
4:8–12	53, 56, 59	5:26	8, 85
4:8b–10a	269	5:27–40	68, 70
4:9	57	5:27–33	269
4:10–12	57	5:29–32	70, 105
4:10	57, 288	5:29	70
4:11	57	5:30	269
4:13–22	53, 57	5:31	311
4:13	59	5:34–39	273
4:14	59	5:36–37	71
4:16–20	59	5:41–42	68, 71
4:19–20	70	5:42	8, 168,
4:19	70	6–8	99
4:21	85	6:1–8:4	11, 354
4:22	59	6–7	96
4:23–31	53, 57	6	75, 79, 80
4:24–30	59	6:1–7	6, 84, 98
4:24	32, 57, 58	6:1–6	100, 120
4:25–26	58	6:1–5	100, 104
4:25	58	6:1	75, 78, 79, 80, 110, 135, 194
4:27	58	6:2	76
4:29	58, 59	6:3	76
4:31	58, 59	6:5–6	96
4:32–5:11	46, 96	6:5	79, 94, 260
4:32–37	63, 64	6:6	144
4:32–35	46, 163	6:8–8:3	84
4:32	63, 65, 75	6:8–8:1	350
4:34–35	63, 75	6:8–7:60	100
4:35	63	6:8–15	85
4:36–37	64, 100, 111, 135	6:8	79
4:36	24	6:9–12	79
5	73, 349	6:14	288
5:1–11	6, 64, 66	7	13, 86, 90, 151, 350
5:3	66	7:1–56	86
5:4	65	7:1–54	100
5:11	69	7:4	86
5:12–16	46, 68, 69, 163	7:8	87
5:12	8, 32, 71, 168	7:25	266
5:13	8, 69	7:35–42	13
5:14–15	8	7:42–43	13

358 Index of Ancient Sources

7:48	198	9:4	273, 274
7:51–52	269	9:5	112, 273
7:51	13	9:6	273
7:57–8:3	88	9:7	110, 115
8	79, 98, 106, 237, 353	9:8–9	147
8:1–13	100	9:8	109, 110, 273, 302
8:1–3	350	9:10–19	115
8:1	80, 88, 135, 139	9:10–18	302
8:3	139	9:10–17	273
8:4–40	84	9:10	274
8:4–25	102, 104, 147, 232, 260	9:11	137, 168
		9:12	109, 144, 274
8:4–13	95	9:13–14	274
8:4	96, 135	9:15	115, 163, 167, 297, 302
8:5–40	10		
8:6–7	237	9:17–18	274
8:6	95	9:17	144
8:7	96	9:19–25	274
8:9–12	237	9:19	110
8:9	95	9:20–25	100
8:10	95	9:20	189, 220
8:11	95	9:22	269
8:13–17	96	9:23–25	113, 116, 205, 220
8:13	95	9:23–24	269
8:14–25	6	9:25	110
8:14–18	131	9:26–31	350
8:14–17	96, 135, 234, 237	9:26–30	79
8:17	144	9:26–27	115, 207
8:18–19	236, 237	9:26	111, 113
8:20–23	99	9:27	59, 135
8:20	266	9:28	59, 111, 113, 114
8:22	96, 311	9:29	79, 80, 114, 135, 269
8:26–40	104, 260, 352	9:30	113, 136, 137
8:27–28	103	9:31–11:18	10
8:34	103	9:31	139
8:35	103	9:32–43	237
8:36	228	9:33	121
8:38	96	9:36–43	250
8:39	105	9:36–41	6
8:40	126, 260	9:36	119, 120, 121
9	80, 108, 110, 116, 119, 131, 274	9:37	251
		9:39	251
9:1–31	109, 273, 302	9:43	127
9:1–30	11	10–11	80, 104, 109, 119, 325
9:1–19	113		
9:1–18	129	10:1–11:18	8, 103, 134, 144, 167, 188, 204, 353
9:1–16	115		
9:1–2	115, 139, 229, 273, 278	10	39, 80, 95, 129
		10:1–48	100
9:1	115	10:1–8	126
9:2	115, 269, 288	10:1–6	199
9:3–6	109, 110	10:2	133, 188, 199
9:3–4	273	10:3–6	129

Index of Ancient Sources 359

Acts		12:7–10	140
10:7	127	12:10	14, 74
10:9–16	127, 128, 129	12:11	141, 269
10:12	129	12:12–17	100
10:13	129	12:12	141, 180
10:14	130	12:13–17	142
10:15	130	12:14–17	140
10:17–23a	127	12:17	139, 140, 170, 262
10:17	130, 140	12:18–23	140
10:19	130, 140	12:22	141
10:23b–33	127	12:24–25	141
10:23	130	12:25–15:35	11
10:25–26	160	12:25	141, 143, 144, 180
10:28	128, 130, 140	13–14	100, 167, 168, 226
10:30–32	129	13:1–14:28	207
10:33	128	13	152, 323, 324
10:34–43	128	13:1–3	100, 332
10:34–35	128	13:1	111, 141, 143
10:36	128	13:2–3	163
10:38	120	13:3	144
10:39–41	131	13:4–12	151, 200
10:39	128, 269	13:4	225
10:44–48	128	13:5	144, 180, 189, 220
10:47	128, 228	13:6	147
10:48	130	13:7	147
11	80, 129	13:8	147
11:1–18	128, 131, 135	13:9	146
11:3	129, 130	13:11	147
11:5–10	129	13:12	147, 292
11:13–14	129	13:13–52	146, 151, 198, 323, 330
11:16	228		
11:17	128	13:13	154, 180, 350
11:18	129, 131, 163, 167	13:14	189, 220
11:19–30	11, 134	13:16–41	151
11:19–26	91, 99, 100	13:23	152
11:19–20	80	13:26	152
11:19	80	13:27–28	269
11:20	80, 135, 143	13:27	152
11:22	135	13:28	152
11:24	136	13:29	152
11:25	136	13:30	152
11:26	136, 288	13:31–32	155
11:27–30	136, 290	13:33	152
11:28	260	13:38–39	340
11:29–12:25	207	13:40	153
11:30	141, 143, 256	13:42–43	153
12	73, 74, 139, 141	13:43	188
12:1–25	144	13:45	153, 218
12:1–24	10	13:45–51	220
12:1–17	72, 139, 143, 350	13:46–47	153, 217, 323
12:2	140, 170	13:46	59, 154, 155, 156, 220, 324
12:3	139, 147, 269		
12:5	139	13:47	154

360 Index of Ancient Sources

13:48–49	220	15:19–29	333
13:50	153, 188, 218, 220	15:19–21	100
13:51	153	15:19	170
14	179	15:20	168, 170, 175, 176, 183, 256, 264
14:1–7	146, 323		
14:1	157, 158, 189, 220, 324	15:22–29	172
		15:22	180
14:2–4	269	15:23	256
14:2	157, 220	15:25	32
14:3	59, 157	15:29	168, 170, 175, 183, 264
14:4	33, 157, 158, 218, 343		
		15:30	264
14:5	157, 220	15:32	180
14:8–20	182, 237	15:36–18:22	226
14:8–10	159	15:36–18:21	207
14:11–18	159, 160	15:37–38	154
14:13	160	15:38	180
14:14–18	316	15:40	180
14:14	33, 343, 344	15:41	180
14:15–17	160, 210, 211	16	194, 197, 352
14:15	211	16:1–5	184, 350
14:19–20	159, 160	16:1–3	190, 246, 344, 348
14:19	160, 204, 220, 266	16:3	182, 183, 263
14:23	164, 256	16:4–5	183
14:27	163	16:6–10	250
15	11, 117, 164, 166, 167, 168, 169, 170, 172, 173, 262, 344, 352, 353	16:6	185, 231
		16:7	185
		16:8–11	250
		16:9	185, 192
15:1–36	262	16:10–18	187
15:1–35	144, 172, 182, 259, 262	16:10–17	185, 246
		16:10	185, 190, 192
15:1–29	207, 333	16:11–17:34	206
15:1–21	172, 173, 175	16:11–40	190
15:1–2	182, 263	16:11–15	120, 194, 198, 204
15:1	175	16:11–12	193
15:2	256, 264	16:13–40	200
15:3	167	16:13–14	199
15:4	167	16:13	189, 266
15:5	279	16:14–15	214
15:6–11	333, 334	16:14	188, 199
15:6	256	16:16–21	240
15:7–11	116, 117, 167	16:16–18	197
15:7	103, 116, 129, 131, 140, 333	16:16	189, 190, 197
		16:17	197, 200
15:8	117	16:18	197, 198
15:9	117	16:19	190
15:10	117, 168	16:20–21	198
15:11	117, 340	16:22–23	199
15:12	168, 264	16:24–34	72, 141
15:13	140	16:25–40	204
15:14	103	16:27	266
15:18	256	16:30	199

Index of Ancient Sources 361

Acts		18:4	189
16:31	311	18:5–17	220, 221
16:35	199	18:5	204, 214, 219, 220, 246
16:37	199, 273		
16:40	120, 194, 199	18:6	154, 217, 218, 220, 231, 324
17	210, 211		
17:1–15	146, 198, 323	18:7–11	220
17:1–9	204	18:7	231
17:1–4	220, 324	18:8	218
17:1	189	18:9–10	219
17:2–3	203	18:12–17	218, 220, 345, 354
17:2	202, 203	18:12–16	222
17:3	303	18:12	218
17:4	188, 204	18:13	218
17:5–9	220	18:14–17	220
17:5	202, 218	18:14–15	219, 284
17:7	203, 218	18:14	218
17:10–15	204, 206	18:15	219
17:10	189, 220	18:17	219
17:11	203, 317	18:18–28	226, 227
17:12	204	18:18–19	220, 223
17:13	204, 220	18:18	225, 263
17:14–15	204, 246	18:19–21	254, 324
17:14	204, 206, 220	18:19	189, 217, 220, 225
17:15	214	18:20–21	226
17:16–34	61, 161, 189	18:22	207, 225
17:16–21	209	18:23–21:16	226
17:16	209, 210, 219	18:23–21:14	207
17:17	61, 188, 189, 209	18:23	226
17:18	61, 209, 210, 213, 218	18:24–28	227, 233, 269
		18:24–26	223, 232
17:19–20	61	18:25	228, 229, 288
17:19	209, 210	18:26	59, 120, 194, 220, 225, 229, 288
17:20	210		
17:21	210	18:28	218, 228, 230
17:22–31	209, 210	19–20	258
17:22	211	19	202, 233, 241, 243
17:23	61, 211, 212	19:1–40	226
17:24–25	211	19:1–10	146, 229, 241
17:26	212	19:1–7	229
17:27	212	19:1	226, 232
17:28	212, 213	19:2–3	231
17:29	240	19:7	237
17:30–31	62, 211, 212	19:8–10	231
17:30	62, 212, 311	19:8–9	234, 254
17:31	212	19:8	59, 189, 217, 220, 254
17:32–34	209, 213		
17:34	214, 215	19:9	220, 229, 231, 233, 288
18	324		
18:1–17	146, 231	19:10	217, 231, 240, 254
18:1–4	194	19:11–20	147
18:1–3	120, 223	19:11–12	237
18:2	219	19:11	236

19:12	235	20:18–35	253
19:13–20	254	20:18–21	254
19:13	237	20:19	218, 254, 266
19:14–16	236	20:20	255
19:17	236	20:21	311
19:18–19	236, 237	20:22–24	254
19:19	236	20:22	264
19:21–40	266, 268	20:23	254, 259
19:21–23	247	20:25	255, 324
19:21–22	241	20:27	254
19:21	241, 245, 294, 320	20:28	256
19:22	241, 246	20:29–31	255
19:23–41	220	20:29–30	255, 257
19:23–40	254	20:31	254
19:23	229, 288	20:33–34	254
19:25	233	20:35	256
19:26	239, 240	20:38	324
19:27	239	21–28	182
19:29	233, 241, 246	21	183, 262
19:31	240	21:1–18	185, 192, 261
19:33–34	240	21:4	259
19:33	240	21:7	259
19:34	241	21:8–9	98
19:35–41	220	21:8	104, 260
19:35–40	240	21:9	194, 260
19:35	233	21:10–11	324
19:37	240	21:10	259
19:40	289	21:11	259, 266, 267
20	247, 256	21:13	259
20:1–16	257	21:15–23:30	207
20:1–12	257	21:17	260
20:1–4	247	21:18–25	170
20:1–2	245	21:18–19	290
20:2–3	269	21:18	140, 262
20:3	218, 245, 266	21:20–21	225
20:4	240, 246, 250, 266	21:20	267, 269
20:5–16	185	21:21	182, 183, 262, 263, 266
20:5–15	192, 248	21:23–24	263
20:5–6	246, 250	21:23	267
20:5	200	21:25	170, 175, 263
20:6–21:8	305	21:26	269
20:6	246	21:27–26:32	220
20:7–12	250, 253	21:27–36	260
20:7	250	21:27–31	269
20:8	250	21:27–30	289
20:9	249	21:27–28	263, 290
20:10	249	21:28–29	266, 282
20:11	249	21:28	266, 289
20:12	249	21:29	246, 267
20:13–16	253	21:30	267, 351
20:16	257, 259	21:31–33	319
20:17–35	6	21:31–32	267
20:17	256		

Acts
- 21:33 — 275
- 21:37–40 — 275
- 21:37 — 272
- 21:38 — 272
- 21:39 — 137, 267, 273
- 21:40 — 272
- 22–28 — 23
- 22 — 114
- 22:1–29 — 302
- 22:1–21 — 275
- 22:1–16 — 109
- 22:2 — 272
- 22:3–4 — 273
- 22:3 — 115, 273, 276
- 22:4 — 115, 229, 288
- 22:5 — 273, 278
- 22:6–16 — 129
- 22:6–7 — 273
- 22:7 — 273
- 22:8 — 115, 273, 288
- 22:9 — 115, 274
- 22:10 — 273
- 22:11–13 — 115
- 22:11 — 273, 302
- 22:12–16 — 273, 302
- 22:12 — 274
- 22:13 — 274
- 22:15 — 302
- 22:16 — 274
- 22:17–22 — 274
- 22:17–21 — 115, 274
- 22:17 — 115, 269
- 22:18 — 274, 279
- 22:21 — 274, 302
- 22:22 — 269
- 22:25 — 273, 284
- 22:28 — 273
- 22:30–23:11 — 283, 287, 297
- 23:1–10 — 56
- 23:1–5 — 277
- 23:1–2 — 277
- 23:1 — 278, 280
- 23:3 — 278
- 23:5 — 8, 278
- 23:6–10 — 277, 279, 283
- 23:6 — 279, 302, 319
- 23:7 — 289
- 23:10 — 289
- 23:11 — 277, 279, 294, 295, 320, 321, 325
- 23:12–22 — 293
- 23:12 — 269, 282
- 23:13–14 — 285
- 23:13 — 282
- 23:14 — 269
- 23:16 — 282, 283
- 23:17–18 — 283
- 23:21 — 269, 285
- 23:22–24 — 283
- 23:23–24 — 283
- 23:24–26:32 — 292
- 23:26–30 — 297
- 23:26 — 267
- 23:27 — 284
- 23:29 — 284, 303
- 23:33–35 — 285
- 24–26 — 324
- 24:1–27 — 287, 297
- 24:2–3 — 288
- 24:5 — 288, 289
- 24:6 — 289
- 24:8 — 289
- 24:10 — 288
- 24:11–21 — 294
- 24:12 — 289, 290
- 24:13 — 290
- 24:14–15 — 290
- 24:14 — 8, 229, 288, 303
- 24:15 — 8, 291, 319
- 24:17–18 — 8
- 24:17 — 264, 290
- 24:18 — 289
- 24:19 — 290
- 24:20–21 — 290
- 24:22 — 288, 291
- 24:23 — 291
- 24:24–25 — 291
- 24:26–27 — 291
- 25:1–12 — 287, 297
- 25:1–3 — 297
- 25:2 — 301
- 25:3 — 294, 297
- 25:4–5 — 298
- 25:4 — 297
- 25:6–8 — 297
- 25:8 — 8, 294
- 25:9–12 — 319
- 25:9 — 294, 297, 298
- 25:10–11 — 294
- 25:10 — 8, 294
- 25:11 — 294, 297, 303, 320
- 25:12 — 295, 320
- 25:19 — 298
- 25:20 — 298
- 25:23–26:32 — 288, 297
- 25:24 — 301
- 25:25–27 — 301

25:25	303	28:3–6	320
26	114, 274	28:4	317
26:2–29	302	28:6	316
26:4–8	8	28:7	317
26:4–7	269	28:8–9	316
26:5	115, 302	28:11–16	320
26:6–7	302	28:14	320
26:6	319	28:16	320, 321
26:7	319	28:17–31	327, 353
26:9–18	109	28:17–28	217
26:9	288	28:17–22	319
26:10–11	302	28:17–20	319
26:10	115	28:17–19	326
26:12–18	129	28:17	319
26:13	302	28:18–19	319
26:14	73, 302	28:20	319
26:15–17	115	28:23–28	319
26:15	115	28:24	322
26:16	302	28:25–28	217, 323
26:20	115, 311	28:28	154, 156, 220, 323, 324
26:22–23	103, 303		
26:26	59	28:30–31	324
26:28	136, 288	28:30	324
26:31–32	319	28:31	59, 326
26:32	295, 303	Romans	
27:1–28:16	185, 192, 305, 306, 313, 346, 352	1:1	35
		1:13	114
27:1–28:10	295, 314	1:14	317
27	14, 311, 312, 313, 314, 352	1:16	146, 156
		9–11	156
27:1–44	313	11:1	148
27:1–12	306	11:2	156
27:3	310, 317	11:13	35, 114
27:9	306	14:1–15:13	132, 173, 333
27:10–12	307	15–16	241
27:10	310	15:22–29	334
27:13–17	307	15:23–29	247, 295
27:20	310	15:24–29	320
27:21–26	307, 310	15:24–25	241
27:23–26	315	15:24	321
27:23–24	321	15:25–33	290
27:24	312, 320	15:25–32	207, 345
27:31	310, 311	15:25–28	259
27:32	310	15:30–32	335
27:33–34	310	15:30–31	264
27:34	310	16	194, 224
27:35	311	16:1–2	195, 226
27:41	315	16:3–5a	223
27:43	310	16:4	195, 224
27:44	310, 311	16:6	195
28	316, 319, 323, 325	16:7	35, 195
28:1–16	321	16:12	195
28:1–10	316	16:13	195
28:2	317	16:15	195

16:21	345	1:1	33, 35
16:23	241	1:6	117
1 Corinthians		1:11–23	116
1:1	35	1:11–17	332
1:12	148, 229	1:13–23	114
1:13–17	229	1:13–17	114, 229
1:14–16	174	1:13	114, 115
1:16	215	1:14	114, 148
3:6	226, 229	1:15–24	112
3:22	148	1:15–20	331
8:1–13	132	1:15–17	30
9:1–2	33	1:15–16	111, 115, 332
9:1	35, 114	1:15	117
9:2	35	1:16	114, 333
9:5	148	1:16b–17	114
9:6	35, 65	1:17–18	27
9:25	91	1:17	113, 330
11:17–34	49	1:18–21	207
11:25–26	312	1:18–19	35, 113, 114
12	49	1:18	113, 148, 330
12:12	35	1:19	35, 140, 170
14	49	1:20	114
14:11	317	1:21	113
15:4–8	30	1:22	89, 113, 114
15:5	33, 148	2	11, 133, 167, 353
15:7	33, 140, 170	2:1–14	145
15:8–9	114	2:1–10	11, 132, 170, 173, 174, 175, 176, 207, 330, 333
15:8	115, 155, 332		
15:9	35		
15:32	233, 253	2:1	65, 101
16	241	2:3–5	183
16:1–4	246, 257, 259, 264, 290	2:3	182
		2:6	117
16:2	249	2:7–9	131
16:3–4	345	2:7–8	116, 132
16:3	241, 247	2:8	35, 333
16:5	204, 241, 247	2:9	65, 99, 117, 140, 148, 170
16:8–9	257		
16:8	226, 233, 241	2:10	333
16:15	215	2:11–14	101, 132, 333
16:19	226, 233	2:11	148
16:19b	223, 224	2:12	132, 140, 148, 170
2 Corinthians		2:13	65, 154, 179, 180
1:19	181	2:16	117
8:1–9:15	259	3:2–5	117
8:1–15	290	4:15	278
10:10	214	5:1	117
11:25–26	313	5:11	182
11:25	276	6:11	278
11:32–33	116	Ephesians	
11:33–34	113	2:3	112
Galatians		3:8	112
1–2	111	6:21	345
1	113		

Philippians		4:14	145
1:1	256	5:17	164, 256
2:25	35	5:19	164, 256
3:4–6	114, 148	2 Timothy	
3:5–8	279	1:6	145
3:5–6	279	1:15	255
3:7–8	280	4:8	91
4:2	194	4:11	9, 193
Colossians		4:19a	223
3:11	317	Titus	
4:7	345	1:5	164, 256
4:10	181	1:7	256
4:14	9, 193	Philemon	
1 Thessalonians		24	9, 193
1:1–2	181	Hebrews	
1:1	207	13:2	162
1:6–10	205	James	
1:14–16	205	1:12	91
2:1–2	204	5:14	256
2:2	206	1 Peter	
2:17	214	2:25	256
3:1–6	206	4:16	136
3:1–2	214	5:1	256
3:1	204, 206, 214	5:5	164
3:2	214	2 Peter	
3:6	214	3:16	331, 337
2 Thessalonians		2 John	
1:1	181	1:1	256
1 Timothy		3 John	
1:12–17	112, 114	1:1	256
1:18	145	Revelation	
2:15	193	2:10	91
3:2	256	3:11	91

Other Christian Literature

Acts of John   243, 258
Acts of Paul   5, 14, 331, 334
1 Clement   337
Gospel of Thomas   193
Gospel of Mary   194
Ignatius   6, 337, 338, 346, 352
  Ephesians   346
  Magnesians   346
  Philadelphians   346
  Polycarp   346
  Smyrneans   346

Trallians   346
Irenaeus   5, 7, 9, 91, 96, 335, 343, 344, 347
  Against Heresies   343, 344
Justin Martyr   98, 338, 344, 347
  Dialogue with Trypho   347
  First Apology   344, 347
Marcion   6, 7, 8, 9, 36, 55, 183, 211, 223, 337, 343, 353
Polycarp   6
Tertullian   7

Greek and Latin Authors

Aratus   212, 213
  Phaenomena   213
Dionysius of Halicarnassus   45
Euripides   13, 14, 72, 200, 344, 347

  Bacchae   13, 14, 72, 73, 74, 200, 344, 347, 352
Galen   148

Homer   3, 13, 73, 141, 142, 185, 187, 192, 248, 261, 305, 307, 312, 313, 315, 344
   Iliad   73, 141, 143, 344, 347, 350
   Odyssey   23, 186, 187, 192, 248, 261, 312, 313, 314, 315, 344, 345, 346, 347, 350
Lucian   312, 346, 347
   On Salaried Posts in Great Houses   346
Ovid   161, 162, 344, 347
   Metamorphoses   344, 347

Plato   60, 61, 62, 209, 343, 344, 347
   Apology   61, 62, 343, 347
Plautus   237
   Casina   237
Pliny the Elder   242
Plutarch   223
Polybius   45
Strabo   242
Vergil   3, 119, 120, 193, 312, 313, 348
   Aeneid   120, 192, 193, 312, 313, 348
Xenophon   61, 343, 348
   Memorabilia   61, 343, 348

Index of Modern Authors

Arndt, W. F. 348
Attridge, Harold W. 351
Babcock, William S. 346, 348
Barrett, C. K. 153, 214, 236, 344, 345, 348
Bauer, Walter 336, 344, 346, 348
Blickenstaff, Marianne 353
Bonz, Marianne Palmer 313, 348
Boyarin, Daniel 336, 340, 346, 348
Bultmann, Rudolf 15, 16, 343, 348
Cadbury, Henry J. 135, 344, 348
Cameron, Ron 343, 348, 350
Campbell, William Sanger 345, 348
Cohen, Shaye J. D. 344, 348
Daniélou, Jean 17, 343, 349
Danker, F. W. 344, 348
Dewey, Arthur J. x, 345, 349
Dibelius, Martin 255, 345, 349
Dillon, John J. 347
Dimock, George E. 347
Donaldson, James 347
Dupertuis, Rubén ix, 60, 156, 343, 349
Ehrman, Bart D. 347
Epp, Eldon J. 343, 349
Falls, Stephen B. 347
Foakes Jackson, F. J. 348, 349
Fowler, Harold North 347
Frend, W. H. C. 17, 343, 349
Funk, Robert W. x, 53, 343, 344, 349
Gingrich, F. W. 348
Goold, G. P. 347, 348
Haenchen, Ernst 26, 55, 241, 324, 343, 345, 346, 349
Hanson, K. C. 349
Hardy, Edward Rochie 347
Hare, Douglas R. A. 350
Harmon, A. M. 347
Harnack, Adolf 10, 11, 99, 343, 349
Hemingway, Ernest 5
Hills, Julian V. ix, 66, 349
Hoover, Roy W. x, 349
Käsemann, Ernst 232, 345, 349
Kea, Perry V. ix, 10, 78, 79, 89, 113, 145, 173, 349
Knox, John 207, 345, 346, 350
Koester, Helmut 334, 346, 350, 352

Kovacs, David 347
Kraft, Robert A. 348
Krodel, Gerhard 348
Lake, Kirsopp 348, 349
Levine, Amy-Jill 353
Livesey, Nina E. ix, 172, 175, 184, 350
Lloyd, Alan B. 352
Lüdemann, Gerd ix, 17, 321, 327, 343, 350
MacDonald, Dennis R. ix, 13, 72, 141, 142, 186, 191, 200, 248, 313, 343, 344, 345, 346, 350
McGaughy, Lane C. x, 349
Marchant, E. C. 348
Marrou, Henri 17, 343, 349
Martin, Luther H. 17, 343, 350
Matthews, Shelly ix, 43, 89, 90, 193, 268, 350
Miller, Frank 347
Miller, Merrill P. 341, 348, 350
Miller, Robert J. x
Moreland, Milton ix, 28, 44, 351
Murray, A. T. 347
Neusner, Jacob 347
Parsons, Mikeal C. 26, 27, 343, 351
Penner, Todd ix, 43, 351
Pervo, Richard I. ix, x, 2, 5, 14, 27, 28, 43, 45, 60, 69, 71, 97, 98, 99, 105, 112, 113, 117, 121, 133, 137, 141, 156, 170, 173, 183, 184, 185, 225, 229, 233, 237, 251, 257, 276, 285, 343, 344, 345, 346, 351
Phillips, Thomas E. ix, 114, 191, 251, 352, 353
Praeder, Susan M. 346, 352
Price, Robert M. ix, 257, 345, 352
Rapske, Brian 283, 345, 352
Roberts, Alexander 347
Schmidt, Daryl D. x, 349
Schoedel, William R. 338, 346, 352
Seaford, Richard 344, 352
Segal, Alan F. ix, 173, 344, 352
Seim, Turid Karlsen 121, 352
Shea, Christine ix, 22, 121, 148, 242, 313, 346, 352
Smith, Abraham 105, 344, 352

Smith, Dennis E. ix, 5, 9, 28, 29, 48, 49, 60, 121, 162, 173, 206, 222, 343, 352
Spencer, F. Scott ix, 99, 105, 121, 344, 353
Tannehill, Robert C. 204, 246, 345, 353
Taussig, Hal ix, 173, 353
Thackeray, H. St. J. 347
Thompson, Richard P. 353
Tyson, Joseph B. ix, 2, 5, 6, 15, 34, 133, 173, 206, 327, 343, 353
Unger, Dominic J. 347

Walker, William O. ix, 2, 11, 113, 116, 171, 173, 183, 184, 222, 223, 343, 344, 345, 353
Watson, Francis 346, 354
Weaver, John B. 344, 354
White, L. Michael ix, 43, 137, 222, 223, 345, 354
Wiest, Stephen R. ix, 78, 89, 354
Winter, Sara C. ix, 137, 173, 354
Wyatt, William F. 347

www.ingramcontent.com/pod-product-compliance
Lightning Source LLC
Chambersburg PA
CBHW071810230426
43670CB00013B/2419